Manufacturing Militance

*Workers' Movements in Brazil and
South Africa, 1970–1985*

Gay W. Seidman

UNIVERSITY OF CALIFORNIA PRESS
Berkeley · *Los Angeles* · *London*

University of California Press
Berkeley and Los Angeles, California

University of California Press, Ltd.
London, England

© 1994 by
The Regents of the University of California

Library of Congress Cataloging-in-Publication Data

Seidman, G.

14761

1 7 JAN 2002

Manufacturing militance : workers' movements in Brazil and South
Africa, 1970–1985 / Gay W. Seidman.

 p.   cm.
Includes bibliographical references and index.
ISBN 0-520-07519-6 (alk. paper).—ISBN 0-520-08303-2 (pbk. alk. paper)
 1. Labor movement—Brazil—History—20th century. 2. Labor movement—South
Africa—History—20th century. 3. Trade-unions—South Africa—History—20th cen-
tury. I. Title.
HD8286.5.S45   1994
331.88'.0968—dc20   92-35866
                                                                                      CIP

Printed in the United States of America
9 8 7 6 5 4 3 2 1

Manufacturing Militance

*To the memory of
Carol E. Hatch,
1940–1989*

Contents

Acknowledgments   ix

Introduction   1

1. Militant Labor Movements in
   Brazil and South Africa   15
   Historical Differences   20
   Patterns of Mobilization   29
   A Comparative Puzzle   41

2. Conditions for Industrial Growth, 1960–1973   43
   Brazilian Industrialization Strategies   48
   Industrialization in South Africa   69
   Conclusion   89

3. Business Opposition and Its Limits   91
   Brazil: Collapse of an Alliance?   99
   Business Opposition in South Africa   114
   Conclusion   139

4. The Emergence of "New Unionism"   143
   Brazil: "Máquinas Paradas e Braços Cruzados"   150
   South Africa: "The Spirit Lives"   171
   Labor Militance in Brazil and South Africa   193

5. Community Struggles and the
    Redefinition of Citizenship   197
    Brazil: "O Povo em Movimento"   203
    South Africa: Community, Race, and Class   227
    Conclusion   252

Conclusion   255
    Explaining Similar Dynamics   258
    Militant Workers' Movements
        in Comparative Perspective   264
    Labor Movements in Late Industrializers   272

Notes   275

Bibliography   315

Index   351

Acknowledgments

It would take several pages to list all the people on whom I depended during the course of this project; in the interest of brevity, I have decided not to try, hoping most of them know how much I appreciate their generosity.

Some individuals must be acknowledged more specifically. Much of what is good in this book was prompted by Michael Burawoy; like all his students, I have benefited from his encouragement, advice, and criticism, and from having a supervisor who combines intellectual rigor and creativity with passionate commitment to his students and to the people about whom he writes.

Charles Bergquist, Peter Evans, and Erik Olin Wright provided detailed and extremely helpful comments on earlier drafts, as did my dissertation committee members, Tom Gold, Robert Price, and Neil Smelser.

Robyn Rafel generously shared her knowledge and insight into the South African labor movement, as well as her friendship; many lives, including my own, are poorer for her untimely death.

For invaluable advice, assistance and comments, I am also grateful to Lais Abramo, Sonia Alvarez, Maria Helena Moreira Alves, Jeremy Baskin, Teresa Pires do Rio Caldeira, David Collier, Ruth Berins Collier, Bruce Cumings, John Humphrey, Ivan Evans, David Fig, Barbara Forrest, Carolyn Hamilton, Margaret Henderson, Margaret Keck, Devan Pillay, Anne Posthuma, Jenny Schreiner, Eddie Webster, and Wolfgang Streeck.

The Congress of South African Trade Unions and the Metal and Allied Workers of South Africa kindly granted permission to use their archives. Without help from librarians and archivists, this project could not have been completed. I am grateful to Maria Francisca de Brito and Maria Cecilia de Souza at the Centro Brasileiro de Análise e Planejamento, and to Cézar Augusto Ribeiro Alves at the Centro de Estudos de Cultura Contemporânea; and to the staff of libraries of the South African Church of the Province Records; the University of California at Berkeley; the Hoover Institution; Columbia University; Harvard University; the Killie Campbell Africana Collection at the University of Natal (Durban); the South African Institute for Race Relations; the University of São Paulo; and the Roberto Simenson Library at the Federação de Indústrias do Estado de São Paulo.

I am grateful for financial support from the John L. Simpson Memorial Fellowship; the Center for Latin American Studies, the International Studies Institute, and the North-South Project at the University of California at Berkeley; and the Nave Foundation at the University of Wisconsin at Madison.

Finally, Heinz Klug provided the countless cups of coffee, word processing and other less tangible kinds of support that make books possible.

Introduction

In the mid-1980s, activists in South Africa's growing independent trade union movement began debating a somewhat arcane question: what lessons could South African workers draw from Brazil, where workplace organizations seemed to have helped bring about the end of military rule? Most sociologists would assume, as I initially did, that workers' movements in Brazil and South Africa would have little in common; although workers in both countries lived under relatively authoritarian regimes in the early 1980s, it seemed probable, given the obvious differences between their social and political contexts, that activists would employ very different forms of organization and strategies.

South Africa's systematic racial oppression, apartheid, was clearly unique. Predicting that superficial similarities with Brazil would disappear under closer inspection, I began a study that I expected would draw contrasts between the dynamics of labor movements in two newly industrializing countries. The South African labor movement was shaped as much by racial dynamics as class ones, I assumed, whereas in Brazil, I expected to find a stronger emphasis on workplace organization.

Yet as I began to learn more about the history and trajectories of both labor movements, about how unionists themselves conceptualized their struggles and analyzed the challenges they confronted, I could not help but recognize the broad degree of similarity between the two cases. Instead of contrasts, I found remarkable parallels. As each movement gained momentum, with slow transitions toward democratic rule, it seemed more important to understand the dynamics that had shaped what looked increasingly like working-class movements than to focus on what made each case unusual.

In the late 1970s, militant labor movements emerged in Brazil, where corporatist legislation should have channeled workers' aspirations away from politics, and in South Africa, where racial divisions should have inhibited any possibility of a class-based movement. In Brazil, the rhetoric of class defined political conflicts, as the labor movement reinterpreted demands for democracy in terms of economic transformation; even in South Africa, where race has been the organizing principle of state structures, class issues were pushed forward by labor activists, and economic change became a major goal of the political opposition. In view of the overwhelming differences in Brazilian and South African political institutions, racial formations, and labor histories, it is worth asking why such similar labor movements emerged—and what we know about this type of unionism. What dynamics might explain the sudden emergence of broadly similar militant movements in places so obviously different? Can we learn anything from these cases that will tell us more about the broader labor movements in newly industrializing societies?

Although there is a theoretical distinction between political and economic unionism, trade unions generally act in the political arena, if only by supporting electoral candidates who will further unionists' agendas. In strikes anywhere, "whatever the official rationale for a march or a rally, workers generally attend with all their grievances in mind."[1] Recently, however, sociologists and labor historians have begun to differentiate between "political unionism," expressed through support for political parties, and behavior that is sometimes termed "social-movement unionism"—that is, between unions that act within an existing political and economic framework, on the one hand, and labor movements whose constituencies spread far beyond the factory gates and whose demands include broad social and economic change, on the other.[2]

Theoretically, social-movement unionism is perhaps best defined as an effort to raise the living standards of the working class as a whole, rather than to protect individually defined interests of union members. Marx suggested that levels of reproduction of labor power, on which wages and living standards are based, are historically determined, through struggles between classes.[3] Social-movement unionism, broadly speaking, consists of precisely such struggles over wages and working conditions, and also over living conditions in working-class areas—over housing and social services, such as health care, education, transport, and running water. These campaigns link factory-based unions and communities, and they lead to challenges to states as well to as to individual employers. Strikes over factory issues receive strong community support; conversely, community campaigns for improved social services and full citizenship are supported by factory organizations as labor movements redefine their constituencies to include the broader working class.

This discussion begs another question, however: Is there something in the organization of newly industrializing societies that stimulates social-movement unionism? What relationship, if any, might exist between industrialization patterns and particular forms of labor militance? For those who study societies outside the industrialized core, the South African and Brazilian movements are particularly intriguing, because they would not have been predicted by most development theories. Modernization theories predicted that with industrialization, unions would gradually "mature." Drawing on assumptions about labor trajectories from Europe and North America, modernization theorists tended to view "normal" unionism as economistic, likely to remain within the framework of employer-employee negotiations. Union officials would increasingly represent members' narrow interests, while their members, as relatively privileged workers, would pursue workplace issues rather than building links to communities, to peasant groups, or to the unemployed.

Faced with the reality of political unionism—which did, in fact, emerge in many developing societies—modernization theorists nevertheless tended to view non-economistic unions as aberrations brought into being by the intervention of nationalist movements and populist leaders, or by the failure of modernizing governments adequately to incorporate industrial union leaders into policy-making processes.[4] Even writers who have criticized modernization theories have sometimes suggested that unions in developing societies do best when they restrain rank-and-file militance, because industrial workers' self-interest is believed to lie in stability and economic growth.[5] Writers in the dependency tradition generally rejected modernization theories' ahistoricism, but they, too, often assumed that industrial unions would represent only a small labor aristocracy.[6] A few dependency theorists believed industrial workers might take up radical demands, but even these writers generally emphasized obstacles to militance: unions could be co-opted by state policies favoring urban industrial workers over peasant majorities, especially in a repressive context.[7]

Militant unionism, then, hardly seemed a likely outcome in the context of late industrialization: as long as industrial workers remained a relatively privileged minority, analysts rarely saw unions as a source of popular opposition to capitalist states and employers. Both modernization and early dependency theories tended to treat unions as either irrelevant or conservative.

In specific cases, these theories tended to shape social scientists' predictions. For South Africa, analysts have generally argued that nationalist tendencies would weaken trade unions, as leaders would concentrate on political and racial issues rather than on the bread-and-butter issues that would strengthen organization.[8] In Brazil, observers have regularly suggested that corporatist legislation created by past populist governments could channel workers' aspirations, reducing shop-floor militance by offering assistential programs to members of state-controlled unions.[9]

As long as developing countries had little industry, questions about the dynamics of labor organization remained academic. Since the early 1970s, however, blanket assumptions about "peripheral" countries have fallen away, as scholars have recognized that some degree of industrialization, with concomitant changes in social organization, has occurred in several regions that previously mainly exported primary commodities—including both Brazil and South Africa. By the 1980s, development theorists, following authors like Fernando Henrique Cardoso and Enzo Faletto, acknowledged that given different international contexts, different patterns of economic change, and different national settings, nation-states could follow different development strategies, with different possibilities for social and economic change.[10]

Obviously, there is enormous heterogeneity within the Third World; some countries remain essentially producers of primary products for export, while others have shifted to manufacture and industry. Capitalist development has taken different forms, and even among so-called newly industrializing countries, there is wide variation.[11] But recognizing these variations should not obscure the fact that where industrialization has occurred, assumptions about the inherent conservatism of labor unions have been called into question.[12]

For our understanding of labor movements in the late twentieth century, the emergence of social-movement unionism in Brazil and South Africa raises a number of questions. What do the structural conditions of late capitalist industrialization mean for emergent labor movements? What conditions enable these movements to emerge? Under the industrialization strategies available to newly industrialized countries, or NICs, what possibilities—what capacities, what strategies—are available to labor movements seeking to improve workers' conditions? Do patterns of late industrialization affect the internal dynamics of labor movements? Can we identify specific tendencies that strengthen particular forms of organization and action? In short, is there something about the experiences of workers in late industrializers that leads them to adopt a militant discourse of class and class mobilization, that prompts factory-based organizations to take up broad issues of citizenship and inclusion?

Wide variations in workers' experiences and the behavior of their organizations reflect different histories, different cultures, different possibilities. But especially with the expansion of multinational investment in the 1960s, most newly industrializing countries have experienced some variant of what Alain Lipietz terms "global Fordism": heavy reliance on imported capital and technology, with widespread use of mass production processes and semi-skilled workers.[13] Workers in these settings may confront labor processes and industrialization patterns that hold some parallels to workers' experiences in earlier industrializers. Many of the most dramatic moments of labor militance in Europe and the United States occurred when rapid industrialization created urban working-class communities of semi-skilled workers and their families, denied access to labor rights and social resources and lacking the moderating influence of established craft unionism. Around the time of World War I, for example, major industrial cities in Russia and Germany were marked by militant trade unions, with strong ties to new urban communities.[14] In the United States, the famous 1930s automobile workers' strikes were dominated by semi-skilled workers on new production lines, supported by communities of relatively recent immigrants.[15] More recently, in the 1970s, Barcelona's rapid industrialization was accompanied by militant unions, supported by a constituency whose boundaries and demands went far beyond the workplace.[16]

These moments of social-movement unionism in what now appear as earlier industrializers were, however, generally short-lived. Activists around the world have mourned the sudden demobilization of workers, who turn to strategies other than militant union-community alliances to meet their needs; the shift from broad working-class movements to factory-based economics has been pervasive enough to lead theorists as diverse as Ralph Dahrendorf, Claus Offe, Samuel Huntington and V. I. Lenin to wonder whether unions are not inherently prone to represent only narrowly defined interests and constituencies.[17] With the glaring exception of prerevolutionary Russia—probably the first true "late industrializer"—national labor movements sought to compromise between established union practices and new industrial workers and therefore abandoned radical demands. Explanations for this tendency are complex, turning on the historically specific dynamics of each labor movement: divisions within the working class, the role of already-established unions, labor's relationship with existing political parties, labor's ability to win organizing rights and community benefits through institutional change.

Despite some similarities, industrialization in what are sometimes called "semi-peripheral" areas may not mirror the European and North American experiences: patterns of proletarianization, labor processes, and political opportunities may be quite different from those that prevailed a century earlier. First, patterns of industrialization in the late twentieth century have often involved reliance on imported technologies developed in core industrialized areas, as well as on infusions of foreign capital, and have depended on links to international markets. While de-skilling of artisans has occurred from place to place, the new technologies have frequently been put in place without many of the labor process conflicts that apparently marked earlier industrialization. Mass production processes using semi-skilled workers have been in place from the start of industrial growth: workers in newly industrializing countries may be more likely to go through re-skilling than de-skilling as they move from agriculture or informal-sector work to capital-intensive factories. Urban communities may be far more cohesive than a focus on the workplace alone would suggest, and working-class identities may be less exclusionary than where traditions of craft unionism persist.

Under these conditions, what kinds of demands are likely to emerge from factory-based organizations? What will be the relationship between factory workers and those for whom industrial work presents a relatively well-paid alternative to urban poverty? In nineteenth-century Europe and North America, artisans already organized in craft unions often shaped the discourses of emergent industrial unions,[18] but several studies of working-class formation in industrializing societies suggest that the links between industrial workers and urban communities may be much closer in more recent industrializers. From India to Egypt to Chile, industrial workers may be more responsive to militant unions than sociologists have tended to assume. So frequently that it cannot be simply an aberration, labor movements in late-industrializing countries have responded to the demands of a relatively undifferentiated work force, in the context of rapidly changing circumstances and identities; repeatedly, union members have refuted assumptions that they or their organizations will remain passive, controllable, or co-optable.[19]

Second, the dynamics of late industrialization, at least under capitalist development strategies, almost certainly affect the relationship between national policymakers and capitalists. In the nineteenth and early twentieth centuries, nations sometimes faced competitive international contexts, and states sometimes sought to attract or placate local bourgeoisies; but governments following capitalist development strategies and responding to what Peter Evans calls "transnational linkages" have played an even more explicitly economic role in the late twentieth century than states did in earlier industrializers.[20] Since World War II, developmentalist states working together with domestic and foreign capital have engaged directly in production, supported joint ventures, and borrowed heavily on international capital markets to promote industrialization.

In addition to shaping states' development strategies, the international context of the late twentieth century has also affected domestic dynamics, often strengthening the capacity of industrialists to insist on a voice in policy-making, while increasing national economies' vulnerability to international pressures. Early industrializing states were certainly affected by international competition, but newly industrializing societies, dependent on capital, technologies, and markets outside the control of any one state, may be even more prone to domestic crises induced by changes in international dynamics. Successful industrial strategies in the 1970s, Lipietz writes, reflected

a genuine Fordism, based on the coupling of intensive accumulation and expanding markets. Yet it is still *peripheral*, in two crucial senses. First, . . . the work patterns and product mixes corresponding to the levels of skilled production, and above all engineering, remain largely outside these countries. Secondly, the market outlets involve a distinctive combination of local consumption by modern middle classes, partial access to household equipment by workers in the Fordist sector, and cheap exports of the same manufactures to the center. It is certainly expected that *world* social demand will grow, particularly for household durables. But such demand is not institutionally regulated on a national basis, as a function of productivity gains in *local* Fordist branches.[21]

Lipietz suggests that the new international context may reduce the willingness of dominant classes in newly industrializing countries to raise wage levels, because they do not require a domestic market. But in most variants of capitalism, producers and consumers are not identical, and few employers anywhere have willingly raised wages; several authors have suggested that Lipietz exaggerates the novelty of the geographic separation of production and consumption.[22] Yet as Lipietz points out, nation-states in the late twentieth century undertake industrial growth in a very different context than that in which earlier Fordist relations were developed: new international economic linkages create new vulnerabilities and have reduced producers' dependence on specific geographic locales. How do these vulnerabilities and changing dependencies affect class relations? How are internal class dynamics likely to be affected by peripheral industrialization?

From the late nineteenth century on, capitalist states in Europe and North America began gradually to respond to workers' demands: from minimum wage laws and bargaining rights to public expenditures on health, education, and housing, political coalitions were built around policies to improve the living conditions of citizens, including workers. But these redistributive programs required some degree of confidence that private capital would not flee, and that higher wages would expand, rather than reduce, markets. That confidence may be eroded in the late twentieth century, when capital is increasingly mobile and markets are increasingly competitive. For capitalist NICs, redistributive programs appear to be especially problematic: in the attempt to attract investment or increase sales in a competitive international environment, industrializing states have often tended to privilege capital accumulation, industrial expansion, and low wage bills over social welfare and labor rights, viewing the latter as benefits that will trickle down with economic growth. Where it has occurred, capitalist industrialization in the Third World has generally been marked by intensified inequalities: states seeking to attract or retain capital have often turned to political and labor repression, postponing both democracy and redistribution in the effort to promote growth. These strategies of accumulation have tended to mean that working-class communities in most newly industrializing countries have been denied access to social resources.

This study, then, seeks to examine in more detail the patterns that shaped militant labor movements in Brazil and South Africa, to explore the relationship between late industrialization and unusually militant, broad-based labor movements. Comparative-historical research on labor movements in late-industrializing societies seems to offer the best method of investigating these kinds of questions: rather than drawing assumptions from the experience of earlier industrializers, it allows an exploration of the dynamics of labor movements that have emerged in a very different context than that of the late nineteenth century. Many of the new international labor studies have taken this approach; thus, for example, Charles Bergquist examines the way workers' organizations in Latin American export sectors have shaped specific labor movements, while Frederic Deyo compares the conditions confronting labor in four Asian export-oriented economies. Most of these comparative labor studies, however, limit themselves to a single continent, with relatively similar histories and cultures. They tend to emphasize differences between cases, asking why, given their relatively similar contexts, labor movements take such different forms. Almost invariably, the answers turn on the specific histories of each case, and on how states and workers have interacted over decades. Thus, for example, Bergquist looks at different workers' cultures and labor processes in different export zones; Deyo emphasizes different state relations with labor, and different union philosophies, to explain the differences between unions in Taiwan and South Korea.[23]

Comparative sociology also offers an alternative approach. Rather than contrasting different outcomes in cases that might have similar backgrounds, it is also possible to use comparisons to try to explain similar outcomes in different contexts, exploring the common dynamics that shape social phenomena. Barrington Moore, Jr., compares paths to modernity in places as disparate as England and Japan; Theda Skocpol's classic study *States and Social Revolutions* compares upheavals in wildly unlike societies, seeking common threads of explanation for the Russian, Chinese, and French revolutions.[24] Recently, David Collier and Ruth Berins Collier have combined both these modes of comparison to examine alliances between Latin American unions and political parties, arguing that labor's patterns of incorporation in the political arena can be traced to alliances made in the 1950s.[25]

Social-movement unionism begs the latter type of comparison. Given their very different cultures, any explanation for why similar movements emerged in Brazil and South Africa must begin from structural changes during the course of rapid industrialization. Those changes, I suggest, created new possibilities for worker and community organization and formed the context in which a new discourse about class relationships began to shape individuals' aspirations. By highlighting similar trends, even while recognizing important differences, this study seeks to explore the relationship between structural change and social dynamics, asking, with Charles Tilly, whether the configurations of people, resources, common ends, and forms of commitment "change systematically with the advances of capitalism and large organization."[26]

Chapter 1 seeks to sharpen the definition of social-movement unionism. The comparison between the Brazilian and South African labor movements in the 1970s and 1980s is presented in broad strokes, accentuating what made these movements remarkable. Chapter 2 describes the structural changes associated with late industrialization, focusing on how state strategies from the early 1960s on rearranged industrial production in similar ways. State policies were designed to attract foreign and domestic capital into heavy industry; rapid growth rates created new dynamic industrial sectors and reshaped the industrial working class, while denying workers and their families access to political and labor organizations.

During rapid industrial expansion—during the late 1960s and early 1970s—both South African and Brazilian employers acquiesced in labor repression. During the 1970s, however, growth slowed in both cases; although for slightly different reasons, industrialists began to demand greater access to state decision-making bodies. In chapter 3, I argue that these disagreements created the political space in which labor movements could begin to demand the right to organize factory-based unions. While employers certainly did not help create emergent unions, in both cases, the timing of the appearance of "new unionism" strengthened its chances of survival, as business leaders were confronted with workers' demands at a time when dominant groups were already engaged in debates about democratization and development strategies.

Chapters 4 and 5 describe the processes through which factory-based unions and working-class communities developed discourses of class and citizenship—discourses that clearly distinguished between democratization at the political level and the kinds of social and economic changes that would benefit workers and their families. Small clandestine groups of activists began to organize in large factories; militant strikes and organization soon spread from factories to communities, taking up broad demands for inclusion and redistribution. First challenging both states and employers for the right to organize at the factory, both labor movements grew to encompass broad demands for social inclusion and citizenship.

Social-movement unionism arose from the lived experiences of workers: from the geography of new industrial cities to the changing gender composition of the work force, from restraints on labor organizations to high unemployment, the patterns of rapid industrialization created conditions that gave resonance to a discourse of class consciousness and class mobilization. The specific patterns of industrialization shaped the strategies available to labor organizers in ways that underscored the appeal of a broad, class-based mobilization. Thus, there seems to be a direct relationship between similar patterns of industrialization and a specific form of labor mobilization.

Under the conditions of rapid and authoritarian industrialization, organizations rooted in workplace relations could hardly resist pressures to take up issues outside the factory; similarly, political demands were reinterpreted in light of workplace experiences. Social-movement unionism thus arose out of the historically specific conditions of Brazil and South Africa, but out of conditions that may also apply in other cases where authoritarian states embarked on capitalist development strategies.

Any attempt to explain similar outcomes in very different contexts is unlikely to emphasize workers' cultural repertoires. Different histories and cultural traditions help shape the way individuals respond to their world; but while cultural patterns shape the expression of demands, they need not determine their content. Cultural expression is a fluid phenomenon: individuals may reinterpret older cultural forms as the context in which they live changes. Brazilian workers often organized under the umbrella of the all-powerful Catholic Church, while South African workers used traditional dance forms during strikes. But the forms of organization they used and the demands they made were far more similar than their different forms of expression would suggest. While recognizing that labor movements and community groups draw on unique cultural forms and traditions, I emphasize the ways in which state and employer interventions affected labor movements' constituencies. The Brazilian military regime played an active role in creating an urban *periferia,* a periphery that was denied basic social welfare or security and seemed increasingly homogeneous in its poverty; the South African state consciously created segregated townships occupied almost entirely by workers and their families.

Chapters 4 and 5, then, explore the way in which participation in growing factory-based movements shaped workers' understandings of their interests. Workers brought these understandings to bear on community demands, reinterpreting poverty and segregation as the results of a broader class structure, while community organizations supported labor campaigns as an avenue to increasing political participation. Together, these chapters seek to explain the ways in which popular groups redefined citizenship, challenging employers and the state to give workers, their families, and their neighbors greater access to the benefits of industrial growth.

Finally, in the Conclusion, I explore the implications of the parallels between Brazil and South Africa for our understanding of labor movements under conditions of late industrialization, arguing that while South Africa and Brazil are each unique, the comparison may reveal the dynamics through which militant labor movements emerge, and their potential for challenging authoritarian states. After summarizing the pattern that produced social-movement unionism, I briefly discuss the relevance of these cases to other examples of authoritarian industrialization. Different industrialization strategies may create different possibilities for labor movements; these cases suggest that state-led, authoritarian industrialization strategies in late industrializers may tend to produce militant working-class movements whose demands go well beyond the factory gates.

Michael Burawoy has argued that production processes in advanced capitalist societies have tended to manufacture broad consent to existing social and workplace relations, as workers come to accept, even expect, inequality.[27] In newly industrializing societies, the effects of authoritarian industrialization strategies may be quite different: the politics of production, both inside and outside the labor process, may create new possibilities for broad labor movements seeking to challenge existing distributions of power and wealth. In a competitive international context, where nation-states' growth depends on attracting international technologies, capital, and markets, industrial expansion may not lead to gradually improved living standards for workers. Instead of creating consensus and compliance, authoritarian industrialization patterns—at least of the sort illustrated by South Africa and Brazil in the 1970s—may inadvertently manufacture new sources of militance.

SOURCES

A comparative study that simultaneously seeks to recognize unique configurations and parallel processes must draw on both secondary and
primary sources; the comparison itself sometimes requires reexamining
dynamics that may have been understudied in each case, to explore a
process that seems important in understanding one case that may have
been less obvious, or at least less studied, in the other. Although I used
both secondary and primary sources in all the chapters, I found primary
sources especially useful in chapters 4 and 5; understanding the organizational strategies and goals of labor and community groups required
examining the ways in which workers and community residents understood and analyzed the situations they confronted.

Memories can, however, be deceptive. Labor and community activists, like any other social actors, often reinterpret past opinions and
strategies in the light of current debates. Discussions with researchers
and activists in the late 1980s were often extremely helpful, but where
possible I have tended to rely more on contemporaneous material than
on interviews to understand debates at different points during the emergence of both labor movements: minutes of meetings, widely circulated
discussion papers, recorded interviews with activists, and articles in the
labor and community press often proved more reliable than individuals'
memories—just as articles and speeches by, or newspaper interviews
with, businessmen and politicians often proved more reliable guides to
their responses to new labor movements than retrospective comments,
made after labor laws had changed, could have done.

On the other hand, for much of the period discussed in this comparison, both Brazil and South Africa were controlled by authoritarian governments, and popular movements were liable to censor themselves to
avoid repression. A civilian government had already unbanned all political parties in Brazil at the time I began my research, thus allowing
activist groups to publish their own histories, and activists to publish
memoirs of their clandestine activities during the 1970s and early
1980s. By the late 1980s, it was possible to get a reasonable picture of
historical discussions within the Brazilian labor movement through
public materials, such as labor archives and contemporaneous articles
by labor activists.

South Africa, however, only unbanned political organizations in
1990, when this project was already well under way. For most of the
time I was conducting research, South African activists were reasonably

cautious about committing to paper—or reporting to foreign researchers—any activities that could be interpreted as illegal under apartheid
security legislation. Since "furthering the aims of a banned organization" could carry a five-year jail sentence until 1990, many labor activists simply avoided discussion of such organizations, their traditions,
and their strategies. The full history of South Africa's labor movement
in the 1970s and 1980s has yet to be written: even two years after
the unbanning, past events involving then-banned organizations like the
African National Congress and the South African Communist Party
were still rarely discussed openly, if at all. Recognizing this necessary
self-censorship, I supplemented archival material with interviews with
South African activists. Hoping to avoid either thoughtlessly incrimi-
nating individuals or understating the importance of activities that were
illegal when they occurred—and given the uncertainly that has prevailed in South Africa through the early 1990s—I have preferred to
err on the side of protectiveness, preserving informants' anonymity and
relying on written materials rather than interviews where possible. I am
confident, however, that as South African labor history is revisited in
the future, by activists and researchers less constrained by fears of repression, the general picture I present will prove accurate.

TERMINOLOGY

All racial categories are socially constructed, but in South Africa they
are also legal classifications. Following a common South African practice, I use "black" to refer to all South Africans not legally classified
as "white." When it is necessary to distinguish between people legally
classified in different groups—for example, to discuss the specific experiences of people who are indigenous Africans (legally, "black"), as opposed to those of people classified as "Asian" or "coloured"—I use
those terms.

CHAPTER ONE

Militant Labor Movements in Brazil and South Africa

The trade union movement is a very powerful organization,
and it is not there just to look at the bread and butter problems
of workers. If the trade union organization cannot take on the
liberation of the country, who will? . . . The trade unions have
got to follow the workers in all their travels—to get them
home, and to school, in the education and welfare of their
children, everywhere. The whole life of a worker needs trade
union involvement.

*Emma Mashinini, former South African
union organizer, 1989*

In the 1980s, discussions of the conditions for transition to democracy
tended to focus on strategic questions, on how to persuade authoritarian rulers to relinquish power, and how to prevent their return. These
questions were of more than academic importance: the answers frequently guided political actors during fragile openings as they negotiated democratic reforms.[1] But while these discussions tended to focus
on elite interactions, democratic transitions in the 1980s also included
cases in which authoritarian states confronted broad-based popular
movements, which helped create pressures for democratization.[2]

Such popular mobilizations were sometimes discussed in terms of
negotiation strategies, where an unwise move might provoke another
military coup.[3] For sociologists, however, these social movements
should raise a different set of questions. What created them? What
shaped popular demands for new institutional arrangements, new development strategies, new definitions of citizenship? What enabled
these movements to challenge authoritarian regimes? Militant labor
movements were perhaps particularly likely to articulate visions of transition that incorporated popular aspirations. In both Brazil and South
Africa, such movements were new phenomena: unions organized at the

factory and reliant on community support constituted a new phase of
resistance to the state. From the late 1970s on, workers in large industrial centers formed militant organizations; they were supported by
broad community support. As these movements grew, the discourse of
the opposition shifted to a class-based rhetoric, and in both cases, a
large part of the opposition claimed increasingly to articulate the needs
of the working class, broadly defined.

By the early 1980s, both labor movements, including popular movements allied with trade unions, had become important political actors.
In Brazil, the "new unionism" forced even skeptics to "agree that elements of Brazilian labor have escaped the limits which Brazil's political
elite had so carefully laid out for them."[4] Brazil's military regime faced
a growing popular opposition, which challenged fundamental relations
of power and control. For over ten years, labor and community activists
built up a national organization to represent the interests of Brazil's
working people. In 1989, a charismatic labor leader nearly won the
country's first direct presidential elections since 1960; support for Luís
Inácio da Silva, known as Lula, illustrated the appeal of a different kind
of social order—one in which members of subordinate classes would be
incorporated as full citizens, with economic and social rights as well as
political ones.

In South Africa, a white minority state had systematically excluded
the country's black majority from political and economic participation
in its wealth; in the 1980s, that state faced an opposition that successfully mobilized internal and international support for the redistribution
of wealth and power. Throughout the 1980s, the emergent labor movement, allied to a broad anti-apartheid opposition, changed the country's political terrain. While the broad movement against racial exclusion represented a multi-class alliance, few South Africans denied the
labor movement's centrality: when Cyril Ramaphosa, former general
secretary of the powerful black miners' union, became the general secretary of the leading anti-apartheid group in mid 1991, his election underscored activists' growing tendency to reinterpret racial domination in
terms of class and exploitation. "For the first time in decades," a South
African observer wrote, "the possibility exists of the working class im-
printing its specific demands on the South African political and social
process."[5]

In both Brazil and South Africa, demands went beyond political
change. Popular movements redefined full citizenship to include access
to social resources and to their countries' wealth. Each movement ar-

gued that the authoritarian state had limited the benefits of industrialization to a small elite. To participants, full citizenship came to mean not only the right to participate in politics, but also the right to adequate wages, decent housing, education, and health care. In both cases, popular movements challenged the social and economic inequality that had marked their countries' histories.

Why did these movements emerge when they did—in countries lacking any recent tradition of militance, and in countries that, on the face of it, appear to pose such different problems for labor organizers? What shaped the patterns of popular mobilization, and where should we look for an explanation? This chapter will first consider alternative approaches to understanding the emergence of militant labor movements and suggest that while these perspectives may help us understand important aspects of each case, they may not tell us very much about the processes through which these labor movements emerged and grew, or explain the apparent convergence in the type of unionism that emerged in these two cases. Then, it will examine in slightly more detail the common characteristics of social-movement unionism, seeking possible starting points for a different kind of explanation.

The most obvious approach to explaining the emergence of militant, politicized union movements is authoritarianism itself: it was hardly surprising that trade unions sought expanded political rights. Social theorists have long assumed that in societies where workers are denied the franchise, labor movements will tend to view political rights as a critical first step toward gaining the legal power to bargain with employers;[6] indeed, working-class parties in early industrializers often viewed universal adult franchise as a direct route to socialism.[7] In Brazil, where a military dictatorship ruled from 1964 on, and in South Africa, where the black majority has been denied political rights for most of this century, working-class organizations could hardly ignore political questions. The parallels in the two countries' state structures were underlined in 1981 when the American political scientist Samuel Huntington drew on Brazilian examples to advise would-be reformers in South Africa seeking to design a controlled transition.[8]

But while authoritarianism explains some aspects of both labor movements, it hardly offers a complete picture. Both the Brazilian and the South African regime offered some channels for political expression; especially when elites began to complain about their exclusion from policy-making, both states created new electoral processes that could have reduced political tension on the shop floor. In Brazil, literate citizens, which included most industrial workers by the 1970s, not only had voting rights, but were legally required to vote, albeit in strictly limited elections. While the military retained control over access to parliamentary bodies and choices for the presidency, the Brazilian regime offered more formal opportunities for participation than most military dictatorships, even at the height of repression. In South Africa, the white-minority state regularly attempted to create new electoral channels for black South Africans. From the mid 1970s on, most black adults could vote either for local administrations in segregated black areas known as "homelands" or for municipal councils in segregated townships. Political participation was restricted by race—blacks could not participate in national decisions—but channels did exist. The question is pertinent to South Africa as well as to Brazil: why did popular movements, including new labor movements, thoroughly reject possible channels for participation? Why did both labor movements define very different political processes as too authoritarian, too exclusionary, to permit any influence, and why did this rejection become so widespread?

Neither the Brazilian nor the South African movement put political rights at the top of its agenda; political demands only appeared as mobilization escalated. Organized at the shop-floor level, the new labor movements demanded the right to deal directly with employers, initially focusing on wages and working conditions. Far from first seeking political change, activists sought to reduce state intervention in factory-level processes. Authoritarian rule certainly came to be defined as the target of labor militance, but it cannot explain the emergence of labor militance, or the fact that workers involved in both movements discussed political exclusion in class terms: they viewed political participation not simply in terms of individual political rights but as a strategy for improving conditions for an entire class.

A second approach to union behavior emphasizes the links between industrialization and democracy: the social and economic changes accompanying rapid industrialization are said to increase workers' ability to insist on greater access to the state and to economic wealth. Thus, sociologists since Reinhard Bendix have repeatedly suggested that industrialization—or, more specifically, the creation of an industrial working class—creates new social groups who will demand political incorporation and a greater share of economic wealth.[9] This approach certainly provides some insight into both labor movements, and into why they challenged their countries' highly stratified patterns of economic development—patterns that the unions argued permitted only the dominant classes, in alliance with an authoritarian, labor-repressive state, to benefit from industrial growth. Far from resulting in general well-being, as social scientists had once confidently predicted, rapid growth had heightened unequal income distribution and coincided with intensified repression.

This approach tends, however, to imply that industrial workers are somehow a different breed than the rural migrants who first arrived in urban areas, and that they will return to quiescence once their wages and working conditions improve. Thus, sociologists in both Brazil and South Africa sometimes explained the apparent absence of worker militance in the 1960s in terms of workers' rural origins, and, when worker militance erupted, predicted that industrial unions would shift to a "mature" focus on workplace issues once demands for collective bargaining procedures had been met.[10] The strongest unions within each labor movement could be said to represent some of the most privileged industrial workers in each country, and initial shop-floor organizations seemed to reflect a process Bendix calls "modernization": industrialization redefined social groups, creating new possibilities for subordinate classes to pressure dominant coalitions.[11] Based on several cases in European history, Barrington Moore, Jr., has suggested that worker militance sometimes derives from traditional communal norms of justice.[12] Industrial workers in both South African and Brazil were relatively new arrivals in huge urban conglomerations, however, with few common traditions; while groups of workers sometimes referred to notions of justice, they were more likely to try to redefine norms in terms of "modern" international standards and referred far more frequently to international labor codes than to any hallowed past. In some sense, these unions did reflect changed social relationships—changed identities—directly linked to industrialization patterns.

In both Brazil and South Africa, however, unions' demands escalated during processes of mobilization, and they increasingly represented workers outside the industrial core. Both labor movements rejected the argument that economic growth alone could raise general standards of living. Unions first focused on the shop floor, but when each state began to allow direct collective bargaining, unions took up political demands. Strikers increasingly demanded that their employers contravene state policy and struck over political issues. Employers recognized and deplored unions' growing politicization; as a South African business consultant asked plaintively in 1987, "What happened to those unions that were supposed, when the government gave them legal standing eight years ago, to devote themselves to worker advancement, to be an escape valve for black grievances and to stay out of politics?"[13]

The industrialization approach, emphasizing the way changing labor processes and labor relations alter the possibilities for workers' militance, offers few guides to understanding the links between labor unions and the rise of a broader working-class consciousness. Mobilization around political demands seems to have resulted from labor militance, rather than providing a starting point; but both labor movements spread rapidly beyond the industrial work force. The extent to which industrial workers considered their interests linked to those of rural workers and the unemployed was underlined, in both cases, by unions' coordinated campaigns for political change and for improved living standards for all the disenfranchised. Why, instead of using strikes for narrow economic purposes, did both labor movements challenge the very patterns of industrialization that had created new possibilities for trade union strength?

HISTORICAL DIFFERENCES

A third approach toward understanding labor movements' behavior revolves around the institutional frameworks in which unions emerge, and their past political alliances. Workers' worldviews along with the history of labor legislation, of relations between unions and the state, and of links between unions and parties serve to explain why unions in different national settings behave differently.[14] In their comparative study of Latin American labor movements, Collier and Collier suggest that patterns of state incorporation in early phases of industrialization have shaped the trajectories of labor movements. The degree of political unity among elites, and elite abilities to accommodate a rising middle sector, determined the framework both of labor legislation and of party politics for subsequent decades. In Brazil, Collier and Collier argue, a relatively powerful state repressed and depoliticized labor organizations from the 1930s on, while failing to incorporate a middle-class constituency through populist compromises. The legacy of this failure, they suggest, was a political fragmentation that continues to shape Brazil's political arena: political parties appear fractionalized in the 1990s, as they were in the 1950s, and the Brazilian labor movement remains more independent of central government, and more prone to radicalization, than most Latin American unions.[15]

Other discussions of labor movements emphasize cultural as well as institutional histories. In his comparative study, Charles Bergquist emphasizes the international links of dependent economies, arguing that labor activism has been directly affected by Latin America's export orientation. Yet he too suggests that the best explanations for labor's political alliances are rooted in the past. For Bergquist, patterns of labor mobilization among a country's first proletarians have continued to shape workers' worldviews and their alliances throughout most of this century.[16] Frederic Deyo, comparing East Asian labor movements, stresses both country-specific institutional frameworks and workers' cultural attributes; he explains different patterns of worker mobilization in terms both of state patterns of incorporation, linked to changing economic policies, and of different Confucian ethics in management-employee relations.[17]

While it is persuasive in specific cases, this kind of historical perspective has two drawbacks: not only does it tend to overlook variation over time, but it remains located within the specificities of each nation-state. It leaves little room for exploring changing capacities of labor over time, or the effects of changing international vulnerabilities and pressures on elite coalitions—which, in turn, have a direct effect on the possibilities of worker mobilization.

Above all, the long-term historical approach is unlikely to provide explanations for the emergence of similar labor movements in different settings: given their different patterns of incorporation and different labor histories, how is one to understand the surprising convergence in the nature of unionism in Brazil and South Africa? Before the 1970s, both the institutional framework and the political alliances of the two labor movements were quite different, and it would have been difficult to foresee any convergence in patterns of mobilization. In Brazil, state support for corporatist unions, combined with repression of militant worker demands, seemed to have sapped union strength by the 1970s. Analysts were far more likely to stress union dependence on the state than to predict any upsurge in workers' collective action, and even writers who acknowledged Brazil's history of militant unionism argued that authoritarian corporatism had reduced existing unions to "assistential" bodies, which offered their few members limited material benefits, such as health care and legal advice.[18] In South Africa, on the other hand, observers often suggested that under apartheid's rigid racial stratification, black workers formed a sleeping giant that would one day shake the foundations of racial capitalism. Only state repression and racial divisions within the work force had postponed the inevitable revolt.

Most analysts predicted that black labor unions would focus primarily on racial issues rather than workplace problems: stressing race rather than class, the labor movement would be part of a broader nationalist alliance, challenging political more than economic relationships.[19]

Of course, the crucial historical difference between Brazil and South Africa lies in the almost diametrically opposed racial structuring of class—that is, in the way in which capitalist development interacted with and changed the social meaning of race. The racial orders of Brazil and South Africa are frequently presented as opposite ends of a spectrum: Brazil has been considered a racial democracy, while South Africa remains the world's preeminent example of entrenched racial stratification. The truth is more complicated, but the contrast remains. The Brazilian image of racial democracy has been tarnished by studies showing the depth of discrimination. No reasonable observer could deny clear evidence of racial inequality and social discrimination: differences in incomes, education, and life expectancy reveal the unequal life chances of Brazilians of different colors.[20] Throughout most of the twentieth century, racial discrimination has been legally condoned in housing and employment patterns as well as social clubs; despite the persistence of an ideology of racial openness, even middle-class Brazilians with dark skins have faced obstacles to social and geographic mobility.

Nevertheless, Brazilians' legal status and formal rights have not differed by race since slavery was abolished in 1888. George Reid Andrews concludes:

> To unemployed blacks and those living on the fringes of [the Brazilian] economy, racial discrimination seems the least of their worries. The differences between these people and the poverty-stricken whites and near-whites who live among them are negligible in comparison to those which divide middle-class blacks from their white counterparts. Food, housing, drinkable water, sewers, personal safety, a job—any of these immediate concerns ranks higher on poor blacks' list of priorities than the more elusive, abstract goal of racial equality. . . . Those few Afro-Brazilians who managed to win election [in 1982 and 1986] tended to be people of working-class origin who gave class-based issues primacy over race.[21]

In contrast, all South Africans were legally classified by race from 1948 to 1991, and all legal rights were tied to racial status. Committed to preserving white supremacy, the South African state designed a complex system of segregation, in which racial classification determined where individuals could live, whom they could marry, what jobs they could hold, what schools they could attend. South Africans who were not white were denied political rights and virtually any possibility of upward mobility.

Apartheid was grounded in the principle of racial differentiation; no South African, of whatever pigmentation, could fail to interpret inequality in racial terms. If poor black Brazilian voters have tended to respond to class-based appeals, black South Africans have historically responded with enthusiasm to appeals to black nationalism. Faced by systematic and overt racial oppression, South African nationalists have frequently viewed whites and white supremacy as the source of their problems: in a comment that reflects a recurrent theme in popular protest, Pan Africanist Congress speaker P. K. Leballo said around 1960: "White foreign dogs in our continent! . . . The Europeans must leave us alone. . . . The white people must surrender to the rule of Africa by the Africans." [22]

Not surprisingly, this difference—between a formally race-blind Brazilian state and the South African state's firm commitment to an entrenched racial order—shaped a key difference between the two country's labor histories, determining both the institutional structures in which unions operated and labor's political alliances. For most of the twentieth century, white South African workers could vote. Their racially segregated unions, recognized by the state, could enter collective bargaining arrangements with employers; black workers—the majority of the country's work force—were denied the right to vote as well as the right to collective bargaining. In Brazil, all literate adults could vote—a restriction that meant that three-quarters of adults, primarily rural, poor, and nonwhite, could not vote as late as 1962,[23] but a restriction that was not experienced in racial terms. Even when they recognized authoritarian corporatism's limitations, most Brazilian labor leaders sought to expand an already-existing industrial relations system. Such a strategy was not an option available to black South African unionists: the long history of racial exclusion meant that black activists were far more likely to challenge the state's very structure than to try to work within the existing framework.

Curiously, the demography of Brazil and South Africa in the mid nineteenth century was not radically different: a white elite controlled economic and political power, surrounded by a nonwhite majority. It is tempting, if perhaps simplistic, to attribute the emergence of such different racial orders to different approaches to the creation of a labor supply for the production of primary goods aimed at the world market in the late nineteenth century. When coffee production expanded in

Brazil's south-central region, Brazilian coffee growers prevailed on their government to subsidize massive European immigration instead of bringing native Brazilians—including descendants of slaves and *mestizos*—from the country's more populated northeast. These immigrants and their children made up more than half of São Paulo's industrial work force as late as 1920.[24] When employers tried to enforce control over workers' movements in the early twentieth century, they differentiated between individuals by class, not race. The *carteira* system, under which individuals are required to present their work records to potential employers, was not dissimilar to South Africa's pass system, in that it allowed employers to identify and exclude labor agitators; but once slavery had been outlawed, Brazilian labor controls applied to all workers, not just blacks.[25] When darker-skinned Brazilians moved to the industrial heartland of São Paulo, those lucky enough to find industrial jobs were treated like other workers—at least legally.

In South Africa, on the other hand, mine owners and the state brought skilled European mineworkers to work newly opened gold mines in the late nineteenth century, but most unskilled labor on the mines was performed by Africans, considered only temporary migrants who would inevitably return to subsistence farming. In the colonial setting, only those with education and property—essentially, whites—could vote. Moreover, in contrast to the anarchist philosophies brought to Brazil by southern European workers, the exclusionary craft unionism of South Africa's European mineworkers reinforced racial divisions at the workplace. Even liberal white labor leaders tended to view African workers as peasants, not yet sufficiently proletarianized to be considered true members of the working class or welcomed into their trade unions.[26] Using their political rights to reinforce racial divisions at work, white labor leaders clearly excluded African workers from their constituency: under what they called the "civilized labor" policy, skilled jobs were reserved for whites. Choices of where to seek labor supplies reflected both preexisting racial attitudes and political realities; but once made, these choices also helped shape racial stratification in the future.

Wherever one looks for the origins of racial orders, the fact that access to the state in South Africa was based on race, while in Brazil, it was based on literacy, has been fundamental to each society's labor history. Differences in racial structure are reflected in labor legislation and in labor's strategies. For most of this century, South African unionism has been divided along strict racial lines. From 1924 on, registered unions could represent workers in collective bargaining at industrial councils. As a government commission argued, the existence of such channels induced responsible unionism, where union officers were "much more likely to take the business point of view."[27] The rub, however, was that most workers were denied access to these channels: registered unions could not include African men ("pass-bearing natives"). Like the Brazilian arbitration system, the South African system emphasized industrywide bargaining for registered unions and prohibited union involvement in political activities; but where the Brazilian system excluded rural and casual workers, the South African system excluded workers simply on the basis of race. From 1931 on, African men's wages were set by wage boards of state officials and employer representatives, not by collective bargaining.

By the 1950s, most South African white unions were led by conservative unionists, who insisted on a segregated industrial relations framework.[28] In 1948, when the National Party came to power promising to impose *apartheid,* or strict racial segregation, one of its first acts was to broaden the prohibition on black unions. Partly in response to black worker militance after World War II,[29] a new law prohibited all strikes involving African workers; African workers would be forced to bargain through structures dominated by employers and white unionists, with mechanisms designed to reduce black unions' workplace organization.[30] According to the minister of labour, permitting blacks to form registered unions would allow them to "use their trade unions as a political weapon. . . . I think we would probably be committing race suicide."[31] From 1956 on, registered unions could no longer include workers of different races; those that had mixed memberships (usually of whites, Asians, and "Coloureds") were required to create separate branches and hold separate meetings for members of different racial classifications.[32] From the mid 1950s on, when African women were required to carry passes and thus were redefined as "pass-bearing natives," they too were excluded from registered unions. By the early 1960s, even the few registered unions willing to organize parallel black branches tended to do so only as an effort to control undercutting.[33]

Given the coincidence between those workers who could vote and those admitted to registered unions, it is hardly surprising that organizers in unregistered, mainly black, unions viewed universal adult franchise as the single most important step toward gaining organizing rights for their members. By 1960, black disenfranchisement was complete: the roughly 80 percent of the population classified as "nonwhite" had virtually no political rights. Faced with the highly exclusionary South African registered union system, unionists committed to the broader working class had little choice but to work outside the legal structure. Some unregistered unions, faced with repression and cut off from conservative white workers, managed extraordinary levels of worker organization in individual factories.[34]

But political rights remained the focus of most activists, including those of the unregistered South African Congress of Trade Unions (SACTU), founded in 1955. Influenced by the South African Communist Party's "two-stage" theory, which suggested that South Africa would have to achieve electoral democracy before socialism could even be a goal, many SACTU activists put their energy into national political campaigns as well as, sometimes in place of, shop-floor organizing. SACTU joined the African National Congress and other allied groups in a vigorous campaign for broad reforms, calling for full political rights, land reform, and the nationalization of important national resources. Two Congress Alliance[35] veterans, one of them the SACTU unionist Ray Alexander Simons, concluded:

> The leaders of Congress were intellectuals and trade unionists, but trade unionism was too weak to set the pace. The clergymen, lawyers, writers, teachers, clerks and chiefs who founded Congress or who decided its policies were constitutionalists [who] aspired to political equality within the framework of parliamentary government. . . . [Until the 1950s] Congress was a radical liberal movement which never envisaged anything so far-reaching as the socialization of the land, mines, factories and banks.[36]

Partly in response to urging by the newly formed SACTU, the Congress Alliance included the restructuring of the South African economy as a basic demand in the 1950s; but the focus of most resistance to apartheid was the attainment of political rights for the "nonwhite" majority—a goal that seemed further away than ever as the National Party consolidated its power through the 1960s. Over and over, although some union activists sought to win shop-floor improvements for members, black unions tended to subsume labor issues under the broader banner of black nationalism and liberation.

Brazilian unionists before the 1970s confronted a very different situation. The early Brazilian unions were largely anarchist in orientation, open to all workers; while their publications were as likely to appear in Italian as in Portuguese—reflecting the prominence of recent European immigrants in the industrial labor force—their ideologies were far more inclusive, in terms of skill levels as well as background, than the craft unionism brought by white immigrants to South Africa. Similarly, the Brazilian state never officially divided workers by race or by skill. From the beginning of the century on, Brazil offered legal, if limited, channels for industrial workers' organizations. Especially after 1945, populist politicians offered urban industrial workers material benefits in return for their vote[37]—an offer that in South Africa was limited to white workers. Until the military coup of 1964, Brazil's urban industrial workers could use their electoral power to support politicians who promised to respond to their needs.

Brazil's labor code—instituted by Getúlio Vargas's military regime in the 1930s, and barely changed until the 1980s—was designed to restrict labor organization, not to outlaw it. Under the code, the Ministry of Labor could delineate both the industrial and the geographic reach of all registered unions—that is, all unions active by the 1940s. Moreover, the ministry could invalidate union elections and withdraw funds if it found union activities unacceptable; it had the right to intervene if unions engaged in political activity or illegal strikes. Registered unions' reach was severely restricted: in addition to controlling funds, the government could create "dummy" unions to outweigh militant ones in any industry; rural and casual workers were excluded from unions until 1963. Finally, the ministry retained final arbitration power over collective bargaining arrangements through its tribunals. In return for state control, registered unions received funds through the Ministry of Labor: each worker paid an annual "union tax" (*impôsto sindical*) equal to one day's pay, which supported a massive union bureaucracy. In addition to negotiating contracts, unions were responsible for providing social services such as legal and medical aid and education to their members.

Historians continue to debate how much Brazilian unionists used the corporatist structure to benefit their members and how much they abandoned militance in return for legality.[38] In theory, Brazil's corporate structure was meant to promote class harmony by allowing all classes the right to participate in tripartite fora. Conservative unionists—pejoratively known as *pelegos,* for the blanket that sits between the horse and the saddle—accepted the threat of government intervention in return for legality and state support. But even left-wing unionists tended to work within the legal framework, hoping to win concrete gains for their members.[39] Some writers have even suggested that the combination of the compulsory union tax and the requirement that unions provide social services to members created an incentive for union bureaucrats to limit actual membership.[40]

Nevertheless, by the late 1950s, the labor movement had acquired so much political strength that the Ministry of Labor frequently ignored illegal union activity. Although the ministry sometimes "intervened" in unions that engaged in illegal strikes or undertook directly political campaigns, massive strikes rocked important industrial centers from the late 1950s on. By the early 1960s, when the former labor minister João Goulart assumed the presidency, the labor movement had organized illegal national federations and could engage in political campaigns without fear. Indeed, Goulart's failure to intervene in militant unions and his announcement that he favored land reform and the extension of the franchise to illiterates were major factors in the military's decision to take over government in 1964.

From before World War II to the 1960s, then, where black South African unionists emphasized a general struggle against the state, outside the legal labor relations framework, Brazilian unionists of all political persuasions generally worked inside the state-controlled system, seeking reforms by building political alliances with elected politicians. Given these differences, the similarities between late-twentieth-century labor movements in Brazil and South Africa seem to defy history. Indeed, it is precisely because Brazil and South Africa present such different histories—different working-class cultures, different patterns of social organization, different relations between workers and the state—that the emergence of the social-movement unionism of the 1980s begs comparison.

Moreover, in the 1980s, unionists in both Brazil and South Africa insisted that their strategies differed in important ways from the earlier period, and that their methods—especially their focus on shop-floor organization as the basis of all labor activity—gave their demands a class character that they claimed had been lacking in the earlier period.[41] Both movements developed in the 1980s into "social-movement unionism": shop-floor organizations, originally formed by semi-skilled industrial workers to press employers on wages and working conditions, began to articulate broader working-class demands in conjunction with community groups in poor neighborhoods. Unions supported emergent urban social movements, focusing on the distribution of resources and stamping urban demands and popular opposition with a distinct class character. Through their interaction with working-class community

groups, they helped shape the discourse of a broad opposition, redefining political demands to make working-class inclusion a basic goal. Although the broad opposition included individuals from both middle
and upper classes, the labor movements in both countries prompted
opposition groups to stress the need for changed property relations and
broad economic structures, and for development strategies that would
benefit the previously excluded working class.

The emergence of broad working-class movements, militant and politicized, is unusual enough to demand some explanation: what processes gave these movements enough strength to make the transitions
to democracy in Brazil and South Africa so unusual? Moreover, given
the differences in their history, in their processes of working-class formation, in their labor legislation and racial orders, why should there by
any similarities at all in the processes through which the unions
emerged? Did similar dynamics in the two countries have similar effects
despite very different contexts?

PATTERNS OF MOBILIZATION

Social theorists have long sought to understand the conditions under
which workers seeking to improve their immediate conditions are mobilized into a broad movement. Historically, trade unions acting in their
members' immediate interest have focused on "economic" workplace-
related issues, often appearing unwilling to consider the interests of the
working class as a whole. Industrial workers, united through their employment in single enterprises, are generally believed to have a material
interest in the continuation of capitalist growth, since their wages depend on the firm's continued profitability.[42] Even Marx believed trade
unions were not likely to be radical; industrial workers might compose
a "class-in-itself," but they could only become a revolutionary collective subject when mysteriously transformed into a "class-for-itself."[43]
E. P. Thompson suggests that "class is a social and cultural formation,"
when loosely defined groups of workers come to share the same "conge-
ries of interests, social experiences, traditions, and value-systems,"
which apparently create a "disposition to behave as a class."[44] However, as Ira Katznelson points out, although groups of workers in early
industrializers mapped and interpreted changes in their conditions of
life, in the shift from these shared experiences and dispositions to
"class-based collective action," workers' movements must always over-

come impediments and obstacles; if it occurs, collective action will invariably reflect the peculiarities of a specific social context.[45]

If broad, "class-based collective action" is relatively unusual in earlier industrializers, it is often considered virtually impossible in countries that began industrial development in the mid twentieth century. In countries going through late industrialization, where industrial workers seem privileged in comparison to peasants, trade union leaders often support government industrialization strategies, and trade unions are expected to be relatively conservative.[46] Viewed in this light, both the South African and Brazilian labor movements appear to be anomalies, explicable only in terms of unique national configurations or unusual conjunctures.

How, then, can we explain what appears to be the emergence of militant working-class movements in two such different contexts, where most theories would have led us to expect, in one case, trade unions representing what is often called a labor aristocracy, and, in the other, trade unions that acted simply as a wing of a nationalist alliance? If, rather than treating class formation and mobilization as static phenomena, we view these as developing through longer historical processes—if we examine how workers gradually learn to act "consciously and collectively in the pursuit of common goals" in the context of broader dynamics of economic and social change[47]—the puzzle becomes still more complex. Striking parallels in the decade-long process through which these labor movements emerged—their composition, their forms of organization, their links to community movements, and their challenge to authoritarian states—suggest that the explanation lies deeper than a common rhetoric.

What, precisely, what this common pattern? Emerging in the mid 1970s, the two movements exhibited similar patterns of growth. Defying government prohibitions, workers in important manufacturing industries joined what appeared to be spontaneous strikes over low wages. It was hardly surprising that workers objected to their pay: in both Brazil and South Africa, real wages had fallen since the early 1960s despite high growth rates and increased productivity. But after decades of labor repression, both movements were remarkable for the rapid escalation of strike activity: semi-skilled workers downed tools in factory after factory, spreading into new industries without overt organization or planning. Out of these strike waves, new worker organizations developed, serving as the basis for further mobilization and future strikes.

In both countries, these new organizations immediately placed them-selves outside the legal framework of labor relations. In Brazil, the "new unionism" appeared in a rash of militant illegal strikes. Striking workers argued that legal unions had lost contact with workers' needs; with strikes as their major weapon, labor activists rejected the existing labor relations system as a conspiracy between employers and the state to rob workers of their due.[48] By 1980, nearly three million workers in a broad range of sectors had joined in, and heavy repression by employ-ers and the state could not return the labor movement to its earlier qui-escence.

In South Africa, where black workers had long been excluded from racially structured unions, the choice to organize outside the legal framework was hardly surprising. But the relative success of the 1973 strike wave, in which nearly a hundred thousand workers participated, provided new impetus to the organization of "nonracial" trade unions—unions that organized workers of all races, in contrast to the segregated unions permitted by law. Representing almost entirely black memberships, these new unions and their organizers were subject to severe repression, with dismissals and arrests, sometimes torture, of ac-tivists; the fledgling unions' persistence and longevity surprised even their organizers.[49] Over the next decade, black South African workers would paralyze production, first in individual industries, and later in nationwide general strikes. By the mid 1980s they had built a national movement whose leaders spoke in the name of the entire working class; their power was demonstrated in massive strikes, to the point where some analysts estimated that nearly nine million person-days were lost in 1987.[50]

Strikes are obviously not an indicator of class mobilization: trade unions can take up industrial action without necessarily engaging in political campaigns. However, in both Brazil and South Africa, the rapid spread of what employers called "industrial unrest" both repre-sented and strengthened a broad opposition. Few observers doubted in either case that the rising propensity to strike reflected a broader social conflict. Unfortunately, neither the South African nor the Brazilian strike data are reliable. Not only were factory-level strikes sometimes resolved without public notice,[51] but both governments understated the level of industrial conflict. In the South Africa, for example, the govern-ment in the 1960s sometimes left "work stoppages" out of strike data on the grounds that they were caused by "misunderstandings."[52] There appear to be no published official Brazilian data for strikes in the late

1970s and early 1980s, and while unofficial data have been painstakingly collected by Brazilian researchers,[53] large gaps in the data make it difficult to produce reliable estimates.

Nevertheless, using even incomplete data, the rapid spread of strikes is unmistakable. Figures 1, 2, 3, and 4 show South African workers' rising propensity to strike in the late 1970s. It must be underlined, however, that these strikes refer only to industrial conflict: *they do not include strikes organized on a purely political basis.* This means, for example, that the 1985 figure of person-days lost leaves out the effects of a two-day general strike in the Johannesburg area, which involved anywhere from 300,000 to 800,000 workers.[54] By 1987, person-days lost to political strikes rose to about 3.2 million.[55]

Strikes are traditionally measured along several dimensions: frequency, intensity and duration.[56] Figure 1 shows the official annual totals of strikes and strikers for South African workers in 1950–85. Figure 2 shows the annual numbers of total strikers and the annual number of person-days lost to strikes between 1970 and 1985. Figure 3 shows the same data (total strikers and person-days lost to strikes) in relation to the non-agricultural economically active population. Figure 4 shows the average size of strikes measured in person-days lost per strike, and the average number of person-days lost per striker. Together, they demonstrate a clear rise in the propensity to strike, in terms of numbers of strikes and strikers, size of strikes, and proportions of workers involved in strikes.

Brazilian strike data are at least as sketchy as South African. In general, strikes are underreported, individual factory stoppages are rarely included, and rural strikes are rarely recorded.[57] Nevertheless, the pattern revealed after 1977 is quite similar to that in South Africa: rapid increases in the number of strikes and person-days lost to strikes, indicating a dramatic increase in labor activism. Figure 5 gives an indication of Brazil's annual totals of strikes and strikers for the period between 1978, the first year of broad strike activity after the military took power, and 1986. Figure 6 shows the person-days lost to strikes reported in urban areas, while Figure 7 shows the extent to which strikes were concentrated in Brazil's industrial heartland.

Despite problems in measuring strike intensity, the pattern of mobilization is unmistakable. In both Brazil and South Africa, after initial strike waves, strike activity dropped slightly. Within a few years, however, as the new unions created organizational bases, strike activity began to mount again—no longer a spontaneous expression of workers' frustration over falling real wages, but in an increasingly organized challenge to employer prerogatives. Despite ongoing recessions in both cases, and despite the constant threat of repression and dismissal, both movements grew rapidly.

In both cases, initial demands stressed wages, working conditions and workers' basic dignity. Tactics were equally focused in the workplace: apparently spontaneous strikes, boycotts of overtime work, and go-slows were restricted to single factories or industries. Labor activists stressed direct negotiations between employers and workers' organizations—negotiations that were not legal in either case. In Brazil, although activists sometimes remained officially associated with registered unions, they called for employer negotiations with factory commissions; generally viewing official unions as unresponsive to workers' needs, they emphasized shop-floor organization and autonomy. In South Africa, where registered unions excluded blacks, the "new unionists" struggled for factory-level union recognition. Unionists insisted on direct negotiations with employers, initially refusing to participate in employer-controlled liaison committees or state-run industrial councils.

Rejecting the prevailing pattern of labor relations meant rejecting state intervention in workplace negotiations. In both cases, shop-floor activists viewed state action as a threat to worker organization; in their eyes, the state had historically represented only the dominant classes, using repression to protect employers from lengthy strikes and production losses. Activists initially sought intervention-free negotiations with employers, against whom they could use shop-floor organization; initially, they avoided direct confrontation with the state, and their publicly expressed demands rarely included political rights.

It was only as the labor movements grew, along with a broader community-based opposition, that unions began to call for the redistribution of political power. As José Alvaro Moisés writes of Brazil, citizenship—redefined—emanated from within the specific arena of labor struggles: "Thus the strategy of struggling to extend rights of citizenship: it flows from the union-specific struggle, but, on the other hand, it enters into the social and political terrain precisely to strengthen the conditions of possibility of the labor struggle itself."[58]

As more workers participated in strikes, links developed between workers in different factories, and then between industries. Union membership soared. In South Africa, membership in nonracial and black unions rose from about 200,000 in late 1982 to about 1 million in

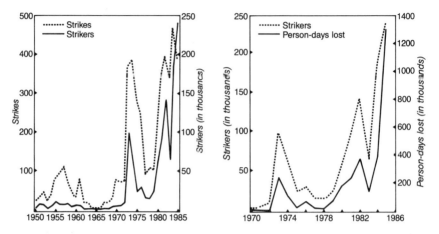

Fig. 1 (*at left*). Strikes and strikers in South Africa, 1950–85.
Sources for figs. 1–4: S.A. Department of Labour and Department of Manpower Year-End Reports, 1960–85; South African Institute of Race Relations, *Survey of Race Relations*, 1960–85; Lipton, *Capitalism and Apartheid*, table 5.

Fig. 2 (*at right*). Strikers and person-days lost to strikes in South Africa, 1970–85.

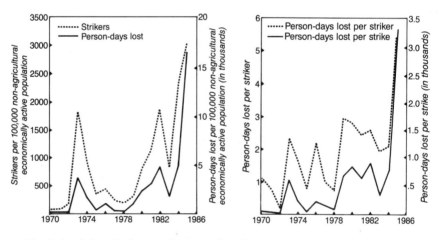

Fig. 3 (*at left*). Strikers and person-days lost per 100,000, non-agricultural economically active population, South Africa, 1970–85.

Fig. 4 (*at right*). Average number of person-days lost per striker and per strike, South Africa, 1970–85.

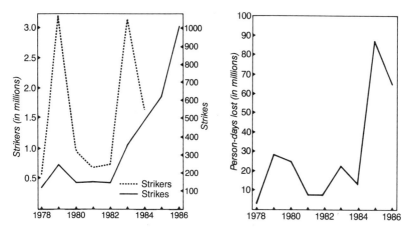

Fig. 5 (*at left*). Strikers and strikes in Brazil, 1978–86. *Sources:* Data on strikers: Alves, *State and Opposition,* tables A-9, A-11. Data for 1985 and 1986 are unavailable. The figure for 1984 includes at least 2 million strikers during the 1984 campaign for direct presidential elections (*diretas já!*). Data on strikes: NEPP/Unicamp; Noronha, *Greve e Conjuntura,* 15; Almeida, "Difícil caminho," 330, 334. These data include strikes mentioned in the press and so give only a reasonable estimate for urban Brazil.

Fig. 6 (*at right*). Person-days lost to strikes in urban Brazil, 1978–86. *Source:* Almeida, "Difícil caminho," 334.

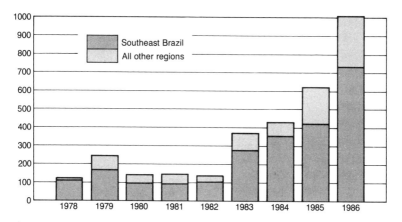

Fig. 7. Number of strikes by region in Brazil, 1978–86. *Source:* Almeida, "Difícil caminho," 334.

1985, a figure that some analysts considered about 30 percent of the realistically "organizable" population.[59] In Brazil, some estimates indicate that union membership more than quadrupled, from 2.7 million before the 1978–79 strike wave to over 12 million in 1983.[60] Workers who began by insisting on their own human dignity in the workplace moved on to demand major changes in the industrial relations system; from there, they began to demand broad participation in political processes.

The new unions generally drew their members from among semi-skilled workers. These workers were not "backward" migrants employed as casual labor: rapid industrialization and changes in the labor force over the previous twenty years had created a stable force of urban industrial workers with steadily increasing skill levels. These skills appear to have protected some strikers from dismissal: in both Brazil and South Africa, industrial employers complained that they could not afford simply to replace striking workers. Indeed, in both cases, strike waves initially occurred when employers were already complaining about skill shortages. During strike waves in the 1970s, when both the Brazilian and South African states threatened repression of strikers, major employers often responded to industrial conflict by seeking to design channels through which workers could express their frustrations and demands rather than risking the loss of trained workers.

Successful strikes in both cases tended to concentrate in sectors marked by especially high growth rates. In both Brazil and South Africa, semi-skilled and skilled workers in the automobile and metal industries—important sectors in both states' industrialization strategies from the early 1960s on—dominated the labor movement. Because the Brazilian government placed a high priority on the production of consumer durables, auto workers in São Paulo regarded themselves as relatively privileged: they believed that both auto manufacturers and the state would agree to negotiate with strikers to avoid production losses.[61] Brazilian auto and metal workers dominated the 1978 and 1979 strike waves, and accounted for about 49 percent of all strikes from 1978 to 1986.[62] In South Africa, unionists initially predicted that multinational corporations, vulnerable to international pressure, would be more willing than domestic firms to recognize black workers' unions. But this strategy proved unsuccessful, as most multinational corporations left labor policies to local managers, who often refused to negotiate, and who were less vulnerable to foreign pressure than the international headquarters.[63] In fact, it was when they began to organize the

semi-skilled and skilled work forces of the economically strategic consumer durable and heavy industries that nonracial unions began to
make concrete organizational gains. As in Brazil, the heavy industries
that had produced South Africa's high growth rates in the 1960s dominated the labor movement. Between 1979 and early 1986, strikes in the
South African metal and automobile sectors accounted for 30.2 percent
of person-days lost to industrial action.[64]

Although labor federations remained illegal, both labor movements
gradually built national, cross-industry groupings. Labor leaders
emerged as national figures, articulating broad political demands. In
Brazil, the labor movement organized a general strike of about three
million workers in 1983, to "sensitize the government to the problems
of the working class" caused by unemployment and austerity measures,
and to support the campaign against military rule.[65] The campaign for
direct elections (*Diretas já!*) did not attain its immediate goals, but it
helped set the stage for a transition to civilian rule. With the return of
civilian rule, labor leaders slowly learned how to engage in the electoral
process, trying simultaneously to maintain an independent labor movement and to build an electoral coalition backing widespread reform.[66]
In 1989 the Partido dos Trabalhadores, or Workers' Party, which grew
out of the labor movement, would produce a solid electoral base for the
automobile union's charismatic leader, popularly known as Lula.

Although the South African state proved far more obdurate than the
Brazilian military—arguably because the state represented racial as well
as class interests—the labor movement emerged by the mid 1980s as a
major player in South Africa's political opposition. On one hand, the
labor movement helped push leading industrialists to support reform
both in labor legislation and in racial controls. On the other, the labor
movement challenged the black nationalist movement to define more
clearly its commitment to economic as well as political change. In the
early 1990s, a transition to a democratically elected government appeared inevitable, and few observers doubted that the labor movement
would continue to help shape popular demands.

Closely linked to the escalation in demands, in both cases, was
broadened support for the labor movement. Close relationships between emergent labor movements and urban working-class community
organizations allowed labor movements to grow beyond their initial
factory bases; indeed, community support was a key factor in early
labor victories, limiting employers' ability to hire replacement workers
despite widespread unemployment—and despite the fact that in both

cases pickets and most strikes were illegal. Community donations created strike funds; community institutions, particularly churches, provided meeting places outside the factory, bringing together workers
from different industrial sites without employer supervision; community organizers increased pressure on intransigent employers, using consumer boycotts and community stay-aways in South Africa and appeals
to politicians and public demonstrations in Brazil.[67]

The links between labor movements and urban community groups
went beyond community support for worker action, however. In both
cases, labor movements emerged in areas where new industrial growth
and concentration had created working-class communities segregated
from higher-income areas.[68] Women workers, who had joined the industrial labor force during rapid industrial expansion, may have been
especially likely to link workplace and community demands. But the
linkage was not simply a reflection of gendered roles. In South Africa,
racial segregation laws meant that nearly all industrial workers were
housed in segregated townships outside white cities. In Brazil's industrial triangle—São Paulo, Rio de Janeiro, and Belo Horizonte—
working-class communities grew up near industrial sites, far from the
wealthier city centers; reflecting this segregation, poor areas are called
the "periphery" (*periferia*). Clearly identifiable, South Africa's townships and Brazil's urban peripheries are distinctive for their lack of basic
urban services. As communities in both countries began to organize in
the 1970s and 1980s—in tandem with emergent labor movements—
they demanded improvements in basic living conditions: education,
transport, health care, electrification, water, sewage services. Lacking
electoral channels, community organizations turned to extra-legal pressure—demonstrations, petitions, boycotts—to demand social services.
Once successful strikes revealed the potential power of workers' organizations, unions were enlisted in campaigns for community improvements and political goals.

In the industrial centers of both South Africa and Brazil, emergent
labor unions helped shape community demands. Generally, community
goals were defined in the course of political mobilization:[69] labor's participation often gave a distinct class character to political mobilization.
In many cases, community "consumerist" demands were directly linked
to workplace issues: struggles over transport services, particularly, are
linked to the distance workers must travel between home and job, the
result, in turn, of urban segregation. In both Brazil and South Africa,
early workplace organizations regularly demanded improved bus ser-

vices between factory and neighborhood,[70] and as the unions grew, they backed a broad range of community goals. In both cases, "neighborhood and factory became, through the experience of the workers, two sides of the same coin,"[71] and union and community demands reflected that convergence.

Together, campaigns for better pay and improved urban services can be described as a broad attempt to raise the historically defined living standards of the working class, and to improve conditions in working-class neighborhoods.[72] Rather than focusing entirely on workplace issues, both emergent labor movements came to view community improvements—social services, housing, education, and ultimately, political rights—as integral to their members' needs. Manuel Castells's suggestion that urban social movements are rarely supported by factory-based labor unions[73] underscores how unusual the strong links between labor and urban community groups were in these cases. In Brazil, the Partido dos Trabalhadores appealed to a broad working-class movement, as Lula promised to ensure organizing rights, provide basic social services to working-class neighborhoods, and redistribute land "from those who have to those who have not."[74] In South Africa, by 1987, national labor federations worked closely with the community-based coalition known as the United Democratic Front, listing political change, a "living wage," and a national minimum standard of living for all workers as their main goals. Joint planning and organization of national stay-aways by labor and community groups cost employers millions of days of lost productivity. Even before 1990, when the state lifted the ban on the previously clandestine African National Congress, the labor movement had entered an overt alliance with the national liberation movement.

In both cases, the links between emergent labor organizations and communities took various forms, ranging from the individual workers who led both factory- and community-based groups to joint actions in support of both workers' and communities' demands. Community groups' active support for unions, and unionists' involvement in community organizations, prompted labor movements to articulate broad working-class demands instead of focusing simply on members' workplace needs. Far from being "populist" in the sense of subsuming specifically class-based goals under general demands, both community-union alliances tended to take explicitly working-class stances, insisting on the importance of working-class leadership and demands, shaping protest in class terms. Links between shop-floor and community organizations underlined the "social-movement" character of both labor movements, giving trade unions an unusually inclusive character and strengthening the discourse of class within popular organizations.

The following characteristics, then, suggest surprising and important similarities between the two labor movements—surprising because they occur in such different contexts, important because they suggest a pattern of worker mobilization that contradicts most theoretical expectations:

1. Sudden waves of strike activity after decades of repression, outside legal labor relations frameworks. Originating in specific factories with a heavy emphasis on shop-floor organization, union activity soon spread to include sympathy strikes, industrywide organization, and shop stewards' councils.

2. Rapid escalation of demands, from directly work-related issues to broad economic and political goals. Shop-floor organizations were soon linked through national federations, which presented direct challenges to the state.

3. Strong links between labor movements and community groups, not only in terms of direct community support for workplace struggles, but in terms of demands linking working conditions and the quality of life in working-class areas. These links were underlined when national labor federations took up political demands that expressed the goals of the broad working class, including community goals. Although their activities were concentrated in urban industrial areas, their reach was far wider, significantly altering the prevailing relationships between the working class, the state, and the dominant classes.

This process of rapid worker mobilization—which could be characterized as the transformation of factory-based unions into militant working-class movements—led to a popular redefinition of democracy in both Brazil and South Africa. Instead of simply calling for political rights and elected governments, both movements demanded wholesale revision of the very processes of capitalist development that had spawned an industrial working class. Authoritarian industrialization had meant exclusion as well as growth; citizenship, as a goal, now came to mean not only participation in political decisions but also access to social and economic resources, distribution of which had previously been limited to tiny elites.[75]

A COMPARATIVE PUZZLE

This, then, is the puzzle for which the rest of this book will attempt to construct an explanation: What shaped the political unionism of the 1980s? What were the processes that allowed these working-class movements to emerge, to grow, and to mount a broad-based challenge to the state? And despite the obvious differences in their histories and racial orders, can we find similar patterns to explain the surprising convergence in both the forms and the discourses of the two labor movements? Finally, if there are similarities, and if a reasonable explanation can be constructed for these two cases, what are the implications for our understanding of labor movements in newly industrialized societies in general?

Where does one begin the search for explanations—explanations that can simultaneously account for the emergence of social-movement unionism, and for a convergence between two cases that appear to be so dissimilar? One could, perhaps, focus entirely on the processes through which the Brazilian and South African working classes, in E. P. Thompson's phrase, made themselves; the ways in which workers interpreted their experience has everything to do with how their unions behaved.[76] One might explain the rise of militant labor movements through the stories of individual activists, the factory-by-factory stories of how worker organizations were built; those histories are well worth telling, and, especially in the South African case, remain largely undisclosed. One could describe the active involvement of students and intellectuals, who brought a Marxist analysis to both movements in their early stages. In the Brazilian case, activists from the Christian base communities of the Catholic Church or from its liberation theology wing provided a framework for discussing broader aspects of trade unionism, just as activists sympathetic to the national liberation movement in South Africa argued that unions could not stop at factory gates. Finally, one could discuss the presence in both labor movements of activists from illegal political organizations, whose clandestine networks linked workers in different factories with one another and with community groups.[77]

Nonetheless, the presence of activists and intellectuals can hardly explain the scale of worker mobilization: while individual activists and clandestine groupings may help shape the discourse of an organization, they can hardly determine how that discourse is received or acted upon. By themselves, low wages or poverty in working-class neighborhoods cannot explain the emergence of social movements; in addition to objective circumstances, one must look at how real women and men interpret and reinterpret reality, how they change their views of what they need for survival, how they readjust their aspirations.[78] Falling real wages do not by themselves explain workers' sudden willingness to face police repression, nor can the presence of individual activists, on its own, explain successful mobilization. As Frances Fox Piven and Richard Cloward point out, broad challenges to repressive authority require some shift in the balance of forces. Before examining changes in subjective interpretations, one must also examine the conditions that allow people to act in new ways, to challenge authority and articulate new demands.[79] Did authority lose its ability to control militance? Was its strength eroded by broader structural change? Or were there structural changes in the ability of specific groups to resist the state?

In the cases of Brazil and South Africa, these questions seem especially pertinent. By the mid 1960s, both governments had turned toward harsher authoritarianism, apparently erasing the possibility of either political or social opposition. What prompted workers to begin the dangerous task of organizing at the shop-floor level? What enabled their organizations to survive the threat of repression? As activists began to organize, was there some change in the relative ability of the state or employers to enforce control at the workplace or in communities, which created the space in which social movements could emerge? And can one find similar changes in two such dissimilar cases that may have shaped emergent movements? To begin with descriptions of individual participation and social-movement mobilization would be to skip over what is perhaps a previous question: what had changed in Brazil and South Africa, before and during the 1970s, that allowed these movements to emerge, to grow, and finally to articulate a powerful challenge to authoritarian capitalist development? It is to these questions that chapter 2 turns.

CHAPTER TWO

Conditions for Industrial Growth, 1960–1973

The biggest contribution of the revolution of '64 to the style of government policy has been the use of all possible rationality in the decision-making process, in methodical planning, in the execution and control of action.

*Brazilian president General
Ernesto Geisel, 1973*

We do not want to stop the economic development of South Africa [but] to reconcile the economic and social needs of the country.

*South African prime minister
H. F. Verwoerd, 1959*

Seeking to explain patterns of mobilization in Europe, Charles Tilly asks, "Which sets of people, which resources, which common ends, and which forms of commitment were involved" in collective action; but he also asks whether "the configurations [of people, resources, and ends] change systematically with the advances of capitalism and large organization."[1] He suggests that the study of collective action should begin with an exploration of long-term changes accompanying industrialization and urbanization, looking at how those changes reshaped potential collective actors.[2] For both Brazil and South Africa, this seems a fruitful point of departure, since it was precisely these processes that became the target of radical labor movements' demands.

The industrial strategies of both states from the late 1950s onward changed the structural terrain on which individual activists and clandestine organizations operated: by the early 1970s, state-assisted industrial growth had changed the conditions confronting workers and created new possibilities of challenging employers and the state. The rapid economic growth, and subsequent impasses, which both countries experienced in the 1960s altered relationships between the state and employers, and transformed the industrial working class. Patterns of industrialization—changes in production processes, in relations between states and working classes, in relations between states and domestic and foreign capital—altered working-class life in ways that helped shape worker organization and workers' consciousness.

Where do we look for structural change? By the 1970s, it was widely accepted that industrializing countries in the postwar era had very different internal structures, and confronted very different international contexts, than countries in North America or Europe. Modernization theorists tended to assume that late industrializers would imitate industrialization patterns of Europe and North America; dependency theorists showed, however, that the historical context of postwar industrialization was completely different, and that new growth strategies would have to be found. Developing, or underdeveloped, nations generally entered the twentieth century as exporters of primary products, dependent on fluctuating international markets and imported manufactured goods; fledgling industries in developing societies had not only to find sources of investment capital and workers, but also to compete with already-powerful industries overseas.

By the late 1970s it had become evident that some less-developed countries had developed significant manufacturing sectors, thus distinguishing themselves from developing countries that continued to produce and export primary products. While debates about definition continue, it is now widely accepted that these newly industrialized countries, or NICs, have shown significant levels of industrial growth[3]—among them, Brazil and South Africa. While they both continued to earn foreign exchange through primary products, and to rely heavily on foreign capital and technology, both developed significant manufacturing sectors during impressive growth spurts in the 1960s, experiencing what has been termed "associated-dependent development"—expanded industrial production, in economies that remained dependent on international markets and imported capital and technology.

In the postwar era, countries that hoped to attract new manufacturing capital rather than mining or agricultural investment generally undertook conscious industrialization strategies. In the Third World, development plans were as common among capitalist states as among socialist ones: from almost any theoretical perspective, industrialization appeared to be the only route to economic growth and labor absorption, and among capitalist industrializers, the general strategy appeared straightforward. From the 1950s on, as multinational capital began to expand into manufacturing, industrializing states sought simultaneously to attract investments and to direct industrial growth through subsidies, protective tariffs, and the provision of infrastructure to key sectors.

It is simplistic, of course, to refer to states as unitary actors; indeed, as I shall demonstrate in subsequent chapters, internal divisions in ruling coalitions in both South Africa and Brazil often led to contradictory policies and conflict. Industrializing states, in fact, may be more subject to fragmentation than most: the attempt to maintain domestic stability while trying to improve the national position within the world economy almost inevitably creates friction, if only because industrial policies inevitably privilege some sectors over others.[4] Brazilian and South African economic policies were no less subject to controversy than most; indeed, I suggest that conflict between industrialists and the state over economic policies helped create new openings in which workers' organizations could emerge.

Nevertheless, through the period of rapid growth rates in the late 1960s and early 1970s—through what in Brazil is called the "economic miracle" and in South Africa is called the "economic boom"—there was remarkable cohesion among elites. In both cases, authoritarian states during the 1960s were relatively free to design economic policy: as long as high growth rates were maintained, and as long as economic elites believed themselves beneficiaries of that growth, state policymakers and employers appeared to form a unified coalition. Economic policy was not always consistent; industrialization policies were often hit-or-miss, and both states sometimes overlooked unintended consequences that would later return to haunt them. But through the 1960s, in both cases, rapid industrialization appeared highly successful; repression of political activity was combined with a promise of rapid growth, satisfying economic elites and leaving policymakers in both states relatively free to reshape their national economies.

Development strategies are obviously multifaceted, and any industrialization process is complex, with policies and players constantly interacting and changing. Nevertheless, as this chapter will demonstrate, the rapid growth rates experienced by both Brazil and South Africa were based on remarkably similar development strategies, which combined state assistance with multinational and domestic investments in manufacturing. Intentionally or not, the Brazilian and South African states adopted similar industrialization strategies to resolve economic crises and to demobilize popular uprisings in the early 1960s. From the 1930s onward, both states had encouraged growth in domestic manufacturing by providing key inputs and protecting domestic production from international competition. From the early 1960s on, both states sought to "deepen" the industrial base by attracting foreign investment to new industrial sectors and increasing state investments in basic industries. In both cases, authoritarian states provided cheap inputs and sought to attract foreign and domestic capital and technology into consumer durables and heavy industry; in both cases, state policymakers consciously combined active incentives to private capital with restrictions on labor mobilization and organization, keeping the general wage level well below increases in productivity. Both countries experienced extraordinary rates of capital accumulation and industrial growth during the 1960s, "economic miracles" that seemed to promise an inevitable "takeoff" toward an industrialized economy.

Most studies of late development have focused on peasants, on the relationships between multinational and domestic capital, or on those between capital and industrializing states, rather than on the experiences and behavior of industrial workers in changing contexts. Nevertheless, sociologists have gradually begun to explore the empirical experience of workers in late industrializers. A growing body of literature has examined processes like the creation of a wage labor force in formerly agrarian societies; the relationships between employed industrial workers and rural or unemployed families; the ability of industrializing states to restrain wage increases through repression or co-optation; and the gendered construction of labor markets and labor processes. By the early 1980s, it was widely recognized that industrial workers in most late-industrializing societies had little hope of upward mobility or higher wages; that wage levels were rarely set in terms of increased productivity; and, finally, that industrial workers in most Third World situations remained components of larger networks, including unemployed and rural family members, making it difficult for analysts to define the working class. Nevertheless, industrialization also affects workers and their families, and sociologists and economists have increasingly incorporated this realization into their definition of "development."[5]

However, most of these discussions remain case-specific: in a particular situation, how was the working class formed? How did this process in a particular nation-state shape individuals' experiences? The conclusion Ronaldo Munck reaches in his detailed review of "new international labour studies"—that capitalist development is an uneven and ongoing process, with wide variation and constantly changing relationships—is inescapable;[6] capitalist relations exist in an extraordinary mixture of forms, and wide variations in workers' experiences and the behavior of their organizations reflect different histories, different cultures, different possibilities. Nevertheless, recognizing that capitalism does not advance in a unilinear fashion need not preclude an attempt to explore and explain common patterns; recognizing that labor movements have different histories, and that workers bring different cultures and experiences to their organizations, need not prohibit an attempt to build a more general understanding of the dynamics that shape popular movements in late industrializers. To rephrase Tilly's question: can we discern any systematic changes during the process of industrialization that may shape the forms of collective action available to subordinate classes?

In this chapter, I focus on how a particular pattern of dependent industrialization—with new technologies, expanding multinational investment, and industrializing states—had specific implications for the labor force. Instead of broadening domestic markets, capitalist industrialization in the postwar era was far more likely to involve low wages, labor repression, and production for a global market.[7] Instead of a gradual shift from artisanal production, the postwar expansion of multinational capital was marked by the widespread application of new production processes, using semi-skilled workers and imported capital-intensive technologies.

In the early industrializers of Western Europe, the switch to mass-production techniques in the postwar era probably strengthened workers' position vis-à-vis the state and employers; using electoral power as well as shop-floor militance, workers could insist on guarantees for labor organizing and the formation of welfare programs.[8] In the second half of the twentieth century, however, the correlation between authoritarianism and industrial growth has been close enough to provoke a serious debate about the economic determinants of authoritarianism: was multinational capital more attracted to countries whose states could ensure low wages and political stability?[9] Albert Hirschman points out that the correlation is not absolute: industrial "deepening" has occurred without repression, while many repressive states have been unable to attract new investment.[10] Whatever the reality, however, politicians in many industrializing societies—including those of Brazil and South Africa—argued in the 1960s that economic growth required political stability, and political stability required repression of "extremist" demands.

Just as any industrialization strategy has specific effects on workers' experiences, part of any state's industrialization strategy, then, is its attitude toward labor. Can any links be drawn between industrialization strategies, including restraints on labor, and subsequent mobilization processes? Starting from the premise that broad changes in the economy may affect workers' ability to organize, it seems almost undeniable that different industrial strategies—with different sets of relationships between states and dominant classes, between domestic economies and the world market, and between states and workers—will create different possibilities for labor movements. Is it possible to explain the convergence between the Brazilian and South African labor movements through similar industrialization strategies, which created new possibilities for labor organization by altering the relationship between labor, states, and owning classes? Can similar changes in structural conditions be shown to be linked to new—and similar—possibilities for worker organization?

This chapter examines the broad effects of both industrialization strategies, showing how, during the "economic miracle," both states and industrialists supported a similar development model; but also how the new policies reshaped both business groups and the industrial working class, in ways that in later chapters I shall argue created new possibilities for shop-floor organization, led to new divisions between the dominant classes and the state, and, finally, laid the basis for intensified mobilization against the state. Throughout the "economic miracles" of the 1960s, rapid industrialization reshaped both societies: a relatively skilled and stable working class, denied the benefits of economic expansion and blocked from access to the state, would discover new abilities to organize at the point of production.

BRAZILIAN INDUSTRIALIZATION STRATEGIES

In the late 1970s, Brazil became one of the first developing countries to produce significant quantities of manufactured goods: in 1978, automobiles and automotive parts made up more than half of Brazil's exports. Although by the late 1970s Brazil was heavily indebted, it was no longer an underdeveloped coffee exporter, dependent on imported industrial goods. In 1982, when growth rates turned negative, Brazilians would be forced to recognize that industrialization had not, after all, ended economic dependence on the international economy; but between 1960 and 1980, Brazil experienced one of the world's fastest industrialization spurts, in what was known as Brazil's "economic miracle."

Brazil's process of industrialization was hardly painless. After stumbling onto import-substitution policies in the 1940s, Brazilian elites viewed industrialization as the only path to economic growth; after 1964, the military regime closed political channels, insulating economic policy from popular demands. Controlled by military officers and guided by technical experts, Brazil's military regime sought to attract foreign and domestic private capital to specific industrial sectors, while expanding the state's productive activities to provide inputs for industry. At the same time, strict controls on wage levels reduced labor costs and increased income stratification. By the mid 1970s, social critics would point out that instead of increasing overall wealth, Brazil's industrialization patterns had created poverty as well as growth.[11] How did industrialization patterns—particularly, changing production processes and concentration in industrial centers—change organizational possibilities for labor at the point of production?

IMPORT-SUBSTITUTION POLICIES

Brazil first adopted a conscious industrialization strategy in the 1930s: successive Brazilian governments argued that domestic industries would solve the country's economic problems by absorbing labor and reducing trade deficits. Heavily dependent on coffee exports, Brazil was hard-hit by the collapse of world trade during the Great Depression: Brazilian exports declined from £95 million in 1929 to £66 million in 1930.[12] The sudden drop in world demand created massive unemployment and poverty. Almost immediately, reformist army officers led by Getúlio Vargas seized the central government, hoping to "make the revolution before the people do."[13]

Historians debate Vargas's intent, but during his first decade in office, the state embarked on policies that simultaneously stimulated industrial growth and brought labor unions under state control.[14] Armed with corporativist philosophies borrowed from Mussolini's Italy, Vargas's Estado Novo gave workers new rights to pensions, vacations, and the like. On the other hand, the government consistently restricted labor leaders, bringing unions under the control of a new Ministry of Labor. Particularly after an attempted Communist putsch in 1935 gave the army an excuse to repress all liberal voices, the government seemed less interested in building class harmony than in enforcing working-class quiescence.

But the depression also prompted Brazil's military rulers to lay the basis for further industrialization. Public works programs provided jobs, and they helped create a national infrastructure. By the mid 1930s, Vargas was also experimenting with subsidies and tariffs to support fledgling industries.[15] After the war, successive civilian governments—including that of Vargas, now elected on a labor platform—considered infrastructural development and the provision of basic industrial inputs to be prerequisites for future growth. By the late 1950s, a network of new roads linked cities in different parts of the country. Basic inputs for industry were under direct state control. Petroleum production was nationalized, and state and federal governments invested heavily in electricity and iron and steel production. Electric power generation rose from about 7.5 billion kwh in 1949 to nearly 24.5 billion in 1961;[16] between 1949 and 1960, iron and steel imports dropped from 198,335 tons to 34,671, while domestic production rose from 1.1 million tons to 3.9 million tons.[17] Werner Baer estimates that total industrial production, including mining, manufacturing, construction, and electricity, nearly tripled between 1949 and 1961; manufacturing production more than tripled.[18]

"Developmentalism"—a constant emphasis on the need for economic growth, primarily of domestic manufacturing—has been described as Brazil's dominant ideology during the 1950s.[19] Political leaders in the 1950s proved adept at building coalitions around growth-oriented policies, persuading labor as well as private industry and agriculture to support industrial growth.

Political participation was severely restricted: Brazil's "experiment in democracy" hardly involved full representation of all sectors, as the Communist Party remained banned and the 1945 constitution excluded illiterates from the electorate. Successive governments retained Vargas's restrictive labor code (after 1943, collectively known as the Consolidação das Leis Trabalhistas, or CLT), giving the Ministry of Labor power to define union memberships, ratify internal elections, and arbitrate between corporatist groupings of employers and unions within single industries. Nevertheless, nationalist labor leaders often argued that workers would benefit from industrialization because it would reduce the power of "feudal" landowners and "imperialist" foreign capital.[20] Even militant labor leaders rarely objected explicitly to the CLT before 1960:

despite its ban on union federations and broader political activities, the CLT also ensured that all workers, even non-members, paid the union tax (*impôsto sindical*) that funded registered unions.[21]

By the late 1950s, policymakers consciously sought to "deepen" the country's industrial base through policies designed to attract foreign capital and to provide cheap inputs. In theory, at least, consumer durables figured prominently in industrial plans. Because automobile imports contributed heavily to a deteriorating balance-of-trade deficit, Brazil began experimenting with steps to promote a national automobile industry—beginning with prohibitions on importing certain parts, then restricting imports of knocked-down vehicles, and finally placing prohibitive import duties on foreign auto parts. From 1956 on, a government-created Automobile Executive Group designed policies to promote local production; although production grew very slowly, by 1962 Brazil was capable of producing a full range of automobile parts and components.[22]

In addition to offering incentives to private industry, the Brazilian state promoted industrialization through state enterprises, providing key inputs at relatively low cost. The civilian government of the late 1950s, like the post-1964 military government, supported private initiatives in industrial growth; but it also argued that state companies could function as profit-maximizing entities in areas that were not yet profitable enough to attract private investment. By 1960, nearly one-fourth of total public investment went into relatively new state enterprises.[23]

In retrospect, many economists would agree that despite their rather ad hoc nature, import-substitution policies aiding domestic private production and direct state investment in new sectors laid the basis for a subsequent industrial boom.[24] At the time, however, new investments in industry brought about both a worsening balance-of-trade deficit and a dramatic increase in labor organization. While coffee prices declined in the late 1950s, the prices of imports needed for rapid-industrialization policies rose; successive governments borrowed heavily to cover the difference, and inflation soared. In 1960, nearly 37 percent of export earnings went to service foreign debt, and elected governments were forced to consider austerity measures.[25]

Even within the limited democracy of the 1950s, the Brazilian government confronted a crisis as the economy declined. In the urban areas, increasingly militant unions protested both inflation and austerity proposals. Rural unions remained banned, but 1,448,151 workers had joined registered unions by 1963;[26] despite the Labor Code's restrictions on political involvement by unions, organized urban workers had become an important political force. Although unionists were divided in their approaches to unionism—Communist and Brazilian Labor Party unionists seeking a coalition between working-class organizations and nationalist politicians, and Catholic and conservative unionists seeking to build more economistic labor organizations[27]—they united in an illegal union federation in the early 1960s, regularly calling national strikes.[28] Despite opposition from some conservative unionists, the national labor movement appeared increasingly willing to support radical demands.[29]

Businessmen and military officers viewed spreading militance with growing alarm; the Cold War provided a prism through which even minimal reformism appeared apocalyptic, as "subversive forces" placed "the president himself . . . in the forefront of the subversive process."[30] These fears of left-wing reforms were hardly groundless: workers made some concrete gains during this period. In real terms, the minimum wage was higher in 1959 than at any point before or since, and many politicians sought popular support by promising significant concessions to the labor movement. Through the early 1960s, repeated national strikes and the rise of peasant leagues in the northeast demonstrated growing organization on the part of a mass movement.[31] On March 13, 1964, then-president Goulart announced his support for the "Base Reforms"—the extension of the franchise, land reform, and nationalization of important resources. Two weeks later, Brazil's armed forces, backed by the Catholic hierarchy and by business groups, removed Goulart from office. Brazil would not hold another direct presidential election until 1989.

1964: REPRESSION AND GROWTH

Given the military's initial emphasis on imposing calm in a highly politicized atmosphere, it is hardly surprising that Brazil's new rulers concentrated first on suppressing political opposition and the labor movement, with successive executive decrees removing channels for opposition. Up to 50,000 people were arrested immediately after the coup; at least 8,000 were still detained six months later. In the first year of military rule, at least 110 individual representatives to national, state and municipal assemblies lost their political rights; 49 judges were removed, 1,408 civil servants lost their jobs, and 1,200 members of the military forces were declared legally dead, losing all pensions and benefits.[32] At a broader level, the military government institutionalized what Maria Helena Moreira Alves calls a "national security state": national security services took control of virtually every aspect of government, installing representatives at every level of local and state bureaucracy. Press censorship was imposed, and with the passage of the notorious Institutional Act Number Five (AI-5) in 1968, the military removed the legal protection of habeas corpus and any hope of an independent judiciary.[33]

The labor movement was an immediate target of the drive against subversion. As a church-funded study argued, the "generals of April" most feared opposition from nationalists in the army and in the labor movement, "who could have messed up the economic model that they were going to impose, in the form of the wage policy and the denationalization" of the economy.[34] Hundreds of individual unionists were removed from office through arrests and *cassações,* or the removal of political rights; the military government took control of the country's major industrial unions, under a 1953 law granting the state the right to replace leaders of registered unions for "crimes against the political and social order." In the first year after the coup, the federal government removed the elected leaders of 433 unions; in 81.9 percent of cases, the reason given was "subversion." Large industrial unions were particularly targeted: nearly 65 percent of the post-coup interventions were in the large industrial and transport unions of the south-central area, while 70 percent of the 73 unions representing more than 5,000 workers suffered interventions.[35] By 1965, any unionist still in office was either government-appointed or considered willing to cooperate with the Labor Ministry.

Industrial growth remained a key objective; indeed, the post-1964 government is a classic example of what Guillermo O'Donnell calls the "bureaucratic-authoritarian state," closing political channels in order to restructure the economy.[36] Over the next decade, Brazil gradually developed a new industrialization pattern, resting on a tripartite alliance between the state and domestic and foreign capital. The state would attract foreign and domestic investors into industry, supporting their investments with tariffs, subsidies, and state enterprise production; simultaneously, by extending credit to upper- and middle-class consumers, the state would create a market for a growing consumer durables sector. Until the effects of the 1973 international economic crisis began to be felt, Brazil's growth rates were truly extraordinary:

industrialists believed the "favorable conjuncture" would continue forever.[37]

The military government was not entirely consistent in its approach to the economy during its first decade. Several different ministers held the portfolio for economic planning, and each emphasized different aspects of growth. Albert Fishlow argues that until 1967, the military's economic advisers attempted orthodox policies acceptable to foreign creditors; paradoxically, after 1967, when the last remnants of an internal political process were closed down, economic policies tended to be somewhat more heterodox. Nevertheless, Fishlow concludes, while specific policies varied, the principal aim throughout was "making market capitalism work." Private capital, both foreign and domestic, was attracted into new sectors of industry, while the state retained control through financial centralization and direct investments.[38] The 1967 constitution, proposed by a military president and passed by a military-dominated congress, summarized the regime's approach to industrialization: strong central control, protection for private investment, and strict control over wages and unions. The state could invest in areas essential for national security and provide investment incentives, but private ownership was primary, and the government could not nationalize corporations. Nationalism was outweighed by the desire to attract foreign investment: any company with a Brazilian subsidiary could buy mining rights, and even petroleum refining, previously controlled by a state enterprise, was now opened to private enterprise.[39]

Begun at a moment when international corporations were investing in industrial enterprises around the world, the military regime's industrial strategy seemed to produce miraculous growth rates. Between 1962 and 1967, annual growth rates in real GDP averaged only 3.7 percent; between 1968 and 1974, however, annual growth in real GDP averaged 11.3 percent. Industrial growth rates soared even higher, with yearly growth rates averaging 12.6 percent.[40]

By 1974, industry accounted for 39.8 percent of net domestic product, while agriculture accounted for only 11.2 percent.[41] As table 1 shows, sectoral growth rates within industry varied significantly: while capital and intermediate goods production expanded between 1965 and 1970, growth in consumer durables was extraordinary. Protected by tariffs and supported by state financing policies, the consumer durables sector also benefited greatly from foreign investment and technology, as well as from an expanded domestic market.

In order to execute its policies, the military government tightened

TABLE 1

SECTORAL RATES OF GROWTH IN INDUSTRY,
BRAZIL, 1965–70 (PERCENTAGE)

	1965–67	1967–70
Durable consumer goods	13.4	21.9
Nondurable consumer goods	3.6	9.7
Capital goods	4.5	13.7
Intermediate goods	10.8	13.7
Exports	5.9	10.7

SOURCE: Foxley, *Latin American Experiments,* 27

federal control over the economy, primarily by controlling domestic finance. First, the federal government took control over tax revenues away from municipal and state bodies. Second, the federal government created new funds, including several to which employees made compulsory contributions, which concentrated large quantities of liquid capital under state control. Between 1965 and 1971, the federal government's running expenses increased by 50 percent, while its real income increased by 80 percent. Furthermore, between 1964 and 1974, 134 new federally controlled funds were created; by 1973, the 55 largest federal funds—not including those administered by the Bank of Brazil—controlled about 3 percent of the national product.[42] By 1974, state-controlled banks held 55.5 percent of total deposits, and almost 65 percent of the loans held by the fifty largest banks.[43]

Through its financial resources, the central state could extend credit to new private enterprises and consumers and fund new state enterprises; thus the state could direct industrial growth both through assisting private investors and through direct investment. Support for state enterprises grew steadily; between 1964 and 1970, annual investment in state enterprises grew at an average rate of 24.5 percent.[44] Brazil had already experimented with state-funded companies to provide goods and services needed for industrialization; under the military governments of the 1960s, however, state companies expanded into new areas. Nearly half of the 231 enterprises created between 1966 and 1975 were in the public service sector, but nearly a third were in industry, construction, or armaments.[45] State companies were particularly dominant in mining, metal products, chemicals, and utilities.

By 1974, state-run companies controlled over 39 percent of the net assets belonging to Brazil's 5,113 largest incorporated firms.[46] While these companies were expected to run on a profit-maximizing basis, they appear often to have sacrificed profitability to broader government objectives such as controlling inflation,[47] and, it could be argued, supporting private capital accumulation by providing cheap inputs to private industries. In part to finance an expanding state sector and to encourage domestic investors, the government relied increasingly on loans, mainly from private banks, to create investment capital: by 1978, the total foreign debt would reach $40 billion, of which about 80 percent was owed to private banks.[48]

State policies also aimed to attract private capital and technology into specific sectors, through subsidies and tariff protection. Although tariffs were generally reduced during the 1960s, Brazil's economic planners sought to balance their desire to open the economy with protection for domestic industry. Tariffs continued to protect the durable consumer goods industry, although the rate declined slightly from 260 percent of nominal value in 1966 to 176 percent in 1969; tariffs on manufactured goods also remained, although they too fell, from 114 percent to 67 percent.[49]

Protection for domestic industry did not always mean protection for domestic capital, however: the consumer durables industry, carefully protected by tariffs, was dominated by foreign capital and joint ventures. It is estimated that in 1970, over 80 percent of investment capital in the consumer durables industry was foreign—compared to about 46 percent in non-durable consumer goods, 43 percent in intermediate goods, and 15 percent in basic industries.[50] By 1974, private foreign capital controlled about 10 percent of total investments and 18 percent of the net assets of large firms.[51]

The dominance of foreign capital in dynamic sectors reflects the military government's approach. Four months after the coup, the military government repealed a 10 percent ceiling on profit remittances; a 204 percent devaluation in 1964 was followed by another 21 percent devaluation in 1965. Foreign capital gradually began to flow in, first as loans, then as direct private investment. The U.S. government lent $50 million in June 1964; in 1965, the World Bank granted its first loans to Brazil since 1950.[52] Although private foreign capital was slower to respond to the changed investment climate, it, too, was gradually drawn in: direct foreign investment increased from a low of $30 million in 1963 to $189 million in 1969, then soared to over $1 billion by 1975. Investments were overwhelmingly in industry: in 1973, 69 percent of total U.S. investments in Brazil were in manufacturing, with 12 percent in the extractive and primary sector and 19 percent in other sectors, including utilities.[53]

From the late 1960s on, then, foreign investment concentrated in the economy's most dynamic sectors: Brazil became the archetypal example of what Fernando Henrique Cardoso and Enzo Faletto call "associated-dependent development," with industrial growth predicated on close relations between the state and domestic and multinational capital.[54] Foreign capital tended to move into high growth, high technology sectors, where Brazilian firms could not compete: half of the Brazilian affiliates of U.S. multinationals reporting to a U.S. Senate subcommittee on multinationals in the mid 1970s admitted they controlled 25 to 100 percent of the markets in which their products were sold.[55] Instead of being antagonistic to this process, state enterprises and private Brazilian companies viewed cooperation with foreign companies, through joint ventures, as a way to take advantage of imported technology, while foreign capital viewed such ventures as a way to gain tariff protection and local links. As Peter Evans puts it, "For multinationals asking 'How can I get in?' and local capital asking 'How can I survive?' the answer seems to be the same—a joint venture."[56] The level of foreign dominance varied from industry to industry, but by the end of the decade, three-fifths of total industrial output, measured in terms of value, came from industries containing significant amounts of both foreign and local capital.[57]

Government policy, then, sought to assist industrialization by attracting investment, protecting domestic industry, and providing inputs and finance. Foreign and private capital moved into new industrial sectors. The state also used its increased economic power to create markets for new goods. Expanded credit for consumer durables was a key aspect of fiscal policy after 1967, with almost immediate impact on Brazil's domestic market. Small cars aimed at middle-class consumers accounted for only 7.5 percent of the 86 percent growth in automobile production between 1968 and 1970, but in the period 1970–74, small cars accounted for 78 percent of the 125 percent growth in automobile production[58]—a clear indication of the relationship between expanded credit and expanding domestic markets.

Many economists have argued that the consumer durables sector, in particular, was also helped by the rise of income inequality during the first decade of military rule. Table 2 shows that between 1960 and 1976, the income share of 80 percent of Brazil's economically active population shrank, with most of that change taking place during the 1960s.[59] Unlike the cheaper consumer goods, such as textiles, that had

TABLE 2

INCOME CONCENTRATION, BRAZIL, 1960–76

Economically Active Population	GNP Share per Year (%)		
	1960	1970	1976
Poorest 50%	17.71	14.91	11.60
Next poorest 30%	27.92	22.85	21.20
Middle 15%	26.60	27.38	28.00
Richest 5%	27.69	34.96	39.00

SOURCE: IstoÉ, Aug. 9, 1979, 65; cited in Alves, State and Opposition, 111

dominated earlier phases of Brazil's industrialization, expensive consumer durables went to the upper and middle classes. Samuel Morley
and Gordon Smith show a direct relation between income inequality
and rates of growth in manufacturing and employment in manufacturing, which they attribute to "the importance of consumer durables, especially automobiles and their supplier industries—rubber, machinery,
metals and fuels—in the budgets of the rich."[60] Luiz Bresser Pereira
argues that the military regime's economic model divided Brazil into
two groups: the upper and middle classes, who made up about 20 percent of the population, and the rest of the country. Under the model,
Pereira writes,

> The [upper class] consumes mainly luxury goods—automobiles, durable
> consumer goods, and services provided by the modern technologically-
> dynamic sector. The concentration of income among the upper and middle
> classes favors an even greater development of large national and interna-
> tional corporations as well as public enterprises. In turn, these large enter-
> prises, highly capital-intensive and technologically sophisticated, increase
> the demand for specialized and administrative personnel, rather than non-
> specialized workers. Middle-class employment increases at the same time as
> lower-class workers become increasingly marginalized. Thus the circle of
> development is completed, as development of the modern sector permits
> concentration among the upper and middle classes, and this concentration,
> in its turn, stimulates the modern sectors' growth. Both the traditional pro-
> ductive sector and the lower classes are excluded, marginalized from this
> process.[61]

Pereira may overstate the extent to which the state aimed to intensify
income stratification, but there is no question that control over wages—
considered by orthodox planners to be essential to controlling infla-

tion—comprised a major part of the military government's economic policies. The effects of the wage policy, known as the "wage squeeze" (*arrôcho salarial*), was felt throughout the economy: average real wages for all sectors, already eroded by inflation, fell by as much as 35 percent between 1964 and 1970.[62] In September 1964, the new government announced that wage increases would be limited to the level of increased productivity. Enforcing this restriction through the Ministry of Labor's tribunals, the state manipulated inflation and productivity indices to lower real wages. Between 1968 and 1973, while real productivity rose 7 percent annually, the government index, on which wage levels were based, averaged only 3.2 percent per annum.[63] As table 3 shows, by 1970 the real value of the legal minimum wage had fallen to 42 percent of its 1959 value, and by 1976 it was down to 34 percent.[64] In 1970, about half of all working Brazilians earned less than a single

TABLE 3

MINIMUM WAGE LEVELS, BRAZIL, 1959—76

	Minimum Wage (in 1976 cruzeiros)	Percentage of 1959 Wage
1959	1,735.29	100
1960	1,204.03	69
1961	1,475.00	85
1962	1,406.38	81
1963	1,304.35	75
1964	724.14	42
1965	840.00	48
1966	849.42	49
1967	744.02	43
1968	737.88	43
1969	732.62	42
1970	724.91	42
1971	723.90	42
1972	690.96	40
1973	681.37	39
1974	623.63	36
1975	600.35	35
1976	590.49	34

SOURCE: *Divulgação* 1/76 (Apr. 19, 1976): 10.

minimum wage per month.[65] Higher-paid workers were also affected: Brazilian wages are usually calculated in multiples of the minimum wage, so any reduction in the real value of the minimum wage immediately lowers all real wages.

CONTROLS OVER LABOR

Obviously, controlling labor unions was crucial to the wage policy's success: a mobilized labor movement would have made the "wage squeeze" impossible. Angela Figueirido argues that from 1966 on, control over unions moved into a second phase: with militant activists already removed, and with prohibitions on political and solidarity strikes and political involvement,[66] the state no longer faced directly political resistance from union officials. Between 1965 and 1970, nearly all of the 104 interventions in union leaderships were attributed to nonpolitical reasons, such as electoral fraud, rather than to overt political motives.[67]

Recognizing that industrial unions could restrain worker militancy as well as stimulate it, the military government required registered unions to provide new services to members. Although the government moved most social security, medical, and continuing educational programs—previously administered by unions—to a national social welfare agency under state control,[68] it raised unions' financial obligations, reducing the state's contribution and forcing unions to spend more of their budgets on these programs. Under the Labor Code, union officials had long been separated from the shop floor, but now union officials could withhold salaries from mid-level officers who attempted to expand union activities beyond "assistential" social-welfare services. Finally, the military government began to register "phantom" unions, bureaucratic entities with no real members, which had disproportionate voices in national federations because their votes counted equally with those of large unions.[69] A study of São Paulo unions conducted in 1972 concluded: "Because of the threat of intervention and the bureaucratic imperatives of the unions, the behavior of radicals who are still in leadership positions is hardly distinguishable from that of bought-off *pelegos.*"[70]

The limits of acceptable union behavior were quite clear. In early 1968, two major strikes—at least partly prompted by a national campaign against the government's wage policy—only succeeded in illustrating the extent to which union strength had been eroded. In April, twelve thousand workers went on strike in Contagem, an industrial area outside Belo Horizonte, in an apparently spontaneous response to wage constraints, layoffs and government intervention in the local metalworkers' union. After a brief discussions with a hastily organized strike committee, the minister of labor ruled the strike illegal; military police took over the industrial park and surrounding residential areas, prohibiting meetings. After the strike, nominal wages were raised 10 percent for workers nationally, but wage limitations—previously treated as a three-year temporary measure—were permanently institutionalized.[71] In July, a thousand workers in Osasco, outside São Paulo, occupied their factory, and several neighboring factories went on strike. Led by a union local president—who secretly belonged to an underground left-wing group, and who hoped to use official union resources to support workers' demands—the strikers were better organized than at Contagem, with clandestine shop-floor networks set up in advance.[72] However, the state responded much more quickly: the Labor Ministry intervened almost immediately. On the second day, the army invaded the occupied factory with machine guns and armored vehicles, broke up a meeting at a local church, and virtually occupied the entire city. By the third day, the strike was over. No demands were won, and leaders were arrested or forced into hiding and exile.[73] Although hindsight allows a reinterpretation of the Osasco strike as foreshadowing the "new unionism"—with its emphasis on independent shop-floor-based unionism, its reliance on community support, and its critique of bureaucratic unionism—the strike's defeat left little room for optimism regarding the potential of working-class resistance.

That year the military regime banned the student movement and promulgated AI-5, closing all avenues of legal organization. In 1969, the theme of the new president General Emilio Garrastazzú Medici, "Security and Development," signaled intensified repression. Along with the Osasco and Contagem strikes, the decision of left-wing groups to attempt armed opposition provided a rationale for the military to systematically detain, torture, and exile individuals suspected of subversion; throughout the early 1970s, union activists faced a very real threat of imprisonment.[74]

There is little doubt that at least some major industrialists supported direct repression. Local and multinational companies in São Paulo—including Grupo Ultra, Ford, and General Motors—initially financed Operação Bandeirantes (OBAN), an army-supported paramilitary organization which became notorious for initiating extra-legal repression in São Paulo.[75] With a network of secret prisons, first in the city and later in the rest of Brazil, OBAN and its successors within the various secret services were responsible for widespread detention without trial and torture during 1969–73, the most repressive period of Brazilian military rule.

In this climate, it is hardly surprising that union officials failed to mobilize industrial workers, or that workers had little hope that unions could alter the situation. In the year before the coup, there were ninety-six strikes recorded in the state of São Paulo, the historical center of union militance; between 1965 and 1969, there was exactly one officially recorded strike.[76] Unionists who sought real improvements in workers' lives tended to focus on assistential services, arguing that a militant stance could jeopardize the unions' very existence.[77] Union membership fell from 49 to 36 percent of the non-agricultural work force between 1965 and 1972,[78] largely because, as one worker told an interviewer in 1970–71:

> The union's not worth anything anymore. It used to have more strength. . . .
> After the military government entered, they arrested and removed the rights
> of union leaders. Today everything's run by the government. . . . It used to
> be that when there was a strike, they had the strength to make a strike and
> demand a raise. . . . With this government, it's over. The workers don't strike
> any more because they can't. Now you can't even talk, because the govern-
> ment arrests you.[79]

Surveys from the early 1970s suggest that many workers had abandoned expectations that unions could improve wages or working conditions, and instead assumed unions would remain bureaucratic, assistential bodies.[80]

Meanwhile, the military government increased the vulnerability of individual workers. First, it virtually eliminated job stability regulations, which had required employers to pay indemnity for unjustly firing workers with more than a year's service in the company. Employers argued that this system—under which workers with more than ten years' service could be dismissed only if serious misconduct were proved in court—lowered productivity; in 1966, the government instituted a new system reducing employers' obligations to workers. Under the new system, the state created an unemployment fund (Fundo de Garantia por Tempo de Serviço, or FGTS). Employers deposited 8 percent of a worker's monthly wage in an account in the worker's name; instead of indemnity payments from the employer, dismissed workers were paid out of this account.[81] However, the FGTS significantly reduced benefits: of the 8 percent of wages paid into the fund, only 2.8 percent reached the dismissed worker. The rest of the fund was paid into several government funds, primarily the National Housing Fund (Banco Nacional de Habitação).

Institutionalized in the 1967 constitution, the FGTS system dramatically increased worker turnover: in one industry, Vera Lucia B. Ferrante found a 200 percent increase in layoffs of workers with more than a year's seniority between 1966 and 1970. She argues that the FGTS was part of the government's effort to attract private investment, facilitating capital accumulation by increasing the mobility of labor, allowing employers to take full advantage of the existence of a large pool of unemployed workers. "With the new law, the government gave businessmen the ability to manipulate the worker's effective productivity, giving employers liberty in the handling of personnel, and creating conditions in which they would confront tensions inside the firm less frequently." [82] While some Brazilian employers benefited more than others, turnover seems to have grown dramatically: in a 1976–77 study of São Paulo automobile firms—admittedly in an industry subject to especially high turnover rates—John Humphrey found that between 33.2 and 54.2 percent of the total labor force left annually. Moreover, the layoffs affected workers with skills and seniority as well as newly hired casual labor: in 1978, 59 percent of all workers leaving five factories had more than a year's service. [83]

RESHAPING THE LABOR FORCE

From the mid 1960s onward, then, a unilinear drop in real wages, coupled with systematic increases in employer control at the workplace— through both a greatly reduced sphere of union action and heightened individual vulnerability—gave some basis for the slightly conspiratorial tinge of many unionists' descriptions of Brazilian state policy. State policymakers may not have explicitly intended to increase income stratification, but the results were unmistakable. Economic policies produced a highly skewed income distribution, which provided an internal market for domestically produced consumer durables and reduced the ability of unions and workers to articulate their demands.

Industrial growth was, of course, accompanied by changes in the class structure. Between 1960 and 1980, Brazil's industrial work force nearly quadrupled, from 2,940,242 to 10,674,977. [84] Using a more complex definition, Paul Singer estimates that between 1960 and 1976,

TABLE 4

GROWTH RATES FOR EMPLOYMENT AND OUTPUT, BRAZIL, 1967–80

	1967–73		1973–80	
	Growth Rate of Output	Growth Rate of Employment	Growth Rate of Output	Growth Rate of Employment
Dynamic industries	16.7	9.9	8.4	4.5
Minerals (non-metal)	13.1	7.7	8.8	4.9
Metallurgy	11.7	8.7	9.3	6.1
Machinery	20.2	21.3	0.0	6.3
Electrical and communications	17.7	8.8	7.5	4.1
Transport equipment	21.8	8.5	6.2	2.7
Paper	13.0	8.1	2.7	3.4
Chemical products	16.5	5.7	7.6	0.8
Traditional industries	9.4	8.1	4.6	3.6
Textiles	9.0	4.2	3.1	-0.4
Apparel	7.9	12.8	4.6	6.8
Food	9.1	9.4	5.1	2.6
Beverages	9.9	3.3	7.5	0.8
Tobacco	5.6	0.5	6.3	3.9
Total	13.3	9.0	6.8	4.0

SOURCE: World Bank, *Brazil: Industrial Policies and Manufactured Exports* (Washington: World Bank, 1983), 16.

the formally employed proletariat grew from 15.9 to 37.1 percent of the population.[85] But the change was qualitative as well as quantitative. Over time, Brazil's rapid industrialization strategy reshaped the country's economy and society: as heavy industry expanded, it changed basic aspects of industrial work and reshaped the composition of the industrial work force and the experience of industrial workers. Using modern technology, often provided by foreign investors, new enterprises tended to be more capital-intensive, more geographically concentrated, and more reliant on semi-skilled workers than older factories were. As Brazil developed a capital-intensive dynamic sector, the experience of most workers would change, in ways that I shall argue later increased the capacity for shop-floor organization.

Throughout the 1970s, metallurgy, motor vehicles, and chemicals—all highly capital-intensive—accounted for over 60 percent of total investment in manufacturing. Changing levels of technology can be seen in the fact that these sectors were marked by high increases in productivity without corresponding increases in job creation. Between 1962 and 1980, traditional industries—textiles, food, wood products, and the like—reduced their contribution to the GNP from 49.2 to 34.5 percent; the share of the consumer durables and capital-goods industries, including metallurgy, chemical products, and machinery, rose steadily from 50.8 to 65.5 percent of the national product.

Sectoral differences within industry were reflected in the labor force. As table 4 shows, after 1967, growth rates in the output of dynamic industries consistently exceeded growth rates in employment; in more traditional industries, employment growth nearly kept pace with increases in output. Patterns of employment did not shift as dramatically as patterns of value produced: while traditional industries' share of industrial employment declined between 1965 and 1980 from 50.7 to 42.9 percent, the share of dynamic industries increased only a few percentage points, from 46.7 percent in 1965 to 53.3 in 1980.[86] Thus, industrial growth in the 1970s did not greatly improve levels of employment: the sectors that received the largest investments, and whose output increased most rapidly, were more capital-intensive than older industries and did not create as many industrial jobs as government planners might have hoped.

The sectoral bias of the "economic miracle" recreated a persistent tendency in Brazilian industry to geographic concentration. In 1976, Brazil's southeast accounted for 77 percent of total value added, and for 70.4 percent of industrial employment.[87] The state of São Paulo

alone accounted for 49 percent of secondary employment in 1970.[88]
This tendency was particularly marked in the automobile industry and
its spin-off supply industries: although industrial growth increased
throughout Brazil during the late 1960s, growth in São Paulo's industrial periphery—collectively known as the ABC or ABCD region because it includes the municipalities of Santo André, São Bernardo, São
Caetano do Sul, and Diadema—was extraordinary. Inasmuch as it was
the preferred site for new factories linked to automobile production,
industrial production in the ABC region more than tripled, rising from
741 factories, employing an average of 62.6 workers per factory, in
1950 to 3,394 factories, employing an average of 84 workers in 1978.[89]

Not only were plants capital-intensive and geographically concentrated, but growth in the 1970s involved larger units. The average size
of factories in all non-extractive industries more than doubled between
1960 and 1980, growing from 16.2 workers per establishment to 39.3
workers. Again, this pattern was especially noticeable in more dynamic
industries: in the motor vehicle industry, factories grew from an average
of 39.1 workers in 1960 to 90.8 workers in 1980.[90] About half of all
auto workers in the São Paulo region worked in factories of more than
500 workers.[91] Perhaps because the metal industry employed so much
of the industrial force, the experience of many Brazilian workers by the
early 1970s would have been shaped by work in enormous enterprises.
In 1969, 1,645 firms employed 80 percent of all Brazil's workers,[92] and
by 1970, about 41 percent of all workers worked in factories of more
than 250 people.[93]

New technology can change skill requirements in different ways, but
in Brazil dynamic industries apparently tended to hire increasing percentages of semi-skilled workers. Humphrey's careful study of internal
labor markets in Brazil's automobile industry suggests that the general
tendency in the mid 1970s was for factories to hire roughly 40–50 percent semi-skilled, 20 percent unskilled, and 20–30 percent skilled workers, with probably increasing percentages of semi-skilled and unskilled
workers. Humphrey concludes that the line between unskilled and
semi-skilled workers was blurred: the major qualification for a job as
a semi-skilled worker was previous factory experience, and unskilled
workers could expect to be promoted to a semi-skilled job within eighteen months. On the other hand, promotion from semi-skilled to skilled
jobs was rare. Nevertheless, Humphrey argues that low salaries and
high turnover for all automobile workers meant that skilled workers
were increasingly treated as semi-skilled workers; constant layoffs

meant their position was hardly more secure than that of semi-skilled workers.[94] By the early 1970s, skilled workers within the auto industry could hardly feel more privileged than semi-skilled ones: their pay was equally eroded by inflation, and their jobs, equally subject to cyclical layoffs, were scarcely more secure.

Growth in the ABC region served as a magnet for would-be industrial workers: the population of Santo André, São Bernardo, and São Caetano do Sul nearly doubled between 1960 and 1970, and would nearly double again by 1980; for comparison, the population of Brazil as a whole only doubled once between 1960 and 1980.[95] Humphrey argues persuasively that despite its attraction, the auto industry does not show many of the characteristics normally associated with primary labor markets: far from being secure or highly paid, all auto workers in the early 1970s suffered declining real wages, instability, and reduced skill classification. Nevertheless, in the context of Brazil, auto workers were almost certainly better off than most: they were generally well paid compared to other industries, and although they were laid off during slack periods, they could expect to be rehired within the industry. If auto sector workers could hardly be considered a labor aristocracy, they were certainly better off than workers unable to get even semi-skilled jobs. For workers restricted to traditional industries or to the "informal" sector, unemployment was a more threatening reality than it was even for repeatedly laid-off auto workers, and workers in the São Paulo area generally considered jobs in the automobile industry attractive.[96]

But not all Brazilian workers could hope to work in the dynamic sector: many lacked the fundamental requirements for employment. Regis de Castro Andrade argues that in Brazil, urban poverty is not a short-term phenomenon but rather "rural indigence recycled."[97] Capitalization of agriculture during the 1960s changed labor requirements and land availability; by 1970, 56.4 percent of Brazilians lived in urban areas, up from 36.1 percent twenty years before.[98] For many recent migrants, industrial employment is virtually impossible. Some workers do not have the *carteiras,* or personal work records, required for industrial employment or access to the social security system: recently arrived migrants, often illiterate and lacking birth certificates, complain of their difficulties in getting the documentation required for steady industrial employment.[99] Wanderley Guilherme dos Santos calls the *carteira* "a certificate of civic birth";[100] originally designed in the 1920s to identify São Paulo union activists, the *carteira* has been required for jobs in the formal industrial sector since 1932.[101] Between 1967 and 1971, *carteiras* became compulsory for rural workers as well, reflecting the military government's concern with the system of documentation.

From a comparative perspective, *carteiras* are analogous to the passes carried by all black South Africans: they contain a record of training and previous employment, with employers' comments, and designate workers as "trained" or industrial, "rural," or "minor," thus channeling workers into general areas of employment. The words of a former labor minister printed in the front of each *carteira* illustrate its role: "Who examines this, will soon see if its bearer is of a calm or volatile temperament; if he loves his chosen profession or still has not found a vocation; if he moves from factory to factory, like a bee, or remains in the same establishment, climbing the professional scale." [102] In the 1970s, São Paulo employers apparently used *carteiras* to identify union militants: employers' signatures in particular colors of ink indicated suspected troublemakers.[103] Although individual Brazilian workers have found various ways to get around the problems posed by the *carteira* system—including fabricating or "losing" the actual document—a lack of documentation can present a legal obstacle to joining the industrial labor force.

Illiteracy, however, presented an even more formidable obstacle for many new urban arrivals. From the late 1960s onward, the military government embarked on an ambitious program in primary education, seeking to train workers for the new industrialized Brazil. Illiteracy rates dropped from 53 percent in 1950 to 23.7 percent in 1977.[104] However, illiteracy rates remain higher in rural areas, so that recently arrived migrants—especially older workers—were likely to be illiterate and were often ineligible for semi-skilled work.

Who, then, were the workers in the large, capital-intensive factories that grew up in Brazil's southeast? In 1976, about half of all workers in extractive and manufacturing industries were between eighteen and thirty years old, and a third were between eighteen and twenty-one. By the mid 1970s, Margaret Keck concludes, "for a very large percentage of the Brazilian working class, the pre-1964 period was at most a childhood memory." [105] José Alvaro Moisés suggests this is especially true for the ABC region: by the mid 1970s, the work force was generally composed not of migrants but of the children of migrants, who had grown up in urban areas. As a result of the pattern of industrialization, it was in the regions where "large national and multinational firms of the economy's most dynamic sector concentrated, taking advantage of the economic and social policies implemented by the regime of 1964," that "a new stratum of more qualified, more prepared workers" emerged. Auto workers were better paid than most, but they also were "more or less precisely aware of the fact that the firms where they worked were exactly those that were most able to pay the labor force more."[106]

Over the 1960s, then, Brazil's "economic miracle" produced a different kind of economy: state policies and international investments shifted industrial production toward more capital-intensive goods, aimed at a stratified market and requiring a more skilled labor force. With the military regime's erosion of union organization and protection for individual workers, workers in this sector could hardly be described as a labor aristocracy; but from the mid 1970s on, they gradually translated an increased capacity for shop-floor organization into a broad challenge to employers and the state. As I shall show in subsequent chapters, workers concentrated in large factories in urban centers—in precisely those industries that formed the cornerstone of the country's economic growth—learned to take advantage of new possibilities for organization created by authoritarian industrialization.

INDUSTRIALIZATION IN SOUTH AFRICA

If successive Brazilian governments chased after industrial development, leading South African politicians tended throughout the 1960s to focus on a very different issue. In the postwar era, political debates revolved not around economic growth but around the threat to white minority rule posed by the growing urban black labor force and spreading political organization among the disenfranchised black majority. Instead of Brazil's "developmentalism," South Africa's political arena was marked by discussions of "separate development," where each racial category was to have a separate geographic area for development.

Nevertheless, like the Brazilian military, the South African state stumbled onto a set of policies that could be called an industrial development strategy. By the 1960s, South Africa's industrial strategy included the same basic components that created Brazil's economic boom: a close alliance between foreign, domestic, and state capital, concentrated in heavy industrial expansion and oriented toward a stratified market. Although inflation was hardly an issue, since mineral-rich South Africa generally had adequate foreign exchange for its imports, the rapid growth in GNP was accompanied by static wage levels; more-

over, black workers' organization and political expression were severely restricted. Nevertheless, as in Brazil, changes in technological
level and the labor process changed workers' capacity for organization:
in the mid 1970s, the basic assumptions on which grand apartheid
rested—that blacks were unskilled workers, temporarily residing in urban industrial areas while their families remained in rural bantustans—
were increasingly problematic. With industrialization, and especially
with an increase in the percentages of black semi-skilled workers, the
racial composition of the industrial labor force changed; by the 1970s,
black workers predominated on the shop floor.

SEPARATE DEVELOPMENT

Capitalist development in South Africa always had an explicitly racial
content, but in the postwar era, control over the country's African majority became the rationale of government policy. As in Brazil, early
industrial growth was concentrated in a few urban areas, largely in response to growing internal demand. By World War II, state policies had
limited the possibilities for African agriculture, while industrial
growth—which offered more attractive options than working on white-
owned mines or farms—had created an urban black population. Increasingly, white politicians viewed that population as a threat to white
control. When the National Party came to power in 1948, it promised
to enforce strict racial segregation, and to block any demands for
black citizenship.

Apartheid, or separate development, promised to allow the African
majority political expression only in areas once called "native reserves."
Black voters were removed from voting rolls, while influx control laws
were redesigned to prevent the rise of a permanent urban black population: passes to live in the 87 percent of the country designated "white"
were granted mainly to Africans employed in white-owned enterprises.
Although even leading National Party supporters recognized that white
South Africa required African labor,[107] government officials argued
that African workers would continue to provide mainly unskilled labor
to mines and industries, and would return to their "homelands" when
their employment ended. Even black education was redesigned to teach
educated blacks that "there is no place for [them] in the European community above the level of certain forms of labor."[108] African workers
in urban areas were subject to strict controls, unable to move between
cities or jobs.

Historians debate the extent to which apartheid laws reflected a new turn in South Africa or simply built on existing patterns of segregation and control developed over four centuries of settler domination. The migrant labor system—the cornerstone of apartheid—developed first in the late nineteenth century, when mine owners sought to create and control a supply of low-paid black workers whose wages would be subsidized by families engaged in subsistence agriculture. The 1913 Native Land Act created national "native reserves," the basis of what would later be called homelands; influx control laws preventing Africans' free movement date to the nineteenth century and were elaborated in the 1930s. But while the National Party used already-existing institutions to tighten control after 1948, the shift in intent—from controlling a labor supply to controlling the black population's incorporation into industrialized South Africa—was underlined by a battery of security laws passed in the early 1950s, which sought to eliminate organized political opposition. As Harold Wolpe and others have argued, the rise of an urban black population with new levels of political organization threatened white domination. Through the 1950s, the white electorate clearly supported National Party efforts to reduce organized resistance to minority rule by expelling from major urban areas blacks not essential to production.[109]

Historians also debate the extent to which white workers benefited from apartheid legislation. From the 1920s on, segregated white unions sought state protection against employers' efforts to replace white workers with lower-paid Africans; skilled jobs were reserved for members of registered unions, which could not legally include "pass-bearing natives." The "civilized labor policy" protected white workers' jobs and salaries, while allowing employers to hold African workers' wages at low rates set by employer-dominated wage boards.[110] By the late 1940s, leading white unionists generally supported two of the National Party's first priorities in office: the elimination of left-wing influence in black unions, by banning the Communist Party, and the weakening of nonracial unions, by requiring them to segregate members by racial classification.

Hardly surprisingly, the National Party's effort to tighten control over the black majority, coupled with increased repression of organized resistance, provoked widespread protests and popular mobilization, with demonstrations, boycotts, strikes, and civil disobedience. Armed with new security legislation, however, the state banned leaders, arrested "defiers," and outlawed organizations. Passes—the permits required for Africans living and working in white-designated areas—became the symbol of the extension of apartheid. In late 1959, both the African National Congress and the recently formed Pan Africanist Congress called on Africans to defy pass laws. On March 21, 1960, sixty-nine Africans were killed in a pass-burning demonstration at the Sharpeville police station; over the next week, demonstrations and general strikes in Cape Town, Johannesburg, and Durban seemed to represent a crisis for state control. The government declared a state of emergency, outlawing the ANC and the PAC; both organizations declared that they would take up campaigns of armed sabotage, since legal methods of protest had been outlawed.[111]

Existing black unions struggled to retain their identity, but the general climate of repression made organization extremely difficult. Although unregistered unions were not banned outright, many individual organizers were arrested for political activities, and over the next three years, new laws restricted unions still further by prohibiting meetings and banning individual unionists. By 1964, most of SACTU's leaders were in jail or exile, and the union federation no longer functioned openly inside the country.[112] By the mid 1960s, there was little overt resistance to the National Party's vision: a South Africa in which African workers would be only temporary residents in urban industrial centers, providing unskilled labor for white-owned enterprises.

INDUSTRIALIZATION STRATEGIES

If the South African government's major focus was on tightening political control, it nevertheless stumbled onto a set of economic policies that encouraged import substitution, which later looked very similar to the rapid industrialization strategies followed in authoritarian Brazil. Although the racial content of South African industrialization often disguises any similarity, in broad outlines the policies are remarkably like those followed by Brazil and other Latin American countries in the postwar period. First, the South African state constructed a transport network, using public works programs to employ and train poor whites. Second, it raised protective tariff walls, blocking industrial imports from competing with domestically produced goods. Third, parastatal corporations provided the basic inputs required for industrial expansion. Finally, state policies created a highly stratified market. White consumers had access to state jobs and credit; most workers, who were not white, were paid minimal wages. Although state policies were aimed in nearly every case as much at strengthening white domination as at sponsoring industrialization, South Africa had by the 1960s been transformed from a primarily extractive and agricultural society into an urbanized industrial one; during the 1960s, the state would undertake policies designed to "deepen" the industrial base.

The South African state began to build an infrastructure when the depression of the 1930s eroded world prices for agricultural produce, creating widespread unemployment. Gold sales cushioned overall national revenues, giving the state leeway to resolve the "poor white problem" through public works programs and job creation; the problems facing poor blacks during the depression were manifold, but these generally only disturbed the state where they affected the availability of land and labor for whites.[113] Railroads already connected major mineral centers to ports by the mid 1920s, and employment on the railroads was already considered a way to employ and train unskilled whites.[114] In the 1930s, when the international collapse of agricultural prices created a new population of "poor whites," road construction provided jobs and incidentally extended a transport system that would later benefit industrial development. The 1935 National Road Act created a national commission to plan and construct a road grid connecting major centers; funded by import duties on petrol, the National Roads Fund developed a grid linking major urban centers by the 1960s.[115] By the late 1940s, the pool of unemployed whites had shrunk so that even South African Railways employed blacks in the lower manual grades, under white supervisors.[116]

From the late 1920s on, the South African government also promoted the expansion of secondary industry for the domestic market. Protective tariffs were designed to encourage light manufacturing, especially in textiles, paper, wood products, and food and beverages. The depression provoked a crisis in the sector: total income from and employment in manufacturing both shrank by about 20 percent between 1930 and 1933.[117] Industrial recovery was an immediate policy goal, and the state embarked on explicit efforts to protect and support manufacturing. A national commission on industrial policy reported in 1936 that despite its fear that tariffs and the high wages paid to "European" workers might reduce the international competitiveness of South African manufactured goods, protection remained "an essential condition for [the] continued existence of local industry."[118]

Even before the Great Depression, the South African state began to create state enterprises to provide basic inputs to industry; after World

War II, when South African firms began to move into heavier industry, state-owned companies played a major role. In 1928, when private efforts proved unable to build a large-scale iron and steel foundry, Parliament established the state-owned Iron and Steel Corporation of South Africa; ISCOR's first plant began production in 1934. By 1954, metal and metal products had surpassed all other branches of manufacturing in terms of the value of net output.[119]

As in Brazil, where a state-sponsored steel industry supported industrial growth, cheap steel products "facilitated rapid progress in the manufacture of explosives, mining equipment, farm implements and structural steelworks," and, in the late 1950s, aided the growth of a motor vehicle industry.[120] From 1946 on, the Electricity Supply Commission (ESCOM) provided over 90 percent of domestically generated electricity.[121] In 1955, the state-owned South African Coal, Oil and Gas Corporation (SASOL) began to produce oil from coal; chemical by-products from the process stimulated the petrochemicals industry.[122] From 1951 on, FOSKOR produced phosphates, previously entirely imported; by the mid 1970s, it was producing about three million metric tons per annum.[123]

Curiously, considering the outcome, the National Party was as interested in providing jobs to Afrikaans-speaking whites as in promoting growth. From 1948, state policymakers viewed state-led industrialization as a way to assist Afrikaans-speaking businessmen, as well as employing white workers, by granting government contracts to Afrikaans companies and appointing Afrikaans-speaking directors and managers to state corporations. According to a well-known Afrikaans-speaking businessman, the state's Industrial Development Corporation was used after 1948 "to strengthen Afrikaner participation in the industrial progress of the country," while the government generally "fostered the establishment of state-owned corporations as Afrikanerdom's answer to the somewhat overwhelming non-Afrikaner interests in mining and industry."[124] Similarly, state financial accounts were moved to Afrikaans-owned banks; deposits in the Afrikaans-owned Volkskas increased nearly fivefold between 1948 and 1958.[125]

Nevertheless, South Africa's parastatals shaped and stimulated industrial growth. Despite government claims that these companies would sound "the death knell of economic colonialism" by reducing dependence on foreign capital and black labor, parastatals acted much like private enterprises, cooperating with foreign companies to secure markets and using lower-paid black workers to reduce expenses. The state gained a broader industrial base, Nancy Clark argues, while "the private sector kept its profits and control over the market, at least in the short term."[126] As in Brazil, parastatals rarely competed directly with private corporations; instead, they offered their products as substitutes for imports.

Public investment, then, played a major part in shaping South Africa's industrial growth: not only did the state provide financing to new corporations, but decisions about parastatals shaped the kinds of cheap inputs available to private capital. From 1946 on, public enterprises controlled about 50 percent of South Africa's total fixed capital; this figure would increase to 58 percent by 1979.[127] While the mix between protection for private investors and public corporations varied, the importance of the state to South Africa's industrial development in the postwar era should not be underestimated. Although both the South African and Brazilian states provided basic inputs for industrial growth, the South African state was prompted by political as well as economic motives: controlling black workers and supporting Afrikaans-speaking whites were at least as important to the National Party as economic growth. Nevertheless, despite its initial intentions, the South African state had, by the early 1960s, laid a basis for rapid industrial growth.

FOREIGN INVESTMENT AND SECTORAL GROWTH

Despite the Nationalist government's anti-imperialist rhetoric, its support for private capital accumulation is hardly open to question: foreign investments were always welcome. Before winning power, the National Party rejected foreign domination; "Hoggenheimer," an anti-Semitic caricature of an English-speaking capitalist, symbolized English-speaking economic domination, especially by the powerful Anglo American Corporation and its director, Ernest Oppenheimer. Economic themes, especially anti-imperialism, played an important role in the coalescence of the Nationalist movement, as Afrikaans-speaking intellectuals and small businessmen persuaded Afrikaans workers to invest in Afrikaans banks and to shop in Afrikaans-owned stores.[128] Once in power, however, the National Party changed its attitude: slowed growth in the mid 1950s, largely caused by capital flight following the party's 1948 election victory, served as a reminder of South Africa's dependence on foreign capital and technology.

By the late 1950s, Prime Minister Hendrik Verwoerd displayed a new eagerness to attract foreign investors, especially where foreign technologies and access to international markets would aid development:

> There is a natural desire on the part of every country to retain control over its economic destiny. . . . [T]he encouragement of local capital formation was one of the guiding principles of our financial policies during the past decade. . . . But . . . foreign capital can still be of great assistance in the development of our resources. . . . Moreover, in many cases desirable development will not take place without the technical knowledge and business skill which accompany foreign capital. . . . [We] will continue to welcome the participation of foreign investors . . . provided this does not conflict with the general principle of a country retaining control over its economic destiny.[129]

From 1960 on, the South African state would prove eager to attract investments into new sectors of industry.

By the late 1950s, South African government officials were discussing a strategy for industrialization that looked remarkably like that proposed by the Brazilian state a few years later: after an initial import-substitution phase, in which manufacture was assisted through tariff protection, state financing, and parastatal provision of basic inputs, the government would now seek to promote dynamic sectoral expansion through market protection, local-content laws, and tax incentives; state enterprises would provide inputs, foreign capital would bring technology and access to international markets, and domestic capital could participate in joint ventures.

This is not the place to examine the motives for international companies' investment decisions, but it is worth noting that in South Africa, as in Brazil, private foreign investors in industrial production seemed to follow financial capital flows rather than precede them. In Brazil, private foreign investment slowed during the turmoil of the early 1960s, regaining speed only after the new military government successfully negotiated multilateral loans, apparently demonstrating renewed creditworthiness. In South Africa, two events underlined the risks involved in apartheid: the massacre at Sharpeville in 1960 and South Africa's withdrawal from the British Commonwealth in 1961. Following Sharpeville, economic growth slowed to zero: £48 million left the country immediately. By May 1961 foreign exchange reserves had fallen to only £77 million, and the government was forced to tighten import restrictions, impose foreign exchange controls, and limit credit. As Anthony Sampson puts it, "For a few months after Sharpeville Western investors appeared to have voted with their wallets, making their own decisive judgment about South Africa's future under apartheid."[130]

Almost immediately, however, international financiers joined with domestic South African capital to restore business confidence, primarily through loans. In 1961, Britain's Barclays Bank guaranteed a $30 million loan to the South African mining conglomerate Anglo American. Chase Manhattan lent $10 million to the South African government, and formed a new international consortium to lend $150 million more.[131] Foreshadowing what would become a standard business theme, Chase argued that "it would endanger the free world if every large American bank deprived developing countries of the opportunities for economic growth. If one hopes for changes in the Republic of South Africa or elsewhere, it would do little good to withdraw economic support."[132]

By 1965, the government appeared to have reasserted control over the political situation. Direct foreign investment began to rise again. Between 1962 and 1971, foreign capital, including reinvested capital generated in South Africa, was the source of 60 percent of gross domestic capital formation, and one study estimates that with the increases in technology associated with foreign investment, international capital could be considered responsible for about two-thirds of total growth in GDP during this period. Total foreign liabilities, including both direct and indirect investment in the government and private sectors, rose significantly between 1961 and 1965, from R 2,982 million to R 3,398 million; this figure would nearly double again by 1970, reaching R 5,818 million.[133] South Africa appears to have been irresistible; in 1972—shortly before the 1973 strike wave dramatically changed the picture—John Blashill wrote in *Fortune* magazine:

> The Republic of South Africa has always been regarded by foreign investors as a gold mine, one of those rare and refreshing places where profits are great and problems small. Capital is not threatened by political instability or nationalization. Labor is cheap, the market booming, the currency hard and convertible. Such are the market's attractions that 292 American corporations and subsidiaries have established subsidiaries or affiliates there. Their combined direct investment is close to $900 million, and their returns on that investment have been romping home at something like 19 percent a year, after taxes.[134]

Much as foreign capital poured into Brazil following the 1964 coup, foreign investors flocked to South Africa once political stability was restored.

TABLE 5

SOUTH AFRICAN GROWTH RATES, 1954–72

Industrial Sector	Output, R '000		Growth Rates			
	1960	1972	1954–60	1960–66	1966–72	1960–72
Food, beverages, and tobacco	218,541	569,030	6.0	5.7	10.2	8.0
Textiles, clothing, leather, footwear	159,300	440,989	3.5	8.5	8.4	8.5
Furniture, wood and wood products	50,838	130,480	−0.5	8.9	6.7	7.8
Paper, paper products and packaging	98,282	312,317	7.0	8.4	10.8	9.6
Non-metallic products	74,460	227,312	4.0	8.0	10.4	9.3
Chemicals, rubber	142,339	582,412	6.0	11.6	15.4	11.7
Basic metals, metal products	228,256	721,600	6.0	9.1	10.1	9.6
Machinery	117,049	437,387	8.0	11.6	10.4	11.0
Transport equipment	63,923	274,362	4.0	11.0	12.5	12.1

SOURCE: Rates calculated from output figures in S.A. Department of Statistics, *South African Statistics, 1964* and *1976,* and *Statistics for Fifty Years, 1910–1960.*

Although details on the sectoral destination of foreign investment are not officially published, private foreign investors appear to have shifted into South Africa's manufacturing sector: growth in manufacturing led the 1960s economic boom. Between 1950 and 1974, agriculture and mining grew at an average annual rate of 5.4 percent; manufacturing grew at an average annual rate of 9.1 percent.[135] By 1972, manufacturing contributed about a quarter of gross domestic product, more than any other sector of the economy.[136]

Within manufacturing, growth rates in net output varied. While all manufacturing sectors grew rapidly in the late 1960s, heavy industries tended to grow faster than others. As in Brazil, industrial sectors that benefited from state enterprise development and from state financial policies tended to grow most rapidly. State economic planners expected heavy industry to dominate growth patterns throughout the 1970s: the 1972–79 economic plan projected a 9.5 percent average annual increase in output in basic steel products, an 8.5 percent average rate in motor vehicles, and only a 4.3 percent average annual increase in clothing and textiles.[137] As table 5 shows, while all industries grew remarkably during this period, the heavier industries—consumer durables and metals—tended to grow more rapidly than the lighter industries that had dominated South African manufacture through the 1950s.

Perhaps the most prominent example of how South Africa managed simultaneously to attract and control foreign capital is that of the automobile industry, which by the early 1970s accounted for about 14 percent of total manufacturing in South Africa. Like the Brazilian government, the South African state offered foreign automobile manufacturers cheap inputs and a protected market, hoping foreign investment would stimulate domestic industrial expansion. Ford first opened an assembly plant in Port Elizabeth in 1924, followed by General Motors in 1926. As the motor industry grew—aided by ISCOR's expansion in metal and engineering products[138]—more foreign firms created wholly owned subsidiaries and joint ventures, relying on domestic producers for tires, glass, and batteries. From 1960, import duties on cars were strengthened by local-content provisions, protecting locally made components and providing incentives for foreign companies to depend on local manufacture. From 1963 on, auto firms paid nearly 100 percent duties on imported completely-knocked-down engine kits, once the main source of engines, and over 200 percent duties on engines that were less broken down. Days after the new local-content protection was announced, Ford and General Motors revealed plans to build engine machine and assembly plants in South Africa; they were soon followed by other international automobile firms. By 1967, thirteen firms produced twenty-six models of engines in South Africa, and domestically manufactured engines composed almost 85 percent of the local market.[139]

Industrial growth during the 1960s did not so much reshape South Africa as intensify tendencies that had appeared in the 1950s. A high level of economic concentration became so marked that many observers saw South Africa as dominated by "monopoly capital": local firms linked to multinational and parastatal corporations increasingly controlled supplies and markets. The most dynamic sectors—iron and steel, engineering, textiles, chemicals, explosives, cigarettes, rubber—showed especially high indices of concentration, but the pattern held throughout industry. In 1977, the three top firms controlled at least 70 percent of turnover in one-third of industrial subcategories. Overall, the top 5 percent of firms controlled 63.1 percent of turnover.[140]

Most dominant companies were closely tied to foreign companies, through licensing and patent arrangements and joint ventures; their foreign ties gave them access to technology developed overseas and to new sources of capital. Large local conglomerates brought in foreign technology as they expanded into industrial production. Duncan Innes's careful study of the rise of Anglo American—a local mining conglomerate that controlled South African mining from World War I on, and that expanded into industry after World War II—shows the importance of access to foreign technology in Anglo's industrial expansion. In 1963, Anglo American brought America's Newmont Chemical in as a partner in a large-scale steel plant, designed by Britain's Davy United; by 1970, the new company, Highveld Steel and Vanadium Corporation, was the fourth-largest quoted industrial concern in South Africa. In 1964, Anglo American took over Scaw Metals, which purchased Highveld's vanadium pentoxide to make steel parts for the mining industry; Scaw was already linked to the American General Steel Industries, the Abex Corporation of America, and the English Steel Castings Corporation. By 1969 Scaw Metals ranked as one of South Africa's top twenty companies. Anglo's expansion outside the steel industry took a similar path: in 1967, Anglo joined with a British firm, Bowater Paper Company, to build a paper company that would be one of two dominant firms in the paper industry by the late 1970s. In 1966, Anglo's subsidiary African Explosives and Chemical Industry, which "has access to the technical information, patents and process of Imperial Chemical Industries Limited under terms separately negotiated,"[141] opened a large petrochemical plant; in 1969, AECI was the country's single largest industrial concern.[142]

While Anglo's case is extreme—particularly in the level of vertical integration and the degree of control it retained over joint ventures—it is clear that the industrial boom of the 1960s, depending as it did on foreign technology and capital to expand into new sectors, was dominated by large firms, closely tied to international investors. Among the local beneficiaries of this pattern were not only traditional South African economic giants like Anglo but also a few Afrikaans conglomerates that managed to translate access to parastatals and to state financial reserves into industrial expansion. South Africa's path of manufacturing growth led to "the emergence of a small and powerful capitalist class closely linked to foreign interests. This [bourgeoisie] includes elements of financial capital, the mining-houses, capitalists in the Afrikaner nationalist movement, the parastatals and foreign companies."[143]

STRATIFICATION AND CONTROL

In the Brazilian model, the production of consumer durables was apparently correlated to a highly stratified market; in South Africa, the market for automobiles was stratified along racial as well as economic lines. Throughout the 1970s, consumer credit extended to whites created a market for the goods produced in new industries; by 1978, analysts were complaining of market saturation. That market was clearly delineated: Africans accounted for virtually no new car sales. In the mid 1970s, Africans were estimated to own fewer than 210,000 cars of all vintages, in a country where about 300,000 cars were purchased annually.[144] South Africa's emphasis on tariff protection suggests that the state assumed industrial production would be geared toward an internal market: tariffs, designed to protect domestic manufacturing from international competition, could only affect purchases within South Africa's borders.

There was, of course, an alternative. From 1958 on, some economists argued that an export-oriented policy for manufacture would improve South Africa's long-term prospects by avoiding domestic market limitations; but throughout the boom of the 1960s, these warnings went unheeded. Not until the early 1970s, when market saturation became a major problem, would the government be compelled to encourage industrial exports. Until then, little was done to promote exportable manufactures: the South African Department of Commerce, which was responsible for developing an export policy, relied on continued exports of primary products and on a continued flow of foreign investment capital to South Africa to provide the foreign exchange needed to build up the industrial sector.[145]

If the South African state encouraged consumption at the upper end of the market, it also assisted private capital by strictly controlling wages. Although it might not normally be described as part of an industrialization strategy—since it was linked to racial segregation, rather than to economic imperatives—the fact that the state set wages for African workers clearly reduced labor bills for manufacturers as well as for mine owners and farmers. Brazilian development strategies after 1964 explicitly controlled wages: government labor policy prohibited increases in wages above increases in productivity, and real wages dropped precipitously. In South Africa, wage limitation was hardly new. Wages for black workers had long been kept artificially low: while white unions could negotiate with management in national industrial councils, black workers' wages were set by wage boards composed of employer and state representatives. Although workers could technically speak at wage board hearings, they were seldom even notified about the meetings in advance and rarely participated in the discussions. For most of the 1960s, strikes were virtually unheard of. SACTU no longer functioned inside the country, and the only viable organizations left for black workers were segregated branches of registered unions, which generally remained under the control of conservative white unionists. Lacking organizations or fora, with most prominent black unionists in jail or in exile, black workers in the 1960s were scarcely able to articulate wage demands, far less back up demands with worker action—leaving the wage boards free to set wage levels.

Not surprisingly, wage boards tended to keep wages low. Although black wages in both mining and manufacturing probably kept up with inflation, income stratification worsened. Real wages in South Africa are usually discussed in terms of differentials between black and white workers: in 1970, for example, the differential in mining reached a peak, with whites' average wages almost twenty-two times greater than blacks'.[146] In the first years of Nationalist rule, in the 1950s, Africans' average real wages declined while whites' wages rose by 10 percent;[147] by the end of the decade their relative buying power had returned to the 1948 ratio, but the average wages paid to Africans in all sectors remained far below those paid to whites. During the 1960s, Africans'

TABLE 6

AVERAGE NOMINAL WAGES (IN RANDS),
MANUFACTURING AND MINING, SOUTH AFRICA,
1965—70

	African Mining	African Manufacturing	White Manufacturing
1965	174.72	487.66	2,509.31
1966	184.56	514.86	2,708.95
1967	191.91	531.12	2,875.91
1968	197.77	573.65	3,061.17
1969	206.04	623.98	3,214.87
1970	216.08	730.31	3,497.67

SOURCE: Average wages calculated from S.A. Central Statistical Services, *South African Statistics*, 1982, 7.8–7.10.

share of total personal income dropped from 21.4 percent to 19.3 percent.[148] In 1970, whites, who comprised less than 20 percent of the population, earned about 75 percent of total personal income, while the 83 percent of South Africans classified as African, Coloured, and Indian received about 25 percent.[149]

Blacks' wages in manufacturing were consistently higher than in mining, as table 6 shows for 1965–70, and differentials between white and black wages were lower. Nevertheless, whites in manufacturing have earned more than blacks throughout South Africa's history. While some of this differential may be explained by the different skills levels of the two groups, the white:black wage ratio in manufacturing and construction, which averaged about 5:1 in real terms between 1915 and 1982, grew steadily higher from 1954 to 1970, peaking at a ratio of 6:1. The pattern is expressed in racial, rather than economic, terms, but the result appears the same: through the period of highest industrial expansion, income concentration appears to have followed the Brazilian pattern of intensified income stratification; the majority of workers suffered declining or steady living standards, while the upper and middle classes benefited from growth.

RESHAPING THE LABOR FORCE

Industrial growth and urbanization changed the occupations available to African workers. By 1970, 51 percent of the economically active population classified as African worked outside agriculture and mining.[150] But in South Africa, as in Brazil, a reliance on imported capital-intensive technology meant that increased industrial output was not necessarily linked to increased industrial employment. Capital intensity increased markedly: between 1951 and 1976, the average value of machinery per person rose from R 855 to an estimated R 1,639 (in 1970 rands).[151] In all sectors of industry, annual rates of increase in output outstripped increases in employment by two to three times: in basic metals, for example, output rose at a rate of 9.5 percent, while employment rose only at a rate of 4.9 percent between 1960 and 1972. In machinery, output rose at an average rate of 10.9 percent, while employment rose only at a rate of 5.7 percent. Even in the less capital-intensive sector of the food, beverage, and tobacco industries, output rose at 7 percent a year, while employment rose only at a rate of 2.9 percent.[152]

South African economists continue to debate the precise effects of increased capital:labor ratios on the labor process in large firms. The picture is complicated both by job reservation laws and by apparent shortages of available white workers by the early 1960s. The job reservation system, which from the late 1920s on restricted skilled jobs to white workers, limited employers' hiring options: many employers might well have preferred to hire African workers, whom they could pay less, but were legally blocked—especially after the National Party strengthened job reservation laws in the 1950s, preventing blacks from entering apprenticeship programs. However, the growth of a civil service required to administer apartheid policies, and the expansion of parastatals, created new, relatively secure job openings for white workers; free education for whites meant that the children of working-class whites could get the skills needed for civil service jobs. By 1970, more than a quarter of all white workers worked directly for the state, and another 10 percent worked for parastatal enterprises[153]—implying a corresponding decline in the availability of white workers for expanding industries. Racial divisions at the point of production, arguably a crucial aspect of apartheid, became conflated with skill and authority differences, as white workers or their children moved into supervisory positions or out of the factory altogether, and growing industries hired black workers for semi-skilled and skilled positions.

With white workers moving into public sector employment, employers' complaints about shortages of skilled workers during the 1960s were probably justified—as were black workers' complaints that they were regularly asked to do skilled labor at rates for less-skilled work. Surveys in 1969–71 showed skill shortages of 13 percent in construction and clothing, 8 percent in metals and engineering, 11 percent in motors, and 12 percent in furniture. By 1970, even conservative Afrikaans business groups argued that the job reservation system should be applied more flexibly.[154] The job reservation system blocked individual workers' mobility within the plant; worse, from employers' point of view, job reservation prevented them from hiring or training black workers to fill vacant positions.

The overall percentage of semi-skilled workers in industry changed, along with the racial composition of the labor force. The decline in relatively unskilled industrial workers during the period of economic growth is unmistakable. Outside the mines, by 1970, only 3 percent of whites were classified as "laborers," down from 11.2 percent only a decade earlier. Given South Africa's racial stratification, it is probably even more surprising that the percentage of Africans in non-mining industrial occupations labeled "laborers" fell from 84.0 percent to 68.2 percent between 1960 and 1970, with parallel drops among workers classified as Asian and Coloured. The increase in the total percentages of semi-skilled industrial workers was equally evident: by 1969, nearly 20 percent of all workers were characterized as semi-skilled, and another 10 percent as skilled.[155]

In manufacturing as a whole, black workers replaced white: between 1960 and 1976, the ratio of black to white workers in manufacturing increased from 2.75:1 to 3.6:1, a shift that appears to have been associated with increased skill levels among black workers.[156] Between 1969 and 1981, white semi-skilled and skilled workers declined from 173,150 to 154,896, while the number of semi-skilled and skilled African workers rose from 847,444 to 1,300,173; percentage increases in semi-skilled and skilled workers classified as Asian and Coloured would probably be as high.[157]

Before the removal of job reservation, however, as manufacturing industries grew, employers complained bitterly about a shortage of skilled workers. Although South African employers had long complained about such shortages, changing skill requirements with industrial deepening worsened the problem. By the mid 1970s, warnings that industries faced a "huge crisis . . . unless the potential black labor force is unfrozen" and allowed to supplement the shrinking pool of white skilled workers were commonplace.[158] In some cases, jobs formerly reserved for artisans may have been broken up, creating semi-skilled jobs in which blacks could legally be hired; in others, jobs were simply rela-beled semi-skilled, allowing employers to hire Africans.[159] When the labor movement began to take shape in the early 1970s, organizers filed numerous complaints with the Department of Labour about employers who paid workers for less skilled jobs but required them to do more skilled tasks; this widespread practice makes it difficult to measure the effect of increased capital intensity on workers' skill levels.[160] In some industries—including on the mines, where job reservation laws were most strictly enforced—job titles were undoubtedly rearranged to by-pass job reservation laws; in others, especially in expanding industries relying on mass production techniques, black workers moved into newly created positions as operatives.[161]

Racial classification and job reservation laws, then, clearly interfere with the construction of skill categories. C. E. W. Simkins and Doug Hindson offer data showing that from 1943 to 1973 "the most conspic-uous trend is the growth in the number of (lower) semi-skilled African workers" and suggest that the erosion of job reservation clauses in the early 1970s led to an immediate increase in the percentage of African workers labeled skilled and semi-skilled. The speed of the change sug-gests that employers simply relabeled positions, and that Africans had already been doing the work. By 1977, less than ten years after the last job reservation laws were actually enforced, 66 percent of semi-skilled workers and 23 percent of skilled workers were African. Blacks, includ-ing African, Asian, and Coloured workers, made up about 91.5 percent of semi-skilled and 40 percent of skilled workers.[162]

This reliance on semi-skilled workers seems to have been especially widespread in heavy industries. In the metal industry overall, semi-skilled operatives made up 50 percent of the work force by 1977, and about 67 percent of semi-skilled metalworkers were African.[163] A care-ful study of a general engineering plant in Natal found that as output per worker increased in the 1970s, so did the percentages of nonwhite workers who were classified semi-skilled; the numbers of unskilled Afri-can workers dropped by nearly 50 percent, and white skilled workers dropped by 80 percent. The number of semi-skilled nonwhite workers increased by 400 percent.[164]

As in Brazil, then, industrial growth linked to foreign investment and capital-intensive technology changed the levels of output per worker; in South Africa, new labor processes were associated with changing skill levels and the changing racial composition of the labor force. While white workers moved into supervisory and administrative positions, black workers found new openings as semi-skilled workers in growing industries.

However, while more semi-skilled black workers were hired, unemployment rose, especially among workers with less than nine years of education. Between 1960 and 1969, while national output grew 5.9 percent annually, unemployment and underemployment hovered around 19 percent; between 1969 and 1976, output grew at 3.9 percent, and underemployment rose to 22 percent.[165] By the early 1970s, the industrial labor market in South Africa appears to have been stratified by skill level as well as by race. Black workers with at least primary education were far more likely to be employed in the capital-intensive dynamic industries that had expanded during the late 1960s; workers lacking crucial skills could not find jobs, despite rapid growth.

The geographic concentration of dynamic industries was perhaps even more marked than in Brazil, with growth poles around Johannesburg, Durban, Cape Town, and Port Elizabeth. Industrial growth around Johannesburg, in what is known as the PWV (Pretoria-Witwatersrand-Vereeniging) area, accounted for 46.6 percent of manufacturing employment in 1965. This concentration had a definite sectoral bias: capital-intensive industries were concentrated at large industrial sites. Although the PWV's share of industrial jobs declined, its share of industrial output rose: it produced nearly 50 percent of manufacturing output in 1965, and 52.8 percent in 1972. Government policies designed to encourage industrial decentralization were most effective for labor-intensive industries; the industries that remained in the PWV area tended to be the capital- and skill-intensive industries whose output increased most rapidly, including machinery, iron and steel, basic non-ferrous metals, electrical machinery, metal products, and transportation equipment.

Trevor Bell argues that changes in "international competitiveness [and] developments in production technology and organization, may [make] proximity to large markets, to suppliers of basic and semi-processed materials, and agglomeration economies more significant locational factors" for the heavy industries on which the economic growth of the 1960s and 1970s depended than for more traditional industries like textiles, pulp and paper production, or food and beverage manufacture.[166] Thus, the changing sectoral composition of industry associated with the economic boom of the late 1960s reinforced the geographic importance of these industrial centers.

Industrial concentration led to rapid urbanization: despite government efforts to stop African migration to cities and to prevent the rise of an urban black population, the proportion of Africans living in urban areas increased steadily: by 1970, 33 percent of Africans lived in cities, up from 23 percent in 1946.[167] Not surprisingly, the four fastest-growing urban areas were those in which industry was most heavily concentrated. A pool of unemployed workers waited outside the industrial centers: rural "bantustans" were full of anxious work-seekers, who were supposed to be channeled by the state's labor bureaus into the areas that most needed labor. By the mid 1970s, rural unemployment was so severe that one study found that Africans from some areas who lacked passes to work legally in white-designated areas could improve their income by as much as 700 percent by working illegally for nine months and spending three months in prison.[168]

Because passes were linked to particular jobs, African workers would not lightly leave a job. Unless they were in the privileged group with permanent urban residence rights—granted only to workers employed for ten years at the same job or who had lived legally for fifteen years in the same area—they were legally required to return to rural areas to await recruitment at a labor bureau. Under these restrictions, it is hardly surprising that every study of South African industrial workers shows African workers before the mid 1970s had a much lower turnover than workers in other racial classifications. By the early 1970s, many industrial workers were "permanent migrants," whose contracts were annually renewed in bantustans; they could not gain permanent residence rights and therefore risked unemployment in a bantustan if they lost their jobs. Of the 1973 Durban strikers, for example, 83 percent had worked for their current employer for at least five years.[169] However, children born in urban areas, or whose parents worked legally in urban areas, could also gain permanent residence rights; these children would also have been more likely to receive primary education than children raised in rural areas. By the mid 1970s, every African worker at the Port Elizabeth Ford plant held permanent residence rights; such figures suggest that especially in technologically advanced factories in older industrial centers such as the PWV area and the Eastern Cape, a significant proportion of relatively skilled African workers were permanent urban residents.[170]

Low wages, high turnover, and a complete lack of political or workplace rights meant industrial workers could not be considered a "labor aristocracy," any more than workers in Brazil's automobile industry. Nonetheless, relatively skilled African workers holding urban rights would be relatively safe from what in South Africa would be the most serious consequence of employer victimization: unlike "migrant" workers, they could not be "endorsed out" of white-designated South Africa, while their skills would make them harder to replace.

By the early 1970s, then, just as the economic boom was coming to an end, the racial composition and skill levels of the South African industrial work force had gone through significant changes. In Brazil, industrial "deepening" through an associated-dependent development strategy created urban concentrations of large factories, operated primarily by semi-skilled workers. In South Africa, a similar pattern produced a similar result, with a slightly different twist: South Africa's racial policies combined with its industrial strategy to change the work force's racial composition. Increasingly, black workers would move into semi-skilled positions; although unemployment increased through the 1970s, black workers who had attained positions within the industrial work force would prove far less dispensable than apartheid's architects had planned.

CONCLUSION

Throughout the late 1950s and early 1960s, Brazil and South Africa embarked on remarkably similar strategies for deepening their industrial bases. In both cases, they had already created some basis for industrialization through import-substitution policies and support for domestic manufacture; during the 1960s, both states would combine investment incentives with the creation of a skewed domestic market for high-cost goods and restrictions on industrial workers' wage levels. By the early 1960s, both economies could be characterized as having experienced associated-dependent development: through a triple alliance of the state and foreign and domestic capital, the consumer durables and heavy industry sectors of both countries had expanded. While both countries continued to export primary products, they were far less dependent on imported manufactured goods than they had been before the 1960s.

Rapid-industrialization strategies had a marked effect on both societies. First, they reshaped relations within the dominant classes: in both Brazil and South Africa, the state's support for rapid industrial growth helped a new group of entrepreneurs emerge. These local industrialists were far more closely tied to international business than agricultural or mining elites had been; thanks to state policies promoting joint ventures and protecting local production, by the end of the boom period neither Brazilian nor South African business leaders could easily be divided into "domestic" or "foreign" capital.

At the same time, the consumer durables sectors on which industrial "deepening" relied in both countries was highly vulnerable to shifts in the international economic climate. As I show in the next chapter, when the 1973 oil crisis set off an inflationary spiral in capital-goods prices and changed the patterns of international investment, the impact on both economies revealed the shaky foundations on which these "economic miracles" were built.

Second, rapid industrialization changed both the composition of the working class and its capacity for organization. Income stratification, already severe, worsened during the economic boom; not only did authoritarian governments demobilize popular protest and political organization, but they made it virtually impossible for industrial unions to represent workers' demands. At the same time, however, industrial growth expanded the industrial work force. Within the dynamic sector, rising levels of technology were associated with greater percentages of workers who could be characterized as semi-skilled and skilled. The change was especially visible in South Africa, where it altered the racial composition of the industrial labor force; but its implications for labor organization were perhaps equally important for Brazil. By the mid 1970s, it would become clear that in major industrial centers at least, rapid growth changed the relation between workers and employers; despite widespread unemployment, shortages of skilled and experienced workers meant, ultimately, that these workers would be able to challenge their employers and the state.

CHAPTER THREE

Business Opposition and Its Limits

An effective industrial policy of the sort we seek presupposes
the business community's effective participation in its
elaboration. Bodies charged with [industrial policy]
formulation must be open to representation from
industrialists, who could lend their experience and knowledge
to designing the broad outlines of that policy, without
interfering in administrative decisions.

Manifesto of São Paulo business leaders, 1978

In the early 1970s, phenomenal growth rates in both Brazil and South
Africa held out the promise of a rosy future. In Brazil, military rulers
suggested that only left-wing threats prevented democratization; civilian rule would come when Brazilian society had grown economically
and matured politically. Similarly, South Africa's white-minority government predicted peaceful coexistence with "separate development."
Rapid growth would provide jobs and social harmony; industrialization would lead to pluralist democracy, and in time, racial tensions
would disappear.

By the end of the decade, however, militant labor movements in both
countries challenged existing social arrangements; leading businessmen
in both countries would negotiate with the unions that had been consistently repressed. Among those most willing to negotiate, paradoxically,
were prominent representatives of precisely the sectors that had benefited most from authoritarian development strategies.

To some extent, conflicts over development policies can be traced to
a changed international context. As Gary Gereffi notes, the period in
which both South Africa and Brazil grew fastest was marked by "extraordinary dynamism in the world economy. The two decades that
preceded the global crisis of the 1970s saw unprecedented annual
growth rates in world industrial production (approximately 5.6 per-

91

cent) and world trade (around 7.3 percent), relatively low inflation and high employment in the industrialized countries, and stable international monetary arrangements."[1]

But while international opportunities and pressures clearly have a great deal to do with shaping the possibilities available to nation-states, decisions about which strategies to follow are not always obvious. In chapter 2, the relationship between states and business communities was treated as relatively unproblematic—as indeed it appeared to be while high growth rates were sustained. But especially as the effects of the post-1973 international recession began to be felt around the world, there was growing conflict among elites over how to sustain industrial growth. Rapid growth rates and apparent consensus had concealed potential tensions between states and dominant classes; as growth rates slowed, different sectors sought to further their specific interests, revealing the way previous industrial growth strategies had altered the relationship between business leaders and state policymakers.

Why, in a comparative study of the emergence of labor movements, should we pause to examine the relationship between states and industrialists? As this chapter suggests, and subsequent descriptions will emphasize, both the Brazilian and South African labor movements started within the factory, among workers; indeed, it was in their responses to labor militance that leading industrialists first acted publicly on their growing disillusionment with past authoritarian practice. Does a focus on dominant classes unnecessarily distract from the internal dynamics of working-class organization and community? Discussions of oppositional social movements generally place themselves on either side of a divide: should the analyst emphasize changes in the practice and consciousness of participants in movements, or should one begin by examining change in the structures of control? The question is sharper still where there is a history of repression: by discussing the breakdown of regimes or the collapse of dominant class alliances, does one diminish the real courage shown by those who have struggled against the state?

In actual historical cases, however, the possibilities for social movements exist within a broader context: at least in Brazil and South Africa, where popular mobilizations had been severely repressed only a decade before, social movements could only emerge when repression relaxed long enough to allow worker organization to spread. Throughout the decade of rapid growth, worker activism had not come to a complete stop: individual activists in both cases tried to organize fellow workers, risking victimization and arrest, as both the Brazilian and

South African states treated strikes as threats to national security. But ten years later, in both cases, while some industrialists called in police over strikes, others acknowledged that strikers had legitimate grievances, inadvertently strengthening unions by acceding to workers' demands. Why were strikers able to make concrete gains in the 1970s, when their efforts had been so repressed in the 1960s?

Increasingly, sociologists recognize that social-movement activists respond to new political opportunities: the question is not so much why poor people rebel, but under what conditions they do so. How do changes in the "political opportunity structure" create new possibilities, even new resources, for social movements? Like the presence of sympathetic media or support from middle- and upper-class students, conflicts among elites may provide new openings for challenging the existing order. Political opportunities, Sidney Tarrow writes, "cannot make the poor conscious of grievances of which they were formerly unaware, but [they] can help them to detect where and how the system is most vulnerable."[2]

"Political opportunity structures," however, remain rather ill-defined; social-movement theorists tend to use the concept in a somewhat ad hoc fashion, pointing out new opportunities—breaches in dominant coalitions, or shifting forces within society—after they have emerged. Given the wide range in types of social movements and types of political opportunity, general social-movement theories may never achieve greater specificity. For particular types of social movements, however, it should be possible to specify at a theoretical level the dynamics most likely to be involved in the creation of greater political space.

For labor movements, it seems relatively easy to point to the social actors with the greatest theoretical interest in preventing mobilization. Employers rarely welcome demands for higher wages, and have frequently sought state assistance in repressing workers' attempts to bargain collectively. Growth-oriented capitalist states—by which I mean both policymakers and the institutions in and through which policies are made and implemented—probably have fewer inherent structural interests in reducing labor costs, but they do have a long-term interest in continued economic growth, and therefore in preserving business confidence and a profitable investment climate.[3] State policymakers tend to consider a stable industrial work force and consistent profit rates as a way to increase investment, especially in new areas of production.

Although all capitalist states face these imperatives in an era of global capital mobility, policymakers in less-developed countries may be especially likely to privilege the demands of private investors in the effort to create new areas of growth in economies where productivity has been relatively low, or where major products have been subject to fluctuating world prices. Indeed, conservative economic theorists have often argued that developmentalist states should prioritize economic growth before attempting to raise the population's standard of living; the benefits of increased productivity are supposed ultimately to trickle down to the population, but only if the state has been able to guarantee a stable and profitable investment climate.

Authoritarian states may, however, have an additional interest in restricting worker organization and the expression of popular demands. For states that have chosen to rely on coercion rather than popular political legitimacy to maintain control, repressing wage demands and labor unions may be one of the easiest methods available simultaneously to ensure a profitable investment climate and to prevent the emergence of a political opposition. State repression of labor movements, then, may reflect state efforts to maintain stability, both by supporting private capital accumulation and by repressing political expression. Guillermo O'Donnell has labeled the growth-oriented, authoritarian coalition between state and capital that he considers likely in developmentalist states, "bureaucratic authoritarianism"; in order to allow rapid "modernization" of the economy, he suggests, technocratic policymakers may ally with capital. Latin American scholars continue to debate the extent to which the dynamics of bureaucratic-authoritarianism are generalizable,[4] but as chapter 2's description of rapid-industrialization strategies has shown, O'Donnell's characterization is probably appropriate for the governing coalitions in both Brazil and South Africa during the 1960s: business leaders and state officials seeking to promote overall growth agreed on the need for insulated policy-making and repression of political opposition.

But repressive apparatuses may also develop their own momentum, beyond the structural requirements of maintaining economic stability. An emphasis on national security concerns can shape state policies and bureaucracies, so that civil servants and political leaders come to view repression of popular demands as an end in itself. In Brazil, Alves writes, the military government's national security doctrine foresaw "the state's obtaining a degree of legitimacy based on continued capitalist development as well as on its function as defender of the nation against the threat of 'internal enemies' and 'psychological warfare' . . . and in turn produces a climate of suspicion, fear and divisiveness [which] leads to a dynamic of absolute control, the search for absolute security."[5] State policymakers created new structures to restrict political expression, staffed by military officials and civil servants committed to retaining control. The situation was even more dramatic in South Africa, where by 1970, a third of whites were directly employed by the state, mainly in the vast bureaucracy required to enforce apartheid legislation. Above and beyond its race and labor control functions, Stanley B. Greenberg writes, the state machinery "constituted the white community. . . . Even if state officials and the government had been able to relinquish some racial functions [they] could hardly have relinquished the white bureaucracies that accompanied them [nor] could they have afforded to endanger white control of institutions that employed a very large percentage of the white community and that directed government investment into the white sector."[6] In both cases, while the initial phases of labor repression may have been linked to state efforts to build an alliance with capital, the dynamics of state repression created a situation where authoritarianism became an end in itself. In both Brazil and South Africa, employers who were unwilling to negotiate with labor could count on support from state bureaucracies and police under authoritarian rule.

As workers in both Brazil and South Africa discovered, however, repression can vary in intensity—even under authoritarian states committed to controlling labor and political organizations. What are the sources of that variation? Logically, if labor repression reflects the state's attempt to build an alliance with employers, tensions within that alliance seem likely to be a major factor explaining variation in the level of labor repression. Acknowledging the extent to which employer-state conflicts changed the context labor confronted hardly negates the independent dynamics of worker organization; rather, it suggests that shifts in the political arena, as well as in the workplace, help explain why labor activism is more likely to be met by police batons in some periods than in others.

This question about variation in levels of labor repression is almost entirely absent from discussions of industrializing societies. Modernization theories generally assumed that industrialization would bring democracy; this assumption has been contradicted by the real world, where industrialists have frequently supported authoritarian states. On the other hand, discussions in the dependency tradition, which emphasize the obstacles to industrialization, rarely acknowledge the way dominant class alliances can change rapidly during political crises. Instead, they tend to stress the extent to which developmentalist coalitions supported consistent control and repression of workers and peasants. Nor do discussions of labor movements in earlier industrializers help much: although nineteenth- and early-twentieth-century European labor movements were clearly affected by state repression, this issue is usually considered only from the perspective of how repression shaped union responses, rather than why and how dominant class coalitions and labor repression shifted within an existing institutional framework.[7]

One way to approach an explanation for the emergence of militant labor movements is to begin with an examination of changing political opportunities—and, in particular, changes in the relations between states and dominant classes. Is it possible to identify specific tensions in the relationship between capital and the state—tensions that altered, even briefly, the response of the dominant classes to labor militance, in ways that increased the opportunities for labor activism?

The most common explanation for changing employer attitudes revolves around changing labor processes. It has often been argued that as skill levels increase, employers will tend to pay higher wages in return for production and stability.[8] With the introduction of more capital-intensive technology, increased skill levels and higher capital:labor ratios may have reduced manufacturers' willingness simply to fire and replace striking workers. But changes in the labor process alone do not explain the wide variation in employers' willingness to negotiate; even within the same industry, some employers made concessions, while others continued to follow labor-repressive policies. Thus, while labor process changes clearly affected workers' ability to organize, they do not by themselves explain why some employers seemed by the 1980s to accept principles of collective bargaining that they had previously rejected. In both Brazil and South Africa, industrialists' responses to strikes were relatively idiosyncratic, reflecting individual ideologies as much as economic imperatives.

Moreover, changes in the labor process do not by themselves explain why any employers who had previously relied on state control over workers would choose to engage in negotiations with workers, when those negotiations could only raise the labor bills for individual employers, and when state repression could have continued to prevent labor unrest. What is most surprising about the late 1970s, in both Brazil and South Africa, is less the existence of disagreements within the business community over how to respond to strikes, than the way business leaders—who by the 1970s represented a new industrial elite—shaped a business consensus calling for a new labor relations framework, in direct opposition to state policy. In the 1970s, some of the same South African and Brazilian industrialists who had supported, or at least cooperated with, authoritarian rule in the 1960s began to reject state intervention in the workplace—and in that context, to acknowledge the legitimacy of workers' demands for higher wages. After decades of supporting repressive state policies, what could have induced employers to abandon appeals to the state to prevent industrial action? What prompted industrialists to challenge the authoritarian state on which they had previously relied for protection and support? How far did business opposition go, and what were the limits to conflict between the state and industry?

It seems worth asking whether this shift in the relationship between industrialists and the state may have been linked to the effects of rapid industrialization on the composition of business elites. By the 1970s, in both South Africa and Brazil, primary product producers had merged into industry; as chapter 2 suggested, in the course of rapid industrialization, both Brazilian coffee growers and South African mining magnates were directly involved in dynamic industries, and business leadership clearly reflected that shift. In Brazil, the automobile industry, centered in São Paulo, led the country's economic growth strategy; landowners, although still important in local rural politics, no longer dominated the economy or the political scene. In South Africa, major mining companies and Afrikaans businessmen had expanded industrial holdings; the mine companies and white farmers who had shaped state policies before the 1950s either shifted into industry or lost political importance.

In both countries, industrialists now dominated business debates. These business leaders began to view their interests as separable from those of the state—especially when international vulnerabilities and pressures created new conflicts over development strategies. While growth rates remained high, state policymakers could satisfy a range of demands from private entrepreneurs and from within the state apparatus; when growth rates declined, different sectors of capital sought to further specific interests—and to demand greater openness in policymaking processes as a means to furthering those interests.

By the early 1970s, three major issues—each related to the model of industrialization followed in the 1960s—had begun to disturb large industrial producers in both countries. First, shortages of skilled labor made the use of complex imported technology problematic. In both cases, despite high unemployment of less-skilled and casual labor, a lack of skilled workers plagued production. Second, the prospect of a domestic market for consumer durables eternally limited by low wages meant producers of high-cost goods could not expect to increase domestic sales. Although exports to other countries could expand markets, such a strategy would make the economy even more vulnerable to international recessions, and, in South Africa's case, underlined threats of international economic sanctions.

From the perspective of individual industrialists, however, even more serious problems were posed by the power of the state in the economy, related to previous state investments in productive capacity. State policies and enterprises functioned independently, and their goals regularly conflicted with those of private industry. First, large state enterprises demanded increased attention from state policymakers; the parastatals that had initially provided inputs for industrial growth were believed to soak up resources that would otherwise have been available for the private sector. Second, both the South African and Brazilian states had begun to give priority to national security programs as well as to economic growth, spending money on relatively unprofitable state-owned energy and arms industries.

I suggest in this chapter that with the international recession of the mid 1970s, important entrepreneurs in both countries saw themselves closed out of policy-making circles and confronted by policies set by a different agenda than their own. During the period of rapid growth, state priorities had coincided with those of big business. As the economic crises of the 1970s deepened into political ones, business leaders sought to reestablish an independent position within society, challenging state officials' exclusive control over economic policy. In the process, almost coincidentally, key business leaders would acknowledge the legitimacy of workers' demands for higher wages and, ultimately, for incorporation into political processes. While that acknowledgement may have had more to do with business seeking to shape state policies than with individual businessmen's desire to increase labor costs, business leaders in both Brazil and South Africa seemed far more willing in the late 1970s to accept the principle of collective bargaining than they had twenty years before—a fact that would provide new opportunities for labor.

BRAZIL: COLLAPSE OF AN ALLIANCE?

In mid 1978, after fourteen years of military rule, eight leading industrialists in São Paulo declared publicly that "only democracy absorbs social tensions." Arguing that it was no longer possible to ignore "screaming needs" in health, sanitation, and education, they called on the state to modernize labor laws and allow wages to keep pace with inflation. While they clearly considered business and the state the major protagonists in policy-making, the businessmen nevertheless declared:

> We believe that economic and social development, such as we know it, will only be possible within a political system that permits full participation by all. And there is only one regime capable of promoting the full expression of interests and opinions with at the same time enough flexibility to absorb tensions without transforming them into an undesirable conflict—a democratic regime. More, we are convinced that the system of free enterprise and the market economy are viable and can be long-lasting, if we can construct institutions that protect the right of citizens and guarantee liberty.[9]

Coming from leaders of the consumer durables industry—which owed its existence to previous policies of the very authoritarian state they now attacked—the industrialists' manifesto challenged the very basis of Brazil's economic growth. It criticized the military's centralized control over the economy, the closure of political channels, and the inequality that had marked Brazil's industrialization strategy.

The manifesto took most observers by surprise: would the Brazilian bourgeoisie, after all, emerge as a leading force for democratization? Would business, as one signatory suggested, break "the pact that government and business signed after 1964," and "walk on its own feet" instead of leaning on state support?[10]

For decades, analysts of Brazilian society have debated the relationship between the state and industry. Along with political activists, sociologists have argued over how much the state has supported national industrial capital, and which fractions of capital have controlled state policy. In the 1950s, it was widely believed that national industry would help develop the economy, in contrast to "backward" agrarian elites or exploitive international enterprises. By the late 1960s, however, most academic observers agreed that this view of national capital was simplistic: the cohesion and support for authoritarian rule from industrial and agrarian capitalists, and from national and foreign capital, had eroded any grounds for faith in industry's progressive tenden-

cies.[11] Sociologists were more likely to argue that the Brazilian bourgeoisie had depended so heavily on the state for subsidies and economic
protection that it had failed to act politically as an independent class.[12]
From a somewhat different perspective, rank-and-file unionists reached
a similar conclusion: they regularly referred to the military regime as
"the bosses' state" and rarely differentiated between fractions of capital.[13] By the end of the first decade of military rule, few Brazilians
seemed to view either the state or industrial capital as autonomous political actors.

By the late 1970s, however, relations between industrial leaders and
the state were so strained that economist Luiz Carlos Bresser Pereira
described the tensions as the "collapse of a class alliance."[14] By the
late 1970s, major industrial leaders in São Paulo had clearly distanced
themselves from the state, demanding economic and political reform.
As Evans points out, it was a remarkable development: an industrial
bourgeoisie that owed its very existence to previous state policies, "re-
inventing" an independent identity and demanding an independent
voice.[15]

Clearly, the relationship between the state and industrial leaders
changed dramatically during the second decade of military rule. By the
mid 1980s, important business leaders publicly supported opposition
parties, and their contribution would hasten the military's departure
from government. But analysts will continue to debate the underlying
dynamics of the shift: were business leaders merely responding to growing public concern over human rights violations and political exclusion,
or did tensions arising out of economic policy arenas spill over into
politics? Did the industrial elite's behavior reflect a democratic thrust
inherent in industrialization, or were there dynamics internal to the
state-capital relationship that led industry to insist on democratization?

Business opposition to military rule was partly rooted in a growing
awareness of the regime's human rights violations and a sense among
members of Brazil's elite that the military's national security apparatus
had gone out of control. In her careful study of the interaction between
the national security state and popular movements Alves argues that
by the mid 1970s many middle- and upper-class Brazilians who had
previously viewed military rule as protection from the Communist men-
ace began to object to the national security apparatus.[16] Especially after
1973, when General Ernesto Geisel promised a "long, slow decompres-
sion" and controlled liberalization of political processes, the human
rights movement gradually gained visibility. Strengthened by interna-

tional criticism of widespread detention and torture, it became an important component of the political opposition movement in the mid 1970s.[17] The Catholic Church hierarchy increasingly spoke out against human rights violations, and from 1974 onward lawyers and journalists' associations challenged the loss of legal procedures and prior censorship. In 1975, the death during interrogation of the well-known journalist Vladimir Herzog brought thousands to hear São Paulo's Cardinal Arns condemn state violence. In 1977, students at São Paulo's universities reorganized an outlawed national students' union, demanding an end to the infamous AI-5; student demonstrations continued and grew larger over the next few years.

Undoubtedly, the growth of the largely middle-class human rights movement strengthened business opposition in the late 1970s and helped push debates that might otherwise have been restricted to economic policy toward discussion of democratic participation. Nevertheless, I would argue that the growing tension between industry and the Brazilian state in the 1970s arose from the process of economic development, as industrial leaders lost confidence in the state's ability and willingness to protect their interests. Changes in the international economic climate and the domestic political scene exacerbated tensions that had been latent even during the peak years of Brazil's economic miracle, and business leaders increasingly viewed their sectoral interests as separable from the interests of the state. Frustrated by contradictory state policies, and by increasing conflict over state resources, business leaders challenged both state control over the economy and the national security priorities that had justified authoritarian practices. In a climate of growing rancor, threatened by an increasingly militant labor movement and a state that no longer seemed responsive to the private sector's immediate needs, the business community came to believe, in the words of a leading automobile-part manufacturer, that "democracy offers a system of control, of self-defense."[18]

At least as they expressed themselves in business associations, leading industrialists generally restricted their criticisms to economic policy issues, avoiding broader political issues. To some extent, business reticence in challenging the military regime can be explained through fear: in the early 1970s, when government repression was widespread, it was certainly safer for industrialists to discuss economic policies than to question political choices—especially for industrialists who depended on state subsidies and credits. Furthermore, Brazil's corporatist system reinforced business's tendency to focus on economic issues: the channels available for articulating business interests were based on economic identity, not political views. When business began to demand a louder voice in policy-making, it organized within associations designed to express the material interests of specific economic groups, rather than political associations. Individual Brazilian businessmen may have been deeply opposed to the regime's anti-democratic practices during the 1960s and early 1970s, but it was not until the emergence of tensions over economic policies that business leaders openly distanced themselves from the military regime.

What caused these tensions? As many authors have argued, as long as growth rates were maintained, the Brazilian *empresariado*, or business class, did not complain. Once the economy slowed, the state's attempts to resolve economic problems almost inevitably threatened the interests of some sectors of the dominant class. Debates over economic policy would gradually turn into complaints over the exclusion of some sectors from policy-making, and finally into demands for greater political participation.[19]

INTERNATIONAL AND DOMESTIC PRESSURES

Most analysts date the split between the state and business from 1974, when the Brazilian economy began to suffer the effects of the 1973 rise in oil prices. Pedro Sampaio Malan and Regis Bonelli argue that from 1967 to 1973, economic growth came from utilizing excess capacity rather than from an expanded productive base; from this perspective, an economic impasse was virtually inevitable as excess capacity was used up, whatever happened at the international level.[20] But the 1973 jump in international oil prices undoubtedly aggravated Brazil's problems. Although Brazil nationalized its petroleum industry in the 1950s, it had continued to rely heavily on imported oil and capital goods; soaring international prices gave domestic inflation, already high, an additional push. Government figures initially misrepresented the inflation figure for 1973—a lie that would come back to haunt the regime in the late 1970s, when it provided the basis for a highly effective national union campaign for higher wages—but even so, inflation reached nearly 25 percent that year, and would continue at even higher levels for the next fifteen years.[21] In 1980, inflation would reach 110 percent per year, and in 1983, it would reach 200.

The post-1973 international recession had two immediate domestic manifestations, both directly linked to Brazil's model of development.

First, the rate of growth dropped immediately, from about 14 to 9 percent in 1974; in 1975, the gross national product (GNP) grew only about 6 percent.[22] International prices for the imported capital goods required for continued industrial expansion rose rapidly. Between 1972 and 1974, Brazil's foreign debt more than doubled; the government depended increasingly on high-interest loans to fund industrialization. By late 1978, Brazil owed nearly $44 billion. Meanwhile, direct foreign investment declined, and the domestic market, already small, shrank still further. The growing deficit and rising inflation reduced the government's ability to provide loans to consumers, while real wages were eroded. The combined effect of inflation and tight credit on the Brazilian car market was so dramatic that models initially designed for Brazil's middle class were almost immediately discontinued, and manufacturers began to look overseas for new markets.[23] As one observer put it, at least until foreign markets were found, "The automobile's days of glory had ended."[24]

Clearly, the new economic situation required new policies. General Geisel, who had just succeeded Medici as president, unveiled the Second National Development Plan in early 1974, aiming to deepen industrialization further by expanding the capital-goods sector. Through "a new phase of import substitution," Brazil would attain a "new industrial profile" with which to cross the "frontier to full development." An expanded state sector would provide new markets for local producers, while the state would provide new financing. At the same time, Geisel spoke vaguely of future political liberalization, suggesting that with economic growth would come both improved income distribution and increased, although not total, political participation.[25]

Geisel was unable to persuade business leaders to support his plan. Already shaken by a worsening economic climate, business confidence was further eroded by the government's stunning defeat in the 1974 election. Geisel came to power in 1973 through an indirect, military-controlled process; despite his promises of gradual liberalization, political channels remained closed. The AI-5 remained in effect, and the Brazilian Congress was dominated by the military's ARENA party. The 1974 elections revealed new levels of popular dissatisfaction with the military regime. In 1970, thousands of people had been arrested just before the election, and about 20 percent of ballots cast were blank; nevertheless, the ARENA party won an overwhelming majority.[26] Four years later, members of the loyal opposition, the Movimento Democrático Brasileiro (MDB) campaigned as "anti-candidates," using the relatively free political space of the election campaign to persuade voters to vote for the opposition. In the state of São Paulo, MDB candidates received more than three times the votes government ARENA candidates did, although votes for the MDB signified as much a set of "diffuse dissatisfactions" as support for opposition candidates.[27]

THE SECOND DEVELOPMENT PLAN

The dissatisfactions of the *empresariado* were hardly diffuse. In reality, Geisel's promised political liberalization was strictly limited: throughout his presidency, the military regime continued to purge "subversives" and to use emergency powers to remove opposition delegates from Congress.[28] In 1978, the government restricted election campaigning, limiting media coverage and making it more difficult for opposition candidates to reach supporters—although MDB support continued to rise, especially in large urban centers.

Nevertheless, it is probably not overly cynical to believe that industrial leaders would have continued to support authoritarian political leaders if the economic situation had improved: historically, Brazilian industrialists have hardly been reliable allies for popular movements. But Geisel's economic ministry proved unable to recreate the prosperity of the 1960s. Piecemeal policies, partial and contradictory, failed to restore growth. Policies designed to attract domestic capital into the capital-goods sector were contradicted by policies designed to reduce inflation; similarly, policies designed to strengthen private initiatives were undermined by growing state involvement in direct production.

In part, the Second National Development Plan's contradictory policies can be explained through the regime's overoptimistic assumptions: a sluggish market put local firms at a disadvantage relative to foreign capital-goods producers, while the trade deficit further reduced the state's ability to finance new investment or purchase capital goods.[29] Moreover, although industrial exports increased in the mid 1970s, private and state borrowing at fluctuating interest rates left the economy more vulnerable than ever to international economic shifts; Brazil became the first example of "indebted industrialization," and in the early 1980s the foreign debt would become a volatile issue in domestic political debates. With enough investment capital, perhaps local producers could have competed with foreign producers; with adequate credit, perhaps a growing market for locally produced capital goods could have stimulated production. Lacking these resources, however, the Second

National Development Plan was a dismal failure: slowed growth rates, galloping inflation, and a rapidly increasing foreign debt made the "frontier to full development" look further away than ever.

In its attempt to restore growth rates, the Brazilian state became an increasingly independent economic actor. Both in the structure of decision-making and in the execution of economic policies, state intervention in the economy tended to overlook private interests. The decision to strengthen the capital-goods sector by creating state-owned productive enterprises threatened to siphon off resources that might otherwise have gone to private companies. Of 205 state productive enterprises in 1982, 110 were created after 1970.[30] In 1979, 28 of Brazil's largest non-financial firms were publicly owned, up from 17 at the beginning of the decade.[31] Although the new state enterprises were initially meant to stimulate private production of capital goods, they competed with private industry for markets and state resources. Instead of emphasizing support for private capital, state enterprises and agencies tended to follow their own dynamic of expansion; increasingly, business leaders believed that this dynamic "inscribed itself in the very mode of expansion of the state," shaping state policy to meet the needs of state enterprises rather than private industry.[32]

Along with trying to strengthen Brazil's capital-goods industry, Geisel's regime sought to develop specific industries for national security, often through large projects that were too risky or too technologically advanced for Brazilian private capital on its own. Especially when the 1973 oil crisis revealed Brazil's vulnerability to international economic forces, the military regime invested heavily in strengthening the national arms industry and in creating a nuclear power industry for energy self-sufficiency. State decisions to invest in national security projects, like decisions to invest in large state enterprises, limited the extent to which private industrialists could count on the state, especially during a period of economic decline. Private businesses—even the large joint ventures of the automobile industry, previously the economy's key sector—lacked the claims to national security priority that might have allowed them to compete for state support. On the other hand, most national security projects would make no contribution to the economy for decades, and business leaders believed they drained state resources without promising future returns.[33]

Tensions over the distribution of shrinking state resources exacerbated conflict between Geisel's stated goal of political liberalization and the growth in executive prerogatives during his tenure. Under Geisel, financial control over national investment funds was steadily more centralized, through bodies such as the National Monetary Council and the National Development Bank; legislative control over financial policies was reduced, while the executive's role was strengthened.[34] Dependent on state policies for access to foreign exchange and markets, and competing with state enterprises for loans and subsidies, business leaders found the centralization of power in the executive reduced their access to policymakers.

A worsening economic climate underscored the contradictory thrust within state economic policy—what Carlos Lessa calls the "schizophrenic split" in the Second National Development Plan.[35] Although most large private enterprises depended on state contracts and support, they also suffered from competition with state enterprises and frustration over the difficulty in reaching policymakers. The regime's most important policy decisions were insulated from political pressure; even at the social level, a decade of military rule had distanced military leaders from the rest of Brazil's elite.[36] Businessmen seeking help had to find informal contacts with state officials, because meaningful official channels no longer seemed to exist.[37] Policy-making seemed distant even from the corporative business associations set up during the 1930s; various branches of the state, often independent and sometimes at odds with one another, controlled economic decisions, leaving businessmen frustrated over the possibility of influencing specific outcomes. While the Brazilian state "faithfully serves the general and most fundamental interests of the bourgeoisie and makes every effort to assure the advancement of private capital accumulation," Sérgio Abranches noted, "it appears as a menacing Leviathan to most social forces as particular actors."[38]

By the mid 1970s, the economic miracle was over, and popular support for the military regime had fallen to a new low. Faced with a military regime that no longer seemed responsive to their needs, important industrialists began to express their distrust. Economic growth had provided the glue holding all sectors of industry together; with its collapse, individual businesses and entire industries complained that state policies ignored their needs. In 1975–76, a survey of leading São Paulo businessmen found that even in the generally favored capital-goods sector, business leaders resented both the centralization of power and the apparent confusion between state branches. One businessman complained that the president had the final word on all decisions: "You can dialogue with all the world, but the decision is closed . . . and the ultimate word is that of the president."[39] In mid 1976, the journal of the Federation of Industry of São Paulo (FIESP) concluded that contradictory policies, misleading information, and the absence of fixed rules meant that "business always loses in the official game."[40] In early 1977, Geisel dismissed his minister of industry and commerce, Severo Gomes, considered the cabinet member most sympathetic to private industry; business protests over exclusion from state policy-making grew almost hysterical.

Despite mounting dismay at government policies, businessmen had few weapons except noncooperation; as one business leader warned, the "non-participation of business" in policy-making "ends by hurting the government" and its ability to implement strategies for economic growth.[41] But probably the most visible sign of growing business disenchantment came in the form of a campaign against state control of the economy. In 1975, FIESP published a study claiming that state enterprises now competed directly in some areas with private businesses.[42] State enterprises were described as unproductive and inefficient, consuming resources that might otherwise have gone to private industry, and acting only in the interests of corrupt state officials.[43] While the call for privatization reflected the spread of monetarist ideologies, in Brazil complaints about state control over the economy also reflected business leaders' demands for increased access to policy-making processes, and fears that the state was unable to resolve its economic problems.

With monotonous repetition, business groups demanded an end to "statization," calling on the state to reduce its direct economic involvement and to provide more support to private capital. Eli Diniz and Olavio Brasil de Lima Junior suggest that the campaign against *estatização* formed the basis for a new business consensus. Businessmen who normally competed for state assistance could feel some solidarity in the face of a growing state presence.[44] As Pereira commented as early as 1976, the campaign against state enterprises represented a first crack in the alliance between private business and state officials, a crack "through which capitalists [could] express their lack of confidence in relation to events, and seek to affirm a dominant position in the system of power."[45]

By the end of Geisel's five-year presidency, business disenchantment with the military regime had reached new heights. In early 1977, the president of Brazil's National Confederation of Industry warned the government that the country "confronts a time of harsh reality. The country stands at a crossroads. The people are dubious and the *empre-*

sariado worried."[46] Later that year, a national meeting of the Congress of the Producing Classes—a revived corporatist body, which had long avoided political resolutions—called for greater political freedom, decentralized economic power, reduced bureaucracy, and more state support for private initiative.[47] Business leaders complained with Laerte Setubal Filho, director of a large São Paulo industry, that the congress should have demanded political incorporation even more directly.[48] Claudio Bardella, named in a national business survey as 1977's leading industrialist, called on business to help in "defining the paths our country should follow," and former cabinet member Severo Gomes, who was also named in the survey as a leading business representative, said, "The only way out is democracy" combined with greater business assertiveness.[49]

How far did this break between the state and industry extend? In an influential article on the role of business in the transition to civilian government, Fernando Henrique Cardoso points out that, despite their concerns, prominent business leaders refused to join the organized opposition.[50] Severo Gomes called stridently for a shift in economic development strategies away from economic policies geared toward export and a highly stratified domestic market, and toward policies that would reorient production toward a more equitable domestic market, thus reducing vulnerability to international recession. Yet he continued to support the military's party, ARENA.[51] Gomes was hardly unique. Business criticisms of state policy throughout the 1970s had more to do with specific industrial policies, state enterprises, and foreign exchange availability than with broad political participation.[52] Although business leaders sought greater participation and called for democratization, their main concern was with steadying the balance of the triple alliance, increasing business input into policy-making rather than ending military control of the state.[53]

CHALLENGE FROM BELOW

In the midst of an ongoing debate over the relationship between the state and the industrial sector, an explosion of labor militance challenged existing labor relations. In 1978, an unprecedented strike wave paralyzed São Paulo's industrial belt, then spread to include half a million workers in six states. In what appeared to be spontaneous sit-down strikes, workers in all the major factories of the auto industry stopped work; unions were only called in later, when employers realized they could not negotiate with masses of workers.

As the next chapters will show, the labor movement of the late 1970s had its own dynamic: it developed on factory floors and in working-class communities. Since the early 1970s, a growing popular movement had demanded an improved standard of living for the majority of Brazilians, who had been excluded from the benefits of economic growth; supported by that movement, workers' organizations grew dramatically, strengthening shop-floor representation and increasingly demanding direct negotiations with employers. By the time most business leaders were aware of the new labor militance, it was already a reality with which businessmen would have to deal.

This reality—a shop-floor labor movement with wide community support—appeared during a moment of intense debate within the business community over the relationship between state and capital. The debate was vicious: while FIESP officially called for repression, FIESP's vice president called the idea of police action "stupidity" and praised the workers' "maturity."[54] Businessmen who generally supported the military regime viewed the strikes as a threat to order, a disaster for the economy, which would create disrespect for law and authority. Those who sought to increase business participation in policy-making argued that workers had a right to make reasonable demands, especially if the result were an expanded domestic market. Business leaders hoping to reduce industrial dependence on the state generally argued that businessmen should respond to the strikes on their own rather than calling for police intervention. Among industrialists, at least, the divisions appear to have been shaped as much by ideological tendencies as by labor demands; if there was any consistent pattern in individual responses to the strikes, it appears to have been shaped by the extent to which a particular businessman was or was not comfortable with the principle of collective bargaining as practiced in the United States—a model with which most business leaders were familiar by the end of fifteen years of expanding economic ties and joint ventures.[55]

Events in the auto industry changed the pattern of Brazilian labor relations. Faced with sudden strikes, employers in the auto industry entered into direct negotiations with workers' representatives, by-passing the state's labor tribunal and arguing that collective bargaining would resolve factory conflicts faster than state intervention. Like other industrialists who now accepted the concept of direct negotiations, Einar Kok, president of Brazil's Association of Machine Industries, argued that reducing state control over labor organizations would allow employers and workers to enter into dialogue instead of conflict, and that state intervention could only muddy the situation.[56] Through direct negotiations, striking auto workers won raises of 11 percent; more important, perhaps, the strikes allowed workers to express their aspirations for "freedom, autonomy and the right to full citizenship."[57]

With thirty years of rejecting direct negotiations behind them, it seems unlikely that leading Brazilian industrialists accepted face-to-face meetings between unionists and employers because of a new enthusiasm for representative unionism. The president of the Metalworkers' Union, Lula da Silva, suggested the auto industry was simply responding to the loss of production; employer participation in direct negotiations, he argued, was simply a more expedient means of ending the strike than calling in the government would have been.[58] Several sociologists have argued that the strikes caught the Brazilian auto industry at a particularly vulnerable time, just as it was seeking to increase international sales; since the auto industry was to be the key component in Brazil's effort to increase its manufactured exports, neither the industry nor the state could afford to let production stop.[59] More cynical observers suggested that years of low wages had given business room to maneuver against the state: industrialists were willing to accept the prospect of limited wage increases and independent unions in return for more independence from a state that appeared to ignore their interests.[60]

It is probably impossible to measure how much the auto industry's willingness to negotiate arose from immediate concerns over production and how much came from deeper shifts in business attitudes toward an increasingly skilled work force and an interventionist state. Some businessmen had called for liberalization of labor laws even before the strike: in 1977, José Mindlin, voted one of the country's leading business spokesmen in 1978, told a business meeting that trade unions should be allowed to organize freely. After 1978, employers would continue to debate the limits of acceptable unionism: while most supported continued control over corporatist unions, some openly defended workers' right to strike, arguing that independent unions would win higher wages, creating the larger internal market Brazilian industry needed. Others suggested that direct dialogue would reduce factory-level conflict and help reduce labor market distortions caused by high turnover and low skills.

But no business spokesperson wanted completely free unionism. Even business liberals warned that freeing unions without first controlling inflation might "unleash a bomb in business's hands," as unions might be used for political ends.[61] Business leaders who expressed an abstract desire for expanded markets were not always willing to raise workers' wages: when the state changed from a semestral to a trimestral readjustment of wages for inflation, the business community considered the shift a betrayal.[62] Within months of the 1978 strikes, a new business consensus would be restored. While some important firms, notably Ford Motor Company, recognized and negotiated with factory committees, FIESP's industrial leaders expressed the consistent position that only unions that stayed within the corporatist framework were acceptable.[63] By 1979, even liberal businessmen would be less tolerant of workers' demands, accepting as legitimate only strikes carried out by registered unions, without intervention by "priests, students and political activists," who might use workers for "political ends."[64] Businessmen repeatedly argued that social problems could be solved only if industry was allowed to expand, and that independent unions were beneficial only while they restricted their demands to factory-level issues.[65] Recognizing trade unions' presence did not mean completely changing the pattern of capitalist development: economic growth, not redistribution, remained the goal. "Profit and salary," businessmen reminded each other, "are integral terms of the same and inescapable equation."[66]

BUSINESS IN POLICY-MAKING

Although business reached a general consensus rejecting militant labor organization, business opposition to the military regime nevertheless became increasingly vocal, with businessmen demanding access to policy-making bodies. In mid 1978, eight leading São Paulo industrialists published their call for democratization, "Só democracia absorve tensões sociais." Over the next few years, through the end of Geisel's presidency and into the beginning of that of his successor, João Batista de Oliveira Figueiredo, leading industrialists took increasingly critical and independent positions toward the state and state policies.

FIESP, representing Brazil's largest and most dynamic industries, itself became a battleground: in 1980, a leading liberal spokesman was elected president, defeating a conservative government supporter. Suggesting that the business community should not leave the formulation of a new political, economic, and social project to the government, the São Paulo industrialist Luís Eulálio de Bueno Vidigal Filho called for a greater business role in policy-making, roundly rejecting the government's recessionary policies.[67] While FIESP remained at the forefront of business opposition, it was gradually joined by industrial associations throughout the country calling for increased participation in decision-making.[68]

It would be a grave error to take calls for political liberalization and greater attention to social inequality out of context: business concerns over industry's lack of access to policy-making processes only deepened into a broader call for democratization under pressure from new popular mobilizations. Indeed, it is easy to be cynical about business leaders' acceptance of independent unionism: in the early 1980s, when recession and heavy unemployment meant shortages of skilled labor no longer plagued the automobile industry, even the automobile industry would acquiescence fully in police interventions in strikes. From 1979 on, when General Figueiredo replaced Geisel and promised to address business concerns more fully, business leaders softened their criticisms of military rule; the pressure for democratization never included a complete break with the state. Figueiredo's *abertura*, offering amnesty to political exiles and reducing press censorship, satisfied most business leaders—especially when they confronted an increasingly mobilized civil society, whose demands went far beyond "controlled liberalization." Throughout the early 1980s, business opposition tended to remain within the economic arena, and most leading industrialists continued to support the military's attempt to control democratization until the mid 1980s. Only when popular mobilizations against military rule had repeatedly paralyzed the country, and the military proved thoroughly incapable of designing acceptable austerity programs, did Brazilian industrialists as a bloc finally express public support for a transition to civilian rule.[69]

This is not to suggest, of course, that business leaders supported Figueiredo's economic policies. On the contrary, business spokespersons objected vehemently, first to a heterodox approach involving raising minimum wages and reducing export subsidies, then to more orthodox deflationary policies causing declining employment and productivity. Inflation rose steadily; real incomes declined by about 10 percent between 1979 and 1984, while Brazil's international debt rose to about $97 billion. Between 1980 and 1983, real per capita GNP declined by about 10 percent. Fishlow concludes that from 1980 on, the combination of pressure by international creditors and domestic demands undermined the government's capacity to design or execute economic planning. Policy was "very short-term, and frequently altered. . . . Solutions were designed for immediate problems, but frequently introduced new distortions that would later inhibit effective policy."[70]

Whatever their limits, however, business statements about the need for greater democracy in Brazil—coming as they did during early unionization drives and during the lead-up to the 1978 elections—can only have strengthened the broad opposition, giving greater legitimacy to opposition demands and increasing the political space available to political activists. Subsequent chapters will suggest that in Brazil, as in South Africa, popular pressure spread rapidly, making it difficult for capital and the state to resolve their tensions. In 1985, the Brazilian military permitted an opposition candidate, Tancredo Neves, to win controlled elections, paving the way for civilian rule.

Brazilians continue to debate the relative importance of the *empresariado* and popular movements: did the military regime permit the civilian opposition to take the presidency in the mid 1980s because of pressure from the business class or because of intensified pressure from urban social movements? Many observers have argued that business calls for democracy should not be overstated: business leaders sought a voice in economic policy, and were willing to make temporary alliances with popular movements to attain that end; but aside from agreeing vaguely that something should be done about Brazil's "social question," they were not seeking radical transformation in social relations. Even the most outspoken section of the *empresariado* "never wanted to be seen or identified as an adversary of the regime. On the contrary, it always sought to preserve its position as a potential ally, however much it demanded more space for the expression of its interests."[71] For Cardoso, the abstract oppositional identity assumed by business leaders against a dominant state "disappeared, naturally, in the concrete collision of interests [as strikes continued through the 1980s]. When the flame of salary demands set fire to the clear interests of businesses, it undid the civic charm of liberal consensual postures. . . . [B]usiness leaders hid once again behind the state, some ashamed, other hurrying."[72] Similarly, Diniz concludes, "The declarations favoring a return to democratic normalcy represented more the *empresariado*'s adhesion to the government's strategy of controlled liberalization than autonomous action [and] an alternative project of transition."[73] Business criticisms of the 1970s and 1980s did not represent a fundamental break between state and capital: for most business leaders, liberalization meant business would become an equal partner with the state in policy-making, and popular participation would be limited to the choice between alternatives offered by political parties. In contrast, the broad-based popular movements that emerged in the late 1970s demanded a different kind of citizenship, with a transformation of social relations as a fundamental part of political participation.[74]

The state's industrialization policies had created two new sectors, both of which would challenge state control: the most dynamic sectors of industry and a "new" urban working class. Throughout the 1970s, growing tension between the state and key sectors of industry appeared to reduce the threat of immediate repression of emergent worker organization; the shop-floor unions that emerged would serve as an important part of a far broader social movement. State efforts to rebuild legitimacy included controlled elections, which gave further impetus to spreading social protest. Ultimately, that social protest would push the state to negotiate a political transition; an elite opposition victory would avoid risking far more profound social changes.[75] Thus, two types of opposition interacted: business opposition may have had limited aims, but it created an unusual opportunity for workers to express basic demands and to create factory-based organizations at a crucial point in the emergence of popular opposition.

BUSINESS OPPOSITION IN SOUTH AFRICA

In the early 1980s, spokespersons for business sometimes claimed that the nonracial labor movement in South Africa owed its existence to business liberalism, especially to multinationals' more enlightened attitude toward worker organization. The claim certainly overstates the truth: as in Brazil, business acceptance generally responded to, rather than enabled, the emergence of independent unions on the shop floor. Rhetoric aside, South African employers were almost as reluctant as the state to grant black workers independent channels of expression. But in 1979, the government announced that it would recognize unions representing black workers; even more surprisingly, all employers' associations, including conservative Afrikaans-speaking groups, supported the labor law reforms. Why, after fifty years of strict labor repression and racial division, did the state and business finally agree to allow black workers to organize? Were the reforms simply a response to emergent worker organization, or did industrial growth make classical apartheid inefficient? What impact, if any, did changes in business attitudes have on emergent popular resistance to the state?

It has often been suggested that in South Africa in the 1980s, modernization brought democracy: new labor processes changed industrialists' attitudes toward worker organization and black labor, and these industrialists changed state policy toward black political representation. Thus, for example, Merle Lipton insists that manufacturers in the 1970s were prompted by changing skill requirements to urge reforms that allowed new unions to emerge and grow; and that those manufacturers were potential allies for black workers. Lipton insists that those who view South Africa's capitalist development as intricately linked to its racial order fail "to see that capitalists—despite some reservations and ambivalence—are among the pressures for [apartheid's] erosion. . . . The refusal to nurture the feasible alliances across racial lines (such as that between sections of white capital and black labor) and, instead, pursuing the chimera of total non-racialism or proletarian solidarity, will simply intensify racial polarization."[76] Modernization theorists blame apartheid on white (Afrikaans-speaking) workers, who insisted on racial job reservation, and on white (Afrikaans-speaking) politicians, who installed "separate development." In this view, capital (primarily English-speaking) has promoted social change by increasing blacks' skill levels and opportunities and by seeking to remove barriers to free movement. Despite the legacy of racial ideology, industry's changing labor requirements and growing dependence on black workers would power the motor of gradual change.

Such theories tend to treat capital-state relations as relatively static, however, ignoring the fact that capital sometimes relies upon state support—including repression of worker organization—and sometimes rejects it, but that these dynamics are not necessarily linked to "modernization" of a unilinear kind. As this section will show, South Africa's reforms cannot be attributed simply to capital's labor requirements or to suddenly liberalized employers; the process was far more complex than such a view suggests, and requires a more nuanced examination of both the state-capital alliance and the ability of workers to take advantage of strategic openings.

Instead, as in Brazil, the relationship between the state and key sectors of the business community changed when the model of authoritarian industrialization, so successful during the 1960s, ran into an impasse. Despite initial objections to apartheid, industry had accommodated itself to racial planning during the period of economic growth. But from the early 1970s, South Africa's industrialization strategy was no longer feasible; although for slightly different reasons than in Brazil, political and economic pressures undermined the "triple alliance" between state, international capital, and local business. Throughout the 1970s, business leaders and the state debated ways to restore growth rates; industry would demand a larger role for itself in shaping state policy.

As in Brazil, this debate created new political space for emergent worker organization, by changing the public discourse about workers' rights and by slightly reducing the immediate threat of repression. By the end of the decade, the relationship between the state and business would be restructured, as a series of reforms removed features of classical apartheid that industrial leaders considered obstacles to growth. But by then, worker organization had already grown into a fact that employers and the state would have to accept.

In Brazil, political activists often argued with some justification that there was little difference between the state's goals and those of industry: business's support for the coup, and for the subsequent closing of political channels, was virtually unanimous, while state support for private enterprise went almost unquestioned. In South Africa, on the other hand, the National Party came to power in 1948 on a platform explicitly opposed to big business. Nevertheless, for most of the first decades of National Party rule, the state was hardly in constant opposition to industry: state policies were probably never as anti-capitalist as party rhetoric, while business was generally more dependent on the state, and less outspoken against state policies, than most businessmen or politicians claimed in the 1990s. It was not until the 1970s, during an economic downturn that spelled the end of the previous industrial strategy and an international recession that underscored South Africa's vulnerability to international pressure, that business opposition began to coalesce. At that point, the state and business began to restructure their relationship—leading, ultimately, to a new consensus on reforms that might preserve racial capitalism.

There is little disagreement that the South African state actively promoted capitalist development: the state's intervention in the economy consistently supported capital accumulation. Successive administrations not only gave white settlers Africans' land but repressed African resistance and created an African labor supply for white-owned enterprises. Historians generally agree that state control over labor supplies, together with state subsidies and protective tariffs, laid the basis for South Africa's economic growth.[77] Debates about the origins of South Africa's racial system agree on this point: ultimately, capitalist enter-

prises in South Africa benefited from the policies of a racially constituted state.[78]

The Nationalist government that came to power in 1948 was rather
different from its predecessors. Racial policies after World War II were
geared less toward ensuring a black labor supply than toward reducing
popular mobilizations in urban areas.[79] But while apartheid's grand design promised to control Africans' political expression, it also threatened manufacturing capital's ability to train and retain semi-skilled
black workers, or to replace highly paid white workers with lower-paid
blacks. In the 1950s, most manufacturers' associations urged the government to allow employers to recognize and negotiate with unions representing workers of all races, acknowledging the permanent presence
of black workers in industrial centers; but the government took the
opposite tack, making it virtually impossible for mixed unions to enter
the legal bargaining framework.[80]

Many observers have suggested that South African industrialists
were more opposed to the state's racial policies than mining or farming
magnates: industrialists, who require a more skilled and permanent labor force, are generally considered to have been willing to accept a
permanent black urban population, and to allow a measure of political
rights if necessary.[81] How far did this difference extend, and how realistic is it to draw clear lines between representatives of different sectors?

Industries were hardly comfortable negotiating with black unions;
like white union leaders and other business sectors, they generally acquiesced in the gradual repression of militant unions during the 1950s
and 1960s.[82] Even when they did protest against apartheid, industrialists were sometimes joined by spokespersons for mining and finance,
which had very different labor requirements than industry. The motiva-
tion appears to have been as much concern over international reaction
to racial legislation as concern over labor supplies. Business opposition
to the state probably reached its peak in 1960, during the state of emergency following the Sharpeville massacre and the subsequent closing of
channels of popular expression.

Neither the *empresariado* nor the international community voiced
serious objections to the 1964 coup in Brazil; in contrast, South Africa's
major businessmen viewed the post-Sharpeville crisis as a serious threat.
Shocked into action by the sudden withdrawal of foreign capital, South
Africa's five major business associations submitted a joint critique of
the labor system, proposing to give black workers the right to "transfer
from one employer to another in the same urban area without forfeiting

his [sic] right to be in that area," the right to bring "the wife and unmarried children" to live with him, and calling for an end to criminal prosecutions for pass offenses—probably the key legal mechanism controlling African workers' movements.[83] Unfortunately for the strict industrial liberalism argument, however, the critique was not limited to industry. Although manufacturing associations were slightly overrepresented, the proposal was also endorsed by the Chamber of Mines and the Afrikaanse Handelsinstituut—neither of which, in 1960, could be described as representing manufacturers.

A more realistic understanding of the relation between industry and the state is probably one that recognizes how the larger political and economic context shaped business's response. When state policies seemed to privilege the interests of mining and agricultural employers, manufacturers tended to oppose them; but during periods of industrial growth, when the state seemed to respond to industry's immediate needs, manufacturers buried their differences with the government in return for protection, subsidies, and credit. In the mid 1970s, when capitalist development made traditional apartheid problematic for the sectors of capital that had by now become economically dominant— that is, for industry and manufacturing—business opposition re-emerged.[84] The question may be not so much how to explain capital's acceptance or rejection of National Party policy, but why industrial capital and the state finally moved toward carefully controlled reform in the 1980s.

BUSINESS-STATE ACCOMMODATION

In the early 1960s, business concerns about the state's direction were rooted less in objections to racial oppression than in business's fears of exclusion from state policy-making processes and concern over international sanctions and reduced foreign investment. Business leaders clearly feared that the National Party government would ignore the needs of English-speaking businessmen—who probably controlled about 90 percent of South Africa's manufacturing sector between 1948 and 1963.[85] Throughout the 1950s, state enterprises had been rhetorically oriented toward assisting Afrikaans-speaking businessmen and businesses, although English-speaking capital also benefited from cheap inputs and subsidies; but despite a steady rise in the percentage of mining and financial capital controlled by Afrikaans-speaking whites, manufacturing remained almost entirely controlled by English-speakers,

who had little access to the Nationalist cabinet. After Sharpeville, however, Afrikaans capital moved into industrial undertakings, taking advantage of openings created by capital flight, and the lines became
somewhat blurred.[86]

Like English-speaking business leaders, Afrikaans business groups
had recognized early on that economic dependence on "the non-white
worker," meant that "total segregation is pure wishful thinking."[87]
Once reassured that the state would respond to its economic concerns,
both English- and Afrikaans-speaking business groups seemed to accept
the repression of popular organizations, the tightening of pass laws,
and the state's defiance of international pressure, which followed the
Sharpeville crisis. The Afrikaanse Handelsinstituut (AHI), representing private Afrikaans businessmen, made it clear it would "accept the
policy of separate development and strive for close feeling and cooperation with the government and its departments in order to watch
over the interests of the businessman and to be helpful to the authorities
with sober and practical advice."[88] Hardly less accommodating, the
mainly English Federated Chamber of Industry (FCI) emphasized the
need for compromise with government, urging "a more elastic implementation" of influx controls while reminding businessmen *"we have
to work within the compass of what Parliament determines."*[89]

Throughout the 1960s, virtually all business leaders, including industrialists, avoided overt criticism of state policy. Business treated the
political arena as one in which businessmen had no voice: passivity
and accommodation, rather than opposition, marked the relationship
between state and capital. Manufacturers not only stopped short of
calling for majority rule but dropped their objections to controls on
labor mobility or discriminatory pay scales.[90] In 1963, when the FCI
president mentioned that some racial labor practices might be uneco-
nomic, he denied any "intention to offer gratuitous advice or a solution
of the many problems that beset this country on the social and political
front."[91] Even foreign investors, less reliant on the state, refrained from
criticizing racial labor policies. As Unilever commented in 1964, "We
had to take care not to upset the white community."[92]

This wariness may have reflected the state's control over the economy, and individual businesses' dependence on state protection, subsidies, and contracts. Business subservience to the state was frequently attributed to fear of government retribution:

> Is it surprising that directors and managers have tended to become servile to
> the Government? An open opponent of apartheid may well fear, inter alia,

that his competitor will be quietly allowed plenty of African labor whilst he
is allowed little. He will have no appeal to the Courts. And the Government
have not hesitated to remind businessmen of the big stick which the centralization of economic power enables them to wield.[93]

Yet, in reality, the South African state's control over individual businessmen was an integral part of the industrialization strategy that protected and supported private industry: just as it was in Brazil, dependence on subsidies and contracts was the result of a long-standing
alliance between the state and capital.

Were industrialists afraid of reprisals, or did they recognize their dependence on the state—and thus refrain from criticizing the state's racial constitution? In 1964, M. C. O'Dowd, a young executive in the
Anglo American conglomerate, suggested that South Africa was merely
going through the early "stages of growth" before industrial takeoff;
political and economic equality would come later, when industrial
growth would allow more equitable distribution of the benefits of economic growth. O'Dowd promised corporate leaders that with industrialization South Africa would "follow the normal pattern of political,
social, and economic development from minority rule, through a liberal
era, to a welfare state. . . . [In] the process the 'race question' will be
solved, or perhaps will turn out never to have existed except as a cover
for economic cleavages." [94] Thus, political change would inevitably follow economic modernization; capitalism would erode apartheid.

No matter how much some business liberals complained about
anachronistic racial policies, business was able to shape important aspects of state policy during the 1960s, blocking or modifying legislation
that directly affected profitability. South African industry may not have
completely controlled state policy, but it did wield veto power, threatening to halt investment if the state damaged an ever-ephemeral "business confidence." However much South Africa's business community
believed that "free enterprise and officialdom . . . engaged in a duel," [95]
industry could prevent implementation of ideologically inspired policies
when it seemed to threaten profits.

Three examples illustrate industrial veto power. In 1967, the state
tried to decentralize industries, moving them to areas bordering on bantustans; from 1968, expansion or establishment of plants in older industrial centers required government permission. The Physical Planning
and Utilization of Resources Act was designed to reduce the urban African population by moving industrial plants to rural areas where African
workers could live inside bantustan borders. The rationale was straight-

forward. In the late 1950s, Prime Minister H. F. Verwoerd pointed out that if only highly mechanized industries with mainly white workers remained in central urban areas, one "would at least have a chance of industrial peace in the heart and soul of the country, even though you may not have it in some border areas. The danger of economic disruption is much greater when there is a mixed fatherland with the same labor mass everywhere." [96] The FCI viewed the new legislation as an attempt to throttle free enterprise, blaming it for the 1968 stock market slump and a drop in new manufacturing investment. In 1971, "fearing a general investment strike by organized industry," the government modified the policy, removing state controls on the expansion of already-established plants and greatly increasing incentives to industries willing to move to remote areas. [97] The modified decentralization policy tried simply to limit hiring of black workers in white-designated areas, by capping the ratio of black to white workers at 2.5:1.

Despite industrialists' complaints, [98] the policy may not have harmed profitability. Labor-intensive, low-paying industries were most likely to move to bantustans, where they could hire as many black workers as they wished at low, often subsidized wages. Capital-intensive industries, on the other hand, tended simultaneously to increase automation and to seek exemptions from work-force racial ratios. [99] A survey of PWV industrialists in the 1980s found that most had managed to bypass hiring restrictions, either legally or illegally, [100] and total industrial output in the region increased.

Influx control laws provide a second example of state accommodation to business needs. Throughout the 1960s, controls on African movements were tightened: blacks were expected to remain in bantustans until offered year-long contracts through state-administered labor bureaus. State policymakers insisted that any new black workers would be temporary migrants; their families would remain on the reserves, and migrant workers were required to return to bantustans to renew their labor contracts annually. But while these policies were clearly repressive, shaping the lives of African workers and their families and placing Africans under constant threat of harassment for pass law violations, the laws' impact on employers' ability to hire workers relatively freely was probably less dramatic. Many employers ignored complex procedures for hiring black workers, and many state officials simply ignored employer violations. Greenberg concludes, "Somewhere between the [Labor Department's] head offices in Pretoria and the labor bureau offices across white South Africa, national policy has been renegotiated."[101] Bureaucratic incapacity combined with local subversion of national policy meant that although labor policies theoretically restricted urban employers' access to unlimited supplies of labor, these policies were observed only when they did not directly conflict with specific employers' interests.[102]

Racial job reservation clauses exacerbated South Africa's skills shortage; but here again, implementation was frequently erratic. From the early 1960s on, warnings proliferated that white workers would be unable to meet industry's growing need for skilled and semi-skilled workers.[103] Not only did skilled jobs multiply as the economy expanded, but whites were increasingly attracted to jobs in the civil service and parastatal enterprises rather than in private factories. All-white apprenticeship programs shrank: the Iron Moulders' Society registered 205 apprentices in 1949, 49 in 1969, and none in 1971.[104] Throughout the 1960s, white trade unions continued to insist on job reservation clauses; white union leaders suggested that if skill shortages caused problems, the government should subsidize European immigration rather than weaken the color bar.[105] Nevertheless, for most of the 1960s and early 1970s, state enforcement of the color bar depended on labor supplies: except where strong white unions intervened, as on the mines, employers could find ways to hire black workers. By training black workers informally and paying them for work in a lower category, employers could often place them in jobs that were legally restricted to whites.[106] Employers' groups could insist on reclassification: in 1968, the iron and steel industry downgraded many previously "white" jobs, leaving only the top four categories restricted to whites.[107] If no whites applied, employers could get permission to hire nonwhites. Once again, the iron and steel industry provides an example: by 1969, at least 13 percent of production molders were Africans officially exempted from job reservation restrictions. By 1971, the figure had reached 33 percent.[108] By the end of a decade of rapid growth, it was relatively easy for employers to get exemptions to hire African workers: in 1972, nearly 4,700 exemptions—about twice the 1971 figure—were granted. After 1971, no new job reservation orders were introduced, reflecting the state's acquiescence in the changing racial makeup of the labor force.[109]

Like influx control laws, job reservation laws were much harder on black workers than on employers. For black workers, racial job reservation clauses meant that mobility within the factory was restricted, and frequently that they were paid for less-skilled jobs than they actually performed; but these problems hardly inhibited production or profits. For employers, these laws were undoubtedly a nuisance; but where white workers were unavailable, black workers could usually be hired, often at lower rates. While employers could always complain about unnecessary paperwork, they could not reasonably claim that job reservation clauses were strictly enforced. Like the government's decentralization policies and the influx control system, job reservation clauses cannot be viewed as blocking economic growth; indeed, while growth rates continued, business complaints were relatively muted. It was only in the mid 1970s, when growth rates slowed and popular mobilization intensified, that business rediscovered its objections to strict apartheid.

In the early 1970s, business confidence—already strengthened by a decade of economic growth, apparent labor quiescence, and consistent international investment—may also have been strengthened by the growing voice of private Afrikaans-speaking entrepreneurs within the National Party. In the late 1960s, Heribert Adam found only slight differences in the attitudes of white entrepreneurs, members of Parliament, and state officials toward major issues facing South Africa. About 90 percent in all categories believed that "democracy is not practicable" in South Africa; about three-fourths believed Africans were like children, different by nature and needing "centuries" to mature; and virtually all agreed that international communism posed a greater threat to the nation than domestic black nationalism. Afrikaans-speaking entrepreneurs tended to be slightly more supportive of official policies such as racial job reservation, but although Adam initially stressed Afrikaans-English differences,[110] he soon reinterpreted his findings, concluding that "both groups agree on the basic principles of white rule and differ only on tactical measures."

> [T]he historical friction between the English and Afrikaans-speaking populace is gradually being replaced by class contradictions between the two groups. As an entrepreneur, an Afrikaner has more in common with his English-speaking counterparts than with his poorer fellow Nationalists.[111]

By the late 1960s, the government's aid to Afrikaans-speaking private businessmen had borne fruit: no longer reliant entirely on farmers and small businessmen, party leaders responded to "the emergence of a class of aggressive, self-confident Afrikaner capitalists whose interests now went beyond those of the narrow class alliance out of which they had emerged." In 1969, the National Party expelled leading *verkramptes,* or old-style Afrikaans nationalists, when they objected to "open collaboration with 'Hoggenheimer.' "[112]

Recognizing the increasing collaboration between the state and English- and Afrikaans-speaking business leaders by the late 1960s, several prescient observers predicted that *verligte,* or more liberal, Afrikaans politicians—generally presumed to represent the capitalists and professionals produced by two decades of government-aided upward mobility—would join the English-speaking white opposition, seeking "the long-term alleviation of petty apartheid and a less rigid state interference in the labor market."[113] Twenty years later, that coalition was represented in the National Party itself. In the 1980s, a majority of English-speaking whites would vote for the Nationalist government, which responded to business by trying to alleviate petty apartheid and to reduce state intervention in labor markets.[114]

If the 1960s began with an unusual degree of friction between business and the South African state, then, the decade ended in an unusual degree of harmony. In 1971, the FCI's president, S. R. Back, applauded the growth of informal and formal contacts between government officials and industry representatives. With "the usual close contact" ranging from annual golf matches and informal luncheons to an "open-door approach in . . . our dealings with Ministers,"

> We like to believe that such representations and consultations have contributed to the re-introduction of investment allowances for manufacturing industry; the review of industrial decentralisation policy; the directive that banks should give preference to the financial need of industry; the establishment of a standing committee to advise on the better utilisation of manpower; the enquiry into the promotion of exports, and the decision not to proceed with the further relaxation of import control.[115]

While most industrialists had not abandoned verbal opposition to strict apartheid, business ideology generally shifted from concern that job reservation and separate development would impede growth to faith that economic growth and modernization would gradually remove racial divisions. The logic appears to have been irresistible: businessmen and others who found strict apartheid's racial divisions unpalatable discovered they had only to help industry expand faster to do away with them. Changing the migrant labor system—the labor policy that later would be considered so problematic for economic growth—was so far from industrialists' policy agenda in 1974 that senior officials of the FCI and AHI told Lipton "they had not thought through this 'sensitive' question, on which they wished 'to take a low profile.' "[116]

Even foreign executives of multinational corporations repeatedly expressed support for government policies, opposing international condemnations of apartheid and arguing that South African blacks were economically better off than they might be in the absence of foreign investment. In a comment that casts doubt on the depth of business concerns about skills shortages, a Chase Manhattan spokesman told a U.S. Senate hearing that Chase regarded the 1960s in South Africa as "a period of exceptional growth in a highly industrialized and exceptionally productive and efficient society in the utilization of physical and human resources."[117] Throughout the economic boom of the 1960s, foreign and domestic business spokespersons seemed to have reached an easy accommodation with the state, despite the former's expressed distaste for strict segregation and the latter's rhetorical distrust of capital.

THE (RE)EMERGENCE OF BUSINESS OPPOSITION

By the mid 1970s, this apparent harmony had come undone: even prominent Afrikaans-speaking businessmen declared that apartheid policies were anachronistic, atavistic remnants of nineteenth-century attitudes that had no place in the modern world. Business leaders argued that the entire framework of separate development needed to be revised to take into account the needs of an industrialized economy and capital-intensive industry. Far from praising the migrant labor system as an efficient utilization of human resources, business leaders now argued that it reduced productivity and worsened skills shortages, while the government squandered the country's wealth in inefficient state corporations. By the late 1970s, the South African business community, led by the capital-intensive industries built up during the 1950s and 1960s, demanded changes in both development strategies and in political arrangements.

From the early 1970s on, the development strategy of the 1960s ran into what appeared an insurmountable impasse: internal and external pressures forced state officials and industrialists to reconsider the model of development that had previously allowed such extraordinary growth rates. A series of strikes from 1973 on, combined with an international recession the same year, underscored South Africa's domestic and international vulnerabilities—political as well as economic. Spokespersons for capital-intensive industries, strengthened by a decade in an economically privileged position, clearly differed from state planners in their approach to these problems, and in their proposed solutions. The 1976 uprising, followed by intensified international pressure, only further

underlined South African vulnerability and the growing distance between state and key business leaders. By the early 1980s, state and capital would be making even more explicit efforts than in Brazil to restructure their relationship, to find a consensus allowing them to retain joint
control over a process of "gradual liberalization."

Of the two events that began the unraveling of the previous development strategy, the most shocking to South Africans was probably the
Durban strike wave, beginning with a relatively small dockworkers'
strike in late 1972 and erupting in industrial plants in early 1973. By
the end of the year, some ninety thousand workers had struck, and
production had been lost from more than seven times the total number
of shifts lost to African strikes since 1967.[118]

Given South Africa's history of labor repression, employers' responses were even more surprising than in Brazil: although most employers called police to the premises, few strikers were arrested, and
most were rehired; while workers did not get the wage increases they
demanded, most employers did grant small raises. The Institute for Industrial Education concluded that "the most significant change
wrought by the strikes is not in the workers' living standards, but in
their sense of their own potential power."[119] As chapter 4 describes,
over the next years, intermittent strike waves across South Africa suggested that that sense of efficacy and potential power would not easily
be dismissed.

For the first time, the 1973 strikes revealed the extent to which industrial employers relied on semi-skilled black workers. When asked
why strikes did not result in massive arrests, and why even firms who
dismissed their staff had reengaged most workers, one employer's representative responded, "It is too jolly difficult to get a labor force as it
is," and added that "when workers are a bit more skilled employers
no longer want a labor turnover."[120] The strikes also illustrated the
difficulties of negotiating with a leaderless "mob" at the factory
gates.[121] For the first time since the dissolution of unregistered African
unions, industrial employers actively tried to construct channels for
communication, since the strikes showed "it was essential to establish
some means of communication between management and the African
labor force."[122] The strikes, one business journal reported, demonstrated that

> [existing] industrial legislation is inadequate; that strikes are not prevented
> by making them illegal; that existing communication and bargaining chan-
> nels for Blacks have been ineffective if not non-existent; that whatever Ban-

tustan development there might have been, urban blacks are part of the permanent industrial scene; and that the police, having adopted a highly-commendable low-profile approach during the strikes, can no longer be regarded as strike-breakers.[123]

Business liberalism, however, went only so far. Many employers responded like the director of the Steel and Engineering Industries Federation (SEIFSA), who said after the strikes, "In this industry there will be no—and you can underline no—negotiations with African trade unions."[124] In mid 1973, the government changed labor legislation: employers could now choose to recognize unions or negotiate with elected worker committees. But even in the rush to find an alternative to wildcat strikes, employers preferred liaison committees, with half the members appointed by management. In 1972, there were seventeen works committees in the entire country; by 1974, there were two hundred. In the same period, however, over twelve hundred liaison committees had been formed, and a survey found most employers still rejected elected worker representation.[125] In the words of a labor relations specialist, most employers were unwilling to give up even a small part of "what they regard as their prerogative to make *all* the decisions on matters relating to wage and working conditions."[126] Attempted strikes in all sectors in the mid 1970s were met with repression: in 1974 and 1975, eleven striking workers were killed. In 1977, when the government proposed giving liaison committees more bargaining power, employers complained that factory-level bargaining would raise local wage levels; the proposals were withdrawn.[127]

Some industrial leaders might have preferred to recognize racially mixed unions, outside the legal structure, but their arguments centered on control of worker militancy rather than on creating channels for full negotiation. For example, Anglo American's powerful chairman, Harry Oppenheimer, suggested, "The best thing under the circumstances would be to encourage the growth of racially-mixed trade unions in order to prevent, if possible, political action on a racial basis by black trade unions."[128] In 1975, the FCI called for a reappraisal of the Industrial Conciliation Act "with a view to registering and controlling trade unions irrespective of racial composition."[129]

But even Oppenheimer's Anglo American evidently saw no need to recognize unregistered unions. As an acerbic unionist pointed out in 1976, Anglo American's policy allowed each subsidiary to set its own labor relations strategy; Oppenheimer's rhetorical support for unionism did not translate into recognition of unregistered unions at Anglo

American's subsidiaries.[130] Such negotiations were not illegal: in 1974, a British textile subsidiary signed a formal recognition agreement with an unregistered union, and the state did not intervene. Yet in 1979, only four firms—all foreign-owned—had contracts with independent unions.[131] While the 1973 strikes deepened business reservations about classical apartheid, business opposition would only coalesce later in the decade, when the full effects of the economic impasse and international vulnerabilities became evident.

For business, the strikes' immediate impact was political rather than economic. The Durban strikes and their aftermath provided apartheid's opponents with dramatic illustrations of South Africa's low wage scales and repressive policies. From 1973, no South African businessmen could ignore international calls for foreign companies to leave South Africa and for economic sanctions. In Britain, the 1973 strikes prompted new guidelines for labor relations in British companies in South Africa: a parliamentary commission recommended in 1974 that British companies who remained should improve wages, training, and working conditions for African employees, and suggested that since "African trade unions are not unlawful, although they possess none of the normal trade union rights, there is nothing to prevent a company from recognising and negotiating with a trade union representing African workers." [132] (Ironically, the week the British guidelines were published, British Leyland's Durban subsidiary fired 104 strikers, refusing to negotiate with an African union and demonstrating "the extent to which most foreign firms still felt free to ignore pressure in their home countries.")[133] Similar guidelines were later drawn up for American companies, although they included no more enforcement mechanisms than the British code.

Along with labor conflict and international pressure, 1973 raised the specter of higher fuel costs. For South Africa, the oil crisis had political implications: in November 1973, the Arab summit declared an oil boycott against South Africa, cutting off the source of about half of South African oil imports.[134] Much as the Brazilian military responded to the oil price increase by redefining energy self-sufficiency as a national security priority, the South African state sought to reduce its international dependence on a product that could be cut off at the source.

Even more than for Brazil, however, the perceived threat to national security included a military dimension. As South Africa's neighbors gained independence from former colonial rulers, the buffer zone of white-minority states on South Africa's borders looked increasingly porous to both the liberation movement and the National Party. P. W. Botha, then minister of defence, announced:

> Ideological attacks on the Republic of South Africa are progressively being converted into more tangible action in the form of sanctions, boycotts, isolation, demonstrations and the like.... [We have not] yet eliminated the [guerrilla] threat. I do not wish to spread alarm, but I must state unambiguously that for a long time already, we have been engaged in a war of low intensity and that this situation will probably continue for some considerable time to come.[135]

Botha reflected the regime's sense of isolation, as pressure for international sanctions increased, and as neighboring states appeared likely to support anti-apartheid guerrillas. In 1975, South Africa invaded Angola for the first time; over the next decade, its troops were more or less permanently engaged on its borders, occupying Namibia and conducting repeated raids into Botswana, Lesotho, Mozambique, Swaziland, and Zimbabwe.

While it would be overstating the level of conscious reorientation to describe state policies during the mid 1970s as a new development strategy, the South African state certainly redirected its economic activity after 1973, recognizing—though for different reasons than the Brazilian military—that previous economic growth patterns could not continue. Like Brazil, South Africa had based its industrialization on imported technology and capital; like Brazil, it suffered a shift in its balance of trade following the oil crisis. Capital goods—machinery and transport equipment—composed about half of South Africa's imports in 1973, and, like most economies dependent on imported industrial goods, South Africa found its import bills more than doubling over the next five years.[136] The inflationary effect on South Africa's economy was slightly less dramatic than in most dependent economies: a rising international price for gold cushioned the immediate impact on South Africa's foreign exchange reserves. But the threat of galloping inflation was serious enough to lead the prominent Afrikaans business leader Anton Rupert to publish a paper entitled "Inflation: How to Curb Public Enemy Number One" in 1974, blaming inflation on economic bottlenecks and artificially maintained wages.[137] In 1975, the gold price fell; at over U.S. $2 billion, South Africa's 1976 balance-of-payments deficit was more than three times the 1966 figure,[138] and the rand was devalued twice during 1975. Growth rates were negative in the second half of the year. By 1976, South Africa had entered a serious recession, with rising unemployment and double-digit inflation.

As in Brazil, however, the state's national security agenda meant it could not concentrate solely on reviving the private sector. South Africa had already begun to try to develop its energy supplies, stockpiling oil and building coal-into-oil plants. In 1974, the state decided to invest heavily in further energy plants at home as protection against a future tightening of the oil boycott. The process would not reap immediate economic benefits: even in the mid 1980s, South Africa still imported about half its fuel. Similarly, growing calls for a strong international arms embargo[139] led the state to increase its already-sizable investments in the domestic arms industry. By 1977, when the U.N. embargo became mandatory, South Africa claimed to produce more than half its arms and ammunition; while these claims certainly understated South African dependence on imported components and technology, they indicated the importance of the arms industry within the economy. Military expenditures became an ever-expanding part of South Africa's state budget, reaching well over 20 percent by the late 1970s.[140]

Thus, national security concerns became increasingly important in South Africa, as in Brazil. In 1975, Defence Minister Botha called for a "total strategy," mustering political, economic, diplomatic, and military initiatives to protect the country against a social upheaval; within two years, the government declared that that "total strategy" had become essential, that "the principle of self-determination of the White nation must not be regarded as being negotiable," and that white society must be mobilized under the leadership of the Defence Force to protect minority rule.[141]

The conjuncture that prompted the government to take up a national security agenda also prompted prominent leaders of the business community to reevaluate South Africa's economic development model. After the 1973 strikes, Anglo American's Harry Oppenheimer said South Africa needed to move to a new stage, where a stable black work force could eliminate the skills shortage and also create a new market for manufactured goods. His analysis, which is remarkably similar to Severo Gomes's description of the Brazilian economy, is worth quoting at some length:

> Until recently, economic growth was achieved by a process of sucking unemployed or underemployed black peasants into the cash economy. Though their productivity and their wages were pitifully low they still were higher than [those in] the rural areas from where they came. But the possibilities of sustained and rapid growth along these lines have virtually come to an end. The modern sophisticated economy which has been built up cannot grow on

the basis of more and more units of untrained, undifferentiated migrant labour, and the acute shortage of skilled men has made itself felt together with
a worrying amount of unemployment among the unskilled. At the same
time, efforts which have been made to build up the exports of manufactured
goods and to reduce the country's dependence on gold and other extractive
industries, as a source of foreign exchange, on the whole have been disap-
pointing. The reason for this is that it is difficult to build up the export
of manufactured goods except as an overflow after meeting the needs of
a substantial home market, and the South African home market remains
comparatively small. These are our basic economic problems.[142]

Like Brazilian businessmen, South African business leaders responded
to a changing economic environment by questioning the very model of
industrialization that had allowed them to prosper.

At least as regards bringing black wages somewhat closer to white
wage levels, Oppenheimer's views were not unusual. Even some government officials agreed at the time of the 1973 strikes that Africans' wages
were often too low and should be raised.[143] At the 1973 FCI meeting,
the issue was vigorously debated: low-wage industries, especially
textiles, tended to consider higher labor costs prohibitive, while more
capital-intensive companies insisted on higher wage levels.[144] Propo-
nents of higher wage levels generally agreed with Oppenheimer that
workers in modern, capital-intensive industries were more productive
and deserved higher wages; in addition, higher wages would expand
the internal market for manufactured products. A 1972 government
commission had suggested that labor market changes would raise productivity and expand manufacturing exports.[145]

In the South African context, the argument for higher wages had an
implicit political aspect: raising average black wages relative to white
wages would remove a major source of international opposition, and
would reduce the threat of sanctions. This was particularly important in
the mid 1970s, since Britain—previously South Africa's most important
customer—was on the verge of joining the European Economic Community; unless South Africa won preferential status, which was unlikely
given the EEC's political stance toward apartheid, it would have to seek
new markets.[146] Many business leaders believed that changed employment practices would also increase the chances of opening up new African markets; as the continent's largest industrial producer, South Africa
could become an exporter of manufactured goods—if political opposition could be eased. Over the next decade, calls for state efforts to expand the domestic and international markets for manufactured goods
became a business community refrain.[147]

Concerns over new markets, international economic sanctions, and labor unrest led to higher wages for black workers in some sectors. From 1973 on, average wages for whites and blacks in manufacturing grew somewhat closer, moving from a 1970 high of about 6:1 to a ratio of 4.4:1 in 1982. Even in mining, average wages for whites and blacks moved from a 1972 ratio of about 19:1 to 5.5:1 in 1982.[148] Despite rising unemployment, however, whites' monthly wages in manufacturing and mining in 1976 averaged about R 1,700 and R 1,200 respectively, in contrast to an overall average income of barely R 120 a month for black South Africans.[149] Much as Oppenheimer had predicted, increased real wages did expand the domestic market, at least for light consumer industries: from the mid 1970s, more and more businesses began to orient products and advertising to an urban black consumer market.

The changing ratio of black:white wages in manufacturing is related in part to the gradual removal of job reservation from 1971 on: employers who had long urged the removal of racial restrictions on hiring and training stepped up their demands, arguing that the economy could not grow without more skilled workers. In a new effort to expand the pool of skilled workers, business pressure in the mid 1970s prompted the state to pay new attention to formal black education. Compulsory education was introduced for Indians in 1973 and for "Coloureds" (although not for Africans) in 1976, and in 1974 the government changed high school entrance requirements, more than doubling the number of African students eligible to continue their education. But the state remained a reluctant participant: most funds for school expansion came from private donors and corporations, and student overcrowding in African schools contributed to tensions leading to the 1976 student uprising.[150] Meanwhile, state officials—who had previously insisted that there was no point in training black workers, because they would never be allowed permanent residence in white-designated industrial areas—began to set up industrial training centers for black workers, because, as the prime minister admitted, "it would be of little avail if new, more advanced job opportunities were opened up for non-white workers who were not equipped to take advantage of them because of a lack of suitable training."[151]

Throughout the late 1970s, employers actively sought to change the racial composition of the industrial work force. While higher-level apprenticeship programs remained 80 percent white, thousands of black workers participated in private training schemes, usually run by employers.[152] In 1973, government officials announced that blacks, including Africans, would be allowed to do skilled work;[153] although in theory the color bar's complete removal depended on the approval of white unions, in practice employers frequently hired blacks whether or not white workers agreed.[154] Legal restrictions no longer prevented employers from filling skilled positions with black workers: labor market segmentation persisted, but apartheid was less likely to pose an obstacle to an employer's production goals. By 1977, the percentage of skilled workers classified as African had risen from 9.3 percent in 1969 to 23.2 percent. The percentage of skilled workers who were classified as white dropped from 74.6 to 60.3, while percentages of skilled workers classified as Coloured and Indian increased only slightly.

At the level of mass production skills, the change in the racial composition of South Africa's industrial labor force was even more obvious. By 1978, all categories of manufacturing work were open to all workers. The percentage of semi-skilled workers classified as white dropped from 15.7 percent in 1969 to 8.5 percent in 1977, while the percentage of workers classified as African rose steadily, from 54.7 to 66.7 percent.[155] Employers could hardly ignore their dependence on an increasingly skilled black labor force: by the end of the decade, as that labor force became increasingly self-confident and organized, employer associations would no longer view liaison committees as a realistic alternative to more authentic expressions of worker concerns.

BUSINESS RESPONSE TO "UNREST"

What changed individual employers' attitudes during the late 1970s? Rather than stressing manufacturing's inherently liberal leanings or straightforward labor process issues, a more realistic assessment of growing business opposition considered the impact of the 1976 uprising on business confidence. In June and July 1976, student demonstrations and general stay-aways marked the first popular mobilization since the late 1950s; police killed over five hundred people and arrested thousands more. In 1977, Black Consciousness organizations were banned, and Steve Biko, an important Black Consciousness leader, was killed in detention. In the midst of a recession, with rising unemployment and negative growth rates, the uprising marked the end of a long period of relative political quiescence among urban black South Africans.

To workers and community groups, as the next chapters show, the uprising revealed the potential strength of a worker-community alliance. To the president of the FCI, however, watching the flow of foreign investment capital come to a virtual halt, the uprising "cast a shadow over the South African economy, influencing the business mood as well as the country's credit rating."[156] Increased international pressure for change, combined with slowed direct foreign investment, meant foreign investment as a percentage of gross domestic investment dropped from a high of 22 percent in 1975 to just 3.1 percent in 1977.[157] International banks were reluctant to make loans; as far as can be ascertained, *no* medium or long-term credits were extended to South African borrowers in 1977, and figures did not return to previous levels until 1982.[158] Although some of the difference would be made up through direct loans to the government—among them a $571 million loan from the International Monetary Fund, more than to all the rest of Africa combined during 1976 and 1977—private overseas banks faced growing public criticism of loans to South Africa.[159] The *Financial Mail* reported that for business, "the chief concern is the political outlook. . . . Most local businessmen insist that definite political progress is a sine qua non for a return to prosperity."[160]

Business leaders responded quickly to the crisis and to the threat of international isolation. Oppenheimer argued, "Too many men of substance, with so much at stake, still stand on the sidelines, believing that . . . government actions . . . can meet the challenges posed by rapid urbanization, compounded as these are by the racial diversity of our society."[161] In late 1976, a conference of "leaders of industry and commerce" formed the Urban Foundation to "organize and direct the resources and the initiative of the private sector to come to grips with the social problems of the underprivileged." With a board composed of prominent business leaders and chaired by Oppenheimer himself, the Urban Foundation was funded by donations from the country's major business groups. By 1981, although 223 donors had given money to the fund, over half the donations came from nine sources, nearly all among South Africa's largest industrial and financial conglomerates.[162] By 1983, the Urban Foundation had participated in projects worth R 47 million.[163]

The Urban Foundation both shaped and came to represent a new business consensus. It approached the crisis in terms very different from those of the state's national security agenda. Although it was technically nonpolitical, the Urban Foundation lobbied for stabilizing the urban black population by promoting black homeownership and business opportunities, which it argued would help "promote free enterprise values" among urban blacks.[164] Focusing on improving black housing, education and training, employment practices, and the physical environment, especially by providing electricity,[165] the Foundation also designed an employment code, calling for higher wages and increased training for Africans. Moreover, the code suggested rather vaguely that South African companies should recognize the "basic rights of workers," including freedom of association and collective negotiation.

The "men of substance" who formed the Urban Foundation were quite explicit in their goals: as the first executive director put it, "no free enterprise system can survive in circumstances of persistent social disruption and disorder. Thus, investment in social advance and upliftment is an investment motivated by enlightened self-interest."[166] Foundation officers viewed urban black homeownership—which would require changes in urban residential and land tenure laws affecting Africans—as a way to strengthen the commitment of a black middle class to free enterprise; further, black homeownership would permit a permanent black urban population, potentially a source of "the level of skilled manpower we shall need in the future—indeed, that we need at present."[167]

Through the late 1970s, business leaders, supported by the National Party's *verligtes,* continued to press the government to reform classical apartheid. In politics, Oppenheimer and other businessmen helped fund a new opposition initiative, the Progressive Federal Party, calling for a qualified black franchise and the establishment of a permanent black urban labor force. In contrast to their acquiescence during the 1960s, business leaders increasingly argued that racial discrimination and free enterprise were basically incompatible. "Failure to eradicate the one will ultimately result in the destruction of the other," not simply because apartheid restricted economic growth, but because of "the real danger" of capitalism being "rejected for its perceived support of oppression and apartheid."[168]

Business demands for liberalization, however, were not simply altruistic: in South Africa, as in Brazil, they were clearly linked to objections to state policy, and the failure to incorporate business leaders in policymaking. In 1977, just as the Urban Foundation was being launched, the chairman of the largest Afrikaans conglomerate, Andreas Wassenaar, published a scathing attack on the government's growing involvement in productive enterprises, calling the combination of state ownership, price controls, and intervention in the labor market an "assault on private enterprise." Echoing arguments used in Brazil's privatization campaign, Wassenaar argued that the private sector had to mobilize opposition against a state bureaucracy that was "lukewarm if not antagonistic in its attitude toward private enterprise." Politics and economics, he warned, were inseparable, and South Africa's economy would collapse unless its "democratic government" showed "it can tolerate expertise in the inner circles of government in spite of the fact that it will then find that some fossilised political conceptions, some political calf-paths of the mind, are completely incompatible with the most elementary economic and financial requirements of survival."[169] Increasingly, business spokespersons agreed that unless the state took business advice seriously, removing racial constraints, the economic and political crisis would only worsen.

Business complaints about state involvement in the economy would continue for the next decade; as in Brazil, they would wax and wane, depending on the extent to which business leaders believed the state was responding to business policy agendas. But in the long run, how antagonistic was the relationship, and how far did business calls for democratization extend? By the early 1980s, the South African state seemed to have given in. Abandoning its traditional support base among Afrikaans-speaking workers and farmers—groups that were already shrinking demographically—the National Party increasingly responded to industry's reformist demands. In early 1979, party leaders refused to support white mineworkers who struck against a mine's decision to hire three "Coloured" artisans;[170] the impression that the government was shifting its stance was reinforced later that year, when the newly inaugurated Prime Minister P. W. Botha told 350 business leaders that he was committed to "strengthening the free enterprise system and introducing orderly reform." Even more important for businessmen, Botha promised to create "reciprocal channels of communication," allowing business and government to work together for the sustained economic growth necessary to win support from the black population. Reflecting business enthusiasm for the new prime minister, the *Financial Mail* named Botha "Man of the Year."[171]

Major legislative initiatives, strongly supported by business and Western diplomats, removed some of apartheid's most obvious labor controls. In 1977, two major commissions had been set up to look at labor matters and "all other legislation relating to the utilization of manpower."[172] The Wiehahn Commission, looking into labor matters, heard submissions from employers and trade unions, both registered and unregistered. All employers' associations recommended the government allow African workers—especially urban residents—to join registered trade unions.[173] The Wiehahn Commission called for the registration of unions with open membership, as long as they had no links to political groups; the Riekert Commission urged the stabilization of urban blacks and slightly reduced restrictions on black labor mobility. Within a year, both recommendations were implemented, with modifications.[174] From 1979 on, nonracial unions could register, and employers could no longer use the law as an excuse to avoid recognition. Urban residential rights were extended to many more Africans and their families; elected "community councils" even gave urban blacks a modicum of participation in local government.[175]

Why did employers ask the state to register black workers' organizations in 1979, when throughout most of the 1970s they had rejected trade unions in favor of more controllable liaison committees? The emergence of manufacturing as South Africa's dynamic sector may have changed the labor process in ways that facilitated shop-floor organization and reduced employers' willingness to replace a trained African work force, but industrialists seem to have accepted the principle of unionism only because they faced pressure from organized workers and from overseas. As the next chapters will show, employers faced an increasingly organized work force, with strikes called by unions outside state control. As the emergent unions made contact with international unions and with anti-apartheid groups around the world, pressure for union recognition grew stronger: like Brazilian industrialists, South African employers confronted the labor movement as a social fact. The Wiehahn Commission's chairman traveled abroad several times to lobby foreign businessmen and unionists to support its recommendations. The government published an overseas-only magazine describing new labor reforms, "designed to convince its readers that a new era of free and nonracial labor relations had dawned in South Africa."[176]

The changes set in motion by the Wiehahn and Riekert commissions left untouched both white minority rule and the migrant labor system, but as the following chapters show, the changes did create new legal space for nonracial trade unions and for urban black political mobilization. Was the South African business community satisfied? Were business liberals, like the Brazilian *empresariado*, willing to accept severe limitations on democracy as long as state policies suited their immediate needs? On the whole, the South African business community seems to have been convinced that adequate reform was under way. Many businessmen expressed concern over the pace of political reforms, but none called publicly for universal franchise until the combined 1985–87 uprising and debt crisis reawakened concern over the country's direction. Throughout the early 1980s, business and government moved into what Michael Mann calls a "techocratic" alliance, with a greater role for the private sector in designing and implementing economic and social welfare policy, and with businessmen brought into key presidential advisory bodies as formal participants in planning reforms and administration.[177]

The relationship was not perfectly harmonious. At the 1981 Good Hope summit between business and government, business leaders expressed concern over "those aspects in our system which obstruct or delay" economic growth, and with the slow pace of reform; but they rarely expressed public opposition to the general direction of state policy. As Botha moved steadily toward reforming internal obstacles to industrial development and toward reducing international pressure, business generally supported his efforts to make white minority rule compatible with free enterprise. In 1983, when the government proposed a tricameral Parliament—with separate, less powerful houses for Indian and Coloured representatives, but with no representation at all for African South Africans—most business spokespersons supported the new constitution. In early 1984, when Botha appeared to be building diplomatic links with Mozambique and Europe, and to be willing to listen to business advice, Mann reports, "enthusiasm in business circles about Botha's performance in office verged on euphoria."[178]

By the mid 1980s, Anglo American's personnel director, Bobby Godsell, claimed the government had been forced to acknowledge "the power of business to shape reality." With the government creating joint commissions to deal with manpower and training, influx control and labor relations, and bringing business leaders onto committees designing national policy, Godsell believed, P. W. Botha had "emerged as this country's first modern leader who understands that the role of political leadership is not to create a new social order through parliamentary dictates from the top, but rather to coordinate the forces already at work in changing and shaping the social order."[179] The relationship between business and the state had been reconstructed, and some business spokespersons, at least, believed their voices were being heard.

Like the Brazilian business community, South African business leaders remained relatively passive while rapid growth persisted. When further growth was stymied, they challenged their exclusion from policymaking bodies. But in South Africa, as in Brazil, leading industrialists remained unwilling to break completely with the authoritarian state: while they sought a controlled liberalization that would remove obstacles to business profitability, full democratization was not the aim. Rather than removing racial domination, the kinds of reforms business sought were those that would "encourage political support for capitalism while demobilizing potential militancy [and] facilitate the expansion of the black consumer market."[180] In 1985, Oppenheimer, doyen of South African business liberals, offered a four-point plan to end apartheid, to "erase his nation's image as an outcast." Far from calling for universal franchise or significant black political rights, he mentioned only opening up commercial districts to people of all races, allowing blacks to own land, ending forced removals of blacks from white-designated areas, and abolishing the pass system.[181] Controlled liberalization would allow business leaders to participate in policy-making, without removing the basic structures of racial capitalism.

South African business's apparent willingness to enter into collective bargaining did not represent support for workers' rights to free association or democratic rule, any more than Brazilian business's call for democratization reflected a complete break with the state. Rather, it reflected a lengthy process in which the country's industrial leaders—now, following a decade of industrial deepening, the dominant fraction of capital—came to agree that their material interests would be better served by a nonracial capitalism linked to the international economy than by an isolated racial state. As the economic and political crisis deepened through the 1970s, business leaders redefined their economic and political goals and called on the state to listen. Recognizing their dependence on international investments and markets, business leaders hoped to reduce international pressure and contain domestic uprisings without abandoning minority rule; instead of being controlled by a centralized state, business leaders sought to control it. The consensus of the early 1980s would fall apart again under pressure from domestic resistance and international sanctions; but until the 1985–87 uprising again raised the specter of radical social upheaval, even the most liberal South African industrialists seemed willing to accept only a very limited form of liberalization.

CONCLUSION

A curious fact illustrates the parallel between the efforts by business and the Brazilian and South African states to reconstruct their relation-

ship: in 1981, the American academic Samuel Huntington gave the keynote address at South Africa's annual political science conference, ad-
vising South Africa to follow Brazil's example of a slow, controlled
abertura, gradually opening channels for the expression of certain kinds
of demands. His advice—"a little reform here, a little repression
there"[182]—was partly based on his experience as a consultant to Brazil's military leaders, where he had also played down the reintroduction
of classic liberal rights in favor of strong institutional controls to keep
democracy from getting out of hand.[183] In South Africa, as in Brazil,
Huntington's advice was enthusiastically accepted by would-be reformers: it provided an intellectual rationale for a strictly limited liberalization process, where only a small elite would set the pace and content
of reforms.[184]

How far did business liberalism extend? Neither set of business leaders sought full democratization; their concerns were far more limited.
If they accepted workers' organization, they did so because they were
forced to by strikes occurring at a time when there was already tension
between industry and the state over national policy-making issues and
state spending priorities. In both cases, high growth rates had been
achieved through a development strategy aimed at deepening the industrial base, which created a capital-intensive industry dominated by joint
ventures between private domestic, state, and foreign capital. In both
cases, that strategy had involved repression of working-class organization; it had also increased economic vulnerability to international economic trends. When the international context changed and growth
rates slowed, industrial leaders—whose dominance in the economy was
the direct result of the previous decade's state-supported industrialization—began to challenge the state's priorities, demanding their own
voice in policy-making.

In both cases, economic crises deepened into political ones, as industry and state officials reconstructed their relationship. First, both Brazilian and South African industrialists had to create new channels for expressing their demands; business acquiescence in the demobilization of
popular protest during the previous decade had eroded the independence of business associations, and the new capital-intensive industrial
sector had to identify general goals and find channels through which to
articulate them.

As states and newly reinvented business classes reconstructed their
relationships, both sets of industrial leaders criticized the state's basic

development model. Threatened by international economic fluctuations, business leaders criticized levels of income stratification that restricted domestic markets; threatened by rising international prices for inputs, they sought more state support for their enterprises; and threatened by growing national security expenditures, they criticized state enterprises for soaking up resources. In both cases, industrial leaders urged the state to shift toward a model of development that would reduce state control over the economy, reduce international vulnerability, and strengthen local manufacturing by increasing the domestic market for consumer goods—all in the name of returning to a system of "free enterprise."

As the political discourse shifted among the dominant classes—away from the emphasis on national security and growth, challenging the highly centralized, authoritarian state—calls for some form of democratization became more frequent, and labor activists took advantage of a new political opportunity. Why did industrialists in the late 1970s in both countries call for new kinds of labor relations? In both cases, confronted by sudden strikes, prominent members of the business community recognized that state intervention in the workplace might come at the expense of their own independence. Accepting that they needed a skilled and stable labor force, employers in capital-intensive industry hoped direct negotiations would create "safety valves" for shop-floor tensions; without those safety valves, shop-floor conflicts could become quickly politicized, and employers might lose control. Moreover, state intervention would contradict the discourse of economic liberalism, which was increasingly popular in business circles. In a deepening economic crisis, facing growing labor militance and popular mobilization, employers came to view negotiations as a way to avoid further loss of production and assert their own "reinvention."

As the next chapters show, shop-floor changes alone would not end political tensions within the factory: the links between workplace and community organization made it virtually impossible under an authoritarian state to depoliticize labor relations. In a comment that could apply, with appropriate modifications, to Brazil under military rule, Anglo American's personnel manager, Godsell, wrote:

[A]s a consequence of the 1973 Durban strikes, the increasing skill level and political awareness of black workers, the impact of the Wiehahn Commission, and the growth of black workers, we are moving in the mines, factories, shops and offices in South Africa from a whites-first blacks-second labor dispensation to a more open racial order, where advancement and opportunity are based on merit. However, the rate of change outside the factory gate has been very much slower. . . .

A situation where there is reform in the workplace and stagnation outside must create social tension.[185]

Although the tensions between states and dominant classes in the mid 1970s may have had their origins in debates over broad economic policy, they created new political spaces for worker organization—spaces that worker activists were quick to exploit and expand. Had the initial strikes of the 1970s been completely defeated—like the 1968 strikes in Brazil and SACTU's campaigns in the 1960s—it is unlikely either trade union movement could have grown. As the previous histories of both countries had shown, repression can make the cost of political activism to individuals unacceptable. When repression was possible, even probable, but not inevitable, workers proved far more willing to challenge employers and the state. Throughout the early 1980s, emergent shop-floor organizations joined together with community groups based in working-class areas, insisting that they deserved higher wages from employers and more resources from the state, and in the process redefining democracy and citizenship. In both Brazil and South Africa, popular movements would mount a challenge to controlled liberalization; in both cases, industrialists would finally try to distance themselves from the authoritarian state that had allowed them to prosper and would accept a far broader reconstruction of democratization than they seem originally to have envisioned.

CHAPTER FOUR

The Emergence of "New Unionism"

I began to realize that mobilizing workers was not enough—
there is a big difference between being mobilized and being
organized. [On the East Rand] workers were mobilized
because of the ten-cent increase that workers at Hall
Longmore won as a result of strike action. After that success,
we had workers streaming into the union's offices. . . . They
would come marching from their factories and in some cases
they would leave their jobs even before they had approached
management or they were dismissed. I realized those workers
were mobilized, not organized.

> *South African metalworkers' organizer*
> *Moses Mayekiso, speaking about the*
> *1981 East Rand strike wave*

Trade unions are rarely given much consideration in theories of social
movements. Social-movement analysts generally begin by asking how
individuals identify common interests; unions, however, are often
treated as almost inevitable products of industrial society, as workers
combine to struggle for better wages and working conditions.[1] Common material interests seem to explain why workers join unions, while
shared workplace experiences "are central to explaining their collective
capacity to struggle."[2]

Between workplace relations and militant labor movements, however, lies a range of possibilities: even if work relations create the conditions that make union organization possible, individual workers or
groups of workers must nevertheless make choices about affiliations,
forms of organization, kinds of action, and types of militance. As Craig
Calhoun argues, the distinction sometimes made between "old" and
"new" social movements—which treats class-based movements as if
they reflected a ready-made constituency and set of interests—ignores
the way labor activists in nineteenth-century Europe and North

143

America struggled to persuade workers that unions could provide a forum for representing interests that the activists believed they shared.[3] In
Brazil and South Africa, where unions had been weakened and discred-
ited by the 1970s, there was little reason to assume that workers would
make demands on the state through labor organization. In Brazil, political parties continued to exist through the period of the military dictatorship and could have provided a channel for workers' voices, while in
South Africa, the national liberation struggle would seem a more likely
vehicle for popular demands.

How do individual workers come to recognize the potential strength
of industrial action, for both workplace and broader campaigns? What
shaped the vision that emerged during worker mobilization? Under
what conditions did workers take on a larger class identity that reached
beyond individual workplaces?

These questions are particularly relevant to the Brazilian and South
African cases, where worker mobilization occurred almost without
warning, and where worker activists could reasonably deny that they
drew on existing traditions. During the economic boom of the late
1960s, workers' organizations were virtually invisible: older militants
and groups had been repressed, and new forms of organization had not
yet emerged. In Brazil, the 1968 strikes underlined the dangers of overt
worker action; while workers occasionally challenged employers' control through go-slows and absenteeism, organization was generally limited to tiny discussion groups and to the controlled unions permitted by
the military regime. In South Africa, black workers had virtually no
legal organizations after 1964; although a handful of segregated unions
had black branches, industrial action was limited to occasional go-
slows or short stoppages within factories, and the most visible trade
unionists were white supremacists. Attempted strikes—in 1969, at a
Leyland factory, and a 1970 strike of Johannesburg bus drivers—resulted only in arrests and dismissals.

Under these circumstances, despite the growth of an urban industrial
labor force, it was hardly inevitable that either labor movement would
become a central part of the national political scene. Indeed, throughout the 1960s, observers in both countries generally believed workers
would not engage in collective action, either because they feared direct
repression or because they had abandoned any expectation that unions
could represent them. In 1974, Brazilian workers told a researcher they
preferred corporatist union behavior to the confrontational approach
of the early 1960s, evidently because they believed labor militance

could achieve nothing; instead, they looked to unions only for assistential services.[4] Given the constant threat of repression, even the exiled leadership of the South African Congress of Trade Unions seemed to doubt whether authentic shop-floor organization could emerge in South Africa; in 1976, SACTU told the International Labor Organization it should not support the nonracial unions then emerging in South Africa, because their very survival was an indication they had been co-opted by the apartheid state.[5]

In the mid 1970s, however, after years of enforced industrial peace, Brazilian and South African unions suddenly reemerged. In 1973, workers in South Africa rediscovered that they could halt production and win higher wages; over the next few years, they would build a national labor movement at the margins of the established labor relations framework. In Brazil, starting in 1978, repeated strike waves ended fifteen years of industrial calm, and shop-floor activism created a basis for revitalizing militant unionism. In both cases, apparently spontaneous strikes surprised even union officials, leaving employers and states scrambling to regain control. By the end of the decade, both governments had reformed labor relations laws to accommodate a new reality.

In early industrializers, labor repression is sometimes said to have promoted political unionism: when states and employers refused to permit collective bargaining, unions joined in national-level politics to demand a new labor relations framework, hoping to change the context in which unions operated. "To the extent that unions suffered severe and continuous repression," Gary Marks writes, "they tended to rely on political parties for leadership."[6] But workers in nineteenth-century Germany, for example, believed existing political parties would represent their interests. In both Brazil and South Africa, electoral participation was severely limited; few unionists expressed great faith in those parties that were allowed to operate openly. Moreover, before South African or Brazilian unions could support political parties, or even form labor federations, workers first had to join industrial unions; only the threat of persistent shop-floor militance created an atmosphere in which states and employers would begin to call for legislative reform. Broad discussions of unions in politics, then, beg the question: why did workers join unions before they were legal, and why were these unions able to grow so rapidly into a movement strong enough to bring demands to the national political scene?

It is widely acknowledged in sociological discussions of labor federations that, once institutionalized, unions tend to maintain a perspective reflecting their past experience and political alliances; Peter Lange and George Ross conclude that we should consider labor movements as strategic actors, "which analyze and respond to changes in the world through the prisms of [their own] systems of perceptions and purpose."[7] But this recognition begs a previous question: what shapes that initial worldview? Why do some labor movements move from "shared dispositions" to collective action based on a common understanding of class interests—and can we discern any patterns that might lead us to predict when such a move is possible, even likely?

One common approach to this question, especially in relation to labor movements in early industrializers, is historical, focusing on the ways in which communities of workers draw on existing traditions and identities in the creation of labor organizations. Barrington Moore, Jr., for example, suggests that in the process of rapid economic and social change, groups of workers in nineteenth-century Europe were held together by common conceptions of justice and fair returns to labor. Isolated communities of coal miners seem to have been more likely than newly urbanized immigrants to build strong labor movements, for example, because they already shared a collective identity and could easily develop common understandings of their interests.[8] Often, emergent unions drew on preexisting cultural meanings: Richard Biernacki shows that workers in Germany and England understood "labor" and "labor power" very differently; the organizations they formed, and their unions' demands, reflected different understandings of a "just return," based in different experiences during the transition from feudalism.[9] Groups of workers can sometimes reinterpret traditional organizations and beliefs to meet new situations—as French workers reinterpreted the guild to protect journeymen-laborers in post-revolutionary France; as American workers reinterpreted craft associations in nineteenth-century New York; and as workers in northern Nigeria have reinterpreted Islam to promote participation in unions.[10] But even these cases, analysts have suggested that preexisting ties of community and tradition explain the process through which workers recognize shared interests.

In newly industrialized countries, however, the development of a collective identity—the acknowledgement of shared interests based on workplace relations, and on broader class relations—is generally considered more problematic. Where rapid industrialization has occurred, workers are rarely drawn from strong, cohesive communities; instead, they tend to be recent migrants to new industrial areas, often bringing with them a range of different ethnic or regional identities. Within the modernization paradigm, Alex Inkeles and David H. Smith recognized that individuals' attitudes and behavior could change relatively quickly when they entered industrial settings,[11] but this approach was relatively unusual: most modernization theorists were more likely to conclude that newly proletarianized workers lacked any basis for collective identities.

From this perspective, the recent migrant's ties to rural areas, or the new worker's lack of familiarity with industrial organization, would be expected to prevent cohesive organizations at work. These new workers, it has often been suggested, were unlikely to respond to appeals for solidarity with fellow workers. Especially where labor market differences overlap with differences of origin and identity, José Albertino Rodrigues writes, the qualified worker, "carrier of greater class consciousness," is likely to have little in common with "the unskilled worker, who, because of his recent rural origins, has no great class consciousness and only seeks some protection from the employer, the law, or the union."[12] While some observers noted that even newly arrived migrant workers could participate in "hidden" workplace resistance—through sabotage, absenteeism, and the like—they nevertheless tended to assume that recent migrants were unlikely to recognize, much less act upon, broad class interests.[13]

More recently, several authors have recognized that workers in industrializing societies have created their own traditions during the century or more since their societies became increasingly marked by wage labor. Charles Bergquist suggests that Latin American workers' experiences in the earliest stages of proletarianization—generally, in the export sector of dependent economies—have continued to be reflected in the way labor organizations interpret and shape workers' interests; for Bergquist, it is workers in export production, "a class formed in response to the expansion of the world-capitalist system after 1880, who did the most to make the Latin American labor movements [and] whose struggles most deeply influenced the modern trajectory of the various national labor movements of the region."[14] Similarly, for Africa, Jeff Crisp's description of Ghanaian miners' organizations and John Higginson's history of Zairian miners emphasize the way the experiences of export-oriented sector workers can shape late industrializers' labor movements.[15]

Looking at a somewhat later period, Ruth and David Collier argue that patterns of labor incorporation into national political arenas continue to shape labor's organizational and political strategies. The expansion of Latin American economies in the late nineteenth and early twentieth centuries stimulated new urban and industrial growth, in turn provoking crises in the political arena when newly formed middle-class groups and labor challenged existing political arrangements. The resolution of those conflicts shaped patterns of incorporation that have continued to dominate political alliances throughout this century.[16]

Both these perspectives clearly offer an important reminder: workers in many late industrializers are not simply ex-peasants; they may have developed organizations, traditions, and identities over decades of industrial labor. On the other hand, the emphasis on shared historical experiences may lead observers to overlook a different phenomenon: workers in some situations appear to have developed a collective identity relatively quickly in response to the new situations in which they find themselves: rather than drawing on old identities, or even following old trajectories, workers in some situations appear able to find new strategies, to take advantage of new situations.

In the 1970s, workplace militance in Brazil and South Africa was extraordinary: generally led by younger workers who devised new strategies to deal with factory and state repression, strikes spread so fast that neither unionists nor employers were fully in control. Coming at a time when the business communities in both countries were already disenchanted with state policies, the "new unionism" successfully challenged the framework of labor relations: before unions and employers' associations began to lobby officially for new labor relations laws, workers at specific factories were already beginning to negotiate informal arrangements with employers. Strikes spread from region to region and from sector to sector; workers demanded increased wages, recognition of shop-floor representatives, and employer acknowledgment of workers' dignity. Within less than a decade, both labor movements had moved to a far broader understanding of their constituencies and goals. In Ira Katznelson's typology, Brazilian and South African workers formed social classes not only in the sense of shared economic relations, but as "groups, sharing dispositions," where "cognitive concepts map the terrain of lived experience and define the boundaries between the probable and improbable"; and they quickly moved to collective action, in which classes "are organized [and] act through movements and organizations to affect society and the position of the class within it."[17] Undoubtedly, the most striking feature of the labor movements that emerged in Brazil and South Africa in the 1970s was the creation of working-class organizations and identities that seemed to resist division, to transcend ethnic and economic particularism, and to reflect in collective action a new sense of shared interests and goals.

Why might this have occurred in two such different contexts? One explanation of labor militance in some of the Europe's new industrial centers in the early twentieth century stresses the way the prewar industrial buildup created large groups of semi-skilled workers who shared the experiences of rapid change and of wartime deprivation. These workers created organizations that were more inclusive than artisan craft organizations and were frequently more militant.[18] The key element appears to have been rapid industrial change, not war. Richard Oestreicher attributes the shift in Detroit in the 1880s, when workers began to develop new institutions, new moral codes, and a vision of unions "which transcended ethnicity and economic particularism to recruit workers on a class basis,"[19] to changes in industrial work—particularly the introduction of new labor processes that reduced the labor market and skill divisions among ethnically divided workers. Similarly, Marks suggests that politicized unionism in nineteenth-century Britain, Germany, and the United States reflected what he calls the "organizational revolution," the "immense expansion of economic, social and political life," with "a rapid concentration of finance and production into ever larger units under the influence of innovations in communication, power generation, and mass production."[20]

In this chapter, I suggest that changes in the organization of work and in workers' experiences, linked to the rapid industrialization strategies outlined in chapter 2, laid the basis for a new kind of labor movement in both Brazil and South Africa. Comparing the emergence of labor militance in the two cases, I shall show how labor organization gradually spread, as workers chose strategies that reflected their new experiences at work and in their communities; when the political opportunities described in chapter 3 appeared, these new unions could take advantage of them. While individual unions reflected the characteristics of specific industries and regions, and even of specific organizers, the national patterns are remarkably similar, suggesting a direct link between rapid industrialization and the spread of a broad-based labor movement. In both cases, semi-skilled workers predominated in shaping the labor movement: the rise of capital-intensive heavy industry increased industrial workers' capacity to challenge employers on the shop floor, and the organizations they formed reflected that experience.

These organizations then spread into other sectors, at least in part because the class-based discourse that expressed the shared identity and interests of semi-skilled workers also appealed to workers outside heavy industry; both the Brazilian and South African labor movements sought to introduce workers' demands into the national arena, challenging existing definitions of citizenship and labor rights. This chapter emphasizes parallel trends that help explain the rapid growth of class-conscious labor movements, and suggests that these patterns are best understood as resulting from the way authoritarian industrialization strategies shaped workers' lived experience, laying the basis for broad class mobilization.

BRAZIL: "MÁQUINAS PARADAS E BRAÇOS CRUZADOS"

On May 12, 1978, a hundred workers at Saab-Scania's plant in São Bernardo do Campo punched in, crossed their arms and stopped their machines, demanding a 20 percent raise. The strike spread through the factory; soon Saab-Scania's eighteen hundred workers were all punching in and refusing to turn on their machines. The strikers insisted on direct negotiations with the company, confirming negotiations through plant assemblies and rejecting intervention by union leaders or labor ministry officials because "our fight is with the firm."[21] The strike spread rapidly through São Paulo's industrial belt: by the end of the second week, nearly seventy-eight thousand workers, mainly in the automobile industry, were on strike for higher wages and direct negotiations with employers.

Although union officials denied any involvement, the work stoppages certainly fitted a larger strategy: led by Lula, the São Bernardo metalworkers had decided in March to reject the annual industrywide contract negotiations, believing that only shop-floor militance would prevent Labor Ministry tribunals from ratifying employers' proposals. There had been small work stoppages in the nearby Mercedes-Benz and Ford plants in March and April, and Lula himself had almost certainly been warned that Saab-Scania workers planned a stoppage.[22] The industry itself was vulnerable. As the private automobile sector was not classified "essential," sitting down in front of machines would not constitute an immediate violation of the labor code.[23] Equally important, the industry was a key foreign exchange earner: in 1978, Brazil's auto

manufacturers were seeking markets overseas, and neither manufacturers nor the state could afford to let production stop for long.[24]

The 1978 strike stood in sharp contrast to the strikes of the early
1960s, when national labor leaders called for workers to mobilize in
support of national aims or to protest national issues: a political refer-
endum, galloping inflation, and the like. During the early 1960s, just as
employers sought state assistance, so too did union leaders, who believed their strength lay in alliances with reformist politicians.[25] Under
military rule, however, after over a decade of labor repression, few
workers expected to win gains through appeals to the Ministry of Labor, or through state-appointed union leaders. The form of the 1978
strikes reflected workers' distrust of state-controlled unions and controlled negotiations. At Saab-Scania, a small network of activists quietly
planned a stoppage. "To speak the word *strike* was frightening . . . but
this wasn't a strike. It was a stoppage." When workers throughout the
factory refused to turn on their machines, the company invited in a
representative of the Ministry of Labor; he arrived with an agent of
the security police. The workers' main demand: salary increases, to be
negotiated between the company and an elected factory commission,
and ratified by a factory assembly.[26] This was a far cry from the mass
rallies and demonstrations of the 1950s; it was a strike planned by
workers, without visible outside leadership, and conducted entirely
within the factory itself.

Although workers inside the Saab-Scania factory planned the stoppage, the spontaneous response took even optimists by surprise: the
strike appeared to have been born, as Lula, the recently elected president of the metalworkers' union, put it, "of the necessity the worker
has of breathing."[27] Automobile workers had been considered among
Brazil's most privileged industrial workers. Only a few years before,
Leôncio Martins Rodrigues had described them as prospective members
of a satisfied working class, whose unions would focus on purely economic issues,[28] while Maria Hermínia Tavares de Almeida suggested
that they might be considered a labor aristocracy, with high skill levels
and relatively low unemployment.[29]

On the other hand, conditions within the industry, and the contrast
between aspirations and factory reality, may have reinforced workers'
grievances. Even skilled workers experienced extraordinarily high turnover rates; employers could keep average salaries low by laying off
workers and replacing them with new ones. In 1974, Humphrey found

that up to 30 percent of skilled workers and 40 percent of unskilled workers were laid off in a single month at one factory. Such high turnover could weaken union organization, since employers could, and did, use the constant threat of layoffs as a means of disciplining workers.[30] The skills shortage meant auto workers were relatively protected from long-term unemployment,[31] but the insecurity that accompanied the post-1973 recession compounded the effects of inflation: real wages had eroded, even for metalworkers. Privilege, in this case, was very relative; while other workers in São Paulo may well have aspired to jobs in the auto industry, workers in the industry itself must have felt grievances over deteriorating conditions by the mid 1970s.

Regardless of whether conditions in the metalworking industry had worsened during the "economic miracle," Lais Wendel Abramo argues that, above all, the 1978 strikes represented a campaign for workers' self-respect. During the auto industry's expansion, the drive to raise productivity had directly affected workers' lives, in terms of pressure to accept overtime shifts and in speeded-up lines. Auto workers' descriptions of their daily lives reveal a sense of powerlessness, circumstances in which "there are days in which I don't have time even to smile." One worker wrote simply, "I work at Volks, where I lose 70 percent of my life."[32] Chronic fatigue and psychological pressure contributed to high accident rates. Control over workers' movements in most large factories was despotic: workers' accounts tell of supervisors who strictly limited bathroom trips and of guards whose arbitrary decisions amounted to the humiliating control of high school prefects. As a striker put it, "The strike was more for a guy's honor than for the raise."[33]

Taken by surprise, employers were divided in their response to the 1978 strikes. Although many firms threatened workers with dismissals, assault, or arrest, and although the Ministry of Labor declared the strikes illegal, the army was not brought in.[34] Faced with production losses, employers tried individual methods of ending the strike, through threats and attempts to negotiate with individual workers. Employers may have feared that an invasion of the factories by police or soldiers would lead to widespread damage to expensive machinery. Some multinational companies, including Saab-Scania, were already under pressure from workers in their home countries to negotiate with their Brazilian employees.[35]

Eventually, the automobile industry employers' associations began an unofficial bargaining process with the ABC Metalworkers' Union; Grupo 14, representing employers in the auto and metal industry, granted a staggered wage increase of 24.5 percent.[36] Leading industrialists argued that because "state intervention in labor-capital relations always generates distortions," employers should be allowed to deal directly with nonpolitical strikes.[37]

Employers were hardly ready to abdicate control: most workers who served on factory commissions were fired when they returned to work.[38] But the strike appeared to be a victory for the workers, and its main lesson was a political one. Lula concluded, "One learns that it is easier to negotiate with the machines stopped."[39] João Ferrador, a comic character whose letters in the Metalworkers' Union's newspaper vividly expressed workers' complaints throughout the 1970s, wrote:

> We have won, good sirs, the first great battle in the war with the employers. Because of it, from here on we must be treated as a social force, worthy of the greatest respect by authorities and employers. [In the strikes] lies proof of what we are and what we can do in defense of our rights and against employer injustices.[40]

Workers' comments reveal the significance strikers attached to the success of their factory-based action: rather than relying on union officials, they had forced employers to negotiate with elected worker representatives and to grant wage increases. They had challenged employer control and won.

To many Brazilians, the strikes seemed to herald the return of industrial workers to national political life.[41] By the end of the year, about 540,000 Brazilians—including teachers, bank workers, and textile workers, as well as 350,000 metalworkers—had followed the Saab-Scania workers' lead, striking for better wages and independent bargaining rights.[42] Sometimes strikes were organized by unions, across categories of workers; more often they were organized within individual factories or regions. As strikes spread into industries where employers were less dependent on skilled and semi-skilled workers, and where daily production losses were less problematic for employers, strikers faced mass dismissals. The police and army arrested workers in sectors designated "essential," such as dockworkers and public employees in health and education. A national bank workers' strike, composed primarily of workers in state-owned banks, was also directly repressed.[43]

Nevertheless, in 1978 the military government did not remove any union leaders, even in "essential" sector unions: coming at a time when the government was already under attack from leading businessmen going into the 1978 election campaign, the strikes apparently created further division among state officials. In mid August, the government tried to regain control: a new labor law gave employers more discretion in dealing with strikes, but it also threatened strikers' social security benefits. Like unionists and employers, the state clearly recognized that the 1978 strikes had opened a new era.[44]

LAYING THE BASIS

What formed the organizational basis for the strikes in 1978? By the late 1960s, arrests, interventions, and expulsions had left only the most pliable unionists in office. From 1968 on, "conflicts arising in the plane of labor relations were not considered objects of discussion, only of repression," and repressive state action "was always applauded and frequently solicited by industrialists."[45] Individual activists, however, continued to try to organize, either working within registered unions, accepting the limits of assistentialism,[46] or organizing within the factory. Activists often disagreed over strategy and tactics; while some groups stressed work within the factory, others sought to win official union positions. But despite different emphases, all agreed on the need for more combative workers' organization and shop-floor representation.[47]

Several networks of clandestine worker activists operated in the São Paulo area. One set of activists was linked to the Catholic church. From the early 1960s, members of Catholic Worker Action (Ação Católica Operária) participated in local church efforts to raise awareness about levels of poverty in the São Paulo area.[48] From 1974, Catholic Action redefined its project: stressing that the church should serve the workers' movement, rather than the reverse, the group emphasized building worker leadership and organizing within factories, rather than within communities or even within unions. In some areas, Catholic Action groups worked closely with Popular Action (Ação Popular), a former Catholic student group that had supported the left-wing decision to take up armed struggle in the mid 1960s, but stressed factory-level organization as the basis for class mobilization. "Through arduous and painstaking work," Brazilian sociologist Heloisa Helena Texeira de Souza Martins writes, "these militants were re-linking workers inside the factory, building alliances with other opposition groups . . . trying to carry forward a project of the working class, not that of realizing the reign of God on earth."[49] Heavy repression limited most activity to small clandestine discussion groups and occasional pamphlets,[50] but in the early 1970s, the Catholic church created a Workers' Pastoral, with offices in São Paulo's southern zone. Although it initially focused on community issues in São Paulo's industrial periphery, meetings of the Pastoral provided a relatively safe arena for workers from different factories to meet and to discuss workplace issues. As the next chapter will show, church-related groups also provided a forum in which participants could examine the links between factory and neighborhood issues, drawing out broader political implications of isolated local problems.

A second clandestine network was formed by left-wing activists in illegal parties. Some members of the banned Communist Party remained active despite repression. In the late 1960s, activists from small guerrilla groups tried to make contact with worker activists, although generally unsuccessfully.[51] Especially as the Catholic church shifted to support grass-roots organization, church-linked and politically motivated workers joined in informal factory-based groups.[52]

Perhaps the best-documented clandestine network was that of the Metalworkers' Union Opposition, initially formed to propose an opposition slate of officers for the Metalworkers' Union of the State of São Paulo in 1967, and composed of Catholics, Communists, and independent syndicalists. These opposition candidates raised issues like the strike law, the wage policy, the FGTS, and inflation; they argued that the main lesson of 1950s populist unionism was that factory-based unions would be less vulnerable than nationally identified leaders.[53] The slate lost, and the 1968 repression of the Osasco and Contagem strikes left the Metalworkers Opposition in disarray: in 1968, only about twenty workers from factories around São Paulo attended its secret meetings. Over the next few years, these workers gradually built up tiny nuclei within their factories—five workers in Passini (auto parts), ten in Lorenzetti (electrical materials), thirty in Arno (motors)—talking to fellow workers, visiting them at home, and raising questions of work and opposition.[54]

Always vulnerable to identification, opposition activists were often fired, arrested, tortured: in early 1976, Manoel Fiel Filho, a well-known metalworker activist, died under army interrogation. However, given the metalworking industry's high turnover and shortages of skilled workers, activists fired from one job could usually find employment elsewhere. Indeed, high turnover may have helped spread clandestine networks across São Paulo's industrial periphery, as activists moved from factory to factory.[55]

Once established, factory groups would try to identify specific factory grievances. In Massey-Ferguson's metal plant, a five-person nucleus instigated a 1972 strike against changes in the firm's transportation service.[56] In 1973, three years after the formation of a small nucleus at the Villares metal plant, workers struck for wage increases and against inflationary prices in the factory canteen and bus service. Villares's 2,500 workers stopped work every day for half an hour, insisting that the firm negotiate with an elected workers' commission, with general factory meetings for discussion and ratification. Most strike leaders were fired, but the Villares strikes gave one of the first indications that a different kind of unionism was beginning to develop.[57]

Despite a common theoretical emphasis on building shop-floor organization, many opposition unionists continued to try to influence official union leaders—although success varied, depending on the individual union leader. In São Paulo proper, where the Metalworkers' Union president was a government appointee, an opposition metalworker said "the only contribution of the official union . . . was to bring us to the police."[58] Nevertheless, official union structures could provide space for organizing: in 1972, an opposition slate lost a bid for the São Paulo metalworkers' leadership, but during the campaign, workers discussed alternative forms of unionism at meetings in communities, factories, and even in union offices. By the mid 1970s, these ideas of an alternative shop-floor-based unionism seem to have influenced even government-appointed union officials. A 1974 resolution of the São Paulo Metalworkers' Congress proposed the creation of factory-level union delegates to strengthen links between union leadership and factory base.[59]

Clandestine organization was not the only potential threat to employers' control, however. Although the signs were barely visible, by the early 1970s workers around São Paulo had developed ways to disrupt the labor process without risking repression. In the mid 1970s, workers could tell researchers about various methods, individual and collective, through which they could slow production. Individually, workers could speed up a machine until it broke; shift a machine's position or throw in a wrench to break the flow of line; make defective pieces; balance pieces badly, or misuse machines so that they fell or broke. Such individual methods evidently never involved collective decisions; according to one worker, such actions were "the fruit of the situation. A point will arrive where the worker can't bear it any more."[60]

Even in 1970–71, however, workers could also describe a repertoire of collective methods for covertly slowing production. Workers on automated lines took alternate breaks; they allowed work to pile up at key points on the line; or they increased errors so that work had to be redone.[61] Usually over wages, these go-slows seem to have been informal and factory-based; they were never organized by the union and usually resulted in dismissals or arrests. From 1973 on, however, the growing economic crisis increased the urgency of wage demands. Between 1973 and 1977, there were at least thirty-four recorded strikes or go-slows, mainly over wages or late payment. Of these, sixteen were among metalworkers, and twenty-one were in the São Paulo or ABC region.[62] To some workers, struggles in individual São Paulo auto plants showed the factory to be "a privileged site of conflict," while the fact that government-appointed union officials repeatedly failed to support striking workers underlined the importance of independent shop-floor organization.[63]

THE *REPOSIÇÃO* CAMPAIGN: AGAINST EMPLOYERS AND THE STATE

By the mid 1970s, then, individual activists had formed nuclei within some factories, and had begun to challenge union practices, seeking to develop stronger factory representation and worker militance. In working-class areas of São Paulo, small groups of workers met regularly to discuss working conditions and wages, often in neighborhood churches. Not surprisingly, many of these groups focused on inflation and low wages. Real wages had declined steadily, and slowed growth rates reduced any hope that the benefits of the Brazil's "miracle" would trickle down to workers. From 1974, a church-linked community movement publicized the effects of inflation, and even state-appointed union officials argued for higher inflation indices during salary negotiations.[64]

Almost certainly in response to a changing political climate, and perhaps also in response to slowly growing factory-based militance, union activists embarked on a national campaign in 1977, publicly discussing inflation, wages, and labor organization in terms of social justice. The campaign for *reposição*—for the reinstatement of wages lost through arbitrary indexing—began almost by accident, when an interunion statistics bureau, DIEESE, discovered a World Bank report showing that the true 1973 inflation rate had been about 25 percent, considerably higher than the government's published figure of 15 percent.[65] Led by an energetic new director and staff, DIEESE argued that the government's conscious manipulation of inflation data had limited workers' increases to two-thirds of the correct amount. By 1977, when the government admitted that it had published artificially low figures, workers had lost, on average, 34.1 percent of their wages.

Indexing was a political as well as an economic issue: since inflation indices were set by the state, and official wage increases were restricted to the level of inflation, wage negotiations invariably involved debates over how indices were estimated. The *reposição* campaign was the most successful union effort in a decade. Carried on through large rallies and public petitions, rather than in factories, the campaign was supported by various union papers and by pamphlets and bulletins published by church groups.[66] It was led by a registered union, the Metalworkers of São Bernardo do Campo—a fact that certainly gave its leaders a measure of visibility and protection from repression. Lula, the union's charismatic recently elected leader, came from a younger generation of metalworkers with no direct experience of the populist unionism of the 1950s. Lula had been chosen as the official candidate by the outgoing president, a conservative *pelego* who apparently expected Lula to do his bidding;[67] in office, however, Lula—who himself had little political experience, but whose brother was imprisoned as a Communist the year Lula took office[68]—grew impatient with the "farce of salary negotiations whose final objective is to give legitimacy to [an inflation] index arbitrarily fixed by the government."[69] He and fellow union officers used the official union's resources—publications, researchers, access to the São Paulo newspapers—to support the campaign. Armed with DIEESE's statistics, Lula and other union leaders negotiated with government leaders, forcing the Labor Ministry to concede that salaries should be readjusted. Safer than a strike, the national campaign for the restitution of unfairly denied wages demonstrated the presence of labor activists on the national scene and affirmed the legitimacy of their demands at a time when industrialists were already complaining about government economic policies.

The salary readjustment campaign suggested for the first time since the early 1960s that workers could successfully challenge state control over wage levels. At the same time, it underscored the state's bias in labor negotiations and the problems inherent in Brazil's labor code. A year later, when strikers demanded direct negotiations, the demand did not simply reflect workers' distrust of union leaders; indeed, the auto workers of the ABC region counted on support from the Metalworkers' leadership.[70] Rather, it reflected a growing belief by many union members that factory-based militants were more likely to win concessions directly from employers than from the Ministry of Labor. The labor activism that the campaign reflected and inspired came from the factory, from worker activists who insisted their demands were legitimate.

The debate over union strategy was quite public, as shop-floor militants, or *autênticos,* challenged union officers who were willing to stay within the corporatist framework. At a 1978 Congress of Industrial Workers, shop-floor-based unionists rejected the Labor Ministry's tribunals, arguing that the state only interfered in negotiations on the side of employers, and that workers could not rely on the military regime to protect their interests. In their "Letter of Principles," opposition unionists insisted on direct negotiations, union autonomy, and shop-floor representation—all principles that challenged Brazil's corporatist structure and the practices of most registered unions.[71] The following year, the first open meeting of the São Paulo metalworkers' opposition declared, "The role of the union opposition is to dismantle the current structure and create a new one, independent of employers and of the government, starting with factory organization." [72]

This, then, was the "new" unionism. Developed within factories during the harshest years of military rule, its activists emphasized shop-floor organization and representation and rejected state control over labor. Demanding democratization of union and state practices, worker activists viewed the state's wage policy as a means of assisting private capital accumulation. Insisting on factory-based representation in negotiations, they rejected the populist tradition that had dominated Brazil's labor history: instead of turning to the state for assistance against employers, they tended to consider state intervention a threat to worker organization, and believed their most successful strategy lay in shop-floor militance.

THE "NEW UNIONISM"

From May 1978 on, the "new unionism" spread through Brazilian industries, with worker activists calling for greater shop-floor representation in union structures and direct collective bargaining. Even outside São Paulo's heavy industrial sector, "specific demands emerged with growing radicalization, in demonstrations and strikes. Incisive critiques [were] directed at the current Brazilian model—economic, social, and political." [73] Brazilian sociologists generally agree that although factory-based militance spread to service and rural workers, it was carried primarily by the industrial workers among whom it first emerged: relatively skilled workers, drawn into activism through shop-floor struggles in São Paulo's large factories. In some areas, activists could appeal to local memories of militant unionism to mobilize workers,[74] but in general, the new industrial workers had missed the populist era of the 1950s. In 1984, a survey of auto workers in São Bernardo do Campo found that less than 10 percent were older than forty-five, suggesting that nearly all of them had been under twenty at the time of the 1964 coup;[75] on average, union officers were probably only slightly older.[76]

According to Lula, the strikes occurred in São Bernardo's metal industry because "it was no longer the worker from the interior who was in the factory, but his son." These workers "had had access not only to a primary school but also to an apprenticeship program," he said, and they had come to understand the principles of unionism not by reading *Capital* but "by working at a machine, producing twelve pieces and getting paid the value of two."[77]

The difference between the attitudes toward militance of the "new unionists" and those of the officials who dominated state-controlled unions was readily apparent. After the 1978 strikes, Lula commented: "The worker learned that strikes are not a thing that's prohibited. It must be done, even if there's a law that blocks it." Union officials who had served under the military regime, on the other hand, tended to fear militance as dangerous. Miguel Galhardo, president of São Paulo's union of tobacco workers, asked business to grant a 10 percent raise "in order to avoid any radicalization"; but he added that the anti-strike law must be obeyed, because "we are subordinate to it." Unions, he said, "only seek to serve as mediators in the conflict." Joaquim dos Santos Andrade, the president of the Metalworkers of São Paulo who had been put in office by the military government in 1964, agreed that "the worker knows that under the current legislation he has only the right to work and no more."[78]

Andrade, described by an opposition activist as one of "the most adroit and capable" of the unionists who cooperated with the military government,[79] insisted that Brazilian unions could not survive without state support, and firmly opposed the "indiscriminate use" of strikes.[80] Despite pressure from members, Andrade, like other official unionists, often refused to give strikers and opposition unionists access to union resources and frequently failed to support strikes. Over the next few years, several leading union officials who refused to support striking workers lost internal elections; among those who lost their positions was a Metalworkers' Union official from Fortaleza who was widely believed to have helped employers create groups of strikebreakers in 1980. Others, however, managed to retain their positions, often through adroit manipulation of union resources; in one case, a conservative Metalworkers' Union official from São Caetano managed to retain his seat through maneuvers that included calling the police to block an opposition unionists' meeting in union headquarters.[81]

Factory-level conflicts during the process of rapid industrialization had produced new strategies and new leaders, who had little faith that the state would protect their interests, and who had found that they could use workers' positions at the point of production to back up demands:

> In the vanguard of this ["new unionism"] movement, one finds a working class, largely constituted by the authoritarian period's accelerated process of industrial growth, that had no direct ties with the syndicalism of the populist phase. . . . [Leaders] forged in the atomized struggles that had taken place in the interior of factories, who confronted employer decisions always protected by the regime, experienced intensely the inefficiency of existing union organization.[82]

Working in relatively large, modern enterprises, lacking traditions of traditional populism and memories of past defeats, the new militants insisted that the factory, rather than corporatist union structures, should serve as the major site of struggle.[83]

As workers discovered that they could challenge employers' prerogatives on the shop floor, the "new unionists" only gradually came to reject state control over the labor movement. In 1973, opposition unionists still sought to work within established structures; indeed, the Santos Metalworkers' Union ran candidates for the official opposition party.[84] In 1978, unionists were still debating their relationship to corporatist labor legislation. A year later, however, the 1979 ABC metalworkers' strike revealed the government's inability to control the new unionism and demonstrated the tendency of militance to spread beyond the factory floor to working-class communities.

In early 1979, representatives of all the metalworkers' unions in the São Paulo region met to agree on a strategy for annual contract negotiations. Workers then met by factory to discuss factory-specific demands and elect commissions to coordinate the salary campaign. In addition to a 34.1 percent salary increase, the metalworkers sought job security, a 40-hour week, and elected union delegates in each factory. Job security had become an especially important issue, since after the 1978 strikes, layoffs increased dramatically in the São Paulo region.[85] Employers rejected the demands, agreeing to a pay raise but refusing to grant job security to union delegates. The metalworkers' response was divided. Andrade, the conservative São Paulo Metalworkers' president, accepted the employers' proposal; the ABC metalworkers, representing the rest of the region's heavy industrial workers, voted in mass rallies to strike.

This time, however, employers and state officials were prepared; the latter even warned employers to produce extra inventory as insurance against a long strike.[86] Strikers were locked out of factories, preventing the sit-down strikes that had been so successful the previous year. After three days of pickets at factories and bus stops, the strike was declared illegal; by the end of the week, military and security police were patrolling the streets of the ABC region, sleeping inside factories, and arresting strikers, often violently.

The ABC community immediately expressed its support for the strike. Over 80,000 workers and their families attended rallies at a local stadium, where union leaders announced the creation of a strike fund and the local bishop called on church members to support the strike. When the Labor Ministry intervened in the ABC metalworkers' unions, briefly arresting Lula and other leaders, and police occupied union headquarters, the church offered the Cathedral of São Bernardo do Campo as informal union headquarters. More than 150,000 people celebrated May Day in support of the union's demands and the right to strike, and the union's newly created strike fund fed nearly 32,000 people in 6,384 families.[87] The officially removed union leadership continued to function in temporary offices.

Nevertheless, faced with an unexpected level of police violence, the Labor Ministry's intervention in the union, and threatened layoffs, the strike weakened; through informal direct discussions, the union and employers agreed to a 45-day negotiating period, and the strikers returned to work. When the union membership ratified the negotiated accord, the Federated Industries of the State of São Paulo asked the Labor Ministry to allow Lula and other elected union leaders to return to their positions: ultimately, even employers preferred to negotiate with a union leadership that could control the strike and asked the state to step aside.

The strikes were not generally considered a success. Activists were fired, and police violence had been severe. The 1979 strike, one worker commented, showed that "to strike outside the factory is to serve up a punching bag to the police."[88] Nevertheless, the strike held two lessons for activists. First, it showed that a well-organized union could resist state intervention; employers had continued to negotiate with the elected union leaders even after the state had removed them from their posts. Second, the strike showed the depth of community support for strikers and their demands. Not only had employers been unable to hire replacement workers, but the community—hardly wealthy—had donated the resources necessary "to win autonomy from the state and to keep the strikes going."[89]

Like the 1978 auto strike, the 1979 metalworkers' strike provoked a strike wave that spread across Brazil. During the year, more than three million workers—about 13 percent of Brazil's industrial labor force— were reported on strike, mainly for higher wages. Of these, 40 percent were in the São Paulo region, and about half of these were metalwork-ers.[90] But again, the strike wave spread far beyond industrial centers, and into a variety of workplaces. Bus drivers, garbage collectors, con-struction workers, and teachers joined what an opposition weekly called "a alegria dos peões"—roughly, the happiness of laborers.[91] Many of the strikes were organized over union officials' opposition, demonstrating the attraction shop-floor militance held for ordinary workers.[92]

Few strikers won their demands. Although they were generally sup-ported by a growing opposition movement—by an alternative press, students, priests, opposition members of Congress, and even some busi-nessmen who attended support meetings and raised funds—few strikes won pay raises, and none won noneconomic demands for shop-floor union delegates, job security, or a 40-hour week.[93] Lacking organiza-tion or resources, these more spontaneous strikes sometimes turned into riots involving hundreds of people, and especially outside the São Paulo region, the police often responded with arrests and violence. The Labor Ministry declared strike after strike illegal, and intervened in the Bank Workers' Union.

As the Bank Workers' president put it, the state's frequent repression of strikes clarified "the close connection between objective, concrete demands and the question of the country's social and political organiza-tion."[94] That connection—in essence, the role of the state in labor rela-tions—was further underlined late in the year, when the government gave in to union demands for a semestral readjustment of wages for inflation, instead of the previous annual raise. Although most of the 1979 strikes were unable to win concessions from individual employers, the new wage law was clearly a victory for the labor movement as a whole; the fact that it was the state that granted the concession, rather than individual employers, can only have strengthened the political content of unionists' demands.

POLITICIZATION OF SHOP-FLOOR ORGANIZATION

By the early 1980s, industrialists confronted with shop-floor militance had begun to "privilege negotiation over appeals for government coercion," trying to develop labor relations techniques to reduce the threat of strikes. The old industrywide negotiations were inappropriate for the current situation: nearly 70 percent of the 1,600 strikes between 1978 and 1984 were based in single establishments, illustrating a need for decentralized negotiations and workplace communication. Strikes by bank workers, teachers, and other middle-class categories tended to be broader; strikes by industrial workers were far more likely to be by individual factory, emphasizing shop-floor organization.[95]

This was particularly true in heavy industry: between 1978 and 1984, metalworkers were responsible for about 70 percent of all strikes in Brazil.[96] Over the next few years, several large employers would experiment with factory commissions, with elected delegates who received job security as part of the position. In some cases, notably at Ford's ABC plant, the commission's elected delegates included widely respected activists. In others, the proposed representative structure was unworkable: Volkswagen offered a factory commission so powerless that only half the 42,000 eligible workers voted for actual candidates; the rest wrote in the names of Lula or cartoon characters.[97]

Even business leaders willing to concede new channels for negotiation, however, insisted on limits to permissible union behavior: while more industrialists claimed to agree that workers had a right to choose their own forms of association, many continued to fear that demands would move beyond strictly work-related issues. One survey found that employers believed direct negotiations would permit greater employer flexibility in responding to strikes; but most hoped the state would keep some control over worker organization, "to keep it within strictly 'workerist' limits." Above all, employers feared that labor militance would translate into political strikes, threatening "social order."[98]

Employers' fears were not entirely unjustified. By 1979, many union activists involved in the strikes clearly agreed with Lula's assessment: "The economic and the political are two factors that we cannot disentangle from each other. They are two very interconnected things. . . . The struggle that occurred in ABC was for wages, but the working-class movement, while fighting for raises, had a political result."[99] Over the next five years, repeated strike waves would reinforce two lessons from the strikes of 1979: first, that strikes required strong shop-floor organization, and, second, that under Brazil's labor regime it was virtually impossible for workers to disentangle political and economic demands. Almost invariably, workers striking in factories defined their interests in political as well as economic terms: without access to state resources, without reforms in labor legislation and state policies, workers could not hope to improve either their working conditions or their general standard of living. Even when workers' demands focused entirely on workplace issues, they had an implicit political content: as long as legislation prohibited collective bargaining and union autonomy, labor militance would involve a direct challenge to the political order, by disrupting the state's normal control over wage increases and labor activism.

Recessionary policies in the early 1980s underlined the way grievances against employers could be compounded by grievances against the state. In 1980, the government responded viciously to what had become an annual metalworkers' strike during contract discussions. The Ministry of Labor again intervened in the union, and refused to let employers negotiate directly with workers;[100] the security police arrested Lula and other leaders. Riot squads and police dogs roamed the streets of São Bernardo and Diadema, using tear gas and beating up residents. When union headquarters were occupied by troops, strikers met at the church; a May 1 demonstration drew over a hundred thousand supporters.[101] Nevertheless, after forty-one days, far longer than previous strikes, the metalworkers returned to work without winning concessions.

The metalworkers' 1980 defeat signaled the start of a difficult period for Brazil's unionists. Industrialists may have objected to recessionary policies, but rising unemployment undoubtedly fortified employer and state resistance to workers' demands. Between 1980 and 1983, while the national per capita GDP fell by 10 percent and unemployment soared, strikes became increasingly defensive. Workers in all industries began to strike for security of employment, even against late wages, rather than for higher wages and better working conditions.[102] The labor movement had to acknowledge the impact of a growing economic crisis on the possibility of worker mobilization. Although official figures are certainly misleading, the Department of Labor reported the total number of strikes dropped from 429 in 1979 to 42 in 1980 and 34 in 1981.[103] In 1981, the metalworkers did not strike. In October 1981, a proposed general strike against the government recessionary policy prompted only demonstrations in eighteen cities, not industrial action.[104]

But the strikes of the late 1970s seem to have changed the way Brazilians viewed the possibility of shop-floor militance and the potential strength of working-class organization. Despite its defeats, the labor movement grew rapidly. Union membership soared from 2.7 million in 1973 to over 12 million in 1983.[105] From 1982, industrial action rose despite—or perhaps because of—a worsening recession. In one metal factory in São Paulo, of the 34 strikes between 1957 and 1984, 50 percent occurred between 1982 and 1984.[106] The number of strikers represented by 11 unions for which data were collected increased from 691,673 participants in 142 strikes in 1982 to 1,521,835 participants in 364 strikes in 1984.[107] Rising unemployment, declared the interunion statistical bureau DIEESE, was "largely due to the recessionary policy adopted by the government [and] implies a choice to unload the weight of the crisis on the workers."[108] Leading unionists argued that government policies, coming at a time of relative political liberalization, would turn a movement for wages into class struggle, as workers came to recognize that their economic demands could only be met if there were political change.[109]

WORKING-CLASS ORGANIZATION

As factory-level mobilization intensified, and with economic and political demands increasingly seen as inseparable, two different, if related, organizational tendencies developed, both involving the construction of national entities uniting shop-floor organizations and unions. First, unionists challenged the legal prohibition on interunion organization, creating national federations that could take up national issues. Second, drawing on both the organized labor movement and the broader community-based social movement, unionists joined with left-wing intellectuals in creating a workers' party, the Partido dos Trabalhadores (PT), to challenge elite control over the political process. Moving beyond simply challenging employers, the labor movement began to take on the state.

Since Brazil's labor code prohibited the formation of federations uniting workers of different industries, the federations that emerged in the 1980s were clearly illegal. Their existence testifies to the state's inability to prevent the labor movement's spread: as workers were mobilized, their leaders could safely create an open national organization, defying the law. The lesson, perhaps, had been drawn from employers' reaction to the 1979 Ministry of Labor intervention in the São Bernardo Metalworkers' Union: when the state arrested leaders like Lula, even obdurate employers realized that the ensuing labor unrest could only cause further disruption and complicate negotiations. In 1981, 5,247 delegates representing workers at 1,126 firms met at a Conference of the Working Class, the largest meeting of shop-floor representatives since the imposition of military rule. Although delegates expressed realistic fears of repression, the meeting called on the government to restore democratic rights and recognize workers' willingness "to struggle for participation in national decisions."[110] More important, perhaps, representatives began to discuss the formation of a national labor federation.

As in the 1950s, however, unionists were divided by political and strategic disagreements. Activists continued to debate strategies: should unionists work within the existing union structure, despite its ties to the Ministry of Labor, or should they seek to build entirely new shop-floor-based unions? Should they work with established leaders, or should they challenge them in official union elections?[111]

Two separate labor federations were founded in 1983. The most visible leaders of recent strike waves formed the CUT (Central Única dos Trabalhadores, or Unified Workers' Central), emphasizing worker involvement and leadership, factory-level organization, and independence from existing political parties. In the CUT's view, employers and the state were equally involved in exploiting workers; only independent shop-floor-based organizations, led by workers, could challenge this alliance. Led by the São Bernardo Metalworkers' Union's Lula, and dominated by workers from heavy industry,[112] the CUT emphasized factory-level mobilization. Much as South Africa's FOSATU would be guided by the organizing experiences of workers in heavy industry, the CUT's strategies reflected the increased ability of semi-skilled workers to stop production: the emphasis on shop-floor organization, on political autonomy, and on a broad working-class appeal clearly reflected the metalworkers' experiences.[113] Later, as even middle-class groups joined the CUT, the discourse and strategies developed in the federation's earlier years would help to shape the way individual members understood issues of class and collective action.[114]

A second federation, the CONCLAT (Coordenação Nacional da Classe Trabalhadora, or National Working-Class Coordination), was formed by unionists more willing to remain within the existing structure of labor relations. Many of these were unionists who had held positions in state-controlled unions during the 1960s and 1970s. Later renamed the CGT (Confederação Geral dos Trabalhadores, or General Workers' Confederation), the more corporatist union grouping argued that while the state had protected employers' interests since 1964, this was not inevitable: a different government might behave differently. These unionists insisted that while Brazil's corporatist legislation was implemented after 1964 in ways that hurt unions, workers could use the existing structures to press for reforms; existing unions could mediate between state, employers, and workers. Moreover, they argued that employers should not be considered a homogeneous category, suggesting that "civil society" ought to support national capital rather than assuming there was no difference between multinationals and Brazilian employers. Generally led by officials who had survived the dictatorship, along with unionists associated with the Brazilian Communist Party and several smaller left-wing parties, the CGT tended to stress national political and economic reforms that would allow labor to participate in government alongside "progressive" national capital.[115]

In general, these different strategies flowed from the lived experience of activists in each grouping. Based on a survey of the two federations' leaders, Roque Aparecido da Silva suggests that CUT leaders tended to see reality "through the lens of the interior of the factory—where they had lived most of the authoritarian period"; only workers mobilized at the point of production, they believed, could challenge existing social arrangements. CGT leaders, on the other hand, had generally spent most of the authoritarian period as union officers; instead of seeking to create new shop-floor structures, they generally argued that strengthening existing union structures and ensuring democratic electoral processes would adequately respond to workers' needs, and they were far less likely to emphasize rank-and-file militance.[116]

The growing strength of the CUT relative to the CGT demonstrates the appeal of the "new unionism." Initially, CUT unions had fewer members than those in the CGT, partly because the rural unions' association elected to join CGT. By the mid 1980s, however, no observer could ignore the CUT unions' leading role: they were far more likely to engage in industrial action, to challenge employer and state policies, and to mobilize working-class support than were CGT affiliates. By the late 1980s, CUT leaders could justifiably claim that where the CUT had only been able to mobilize two million strikers during a general strike in 1983, by 1989—after six years of active organization among both urban and rural workers, with support for community activism and a political vision that stressed "class independence"—CUT could mobilize thirty-five million participants in a two-day general strike.[117]

Margaret Keck argues that the CUT's predominance should not be interpreted as demonstrating workers' conscious choice of one broad vision of social change over another; but, she adds, worker activists could see that the CUT's emphasis on shop-floor organization and "its confrontational strategy, combined with its emphasis on direct bargaining, was highly successful in winning concrete gains for the membership."[118] Whatever the reasons, the CUT would come to dominate the labor scene in Brazil, and many former CGT unions would change affiliation, apparently attracted by the CUT's militance and its ability to win wage and work-related demands. (In 1990, the CGT split, and a third union federation was formed, partly reflecting the effects of this kind of pressure.)[119]

The growth of the militant CUT led to the development of the Partido dos Trabalhadores as an alternative form of worker representation within the state. Rather paradoxically, the decision to found an independent workers' party, closely aligned with the CUT, predated the formation of the union federation—paradoxically, because a basic tenet of the CUT was that "parties must be subordinate to unions, not the reverse."[120] At the 1979 São Paulo (state) Metalworkers' Union congress, several workers proposed a resolution asking Brazilian workers to "unify in the construction of a political party" that would "build the political independence of workers as an instrument of struggle for the conquest of political power."[121] The congress did not vote on the resolution, which mirrored a suggestion Lula had made several months earlier,[122] but in the next months, a fierce debate raged over whether a new party would articulate workers' demands or simply split the political opposition to military rule. Although many leading unionists believed the labor movement was not yet ready, in mid October 1979, a meeting of a hundred people in São Paulo approved an interim structure for the PT.

In her detailed discussion of the PT's formation, Keck argues that as the labor movement grew stronger—as it developed a national leadership, an alternative press, and a base among increasingly mobilized workers—its leaders came to believe that the labor movement's goals could not simply be subsumed under broad calls for democratization. A workers' party would articulate workers' interests differently from elite parties and politicians.[123] Rejecting what they believed to have been labor leaders' historically subservient dependence on populist politicians, the founders of the PT sought to "create an effective channel of political and party expression for workers in the cities and in the countryside, and for all sectors exploited by capitalism," which would not simply become an electoral machine to gain working-class votes for established politicians.[124]

The proposal to establish a new political party, founded and led by workers and seeking to offer workers the benefits of economic growth, reflected a relatively recent theme in Brazilian debates: working-class interests were clearly distinguishable from those of a broader multi-class opposition, and only working-class organizations and leaders could ensure the articulation of workers' interests. Despite political liberalization, employers' responses to strikes during the previous years had underlined the differences between workers' aspirations and business goals. The discourse of class interests, stressing the extent to which industrial workers shared interests with rural workers against employers and landowners, was further popularized during PT electoral campaigns. "It should be made clear that we have two Brazils: the Brazil of the [presidential palace], of the [Congress buildings], and the Brazil of misery, of the *favela,* of unemployment, of landless laborers, of marginalized workers," Lula insisted. "Who lives in *favelas* today is the worker of the most sophisticated industries of the country, the worker at Volkswagen, of Philips, of Villares, Mercedes, etc." [125] Working-class interests could be clearly distinguished from the interests of dominant classes: calls for political liberalization from members of the dominant classes did not negate basic differences within the opposition, between those who had benefited from authoritarian capitalism and those who had not.

Although the PT initially claimed to represent a broad social movement, for its first few years it remained essentially an extension of the CUT. CUT unionists held important positions in the party, and the party insisted on taking direction from the labor federation rather than the reverse. The party made few electoral gains at first: as the next chapter suggests, before the PT could win electoral victories, the "new unionism" from which it emerged had to strengthen alliances with the communities in which workers and their families lived, to build a broader support base. On the other hand, in their insistence that workers' shop-floor experiences and organization should shape political activity, CUT and PT leaders challenged the terms on which even left-wing unionism had previously operated in Brazil: instead of asking workers to vote for established politicians, the PT insisted on retaining an independent identity and ideology.

By the early 1980s, after nearly twenty years of military rule, a different kind of unionism had emerged in precisely the industrial sectors created by the military regime's industrialization strategy. As economic conditions worsened, labor activists drew on community support to build shop-floor organizations; especially in large capital-intensive factories, workers could challenge employer control, but they required community support to withstand repression, to create strike funds, and to prevent employers from hiring replacement workers. As the labor movement grew, its emphasis on shop-floor organization—shaped largely by its leaders' experiences in heavy industry—expanded to an insistence on independent working-class organization, led by worker leaders and free of ties to non-worker political groups. This insistence on independence would erode as the recession worsened and the labor movement and the PT sought support beyond the factories of São Paulo's periphery; but as chapter 5 will suggest, the labor movement's initial emphasis on factory-based organization meant that its articulation of a separate working-class identity and interests would shape the way community issues were expressed during the transition from military rule.

SOUTH AFRICA: "THE SPIRIT LIVES"

In 1973, nearly a hundred thousand African workers in South Africa downed tools, taking employers, the state, and even worker activists by surprise. Much as Brazil's *reposição* campaign and the 1978 strikes relegitimized workers' demands in the public arena, the 1973 strike wave initiated a new era of worker organization in South Africa. Over the subsequent decade, black workers painstakingly built the nonracial unions that eventually formed the Congress of South African Trade Unions (COSATU); gradually, despite repression, the unions built a national organization with a strong shop-floor presence.

In their earliest phase, the new unions tended to focus on shop-floor demands. After 1976, however, when a student uprising and a recession created new divisions between employers and the state, the new unions increasingly challenged existing labor arrangements. Economic and political demands were as intertwined in South Africa as in Brazil: the state's constant presence on the shop-floor was unmistakable. Nevertheless, South Africans unionists—shaped by the experience of shop-floor mobilization within the large industrial factories that grew up in the previous decades of rapid economic growth—initially stressed the separable identity of workers, distinct from a broader political opposition. As in Brazil, the discourse developed within the labor movement would gradually come to shape the broader opposition, so that the anti-apartheid movement increasingly became a movement organized around class as well as racial issues. Reflecting that shift, full citizenship—the goal of the broader opposition—was redefined to include economic and social rights as well as the vote.

THE 1973 STRIKES

Like Brazil's 1978 strikes, the Durban strikes of 1973 seemed spontaneous: early on the morning of January 9, 1973, a small group of workers from the Coronation Brick and Tile company woke up fellow workers at the company dormitories, telling them to go to a nearby football stadium instead of the plant. Chanting in Zulu, "Man is dead but his spirit still lives," nearly 2,000 workers marched behind a large red flag to the stadium, demanding the company raise its minimum wage from R 8.97 to R 20 a week.[126] Refusing "to negotiate with 1,500 workers on a football field," and apparently unable to resuscitate a defunct factory works committee, the company made several offers to raise wages before the workers agreed to return to work.

Meanwhile, strikes broke out in several other nearby factories, inspired at least in part by news of the Coronation Brick and Tile strike. "What had been a trickle of strike action began to turn into a wave,"[127] and by the end of the year, nearly a hundred thousand workers had gone on strike. Although the strike wave remained centered in Durban, there were strikes in the Transvaal and the Eastern Cape; workers classified "Indian" and "Coloured" joined African workers on strike at a range of industries and mines. Repression continued: in late 1973, police shot thirty-eight workers, killing twelve, during a miners' strike near Johannesburg.[128] But the strike wave clearly changed workers' perceptions of the possibilities of industrial action. In Durban, a random survey of ninety-five African workers found 42 percent of the respondents had experienced some form of work stoppage; 70 percent reported workers returned to work only when promised a raise. The study found most workers prepared to strike again and concluded that the most important result might lie not so much in higher wages as in workers' "sense of their own potential power."[129] The police failure to break the strikes was equally important: as a sympathetic white unionist concluded, the 1973 strikes "taught workers that the sky wouldn't fall on their heads if they struck."[130]

As in Brazil, a small group of workers within the factory initiated the first strikes, and the work stoppage spread rapidly through the area. No organizer could have predicted success: after nearly a decade of labor repression, organizers could not have known how many workers would respond. But, in retrospect, a series of developments seem to have helped lay a basis for the strike wave. First, several smaller strikes, though generally unsuccessful, had publicly raised the issues of working conditions, wages, and the possibilities of worker organization, much as Brazil's campaign for *reposição* had done. A large strike among Namibian diamond miners in 1971 and strikes by Durban and Cape Town dockworkers in late 1972 demonstrated not only that workers could organize, but that they might win pay increases. Anonymous leaflets had called for a mass train boycott against high fares just before the Durban strikes; although the boycott failed to materialize, and although SACTU organizers probably had no direct involvement in the Coronation Brick and Tile strike, observers at the time saw a possible connection in the timing of collective action.[131]

Secondly, student and clandestine worker activists had begun to initiate workers' organizations in the early 1970s. Some university students, mainly but not all white, began to argue that the key to challenging apartheid lay in black workers' ability to halt production. From 1971 on, student activists used resources available through liberal student groups to help worker organization, providing statistical information about rising living costs and industrial conditions, publicizing legal channels available to black workers seeking to raise wages. The Durban Wages Commission, affiliated to the National Union of South African Students (NUSAS), called meetings to talk to workers about low wages and collective action.[132] Students who had researched conditions on the docks provided information on wage levels before the 1972 Durban dockworkers' strike.[133] In Cape Town in August 1972, students distributed pamphlets informing dockworkers about the upcoming wage board hearing. About a hundred workers, three students, and "last but not least, two members of the Security Branch who . . . only stayed for about half the meeting" attended a meeting where workers told the wage board—which normally heard only from employers—that wages and working conditions had become intolerable.[134] Soon afterward, the Cape Town dockworkers went on strike.[135]

Following this success, university students tried to raise issues of wages and worker organization in industries as diverse as glass and glassware manufacturing, soap- and candle-making, and stone crushing.[136] Off-campus, Durban students joined white liberals and hundreds of black workers in forming the General Factory Workers' Benefit Fund in 1972, "to make workers aware of their rights and to assist them in making representations to the Government Wage Board hearings," calling open meetings where workers could discuss the possibilities of forming unions.[137]

Like Brazilian labor statisticians, then, student activists publicized information about low wage levels, underscoring the legitimacy of economic grievances. After 1973, many of the individuals who had worked with student Wages Commissions or the General Factory Workers' Benefit Fund formed the Trade Union Advisory and Coordinating Council (TUACC) and the Durban Institute for Industrial Education, where Durban workers received training and assistance.[138] In Johannesburg, students were equally involved in helping set up fledgling organizations: when a janitor at the wage board offices told a group of black workers who wanted higher wages that University of Witwatersrand students might help, the workers went to the Wages Commission and were offered help in organizing a union. Partly as a result, the Wages Commission established the Industrial Aid Society to assist "emerging groups of workers." The society eventually hired its own organizers for a new metalworkers' union in the Transvaal region.[139]

Clandestine activity by activists linked to the South African Congress of Trade Unions also played some role in the 1973 strikes, although even in the 1990s, the history of clandestine organizing remained murky. Although SACTU was never formally banned inside South Africa, most of its leaders were in jail or in exile in the 1970s, and links to SACTU exposed one to arrest for "furthering the aims" of the illegal ANC; even in the mid 1980s, SACTU activists and South African Communist Party activists in the union movement kept their identities secret. Because open identification remained dangerous, it is difficult to weigh SACTU's role in the early period of the labor movement. Some organizers inside the country were certainly in touch with the exiled SACTU leadership. In 1972, SACTU quietly opened an office in Durban; since the labor federation was officially legal, organizers hoped to rebuild a labor organization, inviting workers to join a general union.[140] Organizers from that office may have had links to the dockworkers' strike. The SACTU recruitment drive was closed down soon afterward, however, apparently because its organizers decided to work within the less-risky overt unions rather than to set up an underground movement, which might invite arrests.[141] Similarly, in Cape Town, former SACTU activists apparently decided in 1972 that it would be safer to join university students in creating a Western Province Workers' Advisory Bureau than to maintain links with the exiled SACTU structure.[142] Contact between SACTU's exiled officers and activists did not end completely, however; for example, there was clandestine contact between some students in the Wages Commission and SACTU in 1974,[143] and other contacts certainly continued through the 1980s.

Whatever direct role SACTU played in the early 1970s, there can be little doubt that some former activists, and the legacy of previous organizing drives, helped lay a basis for the Durban strikes and the first stirrings of new worker organization in the early 1970s. Former SACTU organizers returned from jail or hiding to help form organizations in the 1970s. In some regions at least, SACTU's earlier efforts had left workers with a sense of the potential power of worker organization: one survey found 11 percent of members of Durban's unregistered unions in 1975 willing to admit they had once belonged to SACTU unions, while nearly 10 percent listed as a leader who "could improve the position of African workers" Moses Mabhida, a SACTU organizer in Natal who later became secretary-general of the South African Communist Party.[144] In its first annual report, TUACC's Metal and Allied Workers' Union (MAWU) attributed "a high degree of consciousness" among Natal workers to SACTU's legacy. Sounding almost embarrassed, the report explains that MAWU had been compelled to accept members from the Sarmcol rubber tire factory in Howick who had previously been organized by a SACTU activist. When the Sarmcol rubber workers heard that MAWU was holding a general meeting in a Pietermaritzburg church, they attended in force, demanding that MAWU admit them under the "allied workers" rubric.[145] (Over the next decade, the Sarmcol plant was marked by a remarkable degree of militance, with a strike in the 1980s that involved an entire community over several years.)

As in Brazil, then, there were several resources for the emergent labor movement to draw on: students and intellectuals publicized information about low wages, legitimizing workers' grievances both to workers and the general public, while worker activists had already begun to lay a basis for collective action within factories. Networks of clandestine factory activists in both countries provided an invisible layer of shop-floor organization among semi-skilled workers. Under these circumstances, employers generally preferred to negotiate, since repression would have required firing entire work forces. The geographic concentration of the first successful strike waves around São Paulo and around Durban certainly reflects the degree of industrial concentration in both countries and the extent to which industrial workers were located in single regions; but it may also reflect the importance of informal clandestine networks in creating "spontaneous" collective action, linking worker activists, and tying together small groups in different factories across a region.

BUILDING ORGANIZATION

Most histories of recent South African labor militance date the emergent unions from the Durban strikes. It is probably more accurate, however, to consider the period from 1973 to 1979 a kind of prehistory, in which activists gradually created a basis for organization but made few concrete gains. Unionists confronted several problems. First, black South African workers had virtually no legal union bodies; where Brazilian activists could sometimes work within existing unions, South African activists generally had to begin from scratch. Over the next six years, workers and organizers around the country would slowly create networks, organizations, training programs, and a labor press. The process was painstaking and dangerous: the minutes of early union meetings are filled with reports of arrests and harassment of organizers, shortages of funds and transport, and the need for basic union education. It took time for employers to accept the idea of negotiating with black workers. Although wildcat strikes occurred regularly around the country, workers who joined unions risked dismissal, and employers often called on the state to identify and arrest "agitators."[146] Many factories went on sympathy strikes when union activists were fired, but victimization weakened organizing drives through the 1970s. Unionists were repeatedly detained, banned, and charged with violating security laws.[147] Many employers cooperated fully with the security police; for example, a Swiss subsidiary informed its parent company in 1978 that it would not recognize black unions because they were "suspect for political aims (Marxist/Leninist),"[148] while many employers continued to insist that "these so-called unions" were mere "off-springs [*sic*] of political bodies."[149] Employer attitudes toward unions would only shift as unions strengthened their organization and ties to workers' communities, and as state-business conflict prompted employers to seek a new accommodation with the country's black majority.

Even among workers, however, attitudes had to change before labor organizations could take root. Most African workers had little understanding of how unions could help them: most legal unions had become bastions of white privilege, and for black workers the threat of repression remained palpable. In 1975, TUACC organizers in Durban debated furiously whether the unions, then down to a trickle of members, should focus on publicizing rising living costs and low wages or simply emphasize the possibility that black workers could form unions: either campaign seemed outside the realm of safety. Finally, organizers agreed to begin with house visits to meet workers and discuss unionization on relatively safe territory.[150] Similarly, in Johannesburg, organizers from MAWU (Transvaal) would meet workers outside factory gates during their lunch breaks, sitting in parks to discuss the purposes unions could serve.[151]

The new unions were always short of funds: even a membership fee of twenty South African cents was too much to ask from many workers. Most nonracial unions were reluctant even to seek stop-orders, fearing that even if employers were to agree, bureaucratization would distance union officials from still-shaky memberships.[152] Emphasizing factory-based support, the nonracial unions were also reluctant to depend on donations from international union federations—although, despite an explicit policy against such donations, most did so when they needed funds for specific projects, such as a legal advice bureau or educational training programs.[153]

Despite these problems, the new movement began to expand from the mid 1970s on. Workers in factories across the country engaged in work stoppages to back up their demands, demanding direct negotiations with employers. Between 1974 and 1979, an average of 27,140 workers struck annually, costing about 45,000 person-days each year. Although the figure includes up to 5,000 white workers on strike each year, the difference from the 1966–72 period, when the annual average number of strikers was below 4,000, was obvious.[154] Even more frequent were shorter work stoppages and refusals to accept overtime, as workers rejected employers' attempts to increase productivity. These strikes and work stoppages were increasingly supported by new labor institutions—a labor press, labor lawyers, shop-stewards' training courses—which helped link the single-factory bases of most strikes of this period. By the mid 1970s, despite continual harassment, small union groupings in Natal and the Transvaal began to organize regional meetings to coordinate local union activities.

As they gained experience, union organizers and workers discovered new organizing strategies. When employers refused to recognize independent unions, union members sometimes ran for election as delegates to employer-controlled works or liaison committees. Although these committees rarely succeeded in winning shop-floor improvements, the discussions provided a forum in which union members could raise issues affecting workers, from wages and transport services to occasional discussions of state policies affecting the workplace.[155] Thus, even though unionists considered the committee system inadequate, many of them used it to express workers' demands—much as activists in Brazil sometimes used the corporatist unions as a channel for raising shop-floor issues.

In the early stages of union organizing, many organizers believed that their best hope for organizing workers lay in heavy industry, especially consumer durables industries. In Brazil, activists recognized the privileged position of the automobile industry in the government's economic development strategy; South African unionists similarly designed strategies with the political context and tactical considerations in mind. In 1974, for example, the Natal metalworkers' union argued that workers in large plants might be safer from victimization talking to fellow-workers about unionizing than workers in small enterprises; furthermore, many of these large plants were subsidiaries of foreign corporations, which might be susceptible to pressure from overseas unions and politicians.[156] Especially in view of the possibility of support from international labor federations like the International Metalworkers' Federation, the metalworkers appeared to have a good chance of employer recognition.

The number of large strikes in metal or automobile factories, involving both male and female semi- and low-skilled workers, is particularly impressive in view of the metal industry's strong opposition to African unionization. In 1973, the Steel and Engineering Industry Federation (SEIFSA), the metal industry's employer association, advised members to call in the police "if at any time it appears that law and order are in danger," and it continued to resist union recognition through the 1970s.[157] No metal foundry recognized a union representing black workers until after the state regularized nonracial unions in 1979, and until SEIFSA appointed a new, relatively liberal, personnel consultant[158]—at a time when job reservation laws were finally removed and plants were becoming increasingly dependent on African semi-skilled workers.

Even in the mid 1970s, when there was little chance of winning union recognition, however, black metalworkers' unions in Natal, the Transvaal, and the Eastern Cape struggled to keep up with workers' demands for assistance and representation. In some cases, African workers mobilized because they were paid less than non-African workers for the same work.[159] In others, workers struck for channels through which to articulate grievances. The fact that Indian and Coloured workers had access to such channels apparently reinforced worker support for unionization and may sometimes have strengthened worker solidarity across racial lines. For example, although Africans and Indians worked on the same assembly line at a Defy Industries factory, in 1975 only Indians could join a registered union. When grievances arose over the bonus system, both Indian and African workers struck, demanding the right to a nonracial negotiating system.[160] This kind of cross-racial organization—strongly encouraged by the newly emergent network of labor institutions—laid the basis for the nonracial labor unions that emerged in the political opening that followed the 1976 Soweto student uprising, challenging South Africa's decades-long history of segregated unionism.

THE AFTERMATH OF 1976

In many ways, 1976 can be seen as a turning point for the new labor movement: as chapter 3 suggested, the student uprising and subsequent repression forced activists and employers to reconsider their attitudes toward worker organization. But even if there had not been a student uprising, the labor movement might still have taken off. In late March 1976—nearly three months before the June 16 Soweto students' demonstration that started the student uprising—workers at a Heinemann Electric factory near Johannesburg struck for union recognition. Led by organizers from the Metal and Allied Workers' Union (Tvl),[161] workers rejected Heinemann's in-house liaison committee because it neither met

regularly nor dealt with issues workers considered important; just before the strike, the committee's worker members resigned. Management
refused to negotiate. With police on the premises, the company first
fired 20 union activists and then dismissed the entire work force, promising that individuals could reapply for their jobs. When they arrived at
the factory for the start of the next work week, Heinemann's workers,
about a third of whom were women, were brutally beaten and arrested
while waiting outside the factory. Two MAWU (Tvl) organizers, both
injured, were charged with breaking security laws; the magistrate found
them guilty of inciting the strike, but argued that their presence did not
provoke the labor dispute. Despite the magistrate's finding, about 300
of the plant's original 606 workers were not rehired because they refused to accept a liaison committee instead of union recognition.[162]

The Heinemann strike received a great deal of publicity, reviving
public debate about South African labor laws. Government officials remained intent on suppressing union organization. In May 1976, the
minister of justice warned that "fully-fledged underground political agitators and organizers [had begun to implement] a centrally-directed
plan for the organization and mobilization of workers" in trade unions,
"not with a view to improving the black man's bargaining position,
[but] to use eventual strikes as sparks to revolution."[163] A leading liberal Johannesburg newspaper warned: "Widespread black labor unrest—which could cripple the economy—is imminent unless immediate
steps are taken to strike a 'new deal' with workers," going on to editori-
alize: "Labor disputes are settled by negotiations, by spokesmen of
management and workers talking around tables as equals. Labour
peace and improved race relations do not come with batons and police
dogs."[164] Trade unionists warned of growing worker militance.[165]
Even Andries Grobbelaar, the conservative leader of the segregated
Trade Union Council, warned that police violence during the Heinemann strike "turned the clock back" on labor relations and would be
seen overseas as "another crude attempt to stifle black workers' aspirations."[166]

In 1976, however, international outrage focused on the repression of
students, not workers. In mid June, police shot students demonstrating
against inferior education; severe repression of the subsequent uprising
prompted an international outcry, causing a sharp drop in foreign investment and renewed international discussion of economic sanctions.
By late 1977 the uprising appeared to have been repressed. The state

embarked on its "total strategy"to contain black resistance, while business leaders scrambled to find more moderate reform proposals.

Although student organizations called on parents to stay away from work in support of student demands, they failed to build organizational links with unions; attempts to mobilize worker support generally failed.[167] Nevertheless, the 1976 Soweto students' uprising had three direct effects on the labor movement. First, many unionists were detained in the wave of arrests that followed the uprising; it could be argued that the security police used the student uprising as an excuse to attack trade unions. Second, however, as part of the outcry against apartheid, international and local business leaders began to insist on labor law reform; even Barlow Rand, the South African conglomerate that owned Heinemann, argued that the industrial conciliation system needed "drastic revision" to allow workers to express their demands in an orderly fashion.[168]

Lastly, the uprising and subsequent repression changed both workers and activists' attitudes toward unions. During the three months at the height of the student uprising, students distributed pamphlets to workers at bus stops and on township streets, calling on them to strike in support of their children; years later, workers on the East Rand attributed increased worker militance after 1976 to anger at repression and shame that students had taken the lead in resisting apartheid. One worker told an interviewer that after the uprising, "We talked a lot. About injustice. About what they are doing to us. About having no self-respect, no dignity in us. It was because of people like us that everybody [was] suffering in this country."[169] Meanwhile, the repression suffered by student organizations—culminating in the murder in detention of the Black Consciousness leader Steve Biko and the bannings of all Black Consciousness and student organizations in late 1977—prompted many political activists to reconsider their strategies, seeking ways to mobilize adults who had failed to participate in the uprising. Recognizing that students were relatively powerless, many activists left school and began to work in factories, where demands could be backed by strikes and work stoppages.[170]

For individual activists, the move to factory organization was often accompanied by a gradual shift in ideological position. Some former student organizers formed all-black unions, following the Black Consciousness philosophy that had generally informed student organizations.[171] But many, perhaps most, former students joined already-existing independent unions, most of which recruited members on the basis of economic position, not race. This emphasis on class—and thus nonracialism—arose largely from practical considerations, as well as from SACTU's insistence on racially mixed unions. By nature, industrial unions tend to emphasize workers' economic position, not racial identity. Racially divided unions would only reinforce divisions in the labor force; many unionists believed that emphasizing the racial classification of members and organizers—distinguishing between the interests of "Coloured," "Indian," and "African" workers, or white and black organizers—could only weaken unions' potential strength.[172] Moreover, the fact that white activists were helping organize militant unions and publish labor journals undercut arguments based entirely on race.

In practice, although most of their worker members were black, and although conservative white unions continued to reject black worker organization, participation in the nonracial unions reshaped activists' discourse around apartheid, toward an emphasis on class rather than race: unionists generally insisted that members should be treated as individual members of the working class, not as members of racial categories. By the early 1980s, the principle of nonracialism became dominant within the independent labor movement. In 1982, the death of a white organizer in police detention prompted the labor movement's first national work stoppage; Neil Aggett's death underlined the contribution of a handful of whites to building the labor movement. The principle of nonracialism was sometimes strictly enforced: in 1982 a (black) general secretary was suspended after suggesting that white intellectuals were manipulating the labor movement,[173] an episode that reaffirmed a growing insistence that class interests, rather than race, were what mattered.

Similarly, unions tended to downplay ethnic differences between members. In many South African factories, workers were divided along ethnic lines: factory subsections were sometimes considered the domain of specific language groups, while dormitory assignments in migrant hostels often reflected administrators' views of fixed ethnic divisions. From early on, however, both Black Consciousness and nonracial unions rejected ethnicity as an organizing principle. Recognizing that the overlay of ethnic divisions on top of labor process distinctions threatened collective action, organizers generally rejected any claim that ethnic identities were fixed, or that they determined workers' participation in labor relations.[174]

In part, the absence of overt ethnic conflict within the new unions might reflect regional migration patterns: most of South Africa's industrial centers tend to draw African workers from particular areas. Thus, Durban's workers primarily come from Zulu-speaking areas, while African workers in the Eastern Cape generally speak Xhosa. In the country's industrial center, around Johannesburg, workers came from several language groups, but labor organizations generally resisted any temptation to appeal to ethnic identities. The extent to which this principle had become dominant in labor organizing, and the extent to which workers rejected ethnic appeals, became clear in the mid 1980s, when the revived Inkatha Yenkululeko Yesizwe—an organization that retained its original identity as Zulu-only—appealed to Zulu-speaking workers to organize a new union federation, the Union of Workers of South Africa (UWUSA). If ethnic identities had been primary, this new federation should have quickly developed branches among Zulu-speaking workers in Natal and in the Johannesburg region. Throughout the 1970s, nonracial unions, especially in Natal, had tried to remain neutral toward Inkatha and its leader, KwaZulu Prime Minister Mangosuthu (Gatsha) Buthelezi, to avoid forcing workers to choose between ethnic and class identities. By the mid 1980s, COSATU members in Inkatha-dominated areas found themselves under attack, apparently because Inkatha viewed the labor movement as allied to the underground ANC, and as a threat to a unified Zulu identity.[175] But Inkatha failed in its attempt to replace COSATU with a Zulu-identified labor movement. Apparently, Zulu-speaking workers who had already joined unions were relatively uninterested in UWUSA's ethnic appeal.[176] Although some COSATU members held Inkatha membership, activism in nonracial unions generally seems to have offered an alternative identity for workers, at least while they remained in urban settings.[177]

SHOP-FLOOR ORGANIZATION

By 1979, when thirteen of the largest independent, or unregistered, unions formed the Federation of South African Trade Unions (FOSATU), the nonracial unions reported an average paid-up membership of 1,200 workers. Several unregistered unions stayed out of the federation, either because they wanted to preserve their structure as general workers' unions, or because they were all-black rather than nonracial. (While these non-FOSATU independent unions were important in the development of the labor movement, their membership tended to be small, and their political direction seemed during the early 1980s to be outside the labor movement's mainstream. The fact that the remainder of this chapter focuses almost entirely on FOSATU unions and leaders should not be interpreted as disparaging the importance of non-FOSATU unions in the nonracial movement; in chapter 5's discussion of community-union relations, many of these unions will reappear as important players.)

FOSATU dominated the first phase of legalized black unionism: its membership and organizational capacity far outweighed those of the other independent unions, and its leaders' philosophies shaped organizing strategies and campaigns in the early 1980s. With the growth of community mobilization, the "workerist" philosophy that was often identified with FOSATU would be eclipsed by a broader definition of organizing goals, and the non-FOSATU unions would play a more prominent role in shaping union philosophies; but to understand the trajectory of the South African labor movement as a whole—particularly the emphasis on class identity and interests—one must first examine the rise of factory-level organizations and FOSATU.

At its founding, the new federation was firmly based in the metal and auto industry—precisely those industries that had grown most rapidly in the previous two decades, and in which black workers had moved into semi-skilled positions. The initial proposal for a national federation came from an auto union,[178] and workers in heavy industry dominated FOSATU's membership and leadership. While the four unions representing metalworkers or automobile workers averaged over 2,500 members each, five of FOSATU's eight other affiliates had fewer than 500 members each.[179] Four of the six individuals considered most influential during FOSATU's first year came from metal unions.[180] Lengthy discussions during FOSATU's formation about metal union mergers suggest the extent to which issues relevant to heavy industry were key in the federation.[181]

Given the metalworkers' numerical weight in FOSATU, it is not surprising that workers' experiences in heavy industry were reflected in its initial strategies. Private metal and auto firms were among the largest in South Africa; they were often partly or wholly foreign-owned; and the fact that they had expanded since the late 1960s had radically altered the racial composition of skilled and semi-skilled work. As in Brazil, metalworkers' unions tended to represent a new generation of workers: younger, more educated black workers who had grown up under apartheid, who had always lived in urban areas, and who had little experience of previous unionism, were most likely to move into the new semi-skilled and skilled positions as they opened up. In language remarkably close to Brazilian sociologist da Silva's description of the CUT unions, South African sociologist Eddie Webster persuasively argues that by the early 1980s,

> [C]hanges in the labour process [within the metal industry] created the conditions for a new form of workplace organization. A mass-based, non-racial, industrial union has emerged. . . .
>
> By establishing independent working class organizations, the emerging unions have created the embryo of a working class politics in South Africa.[182]

Despite SEIFSA's strong opposition to black worker organization, employers with capital-intensive production technology and large plants faced increasing pressure to negotiate with new unions. At the national level, MAWU's changing membership reflected the shifting composition of the labor force and of skill levels of black workers in the metal industry.[183] In 1975 nearly 90 percent of MAWU's five thousand members were classified as unskilled or lower semi-skilled, but within five years its thirty thousand members had moved into positions crucial to meeting production schedules.[184] By 1979, employers in the metal industry could no longer afford to ignore the potential disruption that African workers organized at the point of production could cause.

Two factors may have made automobile workers especially prone to militance. First, in the late 1970s, a growing threat of unemployment may have increased workers' willingness to join strikes: increased automation coincided with falling demand for cars during the recession of the late 1970s, raising turnover among auto industry artisans to 58 percent a year;[185] if Brazilian workers struck at a time when auto firms were expanding productivity, South African workers struck in a recession. Through 1979 and 1980, Port Elizabeth's automobile factories were repeatedly on strike, as workers supported by local community groups demanded union recognition.[186] Indeed, it could be argued that the 1979 strikes in the automobile industry of the Eastern Cape were the final straw prompting the state to legalize nonracial unions completely: although the Eastern Cape was certainly unusual in both the high level of unemployment among industrial workers and the strength of its community organizations, the auto strikes seemed to herald a new and uncontrollable wave of industrial action, which could only be prevented by allowing unions some legal channels for expressing workers' demands.

Second, as in Brazil, multinational automobile companies may have been more willing to negotiate with black unions because of pressure from abroad. Ford promised in 1973 that it would recognize any union representing more than 50 percent of the work force, and in 1977, despite white workers' objections, it allowed black employees to sign stop-orders for union dues.[187] That policy probably reinforced worker militance rather than reducing it: in 1980, Ford workers struck against the dismissal of a popular community leader, ignoring union officers' efforts to mediate.[188] But Ford's union policy may been a realistic response to the changing racial composition of its work force, following changes in the labor process and in job reservation laws: between 1971 and 1979, the number of African and Coloured skilled workers at Ford had increased by 48 percent; even more important, while the overall number of semi-skilled workers had declined by 14 percent, the percentage of semi-skilled workers who were African rose from 7 to 38.[189]

Whether or not its direction can be directly attributed to metalworkers' experiences, FOSATU was remarkable for its insistence on strong shop-floor organization. For much of the emergent movement, faith in a shop-steward system became a kind of credo; elected shop-stewards, united through shop-stewards' councils, were seen as a way to ensure a union presence on the shop floor, as well as the articulation of workers' concerns within the union leadership.[190] While the shop-steward system remained relatively weak through most of the 1970s, once unions were legal and recognized, it became the federation's basic structure.

As part of its emphasis on factory-level organization, FOSATU rejected political alliances, insisting instead on forming an "independent" working-class organization.[191] The reasoning was both strategic and principled. Unionists from Natal often avoided political alliances because they sought to avoid the influence of Chief Buthelezi;[192] unionists from the Eastern Cape's metal and automobile industries, on the other hand, generally argued that it was "only through an understanding of the specific nature of factory struggle, the organizational needs and tactical niceties specific to industrial action" that unions could consolidate their position.[193] Some unionists feared that community or political groups might subsume workers' interests under broader populist slogans, reducing the class content of union campaigns; others argued that community leaders might overlook shop-floor demands, weakening workers' support for unions; still others feared that ties to overtly political groups might invite state repression of still-fragile shop-floor organizations, or divide workers according to political loyalties.[194]

Taking up political issues invited repression. Unlike in Brazil, where the Catholic church had provided a relatively safe arena in which community and union activists could meet, in South Africa there were few arenas in which black political activists could safely discuss broad political goals. On the other hand, the geographic concentration of heavy industry, especially in the Eastern Cape and on the East Rand, allowed unionists to organize in communities as well as in factories. Since the early 1970s, unions had started organizing drives through general meetings in communities: workers who attended were asked to begin organizing within their factories. Once workers had developed some form of internal shop-floor organization, they could then call in organizers to approach employers with their demands.[195]

Even more than in Brazil, the question of national political organization was always present in union discussions: what would be the role of the new labor movement in the national liberation movement? Union relations with black communities were hotly debated. As the next chapter shows, some unions worked closely with communities and framed their demands in terms of community goals; most of these unions did not join FOSATU, partly because it rejected political alliances. But even FOSATU unionists recognized that community support was important to workers who lacked strike funds and the right to picket, and that the demand for union recognition posed an obvious challenge to political arrangements.

By the late 1970s, independent unions had learned to use community support to pressure employers, mobilizing consumer boycotts to support recognition drives. In the 1950s, SACTU and the ANC had called for a potato boycott to protest the use of prison labor, especially pass offenders, on private white-owned farms; although it emphasized labor issues, the boycott was primarily a symbolic protest against the pass system. In the 1970s, unions tended to use consumer boycotts more strategically, over specific, shop-floor-linked issues. The first, and perhaps the most dramatic, example was a boycott of a Cape Town wheat-milling firm that refused to negotiate with the Food and Canning Workers' Union. In April 1979, five union supporters were dismissed; instead of discussing the dismissals, management fired five more workers and called in the Department of Labour to threaten workers. The plant's 250 African and Coloured workers struck. Within weeks, support committees in major urban areas began to raise funds for striking workers— about forty of whom faced being returned to the Ciskei homeland— and to promote a consumer boycott. Leaflets emphasized the strike's political aspects, arguing not only that "workers need a strong and independent voice to speak to management" about working conditions and low wages,[196] but also that this boycott offered "a striking [sic] demonstration of nonracial solidarity,"[197] with workers at the plant "refusing to be separated by the color of their skins, and wishing to be treated *in toto* as employees of the firm—not as African and Coloured employees."[198] The firm attributed some of the fall in its profits to changes in the milling business,[199] but labor organizers were convinced the boycott had worked.[200] During the Fatti's and Moni's boycott, a nonracial sports association called a national consumer boycott of a potato chip company that sponsored white sporting events but refused to sponsor black cricket, successfully forcing the company to change its policy. Although it was over a purely political issue, the Simba Quix protest underlined the tactic's potential strength. By November, Fatti's and Moni's negotiated a settlement offering higher wages and reemployment.[201]

After the victory, unionists debated the extent to which the boycott had strengthened shop-floor organization. Although the union had initiated the boycott, its inability to control the groups that carried it out raised the question of how new shop-floor organizations should relate to larger political agendas.[202] But for employers, the Fatti's and Moni's boycott presented a new threat. Newspapers warned that boycotts were likely to affect other companies,[203] and over the next few years, unions became adept at threatening boycotts to get company recognition: in 1981, Colgate-Palmolive agreed to negotiate with the Chemical Workers' Industrial Union days before a boycott was scheduled to begin.[204] Consumer boycotts worked especially well against companies producing lighter consumer goods for the domestic market, and meant that even less-skilled workers in labor-intensive industries could draw on support from black consumers united by apartheid.

By 1979, then, the labor movement could mount a serious threat to production and sales levels. In 1977, the government appointed the Wiehahn Commission to recommend changes in the labor law, and by 1979, while individual employers continued to refuse to negotiate with unregistered unions,[205] every employers' association in the country—including the Afrikaanse Handelsinstituut—supported the creation of legal channels for workers' grievances. The state and employers were at least as interested in controlling the independent unions as in improving communication: the government's reform proposals initially offered African workers bargaining rights, but insisted on racially segregated unions that would completely exclude migrant workers. When the unions rejected the proposals, the government reversed itself: for the first time, unions would be free to define their own membership, both in terms of racial categories and residence requirements.[206]

Nevertheless, the new labor movement fiercely debated whether or not to register. Distrust of the white minority state ran deep: why should a state that had previously repressed all attempts to organize black workers allow them to operate freely?[207] Many unionists believed that participation in industrial councils—where for decades employers and white union representatives had negotiated industrywide settlements without regard to black workers' interests—would narrow the unions' focus to economic demands and create unrepresentative, powerless bureaucratic entities.[208] In 1981, a conference of nonracial trade unions rejected registration, recommending that unions stay outside the legal framework.[209]

Why, then, did many of the nonracial unions eventually decide to register in the early 1980s? It could be argued that most unionists only agreed to involvement in state structures because they had little choice. The benefits of remaining outside the industrial system were reduced as the state gradually removed the legal distinctions between registered and unregistered organizations. Moreover, rising unemployment threatened shop-floor organization: participation in the system offered some hope of winning concrete gains for members. While the nonracial unions were strong enough to reject state definition of their potential membership—particularly attempts to privilege some sections of the working class over others, by denying union membership to migrant workers—their shop-floor strength varied from factory to factory. Employers often tried to create in-house unions or to promote "parallel" unions (segregated unions allied to registered white bodies) instead of negotiating with nonracial unions.[210] As Chloride's liberal personnel manager pointed out, even employers willing to diffuse shop-floor tensions were often reluctant to recognize unions over which they did not have complete control—especially if those unions might be linked to underground political movements, whose demands might be outside the purview of individual employers.[211]

Once legal channels existed, however, employers tended to insist on them, and unionists tended to use them. For metalworkers, the choice was relatively stark. In 1981, nearly eleven thousand metalworkers struck for union recognition in the Johannesburg area,[212] and by 1982, the figure had reached nearly fifty thousand. Nevertheless, the steel and iron employers' association, SEIFSA, refused to negotiate except with registered unions. Faced with retrenchments of nearly 20 percent of the metal industry's labor force, MAWU decided in 1983 to negotiate through the national Industrial Council.[213] Employers outside the metal industry were only slightly more flexible than SEIFSA. Employers in the relatively liberal FCI and ASSOCOM (Associated Chambers of Commerce) urged registration, reminding unions that recognition remained "the employer's prerogative."[214]

At the same time, many unionists began to believe they could gain some benefits through registration. First, lawyers representing registered unions began to win significant gains in labor courts, defining many standard employer tactics as unfair labor practices: now black workers could fight racial insults or victimization in court rather than through work stoppages.[215] Second, it became clear that the state retained powerful mechanisms for destroying union solidarity: a series of strikes involving primarily unskilled migrant workers, in which striking migrants lost their permits to work in white-designated areas, underlined fears that unrecognized unions would be unable to protect their members.[216] Finally, despite overall economic expansion,[217] rising unemployment reinforced unionists' fears that unregistered unions would be unable protect strikers' jobs. Faced with a choice between registration or continual recognition battles, many independent unions began to consider registration a tactical decision rather than an issue of principle.[218]

Both the debate over alliances with community groups and the registration debate reflected a deeper question confronting labor activists: to what extent, and how, should the labor movement take up the broad political issues created by apartheid? Like employers, union leaders in the early 1980s realized that workers' demands would inevitably focus on the state. However, unions could take up political issues in different ways. Workers could strike for strictly political goals, in coalition with community groups. On the other hand, workers could challenge state policies indirectly; for example, in 1980, workers struck to persuade employers to ask for the postponement of a new pension law.[219] In the early 1980s, when nonracial unions were first learning to use legal mechanisms to win shop-floor gains, many prominent unionists elevated their distrust of political alliances into a principle: engaging in community struggles, they argued, might weaken shop-floor organization and reduce the class content of workers' demands. FOSATU unionists, in particular, tended to insist that workers' organizations should remain distinct from the broader anti-apartheid movement. FOSATU's structure was designed to ensure worker control over policy-making through shop-steward councils and elected workers' leaders. Its officers insisted that the federation should represent members' interests as workers, not as community members.

In 1980, FOSATU's executive committee warned: "As a worker organization we must ensure that the efforts of our members and workers in general will be of benefit to them. All political parties and groups seek the support of workers but this does not mean that they have the interests of workers at heart."[220] At the second FOSATU congress, in April 1982, FOSATU's president, Joe Foster, argued that capitalist industrialization had changed the relationship between economic and political demands. Because "the growth and transformation of capital has created the very pre-conditions for large-scale organization," and required both more skilled workers and strategies to "deracialize" industry, unions could now mobilize workers independently, in a movement that would not subsume workers' interests under populist slogans:

> Workers must strive to build their own powerful and effective organization even whilst they are part of the wider popular struggle. This organization is necessary to protect further worker interests and to ensure that the popular movement is not hijacked by elements who in the end will have no option but to turn against their worker supporters.[221]

"Our concern," Foster said, "is with the very essence of politics and that is the relation between the major classes in South Africa, being capital and labor." FOSATU, he argued, should concentrate on building factory-based industrial unions in major industrial areas, carefully developing worker leadership, who would only later commit their factory-based organizational resources to support political campaigns.

The 1982 FOSATU congress adopted Foster's proposals, and for the next three years, FOSATU unionists avoided participation in political campaigns organized outside the labor movement. Often pointing to Brazil's Partido dos Trabalhadores and Poland's Solidarity as exemplars of the political expression of working-class interests, FOSATU's most prominent figures stressed class position; while they acknowledged the effect of racial domination, they tended to be more concerned about economic exploitation. At times, FOSATU unionists' refusal to acknowledge racial dynamics, or any community of interest based on racial segregation, bordered on the extreme: at the 1983 annual general meeting, the Metalworkers' Moses Mayekiso reminded union members, "The enemy is only one—capitalism—and all other things like influx control are merely appendages."[222]

The rejection of political alliances had real consequences. In mid 1983, FOSATU and most other nonracial unions decided not to join the United Democratic Front (UDF), a coalition of anti-apartheid groups formed to oppose the proposed constitution. The decision was controversial: UDF activists argued that by refusing to join overtly political campaigns, FOSATU unions ignored the way apartheid perpetuated the exploitation of workers who were black, and that a "formula for abstentionism" could indefinitely postpone labor's involvement in political campaigns.[223] But Foster's successor warned that only a movement based inside the workplace could avoid "being hijacked by opportunistic mass movements or political organizations"; alliances with "nonworker organizations" might "hinder or misdirect" the labor movement's strategy.[224] Although many union members actively supported UDF campaigns, FOSATU's leaders insisted that nationalist goals could not take precedence over the class struggle.[225]

Throughout the early 1980s, activists vigorously debated the question. Could unions representing mainly black workers stand aside from community issues? Should the labor movement's strategies reflect the interests only of union members, or did its constituency include workers' families, the unemployed, and workers in still-unorganized industries?[226] Even within FOSATU, some unionists argued that working-class interests extended beyond the factory.[227] But as in Brazil, the labor movement would only take up broad political goals when labor organization spread into new sectors and popular mobilization in working-class communities made it difficult for unionists to stand apart. By 1985, when FOSATU folded into the newly launched Congress of South African Trade Unions, the labor movement had expanded beyond its industrial beginnings to include black miners, service workers, and even domestic workers—workers whose organization at the point of production was almost inherently weaker than that of industrial workers and who required greater community support to win factory gains. Nevertheless, the emphasis on working-class organization and interests remained crucial to labor, and, as the next chapter suggests, the discourse developed in industrial unions continued to shape activists' involvement in community campaigns.

Ten years after the 1973 strike wave raised a new specter of black worker organization, then, patterns of organization in the nonracial labor movement had changed significantly, and, with them, unionists' demands and goals. In the early 1970s, workers demanded that employers recognize their human dignity, pay a just wage, and negotiate with chosen representatives; intermittent state repression underscored the political content of wildcat strikes and organizing drives. As shop-floor organization won legal channels for expression, many unionists expressed workers' demands in terms of factory-based interests, avoiding appeals to racial solidarity. Shop-floor militance, reflecting the experiences of a new generation of industrial workers, provided both a new organizational base and a new vocabulary, which would help reshape the broad opposition against the state.

LABOR MILITANCE IN BRAZIL AND SOUTH AFRICA

No one could argue that unionism was identical in Brazil and South Africa during the 1970s: completely different legal structures and traditions shaped the opportunities available to workers, so that unionists had to choose different organizational strategies and goals. Brazilian activists could use already-existing union structures and resources, although they challenged fundamental aspects of the labor code. In South Africa, where African workers had been excluded from legal unions, activists had first to create the resources on which a labor movement could draw and then struggle for the right to build nonracial unions in a racially segregated society.

Nevertheless, several similarities in the emergence of "new unionism" are unmistakable. First, labor organizations facing a repressive state moved quickly to organize national labor federations that could take up broad issues of national legislation and labor relations frameworks—a pattern that apparently mirrors the experience of early industrializers, where individual unions overcame their differences to insist on new labor legislation at the national level. But the similarities between these cases go further, and are perhaps more complex, than a simple equation of repression and politicization would suggest. In both cases, large strike waves suddenly interrupted a decade of industrial quiescence, with relatively little previous overt organization. Although in both cases students and activists linked to clandestine networks had raised the issues of wages and working conditions, activists seem to have been nearly as surprised as employers at the magnitude of the stoppages. Although they won relatively negligible material gains, these strikes raised worker demands in the public arena and gave workers a new sense of efficacy. Coming at moments already marked by tension between employers and states, the strikes provoked new debates among dominant classes over how to control the labor force; unwilling to repress the strikes, and unable to negotiate, industrial employers called on the state to permit new channels for the articulation of workers' grievances.

In both cases, the initial stoppages and fledgling organizations were centered among workers in the heavy industries that had grown up through authoritarian industrialization strategies. While workers in other sectors certainly responded quickly to new possibilities for industrial action and attempted to organize unions, the semi-skilled and skilled workers whose jobs had been created during the period of rapid growth seem to have been far more successful in making their demands heard than workers in areas like construction or mining, or workers in the large public sectors of both countries.

In both cases, metalworkers' unions shaped the initial strategies of the labor movement. Both labor movements concentrated on organizing at the shop-floor level among industrial workers, arguing that changes in the labor process, as well as vulnerabilities to international economic and political pressure, created new possibilities for winning employer recognition. The prominence of metalworkers in both labor movements may, of course, reflect something inherent in metalworking; organizers in both Brazil and South Africa sometimes suggested that the fact that metalworkers tended to be concentrated in large foundries and factories, and that they were relatively skilled, made it easier to go out on strike. Thus, Eddie Webster writes, "the introduction of machine-based production has undermined the traditional division of skill and race in the [South African] foundry. . . . Through their strategic location in the labor process these workers have been able to challenge the traditional form of control. . . . A mass-based, nonracial, industrial union has emerged for the first time."[228]

It is also true, however, that metalworkers' experiences typified more general changes in both industrial work forces since the beginning of the 1960s: relatively young, and more likely to have had some education, these industrial workers were far less likely than older workers to have experienced earlier labor defeats, or to retain strong identities outside the urban industrial context. Moreover, they confronted employers who were already concerned about labor shortages, who considered themselves relatively independent of state assistance, and who could engage in direct negotiations if they so chose; employers in the automobile industry, in particular, may have faced pressures from international labor groups and their own head offices to deal directly with their work forces.

Once workers had joined in industrial action, once their initial demands had been met by employers, these workers quickly recognized that industrial action held further possibilities and came to see labor organizations as a likely vehicle for expressing a range of demands. In both cases, activists in labor movements emphasized the importance of class interests within the broad political opposition. While they recognized that middle-class groups, sometimes even business leaders, opposed some state policies, the leaders of both labor movements insisted that workers had very different political interests from the rest of the "popular" opposition. In both Brazil and South Africa, labor leaders sought to build independent workers' movements that would express members' interests as workers. Labor leaders of the 1970s argued that industrialization had strengthened the industrial working class—both in terms of size, and through changes in labor processes—so that it no longer required upper- and middle-class allies to make shop-floor gains; indeed, they often suggested that multi-class alliances might weaken working-class movements. Organizationally, the labor movement emphasized worker representation at all levels of union organization and created new federations based on factory representatives. Mobilized within factories, in organizations that stressed class identity, workers defined their interests in terms of class position—even in South Africa, where the racial aspects of the class structure are unmistakable.

If Brazilian and South African workers had been mobilized against authoritarian regimes during the 1970s through some other form of organization—for example, through human rights movements or through broad political parties—would their interests have been so clearly defined by class position? Almost certainly, different forms of mobilization would have shaped workers' understanding of their interests differently; a broad-based popular movement against the state, for example, might have reinforced participants' identity as citizens rather than as worker citizens. But how successful would alternative forms of mobilization have been in the mid 1970s? Attempted student movements in both Brazil and South Africa in 1976–77 were severely repressed and seemed to hold little attraction for workers; community movements against the state were relatively powerless until after the labor movement was already well established.

Alternative channels of mobilization might have led workers to interpret their interests differently, but industrialization appears to have provided a structural basis for working-class mobilization; and perhaps only a movement based in shop-floor organization and industrial action could have been as widespread, as militant, and as resilient as both labor movements proved. Left-wing groups in both countries were informed by a class analysis, prompting them to begin organizing in factories. Did activists shape workers' perceptions of the shop-floor as a main site of oppression, or would the labor movement have emerged on its own? The fact that organizers were taken aback by the sudden spread of worker militance suggests that the wildcat strikes might have occurred even without the clandestine left: the strikes' success had as much to do with changes in the labor process as with underground networks. The emergent labor movement provided both an arena for overt organization and a mode of challenging employers and the state. While students and political activists certainly assisted the unions' organizational growth, in both Brazil and South Africa, shop-floor activism in the early 1970s clearly took root within the factories that had grown up over the previous decades, among metalworkers and other semi-skilled and skilled industrial workers.

With factories identified as a primary site of oppression, union members discussed organization in terms of class identities and interests. Especially when both the Brazilian and South African states prohibited political activism by unions, activists tended to emphasize demands related to wages, working conditions, shop-floor representation, direct negotiation with employers, and the creation of independent working-class organization, led by workers rather than by political activists.

Within a few years, however, both labor movements would shift away from their initial factory-based perspective: in both Brazil and South Africa, unionists would begin to appeal to a much broader constituency, redefining the working class to include a much larger community, and redefining goals to include democratization of the state. As chapter 5 will show, in working-class areas created by recent industrialization strategies and denied basic social resources by an authoritarian state, community organizations grew up alongside factory-based unions, supporting their growth and closely linked to union memberships. In both Brazil and South Africa, while unions initially focused on creating a working-class identity within the factory, that identity would be extended to include workers' families, the unemployed, and even the rural poor: instead of concentrating on workplace issues or representing a labor aristocracy, the new unions would seek to raise the wages and living standards of a broader working class, and to challenge the general exclusion of workers and their families from the processes of industrial development.

CHAPTER FIVE

Community Struggles and the Redefinition of Citizenship

> There is a division in society, and it was not we who created it. The *latifundário*'s plantation house is not the field hand's shack. The industrialist's meal is not the laborer's porridge. The banker's profit is not the salary of the bank employee. The neighborhood where the businessman lives is not the part of the periphery where the laborer lives. If we are separated socially and economically, how can we be united politically?
>
> *Statement by the Partido dos Trabalhadores during São Paulo's 1982 gubernatorial race*

When the "new unionism" emerged in the late 1970s, activists in both South Africa and Brazil emphasized shop-floor organization and developing workers' capacities to negotiate with employers. By the mid 1980s, however, labor activists in both cases had shifted: rather than concentrating solely on factory-related issues, both labor movements targeted the state as well as employers, seeking to increase the share of the broadly defined working class in the benefits of economic growth. Unionists joined in community-based campaigns, and were as likely to call for full citizenship—defined in terms of political inclusion and economic redistribution—as to speak of the right to form independent unions.

These community demands were not new in either case.[1] What was new was the support they received. In Brazil, new unions actively opposed the military government, and during the protracted transition to civilian rule, the independent Partido dos Trabalhadores drew on community support to increase working-class representation within the state. Even in South Africa, where debates over citizenship have historically been framed in racial terms, the labor unions redefined opposition goals to include economic restructuring and redistribution. Speaking for a broad constituency, including workers' families and communities as well as union members, the new unions were radical in the deepest sense, challenging the existing distribution of power as well as of economic resources.

There are hardly the kinds of demands that might have been expected from relatively skilled workers in relatively privileged sectors of the economy: instead of seeking to protect members' interests only at the workplace, labor movements in both Brazil and South Africa sought to represent the interests of the working class as a whole. Far from engaging in restrictive craft unionism, both new labor movements defined their constituency as broadly as possible and took up issues ranging from improved social services for urban communities to land reform and expanded electoral participation. Based in factories and working-class communities, both labor movements clearly enjoyed broad support in their challenge to "savage capitalism"—despite the undisputed prominence in their memberships of workers who might have been expected to differentiate their interests as skilled and semi-skilled workers from those of less-privileged workers and the unemployed.

What kinds of demands were raised in communities? Responding to what Lucio Kowarick calls the "urban spoliation" that accompanied rapid industrial growth—sprawling, impoverished communities denied basic infrastructure and services—urban groups in both Brazil and South Africa struggled for the "collective consumer goods and services that are vital to [subsistence]: transportation, health, sanitation, housing . . . not to mention other components such as electricity, paving, cultural activities."[2] Ruth Cardoso's description of Brazil's urban social movements is equally valid for South Africa: "In the cities . . . came an intensification of popular sector participation, through new forms of associationalism. The periphery of metropolises, presented as a living design of social and political spatial segregation, began to make its presence felt, demanding equal rights and full citizenship."[3]

Labor unions in both cases were directly involved in urban campaigns, through organizational alliances and through individual activists' participation in both sets of struggles; unions worked closely with community-based organizations that sought to improve the conditions in which workers lived. Despite an initial emphasis on workplace organization, labor activism spilled over into the world outside the factory. Aided by activists with broad political agendas, workers' participation in community struggles shaped the way urban residents understood their interests and helped define their strategies and goals. In both Brazil and South Africa, class-based discourse provided a unifying theme, and urban social movements took on a specifically working-class character as they confronted authoritarian states. Wage increases could provide one avenue to improved living conditions; community improvements offered another. By the mid 1980s, however, activists in both labor movements argued that only broad democratization could ensure that working-class voices would be heard in the formulation of state policies. In South Africa as well as in Brazil, the labor movement and the popular political opposition were shaped by their interaction with each other:

> On tying the economic struggle to social demands, it was inevitable that the new labor movement would confront the limits imposed by authoritarianism . . . on the exercise of full citizenship by workers. Thus, beginning from very precise and concrete demands, defined on a specifically syndicalist terrain, the "new unionism" . . . defined itself as a movement for the conquest of workers' social and political rights, qualifying itself as the new (and decisive) protagonist of the very struggle for democracy in the country.[4]

The gradual extension of factory-based demands into the political arena is hardly a straightforward process; indeed, it is rare enough to be considered the very definition of working-class consciousness, when workers come to believe that their individual interests are indistinguishable from those of a broader collectivity.[5] Even in South Africa, although analysts frequently suggest that segregationist policies may have thrown industrial workers, informal-sector and unemployed workers, and members of a petite bourgeoisie together, inadvertently "sewing a much wider web of connection among black South Africans than has yet existed," they rarely examine the way this process was reinterpreted by activists in the 1980s in class terms.[6]

That question—what led unions and communities to interpret their interests in parallel terms and to participate in joint campaigns against both employers and the state—is perhaps the key to understanding the meaning of social-movement unionism. The answer is hardly straightforward. Discussions of labor movements in early industrializers often recognize that union-community links have been fundamental to building strong labor movements, but most analysts consider such links relatively unusual. Manuel Castells, for example, suggests that labor movements generally avoid direct involvement in community campaigns, focusing instead on members' workplace positions; urban social movements, on the other hand, tend to avoid a class-based rhetoric that might alienate more middle-class residents.[7]

In late industrializers, where unions represent a relatively privileged minority of newly urbanized residents, labor-community links can hardly be taken for granted. Surrounded by unemployed or underemployed populations, industrial workers easily recognize the risk that they may be replaced during strikes. Unions representing members' workplace interests are often expected to protect members' privileged labor market position. Thus, divisions in the labor market are often expected to translate into unions' unwillingness to include broader demands in workplace campaigns, while workers outside the industrial core are considered unlikely to support industrial workers' campaigns. Even when industrial workers are linked through families and neighborhoods to less-privileged workers, as Mark Holmstrom found in India, they are probably more likely to press their demands within a workplace framework than through the community: a "rational fear of unemployment explains why factory workers look to their unions, first, to protect jobs; then, if possible, to protect or raise real wages." [8]

In both Brazil and South Africa, rapid industrialization was accompanied by high rates of unemployment, especially from the late 1960s on. When agricultural sectors in both countries shifted to capital-intensive mechanized methods, former peasants flooded into the cities, creating pools of available replacement workers who had little at stake in the factory-based struggles that marked the early phases of both labor movements. Furthermore, as Torcuato di Tella points out, "representatives of the working class ipso facto become rather estranged from their own grass roots"; once involved in complex negotiations, even militant workers tend to be counterbalanced by "officially oriented activists, and by the bureaucratic apparatus anchored in the somewhat passive acquiescence of the majority of members." [9] Why, then, did Brazilian and South African unions apparently encourage members to understand their interests in terms of a broader class—and why did communities respond so willingly to labor's appeals?

This question is even more interesting given the way workers' residential patterns in both countries reflect labor market differences: recent migrants who find work are frequently housed in dormitories, separated from larger residential communities. Seeking to explain the absence of labor militance in most of East Asia, Frederic Deyo concludes that such differences in residential patterns "tend generally to discourage class solidarity. Asian light industry attracts large numbers of short-term workers among whom turnover rates are high and commitment to coworkers, jobs, organizations and unions is low," undermining community solidarity, as the work and community experiences of migrants are quite distinct from those of more stable working populations.[10] South Africa's single-sex migrant hostels were consciously built on the edges of black residential townships, while recent migrants to Brazilian cities, especially workers in less-skilled work like construction, often lived at the work site, unable to find or afford housing even in squatter settlements. Why, under these circumstances, were communities willing to support factory campaigns both through strike funds and by refusing to replace striking workers? Why were community residents—often more vulnerable and powerless than factory workers—willing to join in? Above all, what prompted community residents, whose interests are invariably more heterogeneous and divided than those of union members, to understand their goals in collective, class-based terms?

This is not to suggest, of course, that labor movements in early industrializers were entirely separate from communities. Indeed, as Craig Calhoun points out, nineteenth-century labor movements in Europe and North America frequently exhibited many of the characteristics often attributed to the "new" social movements of the late twentieth century, including concerns about "religion, lifestyle, gender and culture" in addition to their primary focus on economic issues; but as the labor movement became more institutionalized, and collective bargaining became more widespread, an economistic understanding of class relations and social issues came to predominate.[11] State repression seems to provide a reasonably straightforward explanation for the few exceptional cases: state interference in labor struggles seemed to reduce the salience of work force divisions, unifying skilled and less-skilled workers in large federations with similar political aims. Thus, Gary Marks writes, "The perception of shared victimization could create a powerful sense of working-class unity";[12] similarly, Victoria Bonnell suggests that state repression after 1911 prompted unionized workers in prerevolutionary Russia, who might otherwise have behaved as a labor aristocracy, to support more left-wing parties and more revolutionary change.[13]

Under the kinds of authoritarian regimes that existed in Brazil and South Africa in the 1970s, however, union-community links are perhaps more, not less, remarkable. In a situation where any popular mobilization risked state interference, why should unions—representing relatively privileged workers—take up community campaigns when such involvement risked endangering activists and hard-won shop-floor gains? Why should industrial workers have risked losing jobs and security to participate in campaigns where their workplace strength could

not protect them from repression? In both Brazil and South Africa, labor activists had every reason to fear that fledgling shop-floor organizations would be repressed—as they had been repressed before—if they
took up political campaigns. Yet in both cases, prominent labor leaders
who urged unions to avoid "politics" lost rank-and-file support, as
newly unionized members insisted that their organizations should take
up broader campaigns against the state. Labor leaders who encouraged
political involvement, on the other hand, became increasingly popular.
What was it about the situations of industrial workers in both cases
that made such a broad approach appealing?

One set of explanations would revolve around activists' ideologies:
clearly, the worldviews brought by individual activists to meetings
where groups analyzed concrete problems and formulated demands
helped define the way issues were understood and acted upon. Brazilian
Catholic activists informed by liberation theology, like South African
activists poring over illegal copies of *The African Communist*, could,
and did, introduce concepts and rhetoric that linked struggles in different arenas. Yet as any activist should know, if impoverishment and
objective conditions do not automatically produce social movements,
neither do coherent analyses, unless those analyses reflect individuals'
lived experiences. Despite the very different political contexts in which
the two labor movements operated, is it possible to identify some parallel underlying dynamic that increased community support for workers'
shop-floor campaigns, and that increased union members' willingness
to participate in community struggles?

The answer to this puzzle seems to lie neither in the objective conditions of poverty confronting the residents of sprawling slums nor in the
programs of political activists, but rather in the way activists reinterpreted the links between workplace and community concerns. As a
start, it seems reasonable to inquire how workers and activists understood the relation between factories and impoverished communities,
and how their understandings changed as labor and community movements grew into the demand for broader political participation. K. P.
Mosely suggests community-based "consumerist" demands will be separated from wage demands, unless "specific mechanisms intervene to
carry over workplace identities into the residential sphere."[14] I argue in
this chapter that in both Brazil and South Africa, explicit state policies
provided those mechanisms.

Housing issues provided one link: "How workers are housed," Frederick Cooper writes, "has much to do with how they are integrated

into a social order,"[15] and in Brazil and South Africa, housing patterns reflected and created a broad constituency that responded to class-based appeals. State and employer cooperation impoverished domestic and community life in a range of ways in both cases: during the course of rapid industrialization, policies that simultaneously reduced wages and denied services impoverished urban domestic and community life. During the course of worker and community mobilization, activists increasingly described their impoverishment—low wages combined with urban spoliation—as the direct result of inegalitarian state industrialization strategies, and thus as the direct result of political processes that favored employers. Once mobilized in support of workers' campaigns, community activists—who recognized industrial action was a far more successful tactic than community rallies and demonstrations against authoritarian regimes—increasingly interpreted community demands as reflections of existing class stratification.

In the context of severely inegalitarian industrialization patterns, once workers developed a sense of class relations through organization at the factory-floor level, this understanding translated fairly easily into efforts to raise workers' share in resources outside the factory: class struggles in the "sphere of production" spilled over into the "sphere of reproduction," as workers sought to raise the historically defined level of the cost of reproduction of labor. It was this process—the spilling-over of labor activism into the broader community—that shaped community residents' strategies and goals and became the basis for labor movements whose constituency lay beyond the factory gates.

BRAZIL: "O POVO EM MOVIMENTO"

By the early 1980s, community mobilization in Brazil had reached an intensity unimaginable ten years earlier: while sociologists occasionally confused "people in movements"—that is, labor and community activists—with "people on the move,"[16] the level of popular participation in campaigns for community improvements had unmistakably increased since the early 1970s. In the most vivid single manifestation of public protest, millions of Brazilians stayed home in support of the 1984 campaign for direct elections; but during the previous five years, many more had participated in local campaigns around more concrete issues. Strongest in, but not restricted to, the country's industrial heartland centered on São Paulo, campaigns to improve public transport, to regularize title deeds, and to provide day-care facilities for working mothers challenged public authorities to provide specific services to working-class neighborhoods, while broad campaigns against the high cost of living publicized the impoverishment of poor urban areas.

Campaigns around local community issues took different organizational forms. In the mid 1970s, what began as isolated spontaneous explosions over slow public transport—the *quebra-quebras,* or "break-breaks," against expensive buses and trains—erupted in every major urban area, often culminating in pitched battles between passengers and police; despite their chaotic nature, they served as the basis for a more organized movement demanding better transport services for areas on the edges of Brazil's large cities. *Quebra-quebras* tended to be associated with the emergence of an organized community-based urban movement and to reflect concern over work-related issues such as the loss of wages because of tardiness.[17]

Other movements had more orderly beginnings. Within neighborhoods, residents' groups multiplied. In many urban areas, participants in Christian base communities and Bible study groups—initiated to counteract shortages of priests, but by the late 1960s often infused with ideas drawn from liberation theology—began to identify community needs, drawing on church resources to develop responses. Sympathetic local priests often helped residents of slum tenements (*cortiços*) and squatter settlements (*favelas*) draw up petitions for improved services; university students researched local needs for clinics, water, drainage systems, even recreational facilities; base community groups carried out surveys to identify nutritional, educational, and other needs.[18] Church-linked "Mothers' Clubs" assisted members individually and mobilized residents to demand social services for communities.[19]

Some urban movements challenged fundamental assumptions about the property rights of the urban poor. Especially in São Paulo, Rio de Janeiro, and Belo Horizonte, haphazard growth over previous decades had involved semi-legal squatting and sometimes fraudulent land sales; in the late 1970s, church-linked community groups campaigned to regularize title deeds for poor households. By 1983, some municipalities had agreed to grant squatters the right to permanent residence, and the National Congress was considering the problem.[20] Seeking land for houses, community groups in the early 1980s invaded vacant lots, simultaneously demonstrating the need for more low-income housing areas and creating space for squatting: between 1981 and 1984, more than sixty thousand people in nine thousand families participated in sixty-five invasions in São Paulo. In Rio, there were twelve organized "invasions" in the first six months of 1983 alone. Primarily organized by newly unemployed people who could no longer pay rents in tenements or afford to purchase land, "all these mobilizations denounced the total inefficiency of existing institutions for guaranteeing necessities and security for the population."[21]

The regularization of property rights changed the relationship between poor residents and the state, serving as a crucial first step toward demanding social services—water, electricity, drainage systems, public transport.[22] In 1979, São Paulo *favela*-dwellers formed a citywide organization to press authorities to provide water and electricity to squatter areas;[23] similar organizations were soon formed in other major industrial cities. Older community associations were revived. In the early 1980s, one estimate counted about 8,000 residents' associations in Brazil, including 900 associations in São Paulo and about 550 in Rio.[24] While these "Friends of the Bairro" and *favela* associations varied widely—sometimes acting as pressure groups, sometimes merely providing electoral machines for local politicians—by the early 1980s many were articulating community demands, mobilizing an informal network of activists outside the institutional structures of the military government. In the 1982 municipal elections, community organizations helped to defeat candidates who supported the military government; in the mid 1980s, they helped mobilize popular support for the transition to civilian rule.[25]

Community-based groups tended to orient demands toward local government, a safer route than challenging the national government. (Even so, community activists, even priests, still risked imprisonment and torture during the late 1970s and early 1980s.)[26] Municipal authorities seem to have been more likely than the federal state to respond to public protest, probably because elections to municipal offices were less tightly controlled by the military than the indirect presidential process. A local focus also enabled activists to work with people they knew well: Vinícius Caldeira Brant argues that repression in the early 1970s prompted residents to view personal and neighborhood ties as less risky than acting alone or relying on strangers in confronting authorities.[27]

In São Paulo, however—by the early 1980s, a megalopolis of some ten million inhabitants—citywide campaigns linked local demands for health clinics and day-care centers across neighborhoods. Often led by women, these larger movements tended to focus on domestic needs, successfully publicizing the difficulties poor parents faced in caring for their families. By 1983, the São Paulo municipal administration had built fourteen new clinics in response to pressure from the Movement for Health;[28] between 1979, when the movement for day-care centers was organized citywide, and 1983, the number of municipal crèches in São Paulo tripled.[29] National consumer campaigns demonstrated the effect of declining real wages on working families. Founded in 1973, the São Paulo-based Cost of Living Movement (Movimento do Custo da Vida) held enormous rallies in the late 1970s to express concern over inflation; it collected well over a million signatures on a 1978 petition for higher real wages, and helped elect two opposition deputies to Congress. Although they maintained its identity as a nonpolitical, church-linked campaign, the movement's leaders clearly directed their complaints to the makers of national economic policy, arguing that workers' growing impoverishment was the direct outcome of the past decade's capitalist industrialization strategies.[30]

Participants in these groups did not necessarily develop a broad political vision. The campaigns around which urban social movements formed often focused on very local issues, and many observers suggest it was difficult for activists to expand beyond the day-to-day issues that united communities.[31] In his study of a residents' group in central Rio de Janeiro, Carlos Nelson Ferreira dos Santos concluded that residents justified their struggle against the state as a community of citizens in need, rather than as members of a class.[32] Similarly, in her careful study of a neighborhood on São Paulo's periphery, Teresa Pires do Rio Caldeira found only political party members expressed a clearly political vision.

Nevertheless, Caldeira's respondents described their world in terms of relationships of power and exploitation:

A baron is he who has capital. Us folks are those who don't have capital. . . . We who have no capital, the money that we have is only to spend: earn in the morning, eat at night.

The owners of industry, they do nothing, they only order and then I think they live just waiting for others . . . to do things for them. And the worker will do it. If not, poor thing, he'll be in the street.

I don't believe that a rich man could live except on the back of the poor; he only lives on the back of the poor. Because how could factories run, these factories everywhere, if not for the poor, the worker, how could they run?

The rich get rich by exploiting the poor.[33]

Caldeira's respondents acknowledged the presence of different strata within their communities; but they seem to have recognized unambiguously that as workers they could not aspire to the kind of wealth or power of those who lived in the city center. Similarly, while the textile workers interviewed by Vera Maria Cándido Pereira displayed a slightly more complex worldview—with bourgeoisie and wealthy landowners on one side and workers and peasants on the other—they described the relationship between rich and poor as one between exploiter and exploited.[34]

In a context where class relations were clearly evident to community residents, and where unions were achieving real successes by the late 1970s, it is hardly surprising that activists would seek to strengthen links between urban social movements and the labor movement. At times, the links were at the level of individuals: Conceição Peres, a central figure in the Mothers' Clubs, was married to Aurelio Peres, a prominent figure in the Workers' Pastoral, who was arrested in 1974 and elected as an opposition congressman in 1978.[35] Christian base communities in working-class areas frequently encouraged members to participate in labor unions, arguing that unions and industrial actions provided one of the few weapons available with which workers could try to improve their situation. Similarly, sympathetic priests and church groups provided unions with meeting spaces that were relatively safe from police and employer surveillance.[36] Community leaders, particularly those with the broader political vision associated with Christian base communities or political parties, clearly viewed factory- and community-based organizations as different aspects of a related effort to raise the living standards of workers and their families.[37]

In turn, labor activists supported vulnerable community organizations. The "new unionists" encouraged union members to support community campaigns, which they considered directly related to the erosion of real wages and the declining material conditions of working-class and poor neighborhoods. As the labor movement developed a stronger shop-floor base, many unions, especially the Metalworkers' Union, included social issues in their annual contract negotiations.[38] For example, the "new unions" helped mobilize residents to protest inefficient transport services, as well as taking up these issues in factory-level negotiations; indeed, opposition unions' protests over transport services preceded the explosion of *quebra-quebras* in the mid 1970s, beginning with a 1973 strike over bus service at Villares. Similarly, the

ABC Metalworkers' Union's 1977 "repositioning" built on the Cost of Living Movement's campaign of the preceding three years and helped mobilize support for that movement in subsequent years. Of course, some campaigns linking workplace and political reform failed, such as the attempt by the newly launched Central Única dos Trabalhadores to call a general strike in 1983 against unemployment, long work days, and salary restraints, and for agrarian reform, for protection of state industries, and for democratic liberties[39]; but the "new" unionists generally sought to mobilize worker support for broader community and political issues.

Labor activism from 1978 on helped stimulate greater activism in working-class communities by dramatically demonstrating the possibility of winning local improvements; but community organizations also strengthened the labor movement. Through donations to strike funds, and by refusing to replace striking workers, neighborhood residents helped ensure that workers and their families could survive strikes that dragged on for weeks. Widespread refusal to scab was particularly impressive, given the levels of unemployment in major Brazilian cities, which increased during the recession of the 1980s; while some employers used the layoffs associated with the recession to fire individual union activists,[40] there were few instances of entire striking work forces losing their jobs to replacement workers. The extent to which neighborhood residents interpreted campaigns for higher wages in some industries as ultimately benefiting all workers was repeatedly reflected in discussions in community groups, in rallies, and in petitions supporting strikes. Unions and community groups viewed wages and living conditions as socially and historically defined; by the early 1980s, rather than viewing wage campaigns simply in terms of negotiations between workers and employers, working-class community groups considered workplace campaigns part of a larger effort to challenge existing definitions of the standards required if industrial workers and their families were to survive—that is, of the cost to employers and the state of reproducing workers' labor power, both from day to day and across generations.[41]

This interaction between unions and community was probably strongest in São Bernardo do Campo, where more than half of industrial workers were members of the Metalworkers' Union,[42] and where from the late 1970s on "the strike movement took hold of the city, creating new spaces for organizations and developing solidarity within the movement as well as with other supportive sectors of society, with entities that reinforced the legitimacy of the strike."[43] Especially in the

1980 strike, when the military government tried to remove union leaders from office, community support was crucial for the metalworkers. Mass rallies and "flying pickets" publicized demands, while churches provided meeting spaces and community volunteers made up food parcels for strikers' families. But even beyond São Bernardo, electoral support for the Partido dos Trabalhadores around São Paulo throughout the 1980s indicated the degree to which community groups identified with the labor movement: in communities in São Paulo's vast industrial periphery, the PT, led by the Metalworkers' Union's Lula, won about a third of the vote in the 1985 municipal elections, and that share would rise in future elections.[44] In 1988, less than a decade after the party's founding, a PT candidate, herself closely identified with urban squatter movements[45] was elected mayor of São Paulo's fourteen million people.

At the same time, the extent to which the PT took up community issues reflected the labor movement's growing involvement in issues outside the workplace: PT candidates called for land reform, educational opportunities, health care, and debt renegotiation, as well as for more traditional workers' rights like the right to strike, parental leave, and improved occupational safety enforcement. In Lula's 1989 campaign for president, the message was relatively simple: the PT came within percentage points of winning the presidency by promising to "give to those who have not." Building on ten years of labor and community organization in poor neighborhoods, activists could reasonably claim that politics in Brazil had changed. Instead of asking poor Brazilians to vote for clientelist politicians who could offer patronage, candidates in 1989 could draw on a broad working-class identity, which had been strengthened through ten years of labor and community activism on the edges of Brazil's great cities.

PROCESSES OF PERIPHERALIZATION

Obviously, no community is entirely composed of members of a single class: Brazilian communities are no more purely working-class than are communities elsewhere. How, then, can we explain the wide support for the labor movement shown by community organizations and activists, and the labor movement's willingness to place community issues so high on its agenda? This question is particularly interesting in view of the predominance of semi-skilled and skilled workers in the "new unions": most industrial relations theories would suggest that especially in the recession of the early 1980s, exclusionary craft unionism might have been a more appropriate strategy for unionists seeking to protect members' interests. Why did the labor movement focus on the state, uniting with community groups to challenge the dominant model of capitalist economic development? What moved unions' focus outside the factory gates?

The answers to these questions seem to lie in the interaction of two related tendencies in Brazil's patterns of industrialization: first, the geographic concentration of major industries and the industrial work force in the industrial triangle between São Paulo, Belo Horizonte, and Rio de Janeiro, and, second, the state's involvement in reinforcing the spatial segregation of the working class.[46] From the early 1950s on, Brazil's rates of urbanization were dramatic: as expanding capitalist agriculture reduced the land and resources available to peasant sharecroppers, migration to urban areas continued.[47] By 1970, 37 percent of the total population lived in cities or towns of more than twenty thousand people, and there were eleven cities with more than half a million residents, compared to only one in 1940.[48] As chapter 2 suggested, industrial growth was heavily concentrated in the major cities, for reasons connected to the transfer of technology, availability of inputs, and access to markets. At the center of industrial growth, metropolitan São Paulo expanded rapidly, reaching a population size of about twelve million in 1981.[49] São Paulo's growth pattern dominates discussions of Brazilian urban trends and illustrates similar trends in other industrial centers; São Paulo "flagrantly displays a summary of the contradictions and tensions resulting from rapid and unequal growth."[50]

Much of the city's population growth came from in-migration. In 1970, more than half of São Paulo's residents had been born elsewhere.[51] Migrants were concentrated in low-income occupations: in the early 1980s, 90 percent of industrial workers had been born outside the city, and over 80 percent reported that neither parent had been an urban wage worker.[52] During earlier periods of São Paulo's industrialization, in the first part of the century, many factories provided company housing, both as a subsidy for skilled workers and as a means of allowing employers greater control over the work force. But as the city grew, employers left workers to find their own housing.[53] Poor and working-class residents were steadily pushed out to the city's geographic and social edges, whence they commuted to work either at nearby industrial sites or further in toward the city center. In the early 1980s, almost half of metropolitan São Paulo's population lived on the urban periphery.[54]

Brazil's spatial segregation certainly has racial undertones: in the creation of working-class residential areas outside the city center, class and race interact in ways that Brazilians have only recently begun to explore. Although segregation in the twentieth century was not legally enforced—in contrast, for example, to South Africa—and despite the still-popular Brazilian mythology of racial democracy, few sociologists deny that race plays a part in determining where people find housing, or that darker Brazilians are overrepresented among the poor. On the other hand, while spatial segregation involves a degree of racial discrimination, the fact that many residents of the periphery are light-skinned—especially in the industrial heartland, where the working class includes descendants of Italian and Portuguese immigrants—underlines the economic processes that direct individuals to particular neighborhoods. In rural areas, segregation may be more explicitly based on racial identities;[55] in major urban areas, the dynamics shaping the periphery are experienced as economic ones. Residents of all colors generally understand their circumstances as the result of poverty as much as of race: "racial prejudice is associated with economic marginalization," not separable from it.[56]

The tendency of poorer residents to move to the edge of the city generally reflects São Paulo's peculiar pattern of growth, in which the poor served as urban pioneers. Throughout this century, land speculators purchased parcels of land on the edge of the city, sold land to people who built their own houses, and then—after electricity, water, and roads were brought in, often in response to popular protests[57]—either sold vacant lots for higher sums or, worse, used irregularities in the initial sale to remove the original homeowners from their plots.[58] In the 1970s, the choices facing low-income residents in major urban areas were bleak: tenements; *favelas,* or squatter areas; or the periphery, which usually meant constructing houses using family labor on illegally subdivided lots where real estate codes were ignored and title deeds could not be officially registered with the municipality. The government consistently closed its eyes to illegal land deals. Between 1972 and 1980, although the city's population grew by nearly 50 percent and subdivisions were probably the major form of expansion, only seven subdivisions were opened and sold in a completely legal manner;[59] residents in all the rest were subject to the very real possibility that once the area received urban services, a dishonest subdivider, or *grileiro,* would take back the property through some legal trick.[60] The legal process of filing title is expensive and complex; in 1979, a study of four thousand plots on the periphery found 38 percent had irregularities in their titles and the remaining 62 percent had never been registered at all.[61]

As the city grew, land speculation further eroded workers' ability to find adequate housing: while real wages were cut in half between 1959 and 1976, real estate prices soared nearly 300 percent.[62] The state's failure to control real estate speculation—a failure that has repeatedly resulted in workers losing houses once the property has been improved—has been a form of policy-making by omission; the periphery is "the unequivocal result of a housing policy that fails to recognize the housing needs of most of the population and of a process of urban growth" involving unrestrained speculation.[63]

The process of peripheralization was not simply the result of state failure to control private enterprise, however. From the mid 1960s on, the state explicitly transferred workers' earnings directly to middle- and upper-class communities and employers in ways that further underlined the political creation of working-class poverty. Perhaps the most tangible example of the state-created links between production and reproduction lies in Brazil's public transport system: the choice of the military state throughout the late 1960s and the 1970s to invest in productive enterprises rather than in social services resulted in visible deterioration of the trains and buses that carried workers between home and work. While state wage policies restricted pay increases, state-owned or regulated public transport companies continued to raise fares. By 1973, on average, one train passenger died every five days, usually by falling from the outside of overloaded trains. The deaths of illegal *pingentes,* who like South African "staff-riders" avoided fares by traveling outside, provided a dramatic illustration of how declining real wages affected workers' ability to pay transport costs. Meanwhile, as cities grew, so did the time workers spent in transit: through the 1970s, travel time for individual workers in São Paulo rose about 30 percent, to three or four hours daily.[64] Overcrowding, delays, and accidents clearly provoked the *quebra-quebras* of the 1970s. Unionists explicitly recognized that employers' refusal to provide travel subsidies or to pay for time workers spent in transit reduced real wages, while the state's failure to maintain services to "peripheral" areas only reinforced the geographic segregation of class.[65]

Daily irritant though it might be, however, transport was only one example of how state policies actively transferred resources from working-class communities to Brazil's upper and middle classes. Far more blatant were the policies of the National Housing Bank (Banco National de Habitação, or BNH), which used workers' wages to fund middle-class housing.[66] Created in August 1964, only months after the military took power, the BNH was meant to "promote the construction and acquisition of homes, especially by the lower-income classes,"[67] and was initially funded through voluntary savings. After 1967, however, the BNH drew on the Guaranteed Fund for Time Served (FGTS)—the 8 percent of workers' wages compulsorily withheld as a form of unemployment insurance. By 1973, the BNH controlled nearly 6 percent of the gross domestic product, with nearly $5.7 billion.[68] As a federal body with enormous resources, the BNH removed much of the decision-making power over urban policy from municipal executives, strengthening central and state governments.[69]

In the late 1960s, the state had an explicit goal: to remove *favelas* from major urban areas and move their residents to cities' peripheries. In Rio de Janeiro, where *favelas* existed next to downtown upper-class areas, state agencies removed 6,875 housing units between 1963 and 1968; from 1968 to 1972, despite widespread protests, the BNH destroyed another 16,467 units. Most of these removals occurred in Rio's inner central and southern zone—the downtown and southern coastal areas favored by upper- and middle-class residents. Promising to replace *favela* shacks with modern housing, probably in the outer zone of the city, the BNH planned to stimulate "upper and middle class residential construction by clearing the most desirable areas of the city of the presence of the poor."[70] While *favela* residents often tried to resist, removals continued until Rio's southern zone was at least temporarily effectively cleared of squatter settlements in the mid 1970s (although new *favelas* sprang up in other, less-coveted areas of the city).[71] Former *favela* residents were supposed to be offered units in housing projects, usually far from the original *favela* site, from their workplaces, and from their old neighbors, and lacking the roads, transport services, sewage systems, and other amenities available closer to city centers.[72]

Did the BNH fund new housing for the expanding urban work force? Given the nature of Brazil's government during the "economic miracle," it is hardly surprising that it did not: BNH funding for low-income housing declined until it was almost nonexistent. From the BNH's founding until 1975, 27.2 percent of BNH resources went directly to middle- and upper-income loans, and another 20.4 percent went toward private construction of higher-income units. About 34.5 percent went to "social interest" programs, but 68 percent of these funds went to private cooperatives, social security institutes, and military mortgage funds; ultimately, less than 9 percent of the BNH's total expenditures by 1976 had gone into housing destined for the 80 percent of Brazilians who earned less than five minimum salaries. In 1975, the BNH spent only 3 percent of its total investment budget on low-income housing.[73]

Ironically, this failure to provide housing for working-class Brazilians was the result, not of conscious policy, but of the decision to structure the federal housing agency as a bank making loans to low-income clients. Initially, BNH "social interest" programs were expected to be self-supporting: even former *favelados,* moved against their will, were expected to repay loans for new housing in *conjuntos,* or low-income projects. Charged up to 6 percent in interest and another 7 percent in administrative fees, poorer residents rapidly fell behind. Nationally, units behind in their payments rose from 50 percent in 1971 to 67 percent in 1974; 30 percent were more than three months behind.[74] The BNH then made the financially sound choice to further reduce funding for low-income housing and loans. As one worker said in the early 1970s, even well-paid workers could not afford BNH loans; instead, the BNH "solved some problems for the middle class," who could repay unsubsidized government loans.[75]

Nor did the state make any real attempt to build low-income units, despite rapid urban growth. The national housing deficit in the early 1970s was estimated at eight million units, growing at a rate of 5,000 units a year; by 1975, after nearly a decade of FGTS contributions, the BNH had completed only 615,900 units of low-income housing.[76] In São Paulo, the BNH's low-income agency had constructed 9,000 units by 1974, of which only 3,459 had actually been handed over to residents; "almost all the rest consisted of houses and apartments on which construction stopped a long time ago, and which were in an advanced stage of deterioration." Indeed, private contractors were allowed to take so many shortcuts that residents had to evacuate several completed housing projects when serious construction flaws were revealed.[77]

During the early 1970s, spending on basic infrastructural improvements—roads, water and sewage systems, and the like—increased, and it could be argued that public agencies helped create an urban environment in which improved low-income housing could later be constructed. However, users paid dearly for these services: while BNH agencies did improve sanitation and sewage systems, helping to reduce urban infant mortality rates, the rates charged by federal agencies for water and drains in São Paulo were 139 percent higher than the rates charged by nearby municipal agencies.[78]

In this context, organizers could easily mobilize a collective sense of deprivation in poor areas. Church, party, and union activists could not assume that a collective identity already existed in the late 1970s, but the visible processes of peripheralization meant that residents would develop a broader understanding of the relationships that shaped their daily lives relatively quickly. Needs are defined in a particular social context, not automatically given;[79] but in a city like São Paulo, where the majority of residents are denied access to services provided in the city center, and especially with activists offering a broader vision in group discussions, urban protest movements could "make manifest an identity which became concrete through the collective construction of a notion of rights, which, directly related to a widened space for citizenship, gave rise to public recognition of needs."[80]

CLASS IDENTITY AND LEVELS OF REPRODUCTION

For industrial workers, the mechanisms of peripheralization were transparent: the authoritarian state's overt control over wages, its refusal to service lower-class communities, and its willingness to shift resources from poorer to wealthier areas reinforced the tendency for labor unions to interpret both factory and community problems as political issues. Housing shortages were worst in rapidly expanding industrial areas: in São Bernardo do Campo, center of the automobile industry, nearly 60 percent of wage workers had to commute to São Bernardo from other parts of the periphery,[81] while in São Bernardo itself, an estimated one in four lived in *favelas*.[82] (In Rio, the situation was worse: one-third of the city's residents were believed to live in *favelas*.[83]) Licia do Prado Valladores lists these principal factors contributing to the process of spatial segregation of the working class: low wages, direct expulsion from urban centers, indirect expulsion through legislation and taxation, and unrestrained real estate speculation.[84] In each of these factors, the state's role was unmistakable.

On the periphery, urban services were generally inadequate. During the 1960s, urban São Paulo's infrastructure fell far short of its borders: social critics described the "logic of disorder" by which high-income areas received the lion's share of public investment.[85] Despite the economic boom of the late 1960s, in the mid 1970s, only 40 percent of the metropolitan region's 8,000 kilometers of road were tarred; only 30 percent of its houses had drains, and only 53 percent had piped water. Services were worst on the periphery: only 20 percent of peripheral homes had drains, and 46 percent piped water.[86] Transport systems were slow and expensive: on average, periphery residents spent nearly 9 percent of their income on transport.[87]

In an influential study in the mid 1970s, sociologists argued persuasively that the city's failure to provide adequate services was related to state decisions about investments, to the closure of political channels through which residents could articulate demands, and to a model of capitalist industrialization that encouraged income stratification and the erosion of real wages. As further evidence, they pointed to an 80 percent increase in São Paulo's *favela* population between 1973 and 1975: the immediate effect of the economic crisis underscored the inadequacy of urbanization rates as an explanation for the process called peripheralization.[88] Poverty and unemployment alone could not fully explain the rise of clearly identifiable working-class and poor communities, even squatter settlements. Fifty thousand *favela*-dwellers worked in the ABC region, mainly in the automobile industry.[89] In São Paulo's eastern zone (Zona Leste 2), where average per capita incomes are just 20 percent of incomes in the city's wealthier central neighborhoods (Centro Expandido), 44 percent of residents with jobs worked in industry, and 54 percent of these were in semi-skilled work in 1977.[90]

The failure of the state and employers to ensure that industrial workers could find adequate housing in neighborhoods with appropriate urban services had several implications. It created income-segregated communities, where poor Brazilians lacked basic amenities provided to wealthier neighborhoods. Working and unemployed Brazilians live side by side in these peripheral areas, both in lower-income neighborhoods and *favelas:* while residents recognized social differentiation, they lacked services equally. Urban campaigns united what might in other circumstances have been groups with somewhat different material interests. "What homogenizes these areas," Caldeira writes, "is poverty and neediness."[91] Uniformly excluded from access to most of Brazil's resources, semi-skilled workers shared an interest in redistribution and democratization with other residents of the periphery. "The complex social content of [urban social struggles] can only be understood in terms of their place in the global process of capitalist accumulation and its underlying class divisions," where campaigns over urban social services are linked to issues of inequitable distribution, and where the distinctions between skilled, semi-skilled, and unemployed workers living on the periphery become less pertinent to collective identities.[92] Community groups were frequently assisted by middle-class activists, including students and priests; but under Brazil's "savage capitalism," especially in the context of a growing labor movement, residents were perhaps especially likely to perceive direct links between exploitation at the workplace and eroded living conditions at home. Community groups thus regularly described their campaigns in terms of class. "The collective character of consumption of urban goods and services shapes a collective struggle"; the struggle for state investments in public works or urban services "opposes workers, who need [these services] to survive or to improve their living conditions, and those who appropriate income."[93]

Given these patterns, it is easy to see why activists in Brazilian urban movements and trade unions understood the construction of their material situation in terms both of class and of the relationship between civil society and the state, whose role in reinforcing class relations took on a physical character, which workers—already aware of the state's role in reducing real wages—experienced concretely in long commutes and inadequate services. Throughout the world, workers have been housed in areas lacking basic social services. But in Brazil—particularly in major urban areas—some aspects of peripheralization have underscored the relationship between factory and community and the way in which household labor ultimately subsidizes employers.

As workers organized in factories, they discussed community problems in terms of the wage relationship and of the ways in which community needs were linked to the accumulation of capital by employers. Several metalworkers concluded in their analysis of the 1978 strikes:

> Workers' eyes were opened wider and wider at all times and in all places: in the factory, when being paid, when paying bills, in the street traveling, in the house paying rent, with taxes, gas, light, on vacation with prices always rising, etc. . . . What they received was only enough to keep them on their feet another day in order to continue.[94]

In São Bernardo, a *favela* resident analyzed illegal (but free) squatting in terms of how it reduced the wages employers had to pay to ensure reproduction of the labor force:

> Folks were discussing the other day in whose interest the *favela* was. For us who live in it free, without paying rent? No. We figured that the businesses have a direct interest in the *favelas*. . . . If we live in a *favela*, we'll submit to a tiny salary [because we don't have to pay rent], and thus this means that, wherever there's a *favela*, they'll have cheaper labor.[95]

Transport problems were also described as a result of class relations: a
cartoon booklet aimed at workers, for example, told the story of a
worker who arrived late to work because of transport problems, lost
his job, participated in a *quebra-quebra,* and then became politicized;
employers, the booklet argued, were the "owners of regions" (*donos
das regiões*), who refused to pay for adequate transport because workers had to make do with whatever was provided.[96] Community activists
interpreted even homeownership in terms of labor exploitation. Few
Brazilian workers could afford to buy ready-made houses, instead
building houses over weekends and during vacations, using cheap materials and often living in substandard buildings meanwhile. For workers,
community activists argued, "the self-construction of residences developed in hours of leave-time in many distant 'peripheries' of the metrop-
olis, on plots lacking basic infrastructure and, usually, situated on
illegal allotments," stretched family incomes;[97] but it also effectively
subsidized wage bills by stretched the amount of labor required to
house and feed a family. Time devoted to long commutes or to building
substandard housing—to family reproduction—is time for which the
employer need not pay. Like overtime work during peak seasons—a
constant feature of industrial life during Brazil's economic boom—the
processes of peripheralization directly affected workers' family lives.[98]
To workers unable to find affordable housing, the policies of the military regime tangibly demonstrated the state's willingness to impose the
costs of rapid expansion on workers and their families. In the course of
analyzing their experiences on the shop floor, workers quickly recognized links between their lack of basic services and employers' profit
margins.

FAMILY LABOR AND CLASS IDENTITY

By itself, the deterioration of living conditions is probably unlikely to
forge a durable link between workplace organizations and community
struggle; workers in many parts of the world suffer material deprivation
as the result of low wages and state neglect, but they rarely adopt the
militant class rhetoric that marked many Brazilian community groups
in the early 1980s. What prompted community activists to view their
needs in class terms? Certainly, a class-based analysis was based in part
on the discourse articulated in unions and in Christian base communities: union activists emphasizing class relations, and Catholic activists

informed by liberation theology, encouraged participants in community groups to explore the ways in which employers benefited from an unequal distribution of state resources and services.[99]

But these discussions also reflected a growing awareness on the part of workers and community members of how employers benefited from community deprivation, based in a changing relationship between household and factory. That change—a growing dependence for survival on wages paid to household members—is perhaps most clearly illustrated by the steady increase in female labor force participation from the mid 1960s on. Between 1970 and 1978, the proportion of women over 10 participating in the labor force nearly doubled, rising from 18 to 35.5 percent. While older, less-educated women tended to cluster in domestic or informal work, younger, more educated women began to move into clerical and production jobs in the industrial sector. In the 1970s, women workers increased from 14.9 percent of the industrial labor force to about 30 percent—a growth rate of about 181 percent, which accounted for about 40 percent of total growth in the industrial labor force in this period.[100] By 1986, women made up 42.5 percent of São Paulo's labor force; although they remained concentrated in lower-paid occupations, they were increasingly represented in the formal rather than the informal sector.[101] Brazilian women had long worked in textile factories, but in the 1970s, they began to find jobs in the capital-intensive heavy industries concentrated in São Paulo: by 1979, women made up 9.8 percent of workers in the metal, mechanical, and electrical materials industries.[102]

Most observers attribute the increase in female labor force participation—a trend that directly challenged traditional Brazilian gender ideologies—to two factors. First, after 1973, the drop in real wages required more members to contribute income in order for families to survive. Several analysts argue that in peripheral neighborhoods, women's work outside the home served as a survival strategy, cushioning households against the effects of inflation and recession.[103] Second, industrial growth created new jobs in heavy industry. New positions opened up in heavy industrial sectors in the late 1960s and 1970s at a time when more and more women were seeking industrial employment.[104] Women seeking work were especially likely to find openings in expanding factories as less-skilled workers. Male workers in the late 1970s sometimes complained that employers preferred to hire women, believing they would be more docile and controllable.[105] Certainly, employers tended to control women workers' movements more strictly than those of male workers, often regulating choices as personal as whether or not a worker could put on a sweater or go to the bathroom.[106]

Despite their reputation for docility, women workers joined unions at a rate higher than men. Between 1970 and 1978, female membership in unions rose by 176.3 percent, while male membership rose by only 87 percent. In the late 1970s, when union membership began to soar following the 1978 strikes, the increase in female membership outstripped the increase for men, although there was wide variation in the extent to which unionists consciously targeted and included women workers. Between 1977 and 1978, the percentage of women workers who were union members increased by 33 percent, while the percentage of women in the labor force increased by only 9.2 percent; the percentage of male workers joining unions increased by only 20 percent. By 1979, although women composed only 9.8 percent of the workers covered by Metalworkers' Union agreements, 25.2 percent of female metalworkers had joined the union.[107]

Women may have been attracted by the assistential services unions provided. The military government had increased union responsibility for education, insurance, and health care for workers, and women workers concerned about meeting family needs may have been prompted to join unions for those reasons. However, in one of only a handful of studies of Brazilian women union members, Leda Gitahy, Helena Hirata, Elizabeth Lobo, and Rosa Lucia Moyses suggest that unionization rates in the late 1970s support an alternative thesis: perhaps women workers were attracted to militance.[108] As unions began to develop a shop-floor base, union leaders changed their attitudes: rather than viewing women workers as marginal, leaders made a conscious effort to incorporate women's demands. The 1978 Congress of Women Metalworkers demanded equal pay, an end to gender-based discrimination, day-care centers, and maternity leave, and these demands were incorporated into subsequent union campaigns. The next year, women workers' "high level of participation in the 1978–79 strikes constitute[d] an outstanding example of learning, of the possibilities of participation, and of overcoming some of the barriers imposed by female socialization in exercising political activities."[109]

The increased participation of women in unions also reflected the growing participation of women throughout Brazilian society in political movements through the 1970s. Women participated actively in the movement for amnesty for political exiles and in the small, but visible, feminist movement; women from primarily working-class backgrounds led the Cost of Living Movement, as well as local campaigns for day-care centers and health clinics. Perhaps for the first time in Brazilian history, working-class women entered into public debate and success-fully mobilized community support, as visible leaders in Christian base communities, in Catholic Mothers' Clubs, and in campaigns for im-proved social services. Although this activism was not necessarily un-dertaken in support of explicitly feminist demands, even in all-female groups oriented toward fulfilling domestic roles, "participation [was] linked not only to a number of meanings relating to the domestic and female universe," but also allowed the creation of "a new space [which] not only [enabled] women to share the equally pervasive oppression and to identify common problems but also to construct an agreeable alternative."[110] Moreover, it provided "the organizational context for networking among women of the popular classes."[111]

In this context, it is probably not surprising that women workers, whose needs had been traditionally ignored by union leaders, hoped the "new unionism" might incorporate women's needs in the larger list of union demands.[112] Women's organizations were often marked by divi-sions between different classes, with different interpretations of gender-specific interests; but in a detailed study of the Brazilian women's move-ment, Sonia Alvarez points out that working women sometimes made more explicit links between domestic gender relations and class issues than either feminist organizers or church-linked liberation theologists expected.[113] Women activists raised personal issues and issues of repro-duction of the labor force to an explicitly political level. In 1979, forty-six women's organizations in São Paulo subscribed to a manifesto ar-guing that domestic work subsidized private capital by reproducing labor, and demanding that the state and employers assume responsibil-ity for childcare. Women's work at home creates "the conditions for everyone to rest and to work . . . [and] creates more profit that goes directly into the pockets of the boss," although women were paid less than men for their time in the factory.

> We are workers who are a little different than other workers . . . because we are not recognized as workers when we work at home 24 hours a day . . . [and] because when we work outside the home, we accumulate two jobs— at home and in the factory. . . . We want crèches that function full-time, entirely financed by the State and by companies, close to workplaces and places of residence, with our participation in the orientation given to chil-dren and with good conditions for their development.[114]

Many of the demands articulated by women unionists—especially campaigns for day-care centers and for paid maternity leave—reveal the extent to which at least some women workers viewed their position in the labor force as permanent: rather than foreseeing a future in which they would return home, they sought changes that would make it possible to sustain family life while they worked.

In the context of increased mobilization, the interaction between declining real wages and the absence of social services must have been transparent to most union members; but to women workers, who bore much of the responsibility for family maintenance, the relationship between workplace and community-related demands must have been unmistakable. Lula regarded women's involvement in labor struggles, both at home and in the factory, as essential to the success of the 1978 strikes: "If the women hadn't pressured the men at home, there wouldn't have been a strike. In the end, they know what the cost of life is."[115] Under Brazilian gender patterns, as in most of the world, women are identified with home and community, but low wages and low levels of services eroded any possibility that women could fulfill the domestic tasks assigned them as women. Some feminist scholars distinguish between practical gender interests, which reflect women's efforts to fulfill gendered obligations, and feminist ones, which challenge gender subordination.[116] During the course of political mobilization, some working women certainly developed a feminist critique of gender inequality; but the practical problems confronting poor families meant that support for broad community-based campaigns like the Cost of Living Movement arose directly out of the concrete, gendered conditions of family life. Women workers may well have understood more clearly than most the inadequacy of the level of reproduction of the Brazilian working class; women workers participating in both the industrial labor force and in the shaping of union agendas may well have been especially likely to view community issues in class terms, underscoring the links between production and reproduction.[117]

CLASS AND CITIZENSHIP

Brazilian sociologists and political scientists watching the emergence of both the labor movement and urban social movements since the late 1970s, with their broadening social bases and the expansion of their demands for economic, social, and political inclusion, frequently discussed these movements in terms of the redefinition of citizenship. Following, at least implicitly, T. H. Marshall's classic definition of citizenship as a combination of civic, political, and social rights,[118] activists tended to interpret community deprivation as the effect of an inegalitarian class structure, reflected in, and reinforced by, a state whose policies consistently favored private capital accumulation. Under the populist governments after 1945, individuals were denied political participation through the disenfranchisement of illiterates, and working-class participation was inhibited through state control over labor unions; but after 1964, the military government's denial of the right to full participation was even clearer, combining repression and coercion to block workers' organizations and individual workers from articulating their interests. The strikes of the late 1970s and early 1980s simultaneously offered visible evidence of workers' ability to articulate demands and reinforced the identity of this "new subject" in Brazilian society.[119]

Francisco Weffort argues that in Brazil, "Politics has always been a privilege of the few; . . . until now, there was barely a public space where political activity, almost always limited to the dominant classes, could be differentiated from the activities of private life. [Brazil's] is a history in which the conservatives are the eternal winners."[120] For the first time in decades, the rise of an urban social movement based in factories and in working-class communities raised the possibility that working-class Brazilians could challenge their country's long tradition of elitist politics.

Perhaps the easiest way to measure the extent to which the discourse of class identity and mobilization came to dominate political debate in working-class areas is to follow the rise of the Partido dos Trabalhadores, which insisted on a political strategy based on working-class organizations and neighborhoods. Initially, the new workers' party appeared unlikely to play a major political role: even poor voters sought a more effective channel through which to express their aspirations. In the context of a highly restricted election process, mounting a pragmatic challenge to military rule was undoubtedly attractive. The Partido Movimento Democratico Brasileiro (PMDB), the largest opposition party in 1982, offered a reformist route that was far more likely to succeed—especially in the recessionary period of the early 1980s, when leading businessmen declared support for the PMDB's project of political change and moderate reforms. Urging voters to cast a "useful vote" (*voto útil*), the PMDB appealed to disaffected middle- and working-class voters to support its candidates. Although its leaders were almost entirely drawn from the upper class, the PMDB offered a populism not unlike that which had dominated Brazilian politics in the 1950s: urban workers would be represented by wealthier politicians, who promised to permit greater political participation and at least the possibility of reform.

If voters in 1982 "deemed the overall gains from a PMDB victory at the state level to be more important than local loyalties," however, local party organizing also played a role: where the Partido dos Trabalhadores had local organization, Caldeira found, it gained a much higher percentage of votes.[121] Even in 1982, urban areas that had supported militant labor struggles were as likely to support the fledgling PT— which viewed participation in the election campaign "as a tool in the organization and mobilization of workers and the construction of popular power" rather than as an immediate route to power—as the more pragmatic PMDB.[122] In metropolitan São Paulo, there is a strong correlation between income levels, percentage of population in the industrial work force, and voting patterns; the party received 14.9 percent of the city's votes overall, but its support was concentrated on the periphery, especially in the industrial southern section. The close relation between party organization and PT support shows that income levels alone are less important in explaining the election outcome than the combination of income levels with previous community mobilization, which meant there were more likely to be activists who would form a PT branch in the area.[123]

Despite charges that a separate party identity would split the opposition, the PT, using slogans such as "Vote PT. The rest are bourgeois," continued to insist that "the only policies that are effectively oppositionist are those that express the interests of the workers."[124] Party activists argued that only a party based on grass-roots mobilization and linked to independent trade unions would be able to avoid being controlled by upper-class politicians or crushed by a repressive state.[125] Instead of supporting a broad reformist front, the PT cooperated with elite parties only to mobilize demonstrations against the military regime, as in the enormous 1984 rallies in support of direct presidential elections.

It is worth underlining, however, that although the Partido dos Trabalhadores grew out of an industrial labor movement, PT theorists viewed its constituency as broader than simply industrial workers: while Brazil's capitalist growth had made industrial workers the fulcrum of the popular strata "by its homogeneity, and its experience with organization and struggle," capitalism had also denied minimally acceptable living conditions to a much broader population, laying the basis for a "broad anti-capitalist front made possible by the very exclusionary characteristics that the process of accumulation has acquired in our country." [126] Reflecting its history and its strategy, the Partido dos Trabalhadores cooperated less with other political parties than with the CUT labor federation, encouraging the CUT's organization among the landless rural population. First winning municipal elections and governorships, PT candidates claimed to offer "a new relationship of the people to power [which] continues to be with the movements, and will always be where the people and their struggles are." [127] During the Constituent Assembly of 1987–88, when an elected congress designed the framework for a democratic transition, the sixteen PT deputies were a small, if visible, minority, which supported only measures it believed would broaden "democratic space and popular participation" for workers and rejected legislative compromises it considered "manipulation by other political forces." [128] The PT emphasized both changes in labor and social welfare legislation and in the ability of grass-roots organizations to propose legal changes.

This is not the place to describe in detail the growth of the Partido dos Trabalhadores during the second half of the 1980s. As it gradually expanded beyond its initial São Paulo base, it redefined its constituency to include the broad working class. [129] Although the PT's uncompromising stance had appeared unlikely to gain significant support in the mid 1980s, the ruling PMDB's inability to deliver on its initial promises apparently underscored the validity of the PT's insistence on a different approach to politics, centered on challenging elite control of the state.

The shift was especially visible in the labor movement: CGT unions allied with the PMDB gradually lost rank-and-file members, and by the late 1980s, the CUT was the dominant labor federation apparently because its insistence on shop-floor militance and its support for landless rural workers' campaigns were more appealing than the CGT's corporatism. But urban workers' growing disillusionment with politics based on class compromises was also visible in electoral patterns, as the PMDB, increasingly responsive to its business supporters, divided over issues like labor law reform, inflation controls, and land reform. By the late 1980s, the PT's electoral successes suggested that its claims to seek the redefinition of citizenship to include socioeconomic rights as well as electoral democracy resonated with Brazil's poor.

By 1989, when Lula ran for president, he was able to appeal to an extremely broad base. Initially considered a marginal candidate, Lula promised to ensure labor rights, to enforce minimum wage laws, to carry out land reform, and to renounce the foreign debt. Lula's main support clearly lay in urban working-class areas. The fact that Lula's wealthy opponent, Fernando Collor de Mello, apparently tended to win slightly more votes in the poorest urban slums underscores the relationship between prior organization and party strength: Lula's support in slightly more stable working-class areas—in "poor but not miserable neighborhoods"—showed that "the Partido dos Trabalhadores is today more rooted in the penultimate [rather] than the ultimate periphery,"[130] where absolute poverty may have inhibited the growth of labor organization or party structures.

Rather than understanding the relationship between factory and community as the result of traditional social bonds or communal ethos, I have argued that the close ties between labor and community organizations in Brazil's urban centers are built on a more immediate class identity, born of workers' lived experiences, and in particular their experience of mobilization within specific kinds of organizations. Interests were identified and organized through campaigns combining labor and community struggles, and the outcome was the formation of a broadly defined working-class identity. In the context of peripheralization, workers, unions, and community activists could easily identify specific processes through which working-class communities were first created and then denied access to social resources. Mobilized through local campaigns, individuals could quickly come to see the state's role in reinforcing stratification at a more abstract level: individual employers, and upper-income Brazilians in general, benefited directly from artificially restrained labor costs, while state policies further eroded the conditions of poor communities. Through policies that steadily reduced workers' incomes and urban services, the state and employers jointly undermined the possibility that workers would see themselves as relatively privileged, compared with the unemployed; as worker mobilization spread, so too did community support for workers' demands and labor involvement in community campaigns.

Especially as workers brought a factory-based understanding of economic relations to bear on community issues, the urban social movements that emerged in the late 1970s had a distinct class character; but at the same time, the labor movement could not ignore the importance of issues beyond the factory gates to its members and their families. As a demand, citizenship—redefined to include political participation, labor rights, and entitlements to state services—became a code for challenging the exclusion of most Brazilians from the benefits of capitalist development. At a time when the state and the dominant classes were already debating the nature of their own alliance, urban social movements reinforced and broadened the class identity that had already been developed in workplace organizations, challenging Brazil's inequitable distribution of wealth and power. Over the next decade, activists in the independent labor movement and in the Partido dos Trabalhadores popularized the language of class and citizenship, and increasingly appealed to a constituency that found itself excluded from the benefits of capitalist growth.

SOUTH AFRICA: COMMUNITY, RACE, AND CLASS

As perhaps every sociologist writing about South Africa has warned, the relationship between race and class under apartheid is terrifyingly complex: apartheid involved both racial oppression and labor controls, and state legislation affected people classified black both as blacks and as workers. Apartheid's severe racial discrimination was certainly its most notorious feature, and international opposition focused on the way political and civil rights were linked to racial categories. Nonetheless, by the late 1980s, an understanding of class relations played an important and explicit part in popular demands, as the labor movement's emphasis on altering class domination was generally incorporated into proposals for the future. By 1989, the broad opposition considered workers' rights a crucial part of constitutional proposals, while the first inclusive meeting of opposition groups inside the country was carefully designed to ensure that labor representatives composed the largest contingent of delegates.[131] Even after ANC leader Nelson Mandela was released from prison and other ANC leaders returned from exile, the labor movement remained a key element in the transition process: for most South African activists, democracy had effectively been redefined to include a stronger voice for workers, as well as political inclusion for black South Africans.[132]

Harold Wolpe has argued that rather than seeing class and race as two separate dynamics, "external and opposed to one another," South Africans in particular should recognize that "race may become interiorized in class demands," in a situation where the two have been historically mutually constitutive.[133] Racial considerations entered into the structuring of class relations in South Africa; under rapid industrialization combined with racial controls, unions have found it difficult to separate economic and racial demands, because workers are denied political rights on the basis of racial classification.

This recognition calls for an exploration of the processes through which demands are formulated and expressed: in a situation where racial oppression is so blatant, why would activists mobilize support along class lines, rather than racial ones? Throughout the late 1970s and early 1980s, community organizations began to form in South Africa's black townships, focusing primarily on local issues such as bus fares, rents, and municipal governance. Often starting from efforts to change state policy on specific aspects of segregated township life, community groups managed to mobilize township residents, gradually growing until, by the early 1980s, "active political protest, organization, and direct action emerged" as black activists sought a role in decision-making at the local level.[134] Building on the post-1973 strike waves and the 1976 student uprising, local groups gradually formed a broad coalition to challenge minority rule. In 1977, following the repression of the 1976 student uprising, there were few visible signs of community organization; but by 1983, delegates from 320 groups formed the United Democratic Front (UDF) to oppose government proposals for a racially divided tricameral Parliament. Within six months, the number of UDF affiliates had almost doubled.[135] Despite regional variation, community groups generally managed to overcome residents' fears, mobilizing broad support for an anti-apartheid opposition.

As in Brazil, each community group had a different genesis and dynamic, making generalizations difficult. Students' groups were formed during the 1980–81 schools boycott, when high school students once again rejected inferior education. Civic associations formed to represent residents' demands to municipal authorities, and at a time when the state hoped to restructure its relationship with urban blacks, these groups could sometimes petition successfully for improved services, persuade private corporations to fund local community programs, or, after 1984, organize widespread rent boycotts. In squatter settlements, residents' associations could sometimes mobilize community resistance to forced removal. By the mid 1980s, women's groups, health groups, and even sports clubs had organized challenges to specific aspects of state policy.

Many of these organizations were assisted by sympathetic church workers or by community workers, who provided meeting spaces, expertise, and access to the press. The organizations were rooted in com-

munities; but apartheid meant that even very localized attempts to reform state policy quickly escalated to more overt political demands.
"Residents' struggles [have] entailed chronic conflict with the state over
both the broad political and the specific fiscal relationships" of black
townships to the state.[136] As in Brazil, community residents may have
been initially mobilized through local grievances, but to an even greater
extent than in Brazil, perhaps, activists often brought with them a larger
agenda: individuals who secretly belonged to the ANC's illegal networks used the movement's symbols and rhetoric and drew on ANC
strategies and analyses, but by avoiding overt political affiliation, they
could hope to avoid repression.

As legal organizations and localized protest movements spread
through urban communities, the state sought to reassert control. Starting in the country's industrial core, and spreading rapidly through the
country, groups stressed specific grievances, but the generalized repression they experienced increased popular support for more general political demands. Jeremy Seekings observes:

> During 1985 and early 1986, high levels of mobilization were sustained and
> generalized, with chronic resistance through rent and consumer boycotts
> erupting on occasions into virtual civil war. . . .
> Behind this generalization and entrenchment of resistance lay [a] process
> of radicalization and convergence of political cultures. Educational griev-
> ances, rents, evictions, [local administration], and repression were not seen
> as unconnected issues. . . . Heightened repression, as an overtly political re-
> sponse to discontent, tied all the issues together through developing the ex-
> plicit political content in the . . . political cultures of township residents.[137]

In July 1985, the government declared a state of emergency in most
of the country's industrial centers, using its powers to detain thousands
of activists without trial. Except for a brief period in 1986, these emergency powers remained in force through the rest of the 1980s, and
membership in many of the community organizations that had emerged
in the first part of the decade was declared a criminal offense. Under
threat of military or police intervention, levels of community mobilization varied widely. In many urban townships, residents organized street
committees to take on responsibilities for local administration and to
mobilize communities. (Although it is sometimes suggested that street
committees imitated union structures, with a block-by-block system
paralleling shop-floor organization,[138] community activists more com-
monly believed these committees would allow them to maintain basic
local organization without exposing visible leaders.)[139]

During the 1980s, trade unions became increasingly prominent in the anti-apartheid opposition. Especially when detentions silenced community activists, their campaigns were continued by trade unionists, who could hope for some protection from shop-floor organizations' ability to pressure employers. When union leaders were detained, workers struck, individual businessmen suffered losses, and business associations complained about state interference in labor relations.[140] By the late 1980s, South Africa's largest labor federation, COSATU, dominated the legal opposition movement. Strikes, or general stay-aways, were prominent in the repertoire of protest actions, and labor activists were among the most visible opposition leaders.

When nonracial unions were legalized in 1979, many industrial union leaders sought to build shop-floor organizations and unify the independent unions before joining political movements, to avoid submerging workers' aspirations in broad popular coalitions. But by the mid 1980s, as community mobilization intensified, unionists increasingly argued that community and factory issues were inextricably linked. Even in the early 1980s, a minority of unionists argued for a closer alliance; in 1983, twelve independent unions joined the UDF, which resolved "to work for a South Africa in which the oppression and exploitation of workers will cease" as a fundamental part of political change.[141] In 1984, when 90 percent of workers in the PWV area boycotted work to protest detentions of community and labor leaders, FOSATU's newspaper editorialized:

> Worker parents are naturally sympathetic to their children's struggle and in many townships joint parent-student committees have been set up to offer support. On top of this, workers are having to meet ever-increasing rent, food and transport costs at a time when employers are using the recession as an excuse to block wage increases.[142]

As the community-based uprising of 1984–87 deepened, national labor leaders increasingly supported union participation in community struggles, describing their task as one of articulating "the politics of the working class, the politics of the democratic majority,"[143] and warning that if workers stood aside from community organizations, they risked isolation.[144] The labor movement increasingly supported township "stay-aways"[145]—a tactic that unionists had previously feared might weaken shop-floor organization.[146] In 1983, unions that joined the UDF did so out of a conviction that only political organizations could deal with the intersection between state policy and workplace exploitation represented by the migrant labor system;[147] at the 1985 launching of COSATU, this view was clearly prevalent within the labor movement's leadership.[148]

Through the 1970s and early 1980s, relationships between community organizations and trade unions, and the class character of community demands, varied enormously. Some of the variation was regional, and it often reflected trade unionists' suspicions of better-educated, wealthier community leaders. In Cape Town, many community groups started in response to union organizing drives, organizing consumer boycotts of products from companies refusing to negotiate with nonracial or black workers' organizations; yet trade union leaders there generally remained wary of community activists, fearing the erosion of worker leadership.[149]

In the Eastern Cape and the PWV triangle around Johannesburg—both areas with a high concentration of capital-intensive industries—unionists who avoided community issues lost support on the shop floor. In most industries, this process occurred within organizations: as members became increasingly active in political campaigns, union officials who sought to restrict activities to factories lost elections. In the most extreme case, Joe Foster, FOSATU's president, who had argued in 1982 that workers should avoid active participation in "community" struggles, no longer held a national position three years later.[150]

In a few cases, unions were divided over how to respond to community campaigns. In the Eastern Cape, relatively educated, skilled workers in the auto industry regularly struck in support of community demands in the late 1970s and early 1980s, abandoning unions headed by factory-oriented officials for unions that were explicitly oriented toward cooperation with community activists. When Thozamile Botha, leader of a community organization concerned with high rents and water supplies in Port Elizabeth's African townships, was fired from Ford, Ford workers struck until he was reinstated—over their union's objections. Union leaders condemned the strike as "political," so the Ford workers formed a factory committee that bypassed the union.[151] Unionism was similarly linked to community activism in East London, where, despite high unemployment, police repression, and highly resistant employers, the South African Allied Workers' Union (SAAWU) first appealed to workers through community meetings, rather than in factories.[152] After militant strikes won substantial wage increases, SAAWU activists organized an extended bus boycott to protest transport costs. Despite severe government repression, SAAWU's active involvement in broader political issues offered a clear alternative to more workplace-oriented unionism: in an area long marked by strong support for the ANC,[153] SAAWU's appeal was based on explicit links to the clandestine political movement.[154]

In the PWV triangle, the relationship between community groups and unions was more problematic. In the early 1980s, after legalization, many union leaders tried to focus on shop-floor organization and recognition drives, arguing that township residents could participate separately in shop-floor and community groups. However, members frequently asked their unions to participate in community campaigns against forced removals or for better services in black communities; the questions became increasingly tense in mid 1983, when most Transvaal-area unions refused to join the newly launched UDF. In early 1984, the metalworkers' union in the area split, at least partly over the question of how unions should relate to community issues; although the new union failed to grow, the split underscored the issue's seriousness.[155]

By the end of 1984, as the community-based uprising spread, union leaders could no longer stand aside: from late 1984 on, even union leaders who had previously been skeptical about taking up campaigns outside the factory began actively to mobilize workplace action in support of political demands. Moses Mayekiso, the East Rand metalworkers' organizer who both exemplified and led this shift, has described the process at some length. In the early 1980s, he told interviewers, the union movement generally

> believed that we needed to build worker strength and to build that strength we needed to concentrate on issues that we could win—bread and butter issues like wages and working conditions. That is not to say we were against politics or political issues—in fact we were paving the way to get involved in politics.
>
> Later in 1984 I began to argue for greater worker participation in community issues. This was not a change from my previous position. I had just come to the conclusion that working class leadership had developed to such an extent that workers were able to sufficiently argue their position in community politics and to assert a worker position on issues. I argued quite forcefully for a change in policy towards greater involvement in community politics. . . . I encouraged [union] participation in community organisations to make sure that they were democratic and represented worker interests.
>
> I emphasised that one could not separate community issues from factory issues. An issue like higher rents was directly linked to the fact that people were earning low wages.[156]

As PWV area community organizations grew stronger, unionists increasingly participated in joint campaigns, often redefining community issues in terms of working-class interests rather than in terms of racial identity. Especially as unionists became prominent in political groups, they raised economic as well as political issues in terms that resonated widely in black communities, whose residents had almost all experienced domination in class as well as racial terms.

In a sense, Natal provides a test case for the argument that experiences of labor mobilization shaped the way communities formed political agendas. To a greater extent than any other region, Natal demonstrated an alternative pattern of mobilization. During the 1970s—at the same time as a nonracial labor movement was emerging in Natal's industrial centers—the KwaZulu prime minister, Chief Buthelezi, organized the ethnically based Zulu cultural movement, Inkatha. Throughout the decade, shop stewards feared that union involvement in political campaigns—particularly campaigns that rejected ethnic appeals— would divide the loyalties of Zulu-speaking workers, threatening the shop-floor unity needed to confront employers.[157] In the 1980s, Inkatha's failed attempt to form a Zulu labor movement illustrated the extent to which unions had offered an alternative vehicle for mobilization, both to workers and to residents in the communities in which they lived. When Inkatha-affiliated gangs began to attack black communities in Natal that failed to support Buthelezi, COSATU members often bore the brunt of these attacks and provided the most organized, visible opposition to Inkatha's claims to represent all Zulu-speakers.[158] This pattern may reflect Inkatha's more general failure to build an urban base, but it also hints at the extent to which involvement in the labor movement may have offered an alternative identity for many Zulu-speaking workers: at least as long as they participated actively in urban labor unions, Zulu-speaking workers were more likely to respond in terms of class, and of a broader South African rather than a Zulu political identity.[159]

If community demands were redefined to include class issues, national union demands became increasingly politicized. In 1987, COSATU's demands included not only a living wage for all South Africans, but also proper housing, full political rights, land redistribution, and educational opportunities;[160] reflecting growing support among union members for the ANC, these demands were directly tied to the ANC's basic statement of principles, the Freedom Charter. COSATU's leaders

still insisted that the working class should play a leading role within
the resistance movement,[161] but unionists increasingly tended to define
workers' needs in terms of a working-class community. By the late
1980s, the labor movement's support for, and involvement in, the
"mass democratic movement" was virtually unquestioned, while within
political groups, demands for a democratic South Africa almost invariably included discussions of redistribution of wealth and working-class
participation in policy-making.

Given South Africa's racial stratification, and the racial aspects of
state policy toward black, especially African, workers, the emergence
of a class-based discourse within the oppositional movement is even
more surprising in the case of South Africa than it is in that of Brazil.
Yet perhaps to an even greater extent than in Brazil, specific mechanisms linked workplace issues to community identity in South Africa:
while the state discriminated against individuals based on racial classification, many forms of discrimination were directly related to relations
of production, and community identity was intimately related to class
position. For decades, employers and the state had cooperated in creating, and benefited from the existence of, working-class communities
that were denied basic social services. The transparency of this relationship shaped working-class consciousness in ways that made the links
between the two types of organizations almost inevitable.

INFLUX CONTROL, GROUP AREAS, AND
CLASS CONSCIOUSNESS

For those unfamiliar with the mechanisms of apartheid, it is worth taking a moment to describe the ways in which racial proscriptions were
intertwined with control over labor supplies. Undoubtedly, the most
obvious method through which the South African state has created,
maintained, and controlled the supply of black workers to white-owned
enterprises has been the set of laws governing where black South Africans may live and work, dividing political and legal rights according to
racial classification. South Africans of all racial categories were affected
by apartheid laws, but the movements and opportunities of those classified as African were especially restricted. Since 1913, although Africans
could physically live and work in the 87 percent of the country set aside
for white residence and ownership, their legal rights were generally restricted to the roughly 13 percent set aside as "homelands" or "bantustans." Throughout the twentieth century, influx control laws have re-

stricted Africans' movements. In white-designated areas of South Africa, African men were required to carry passes from the turn of the century on—initially, to keep them tied to their jobs and later to keep them from forming an unemployed urban population. This system was expanded to include women in the 1950s. The 1950 Group Areas Act designates specific areas in white-designated South Africa for residence by different racial groups; throughout the 1950s, the effort to redesign existing cities along racial lines led to the forced removal of urban black communities. By the 1960s, new black townships had been created on the edges of even small South African cities: whites lived near the city center, blacks lived on the edges, often near the industrial sites where they were expected to work.

Designed to prevent rapid African urbanization, the influx control system was explicitly linked to employment. Designed to keep Africans whom government officials believed were "no longer fit for work or superfluous in the labour market"[162] out of white-designated areas, the passes carried by Africans documented work records, indicating whether the bearer had permission to be outside the "homeland" areas. After 1952, Africans born in rural areas—who constituted a majority in the 1950s—could only attain permanent residence in urban areas by working continuously for a single employer in the same town for ten years, or through continuous legal residence in a single town for fifteen years (which implied consistent employment, since legal residence required employment). African workers with urban rights could keep wives, unmarried daughters, and sons under the age of eighteen with them; however, even after they qualified for legal residence—either through birth or steady employment—Africans could lose these rights if they were found "idle and undesirable."[163] Despite wide resistance in the 1940s and 1950s, by the 1960s, apartheid controls were firmly in place.

Perhaps the least well-known feature of influx control is the extent to which employers were involved in determining an individual's urban residence rights. Before 1979, Africans could not legally remain for more than seventy-two hours in an urban area without a permit—a permit normally granted only when employers asked to hire the individual. Legally, Africans from rural areas could not simply go to town looking for work. In order to allow a continued supply of rurally based migrant African labor, the state developed a complex system of labor recruiters and contracts, allowing employers and the state to maintain the fiction that even long-term workers were only temporary: employers could recruit workers on renewable annual contracts. These contracts removed the possibility of long-term workers gaining permanent urban residence, even if they were continuously employed in the same job. Most employers cooperated actively with state labor officials; as chapter 3 suggests, the system was flexible enough to allow employers to develop a permanent industrial labor force without running into conflict with state efforts to denationalize black South Africans. From the mid 1960s on, to prevent further urbanization, the state built only single-sex hostels in African townships, instead of family housing; although the contract labor system assured employers of a stable work force, Africans were expected to leave their families in rural areas and return there when they stopped working.

The choices facing Africans without permits were bleak: they could remain illegally in white-designated areas, hoping to find work and eventually regularize their status, or live in a "bantustan," where chronic unemployment and land shortages meant almost inevitable poverty. A 1978 study suggested that Africans who worked illegally for nine months in a white-designated area and spent three months in prison might nevertheless improve their income by 702.7 percent over their potential bantustan earnings.[164] In 1980, despite two decades of state policies aimed at decentralizing jobs, nine million of the twelve million South Africans living below the official poverty line were located in bantustans.[165]

Not surprisingly, millions of Africans lived illegally in urban townships, joining their families or seeking work and educational opportunities. In 1976 alone, 216,112 African men and 33,918 women were arrested for pass offenses; of these, 68 percent were arrested in the PWV industrial region.[166] A series of reforms from 1979 changed some of the mechanics of the influx control system,[167] but even when the pass system was officially abolished in 1986, Africans' residence in urban areas remained predicated on housing, work, and on the political status of the bantustan to which they had been assigned. The legal fiction that treated Africans as temporary migrants continued to shape individuals' lives,[168] and it may well have given individuals with urban residence rights greater control over family members, especially women, who had no urban rights, and therefore no legal access to urban services or resources.[169]

Paradoxically, the expansion of the African industrial labor force during the 1970s was predicated on employers' willingness to participate in the fiction that their long-term workers were only temporary visitors. Indeed, the threat of being "endorsed out"—that is, of being returned to rural bantustans—undermined unionization drives, since workers faced with unemployment were more vulnerable to employers' threats. These threats were real: in 1980, striking municipal workers in Johannesburg and striking flour mill workers in Cape Town were packed onto buses and "removed" to bantustans.[170]

But once shop-floor organizations began to emerge, such victimization may simply have reinforced unions' understanding of the links between workplace issues and South Africa's political structure: under the migrant labor system, where even skilled workers were vulnerable to removal, shop-floor organizations were directly affected by the country's political arrangements. The Johannesburg municipal workers' strike, a labor research group concluded, "demonstrated the need for strong political organization, and consistent community organization; the role of the former during the strike being to articulate political demands such as the abolition of the contract labor system, or the release of the union leaders, while the latter could have taken the form of mobilization of the people to provide food and shelter for the dismissed workers."[171] Several studies suggest that "long-term migrants"—workers on renewable contracts, who could never gain permanent urban residential rights, even though they might have worked for years for a single employer—may have been especially active in early shop-floor organization. Such migrants, organized in the single-sex hostels where they were required to live, apparently predominated in the 1973 strikes, and participated actively in union organizing drives in the East Rand metal industry.[172]

For African workers especially, the effect of state policies on shop-floor organization—and employer complicity in state policies that discriminated against black workers—could hardly be ignored; alliances with community organizations could only strengthen unions' ability to resist state intervention at the workplace. Perhaps even more important at the level of creating a collective identity, redefining the labor movement's constituency to include workers' families, the unemployed, and students reflected the framework imposed by apartheid, where all blacks were considered potential workers and Africans' legal rights were predicated on keeping a job.

PERIPHERALIZATION AND CLASS CONSCIOUSNESS

In Brazil, working-class communities were shaped primarily through economic forces, while South Africa's townships were built by overt racial policies. In the mid 1970s, South African community activists were far more likely to analyze their situation in racial than in class terms.[173] Racial segregation meant black townships included residents of different economic and social classes. Apartheid laws prohibited blacks from owning property or operating businesses in "white" areas—by the mid 1960s, including even the informal stands from which black hawkers had once sold prepared food, to the point where industrialists hoping to prevent "the '11 A.M. sag' among non-white workers" were encouraged to introduce factory canteens with menus designed to fit employer conceptions of blacks' eating preferences.[174] Although a few black businessmen managed to accumulate wealth and some black South Africans have managed to gain education to become teachers, lawyers, journalists, clergymen, or doctors, the tiny minority of urban blacks with education or wealth were legally required to live in black ghettos, where they suffered the same inadequate urban services that plagued working-class residents of the same communities. Under these circumstances, the question posed at the outset of this chapter seems especially pertinent: why did community groups view townships' lack of services as problems related as much to class and economic exploitation as to racial discrimination?

In the 1970s, while the labor movement was taking shape on shop floors and at factory gates, outspoken community activists tended to be students and professionals, not industrial workers. Indeed, leading unionists sometimes worried that close alliances with community organizations would undermine working-class leadership, because more educated members of what was regularly referred to as the black "petty bourgeoisie" might control working-class residents' associations, supporting middle-class demands such as the right to freehold homeownership.[175] Certainly, many of the demands expressed by community-based groups in the 1970s reflected aspirations to upward mobility rather than working-class consciousness: while families of all classes sought improved educational opportunities for their children, this demand hardly challenged existing class relations. Was there a shift in the claims put forward by community groups?

Mayekiso and other unionists have suggested that increased participation of workers in community organizations reinforced broad identification with workers' organizations and demands: organized first at the factory, where interests were articulated in class terms, workers brought a nonracial class analysis to discussions of problems in their communities. Shortages of housing and of transport services were discussed in terms of low real wages; workers described disparities between white-designated areas and black townships as the reflection of class relations as well as racial disparities. Local shop-stewards councils discussed community issues in relation to workplace problems. "Workers in the [Germiston] area share many problems," Jeremy Baskin noted. "They use the same buses and trains, they live in the same areas and they know other workers in neighboring factories. The common conditions which workers face at a local level become a major spur to militancy, once organisation gets started."[176] But even as individuals, union activists often helped shape the discourse of the groups in which they participated: they brought with them organizing skills learned in factory campaigns. Community organizers recognized that the possibility that community demands might be backed up by strikes opened the way to new strategies. A 1984 pamphlet of the Congress of South African Students, for example, asked workers to support students' educational demands because, like workers, students sought an end to a "racist and anti-worker" government:

> Workers, you are our fathers and mothers, you are our brothers and sisters. Our struggle in the schools is your struggle in the factories. We fight the same bosses' government, we fight the same government. . . . Workers, we need your support and strength in the trade unions. We students will never win our struggle without the strength and support [of] the workers' movement.[177]

This recognition was certainly reinforced by the underground ANC, which, with the allied South African Communist Party, stressed working-class demands: "The job of the revolutionary fighter is to build the leading force of our struggle—the working class . . . [and] to make sure that the workers' voice is loudest, that the workers' way forward is accepted inside every one of our mass organizations."[178] But the daily experiences of workers and community residents also made community groups responsive. Community campaigns often underscored the links between workplace and community—reflecting the way the mechanisms of apartheid reinforced the class character of black communities, and, in turn, reinforcing black communities' tendency to define needs simultaneously in terms of class and race.

Perhaps more than any other single aspect of black life in South Africa, the experience of commuting daily from townships to white-designated areas to work shaped community identities. As in Brazil, the public transport system, which carried residents of African communities from home to town, demonstrated how black workers were, in the

Brazilian phrase, "peripheralized" by a state responsive only to the needs of a white minority. From the early 1950s on, urban black residents were moved to segregated townships; Africans were especially likely to be placed in townships far from city centers. These townships were even less likely than Brazilian cities' peripheries to otter jobs: state planners and residents alike realized that townships were little more than dormitory communities for those South Africans whose only available asset was their labor power. By the late 1970s, as more of the "homelands" to which Africans were assigned were made independent, this process was frequently coupled with denationalization: boundaries for the "homelands" were frequently redrawn to include large African townships. Thus, many African workers traveled daily, not only from dormitory community to urban industrial area, but across what the South African state considered an international boundary, underscoring their political exclusion.[179] In the mid 1980s, a government research group found that 19 percent of South Africa's 2.1 million African commuters—including commuters from townships as well as those from nominally independent homelands—traveled more than 45 kilometers each way between home and work; another 52 percent traveled at least 20 kilometers each way. About 80 percent traveled an average of 2.5 hours daily; the 20 percent considered long-distance commuters spent between 3.5 and 7 hours daily in transit, with an average of 4.5 hours a day.[180]

As in Brazil, slowing economic growth from the late 1970s on coincided with increased transport costs, and increased fares further eroded wages that were already low. Despite government regulation and subsidization of private transport companies, fares consumed between 5 and 20 percent of average black wages.[181] Even government officials recognized that "in South Africa public transport, particularly public bus transport, is highly politicised. Because large numbers of people are brought together . . . in circumstances in which the group has a shared destiny, it is only to be expected that shrewd observers would see opportunities for making political capital from the situation."[182] These shared experiences were by no means limited to industrial workers; but industrial workers, recognizing that the daily commute both extended long workdays and cut into wages, participated actively in campaigns to reduce fares.[183]

Even more than in Brazil, transport services in South Africa underlined state and employer collaboration in exploiting black workers. The state first imposed a transport levy on employers of African workers in

1952; that levy was extended to employers of workers classified Indian or Coloured in 1972. In 1982, employers paid R 3 per month per worker. Nevertheless, rising fuel costs and greater distances—related, in turn, to segregationist policies—meant that employers' share of the total cost of commuting actually decreased significantly, from 32 percent in 1974 to only 13 percent in 1981–82. In 1984, the state paid 37 percent of the total cost of bus services, employers paid 13 percent, and black workers—already receiving wages far lower than those paid to white workers—paid half the cost of traveling between racially segregated areas and work.[184] Even the state transport subsidy was clearly meant to benefit employers rather than workers: it applied only to tickets bought on a work-week schedule, and workers who missed a workday lost the fare. Indeed, one bus company explicitly resisted efforts to allow workers to miss weekdays without paying, because to do so might spread the subsidy across non-worker passenger fares, which "would defeat the purpose of the government as trustee for the employer and the taxpayer."[185]

In the early 1980s, as inflation rose and transport subsidies declined, bus-fare increases reached as high as 12 percent annually. Workers clearly recognized the effect of rising fares on their budgets. Transport costs were seen as an unfair, inelastic expense: "We are not people who earn fantastic wages. How are we going to afford our food and rent when such a large amount of our wages goes on travelling expenses?"[186] In 1979, poignant images of African residents of relatively rural Ezakheni walking twenty-five kilometers daily to work in Ladysmith, Natal, clearly demonstrated the entire community's support for reduced fares. In Cape Town in 1981, in Durban and East London in 1982–83, and in the Transvaal in 1984, bus boycotts served as the fulcrum for new levels of community mobilization and organization. Residents' associations formed to articulate protests; student groups helped arrange alternative transportation with car pools and drivers; black taxi-drivers' associations ensured that private rates remained steady through the boycotts; union activists helped with organization and mobilization. In several cases, especially when buses were attacked by angry residents, bus drivers' unions refused to allow members to work during boycotts.[187] Boycotts in Cape Town and the Eastern Cape successfully rescinded increases and prompted a government commission to examine tensions in the bus system.[188]

The daily commute reinforced community solidarity and underlined apartheid's definition of black South Africans as providers of labor power. In 1981, 70 percent of Mdantsane's "working-class" residents listed transport as their most serious problem—ahead of crime, housing, educational facilities, and services. But even higher-income residents who were more likely to be able to afford cars or private minibus fares found transport problematic: 36 percent listed transport as the most serious problem confronting them. In Mdantsane, transport was "not merely a necessary inconvenience, but a daily struggle experienced by nearly 25,000 commuters who are processed en masse through a central terminus twice a day and get compressed into 276 buses."[189] By the late 1980s, after a decade of boycotts and strikes, community and union activists had learned to use the commute as an effective forum in which to mobilize residents and workers in support of their campaigns: explaining strikes and campaigns to commuters was an effective way to reach a black audience. In 1987, striking train workers in Soweto mobilized support for their strike in meetings on the very trains they were refusing to run.[190] Even without specific campaigns, as one commuter put it, "freedom songs" became a regular feature of the daily trip to work. "Such transport, dangerous and unsafe as it is, does have one overriding advantage: that of bringing people of roughly the same background together. They share a common bond [which] does ease the troubles of the day and prepare them psychologically for the next."[191]

HOUSING AND THE STATE

If public transport issues graphically illustrated the relationship between work and community and provided a set of common issues for union and community activists, housing campaigns focused black South Africans' demands for a decent standard of living on the state as well as employers. Even more than in Brazil, the state's role in creating peripheral communities, restricting workers and their families to badly serviced townships, was unmistakable. Africans with permanent urban residence rights could not own land or houses until the 1980s, but government-owned rental housing was woefully inadequate: following the 1976 uprising, a government official testified to a shortage of nearly 200,000 houses for legally employed Africans. These figures, however, drastically understate the shortages: at the time, nearly six residents lived in each two-bedroom house in Soweto, and in other areas the average number of residents rose even higher.[192] (In contrast, the 17 percent of the population classified white was said to be lacking only 6,100 houses.)[193] Given the housing shortage's magnitude, along with the state's refusal after 1960 to build new family housing for Africans, it is hardly surprising that during the industrial expansion of the 1970s, squatter settlements grew up on the margins of most townships. Workers lacking legal permanent residence or the money to pay full rent, those whose jobs provided only beds in single-sex dormitories, and those who existed on casual labor found municipal authorities would often ignore illegal squatting—recognizing, at least informally, that as long as industry was concentrated in a few areas, the expansion of the industrial labor force contradicted the apartheid policy of removing African workers to rural areas.[194]

Housing became a major political issue when the state began to adopt a more reformist stance toward the urban black labor force. The business-funded Urban Foundation made housing for African workers its top priority from 1976 on, in the explicit hope of integrating an urban industrial labor force into capitalist South Africa. The state's reforms were moderate: in some cases, rather than building new houses in townships, policymakers redrew bantustan boundaries to incorporate growing African communities, changing urban residents' legal status rather than their actual experience, to reduce their claim on the central state.[195] Nevertheless, by the late 1970s, black communities were split between those who had permanent standard housing and those who either rented rooms or who built their own homes, often in areas lacking even the rudimentary services available in established black townships. In 1979, when the government first proposed to acknowledge legally the presence of a stable urban African population, these divisions between permanent residents and squatters threatened to become more significant. In place of the pass controls, the state proposed to fine employers and township homeowners if they employed or rented space to Africans illegally. Although employers were in practice almost never fined for hiring undocumented workers, the state carried out "unremitting attacks on squatter communities and, in 1982, on illegal occupants of housing within the established townships" during the economic downturn of the early 1980s.[196] At the same time, the state promised to improve services and infrastructure in established townships, and allowed Africans for the first time to take out 99-year leases on township plots—although only 1,727 leases were registered under the scheme by early 1982.[197]

Had the state fully implemented its reforms, divisions within the black community might have restricted the potential of a community-based social movement. Wide regional variations in union responses to

the removal of squatter camps at least partly reflected residential patterns, suggesting that the government could have undercut union support for community campaigns by providing housing for fully employed
workers and their families. In Cape Town, where nonracial unions virtually ignored campaigns against squatter removals in 1981, union
members were mainly housed in single-sex hostels far from squatter
sites.[198] Conversely, on the East Rand, where migrant industrial workers lived in hostels next to the Katlehong squatter settlement, members
of a shop-stewards' council campaigned vigorously against the removal
of residents' shacks in 1983.[199]

Paradoxically, however, the state's shift toward accepting the reality
of permanent African urban populations probably reduced the salience
of socioeconomic divisions throughout the 1980s. New state policies
made housing more expensive rather than cheaper. First, greater emphasis was placed on private construction of new housing and on "informal" housing settlement, increasing the amount residents themselves
were expected to pay toward resolving the housing shortage. Among
other results, this speeded the expansion of huge squatter settlements.[200] Second, and probably even more important, state authorities
decided to make the administration and development of black townships pay for itself. By raising rents and rates for electricity, gas, and
other services, township administrators expected to recover the cost of
providing more services and housing. Near Johannesburg, rents rose
400 percent between 1977 and 1984; in Silobela in the Eastern
Transvaal, rents rose 300 percent between 1981 and 1984.[201] Black
families suffered increased housing costs at a time of rising unemployment: between 1980 and 1985, according to one study, at least 25 percent of all households in the PWV area had falling real incomes.[202]

By the time a new tricameral constitution was implemented in September 1984, both the shortage and the cost of urban housing had become serious problems; even more than in Brazil, the central state's
responsibility for the change was overt. Many township residents already owed back rent, but from the beginning of the 1984 uprising—
an uprising that first became internationally visible through violent repression of rent demonstrations—millions of urban Africans refused to
pay rent. Millions more avoided high rents by moving to "informal
settlements" on the fringes of metropolitan areas, paying less because
services were virtually nonexistent. By the late 1980s, up to half the
Transvaal's population was estimated to live in squatter areas, where,
although generally restricted to a casual labor market and partly depen-

dent on garden plots for survival, they had some freedom from official harassment and "as much access to the benefits of an urban life as they could achieve."[203]

Especially in industrial centers, new community groups frequently linked labor issues to housing questions. In Alexandra, a township in Johannesburg with historically strong local organization, three local committees representing residents protesting rent increases and housing shortages, and residents facing removal, formed a coalition in 1984 called the Alexandra Residents' Association. In its second bulletin, the association told residents that urban redevelopment was aimed at "forcing low paid workers out of Alex. To charge high rent is to select the wealthy for these houses. . . . It is not the fault of the worker if he is retrenched, or if he gets a low wage. That is the fault of apartheid and the capitalist system."[204] Unionists in the township viewed organizations formed around local problems such as the lack of drains or running water as a way to "protect the working class" in the community, "seeing that it is the major one in the entire community"; mobilization around specific details of township living conditions was seen as offering the "ability to assert and defend our class interest, against those of other opposing classes [in] every aspect of our lives—at work; at school; where we live; over the structures of local and national government; over the army, police, courts and prisons; the media; the church; financial institutions and the economy as a whole."[205]

Although groups representing different constituencies within the township sometimes disagreed over strategy, the tendency to use the language of class was marked. Even student activists objecting to adult unionists' insistence that workers should lead community groups argued that "the struggle is for both economic and political power" and agreed that workers' interests should predominate:

> The form and approach of our struggle is a national one. The working class in alliance with other progressive forces will bring about change to the present social order. . . . The recent developments of working class consciousness and political awareness within the progressive movement, demonstrate the interest of the working class. The working class should be involved and take leadership in the national democratic struggle.[206]

As mobilization intensified, the language and analysis proffered by Alexandra organizations—like many around the country—reflected activists' growing insistence on two themes: first, the nonracial ideology of the ANC, and second, the preeminent role of workers in the effort to challenge the state.

By the mid 1980s, unions regularly joined community groups in community campaigns, sometimes using factory-based organizations to back up demands. In the Vaal region, for example, unions threatened to strike when the state asked employers to deduct rents from wages, telling "the chamber [of commerce] that residents could not afford to pay the current rents; accordingly, if rents did not decrease workers would have no option but to demand higher wages."[207] Employers' associations, recognizing the volatility of the issue, refused to cooperate with the new law. Even unions whose members generally lived in single-sex hostels, such as the mineworkers' unions, took up housing campaigns: as the National Union of Mineworkers pointed out, employers could choose to provide workers with family housing rather than retain the migrant labor system.[208]

Like public transport campaigns, campaigns for better housing underscored the state's role in keeping black workers' living standards low. Employers paid low wages, while the state restricted cheap housing. Furthermore, employers benefited from the housing situation, as they did from influx control: housing shortages meant workers depended on employers for hostel beds, while work on self-constructed squatter housing subsidized wages. For the labor movement to reflect workers' lived experience of exploitation, it had to take up community issues; at the same time, it was easy for community residents to understand the link between these issues and workplace relations and to redefine demands and constituencies in class terms.

GENDER IN THE LABOR FORCE

If housing issues merged workplace and political demands and made it easier for community residents to understand political issues in class terms, the extent to which family labor supported wage workers also seems to have shaped community identities. Very little research has been published on the role of African women workers in shaping the labor movement's approach to community issues: as in Brazil, perhaps, where male workers dominate the labor force and most visible union leaders are male, descriptions of the nonracial unions tended to subsume the specific demands of women workers into the whole.[209]

However, workplace and community demands have been eloquently linked by women participants in community campaigns. As in Brazil, women's labor force participation rates have risen rapidly since the early 1970s, especially in the industrial jobs once reserved for men.[210]

During South Africa's industrial expansion, as jobs opened up in manufacturing and commerce, women provided a source of relatively cheap labor: until 1981, minimum wages for women were set lower than those for men. While many black women continued to work in traditionally female occupations, such as domestic work and other service sector jobs, increasing numbers found employment in manufacturing and commerce. Between 1960 and 1980, the proportion of women in manufacturing rose from 15 to 25 percent of the total labor force, and from 24 to 34 percent of the total labor force in commerce.[211] Perhaps as significant, between 1969 and 1981, the percentages of skilled and semi-skilled workers who were black women increased substantially. In the metal and motor industries, for example, black women made up 5.5 percent of skilled and semi-skilled workers in 1969; by 1981, that figure had increased to 12.2 percent.[212]

However, in South Africa, as elsewhere, increased female labor force participation was most apparent in specific industries. From the early 1970s on, under the industrial decentralization program, labor-intensive textile factories opened near bantustans, taking advantage of government subsidies and a cheaper, largely female, labor reserve.[213] In the Transvaal clothing industry, where significant decentralization occurred between 1960 and 1980, African women's participation in the industry rose from 22.8 percent to 74 percent of the total labor force.[214]

The increase in formal-sector female employment was especially marked among African women for several reasons. Overcrowding and erosion in bantustans, where at least half of African women were required to live, meant that subsistence agriculture could not support families adequately, even with migrants' remittances; moreover, the migrant labor system was linked to a significant increase in female-headed households, and throughout the period of rapid industrialization, more and more women moved to urban areas and sought industrial work.[215] But even where both parents were present, a common response to rising costs of living, decreased real wages, and increasing landlessness, was an increase in the number of family members working outside the home. Second, new semi-skilled jobs opening up in expanding industries were increasingly available to women entering the industrial labor force.

Obviously, one would not want to argue that in South Africa, any more than in Brazil, women should bear most of the responsibility for maintaining the home. However, there is no question that under the sexual division of labor in both societies, they do: for women workers, work does not end on leaving the factory. A (male) shop steward told fellow unionists at a 1983 workshop on women workers: "Women are now doing a double job. We say we [blacks] are the oppressed nation, but women are more oppressed. They go to work and then start again at home."[216] Five years later, a COSATU women's conference echoed this view:

> Not only are black women oppressed because they are black and exploited as a class, but they suffer intense hardship due to the fact that they are women. . . . [Black] women, like all the oppressed, do not have the vote. They receive low wages, have no adequate benefits and suffer sexual harassment. The vast majority of women also endure the burden of a double shift—they work a full day in the factory and then go home to another shift of cooking and cleaning.[217]

Just as some women workers in Brazil recognized how exploitation at the workplace shaped their lives at home, women industrial workers in South Africa insisted that the labor movement take up issues with employers and the state that might otherwise have been seen as lying outside the arena of labor relations. At COSATU's 1985 inaugural congress, the labor movement adopted a "women's resolution" resolving to seek equal pay for all workers, including for work of comparable worth; childcare and scheduling flexibility to "make it easier for workers to combine work and family responsibilities"; full maternity rights, including paid maternity and paternity leave and job security; an end to sexual harassment and safe transportation for workers doing overtime and night work.[218] Although unions varied in the extent to which they fought for these demands, some unions, including unions representing metalworkers, chemical workers, commercial and catering workers, and paper, pulp, and wood workers, began to include issues like parental leave, day-care centers, and medical assistance, as well as equal pay rates for women, in negotiations with employers.[219]

Working women were even more visible in community organizations. Although there was a long history of organization among African women in South Africa, including in the labor movement,[220] after the early 1980s "working-class women increasingly formed and participated in women's organizations which played a major role" in communities.[221] Community campaigns were often organized around fulfilling domestic needs; women activists tended to view these issues—education, childcare, rents, housing, and anti-democratic local administration—as closely related to low wages and negligible state services.[222] Discussing the rent boycott in 1984, a member of the Vaal Organization of Women said: "The problem is that people in the Vaal get low wages and can't afford a rent of R 65 or R 78. As mothers we cannot afford the rent. When a child is hungry, the mother is affected and she cannot afford to educate her children because the rent is high."[223] If broad class-conscious movements require an understanding of the inter-relationship of workplace and home, the growing participation of women workers—who recognized a distinctively "feminine" work identity linked to household responsibilities—may have reinforced that expanded vision.[224]

As in Brazil, few women activists considered themselves actively feminist in the sense of challenging gender hierarchies; indeed, women activists frequently suggested that feminist claims could threaten unity within the national liberation effort.[225] After a decade of popular mobilization—especially after the unbanning of political parties in 1990, when the broad opposition began to debate proposals for a reconstructed state framework—many activists would begin to address gender inequalities more directly, but for most of the 1980s, gender-specific issues were more likely to be discussed as a special set of problems facing women as workers. The language of class provided a relatively universal framework for gendered demands: as long as gender issues were raised in the context of working-class families' needs, they rarely provoked dissent from male union or community activists—and they further strengthened a discourse linking workplace and community issues.

BEYOND FACTORY GATES

In the late 1980s, industrial trade unions and community activists focused their demands on the South African state, arguing that only the end of white minority rule would allow working black communities residents to fulfill their aspirations. However, these aspirations were as likely to be expressed in terms of economic change as changing political or social relationships. Throughout the 1980s, workers mobilized in factory organizations brought an understanding of class relations to community debates. For the labor movement to succeed in shaping a future South Africa, Sidney Mufamadi, COSATU's assistant general secretary, argued, "We must make the militant youth in the street of our ghettos, the students in the Bantu Education schools, the housewife in the four-roomed matchbox [government-owned rental housing], the unemployed person who is condemned to starve in the Bantustans understand that capitalism is the root cause of all our suffering." [226] That argument seems to have been persuasive: especially during the recession of the 1980s, when already-low standards of living threatened to decline still further, workers increasingly viewed changes in South African political arrangements as essential to gaining both higher wages and improved social services for their communities.

Black activists shifted away from articulating their demands primarily in terms of race to an analysis that emphasized the need to raise living standards in black communities. Activists who discussed influx control, transport services, and housing problems could not ignore the impact of low wages, any more than workers—especially those responsible for domestic concerns—could ignore the effect of high bus fares and rents on already-strained budgets. By the late 1980s, the broad political opposition included among its goals not only the right to organize and strike but the right to a "living wage." [227] Rather than stressing political incorporation alone, the "mass democratic movement" sought political incorporation as a way to raise living standards for the broad working class. [228]

Probably the most visible indication of labor's importance in the broad political movement came in 1990, when the South African government unbanned the ANC and the Communist Party and began a protracted negotiation process. Over the previous five years, waves of "unrest"—of demonstrations, riots, and stay-aways—had rolled across black townships, despite heavy repression and a state of emergency that ended virtually all civil liberties. In that period, labor unions affiliated to COSATU played an increasingly visible role: although unionists were frequently detained, the threat that union members would embark on national strikes in protest sometimes prompted even employers to ask the government to release prominent organizers. Community organizers, or unionists who could be shown to have direct ties to illegal organizations, were slightly more vulnerable, lacking the threat of shop-floor action. By the late 1980s, after widespread detentions, labor leaders were among the few visible national leaders still relatively free to organize in the black community, and labor meetings provided one of the few legal forums for strategic discussions. In 1988, the government changed the labor law, penalizing unions for political or community involvement; the new law allowed employers to claim damages from unions for "illegal" strikes, sympathy strikes, and even consumer boycotts, in what the minister of manpower described as an attempt to "bring irresponsible and militant unions to heel." [229] The bill's empha-

sis on punishing unions for links with communities reflects the extent
to which those links had strengthened both labor organization and
community activism. Millions of workers continued to participate in
strikes and stay-aways, joining community groups in late 1989 for a
series of demonstrations against apartheid laws. By 1989, Jeremy
Baskin, a COSATU official, observed:

> In the repressive climate COSATU became an outlet for the political hopes
> of far more than its membership. It acted as a political center. Youths and
> students looked to it for guidance; churches asked it for political direction;
> ambassadors, foreign visitors and political journalists canvassed its opin-
> ions—and not because of any particular interest in or support for trade
> unionism.
> To a large extent COSATU spoke for the entire democratic movement. It
> was seen as the voice of the ANC in a situation where the ANC could not
> openly speak.[230]

If COSATU had moved to the center of the anti-apartheid movement, how had the anti-apartheid movement changed as a result? In
1989, when a major COSATU congress reaffirmed the federation's
"strategic alliance" with the UDF (and, implicitly, the UDF's illegal ally,
the ANC), it acknowledged that workers and community groups had
separate identities and interests; at the same congress, it launched a
campaign to draw up a "Workers' Charter" that would "articulate the
basic rights of workers" to be "guaranteed by the constitution of a
people's government."[231] Activists had previously rejected such proposals, fearing that a workers' charter would divide the anti-apartheid
movement along class lines; by 1989, however, instead of viewing
workers' rights as threatening opposition unity, the ANC, SACTU, and
the Communist Party each offered their own versions of a workers'
charter for discussion. During the negotiations that began in 1991,
those rights, and broader demands for socioeconomic change, seemed
likely to be at the center of debates.

The 1991 election of the prominent trade unionist Cyril Ramaphosa
as the ANC's new general secretary only confirmed the extent to which
anti-apartheid goals had been reshaped by labor's involvement. At a
broader level, COSATU continued to insist on its independence and on
grass-roots mobilization, especially through national strikes, as the
most effective means of pressuring the white minority government; the
union federation served "as the ANC's conscience, goad and muscular
left arm" during the transition process.[232] In South Africa, no less than
in Brazil, citizenship had been redefined to include redistribution of

wealth as well as political access and to involve a changed relationship between workers and political power.

CONCLUSION

One of the most striking similarities between the labor movements in Brazil and South Africa throughout the 1980s has been their willingness to engage in broad community campaigns. As they spread, these labor movements, appealing to a broadly defined working class, rather than just industrial workers and union members, challenged the state as well as employers to raise the standard of living in working-class areas. Even more impressive, perhaps, is the extent to which community campaigns were articulated in terms of class: even in racially divided South Africa, activists in poor communities discussed the state's failure to provide services in terms of the way in which the state acted to increase the power and wealth of employers and dominant classes. In both cases, democratization was discussed in terms of incorporating working-class representatives in future governments rather than simply in terms of universal enfranchisement. Citizenship was defined to include improved living standards: community-based political groups and the labor movement argued that democratization must include the redistribution of the country's wealth.

Both labor movements relied on community support, and in turn provided crucial support for community campaigns—essentially, reflecting the emergence of what can only be called class consciousness in poor neighborhoods. I have argued that this class consciousness was the direct outcome of factory-based mobilization, which then spread to community groups; mobilized in the context of a growing labor movement, community residents acknowledged the transparent mechanisms linking workplace exploitation and community impoverishment, and viewed local community problems in terms of class relationships. Working women may have been especially likely to recognize the link between production and reproduction, but few workers could ignore the way that rapid industrialization strategies had peripheralized working-class communities.

As unionists argued, and community activists agreed, employers paid low wages to industrial workers, while the state and employers cooperated to segregate workers and their families from the middle and upper classes. State policies reduced the access of even relatively privileged workers to social services such as education, transport, and health.

While impoverishment alone does not explain the emergence of broad social-movement unionism, in Brazil and South Africa, as shop-floor organizations grew, union involvement in community campaigns underlined the spatial segregation of a rapidly growing industrial work force, and reinforced an emergent class consciousness. In both cases, community demands addressed to the state were increasingly defined in terms of class relationships.

Few of the community concerns raised in the 1980s were new ones: wages, transport, and housing had been the focus of campaigns in the period before authoritarian governments repressed popular mobilizations in the early 1960s. What was new in the 1980s was the extent to which a greatly expanded working class, and a militant labor movement based in heavy industry, demonstrated to communities that they could, too, could challenge domination. Rather than separating members' interests from those of non-members, industrial labor unions expanded their constituencies to include all those who lived on urban peripheries, while community groups adopted a class-based perspective.

Out of this process, politicized unionism was perhaps inevitable. Designed to support private capital accumulation, state policies underscored the links between workplace and communities; in both cases, as labor movements took up community issues, working-class representation in state policy-making became a key demand.

One of the most interesting aspects of this process, theoretically, is the situational nature of class consciousness: rapid urbanization meant that most residents of working-class areas were new arrivals, yet at the end of two decades of authoritarian industrialization, community support for labor campaigns clearly reflected a class identity, built not on traditional bonds of solidarity, but on an understanding of the way employers and the state actively reduced the share of workers and their families in the benefits of industrialization and shifted the burden of recession onto working-class communities. An unintended consequence of authoritarian industrialization strategies was that poor urban communities developed a distinct class character; when, for reasons related primarily to changes in the labor process and in the relationship between employers and the state, labor unions emerged in newly formed industries, the class character of urban neighborhoods strengthened both labor unions and urban movements and provided the basis for a radicalized political opposition. From struggles in the "sphere of production," both labor movements expanded into struggles over the level of reproduction of working-class families.

On their own, structurally based grievances such as inadequate urban services do not provoke mobilization or stimulate class consciousness: countless studies suggest that the residents of poor communities are at least as likely to feel disempowered and marginalized as they are to demonstrate militance. But in these two cases, when emergent labor movements began to win real changes in real wages and labor relations, and as activists brought a larger political vision to bear on discussions of community needs, the broad discourse of class relations provided a framework in which community residents—generally themselves workers or workers' relatives—could understand and analyze the processes of peripheralization as the result of state development strategies designed to support private capital accumulation. In their efforts to improve working and living conditions for workers, their families, and their neighbors, both labor movements interpreted members' interests in broad terms and developed the community-based constituency that is perhaps the defining characteristic of social-movement unionism.

Conclusion

The labor movements that emerged in South Africa and Brazil in the 1970s and 1980s were both remarkable for their militance, their ties to working-class communities, and their ability to redefine the political discourse of their countries; each movement expressed insistent demands for sweeping social and economic changes. In both cases, new workers' movements challenged the patterns that capitalist development had taken in their countries: the severe inequalities that had characterized economic growth and the repression that had accompanied it.

Like all social movements, each movement had its own peculiarities. In 1991, a visiting Brazilian unionist watching a chanting, dancing crowd of delegates to COSATU's national congress remarked that in one sense, South Africa's unions were lucky: they could draw on a sense of solidarity created by decades of state-imposed racial oppression, a unity that would survive disagreements over tactics or strategies, political affiliations or immediate interests.[1] Like all historical phenomena, the Brazilian and South African workers' movements of the 1970s and 1980s reflect the specificities of their contexts. Each has individual patterns, individual peculiarities.

Above all, as any sociological theory would predict, South Africa's overt legalized racial stratification shaped the context of social relations. In Brazil, race certainly plays a role, but in South Africa, race remains a dominant theme in all political discussions. In the 1990s, as well as in the 1950s, the fact that South Africa's apartheid system granted political and economic rights on the basis of racial categories clearly inhibited divisions within dominant classes, whose members were almost entirely classified as white, while strengthening unity among South Africans denied political rights on the basis of pigmentation. In Brazil, where no such glue held together either the authoritarian regime or the political opposition, the coalition between business and the state collapsed faster than in South Africa, but the opposition was also more fragmented.

These different degrees of cohesion help explain many of the differences in the Brazilian and South African transitions to elected civilian governments. In Brazil, prominent industrialists supported the state's control over union organization, and they remained wary of independent unionism in the late 1970s. Nevertheless, when economic crisis loomed, business leaders were relatively quick to join oppositional coalitions, negotiating a controlled transition in which business voices remained dominant. In South Africa, state and business leaders took somewhat longer to conclude that a negotiated transition might be possible: throughout the uprisings of the 1980s, most white politicians, and most business leaders, resisted proposals for far-reaching reform. While business leaders began to call in the mid 1970s for limited reform, they generally restricted their vision to improved housing and union rights.[2] Recognizing that extending citizenship to black South Africans would threaten white domination, few white leaders were willing to call for a system of one-person, one-vote.

Only when the effects of continuing township "unrest" and international economic sanctions began to erode the business-state consensus were business reformists likely to call for an end to apartheid. By the late 1980s, South African business leaders had lost confidence that economic or political stability could be recovered through minor reforms, and leading figures began to challenge state policymakers to offer more imaginative routes out of a persistent stalemate.[3] By 1990, when the new Nationalist president F. W. de Klerk finally unbanned opposition parties and released political prisoners, he gave way to the same kind of multiple pressures that prompted the Brazilian military to leave office.

Ultimately, perhaps, the differences in state-business relations between the two cases were not as great as they appeared during the mid 1980s, when Brazilian elites had joined a multi-class coalition against military rule: by the late 1980s, South African business leaders had formed a "business consultative conference" to propose paths out of the crisis. Nevertheless, it is important to note that the emergence of a white business opposition required ending the long-standing white consensus on maintaining overt forms of racial privilege, and that a business opposition was far slower to come together in South Africa than in Brazil.

As the visiting Brazilian unionist noted, however, racial stratification also strengthened the black population's support for anti-apartheid leaders. In Brazil, community-union alliances appeared demobilized by a lengthy transition in the mid 1980s, and attempts to mount working-class-based electoral challenges to a restricted process seemed relatively weak. Only in the late 1980s, apparently as lower-income voters lost their fear that radical change would prompt another military coup, did grass-roots mobilization in support of an independent workers' movement regain its earlier force. Throughout the late 1980s, as the working-class movement gradually built a solid constituency for more far-reaching reform, the working-class opposition had to overcome political divisions, economic recession, and fear.

In contrast, the South African opposition movement could rely on a basic identity among different social movements and organizations: the fact that a constituency had already been defined by the state's racial classification system did not create automatic support for leaders like Nelson Mandela, but it certainly eased the process of consolidation. While political differences would emerge during the transition process—during election campaigns, for example, as black political groups began to articulate various policy proposals—grievances arising from apartheid's racial divisions clearly created relatively strong community identities. Brazilian worker activists could mobilize residents of the periphery, but they had to mobilize identities, create new organizations and symbols. In South Africa, trade unionists and community activists also had to persuade supporters to redefine interests and constituencies, but they did so in a context of egregious injustice, where certain common interests were virtually undeniable.

Despite these differences, the questions facing the opposition during South Africa's transition to democracy in the early 1990s showed stronger similarities to Brazil's extended process than might have been predicted. Most notably, different strands within the opposition movement debated the relative significance of racial laws and economic inequality rooted in apartheid. Should South Africans be satisfied with a move to nonracial capitalism, with an intact distribution of wealth, or should they press for changes beyond the removal of racially based exclusion? In Brazil, a broad-based workers' movement sought to push reforms beyond simply installing an elected civilian government, to include socioeconomic rights, from land reform to labor organizing rights to parental leave in the new constitutional framework; business leaders who had joined the opposition to military rule were far less eager to alter social relations. In South Africa, similarly, the working-class component of the anti-apartheid movement continued to insist that simply extending the franchise would not be enough to eradicate apartheid's legacies and sought to ensure working-class participation in new political arrangements.

EXPLAINING SIMILAR DYNAMICS

Given their obvious differences, it is the similarities between the Brazilian and South African cases that beg explanation: were there underlying dynamics that help explain the emergence of similar movements demanding citizenship, defined in terms of the distribution of national wealth as well as the political arena? Instead of seeing civilian government as an end point, the Brazilian labor movement saw it as a beginning; instead of viewing universal franchise as its final goal, the South African opposition treated economic and social change as fundamental to its members' interests. This study has tried to identify parallel tendencies that helped create widespread support for these goals, and to explain why, in the 1980s, these demands gained so much visibility.

In 1967, Reinhard Bendix wrote that "modernization"—by which he meant the social changes accompanying industrialization, including structural differentiation, the destruction of inherited privilege, and the declaration of equal rights of citizenship—was characterized by a "process of fundamental democratization by which 'those classes which have formerly played only a passive part in political life,' have been stirred into action."[4] Is this the explanation for the emergence of militant labor movements in Brazil and South Africa: the emergence of new social forces, stirred into action as rapid industrialization proceeded under authoritarian governments?

Undeniably, broad structural processes helped shape the potential capacities of workers' organizations in both cases. Dramatic industrial expansion in the 1960s—in both cases promoted by authoritarian states seeking to achieve rapid growth by directing foreign and domestic capital into heavy industrial production—enlarged both industrial work forces and changed their composition, radically altering unions' ability to mobilize workers and their communities. Industrial workers organized in factories and linked to new working-class communities forced employers to negotiate with workers' organizations. Militant workers' organizations then began to focus on the state, claiming the right to organize and demanding state enforcement of minimum living standards as basic components of citizens' rights—even under capitalism. The parallel with earlier industrializers is hard to avoid: as Bendix, drawing on T. H. Marshall, suggests, from the eighteenth century on, western European workers' protests forced the extension of concepts of citizenship to include rights of collective bargaining and rights to social services, as well as rights of universal political participation.[5]

More than most modernization theorists,[6] Bendix insists that democratization is a process distinct from industrialization, but even he argues that the two are often intimately related: the spread of enlightenment ideas was facilitated by industrialization, which brought workers together, allowed activists to move around the country, and reduced their dependence on a single feudal employer. In Brazil and South Africa, however, the realization of workers' potential capacity to demand fuller participation in national policy-making and resources was more than just a reflexive process, more than just the long-term outcome of industrial expansion. In both cases, authoritarian governments during the 1960s made concerted efforts to control or eliminate militant workers' organizations. Indeed, in both cases, control over labor played a key part in industrialization strategies as authoritarian governments sought to attract foreign and domestic investment by ensuring industrial peace.

Governments of earlier industrializers certainly sought to restrain workers' protests and to limit their demands; but as states in dependent capitalist economies—dependent on attracting foreign capital and technologies, and aspiring to broaden sales to international markets rather than trying to expand domestic sales—Brazil and South Africa appear to have been especially unwilling to respond to workers' demands. From the perspectives of both states, economic growth required high profits to attract foreign and domestic investors to new industrial sectors; and it required closure of political space to protect the stable business climate required to compete with other potential investment sites. In both cases, economic growth based on "savage capitalism" created the basis for an elite consensus: state policymakers and business leaders could disagree over details, but during the 1960s, while overall growth rates soared, repression of workers' protests caused few ripples in elite circles.

On the other hand, industrial strategies also changed both countries' economic profiles, enlarging heavy industrial sectors. Both states provided inputs and incentives to producers of consumer durables, encouraging joint ventures between local and foreign manufacturers and providing support for production of technologically advanced goods. These products were geared to a relatively limited domestic market; income stratification increased during the "economic miracles" of the late 1960s and early 1970s. While most workers received declining or stagnant real wages, an affluent minority could afford new purchases, especially while governments extended easy credit to a relatively privileged middle class.

Here, perhaps, lies the crucial difference between earlier industrializers and newly industrialized countries like Brazil and South Africa in the late twentieth century: in a competitive international context, expanding industries looked to export sales for new outlets rather than treating domestic markets as the main outlet for new goods. Alain Lipietz argues that because it need not rely on domestic sales alone, dependent capital-intensive production in the late twentieth century need not employ the logic of classic Fordism, where industrial workers provide new markets; instead, "peripheral" Fordism combines new production processes with a less generous labor regime.[7] Lipietz's generalization is probably overstated: even in early industrializers, few industrialists agreed to raise wages for their workers without protest, while there are certainly examples of late industrializers in which state policies and business communities have been somewhat more oriented toward creating a domestic market than they were in either Brazil or South Africa.

For these cases, however, Lipietz's description seems to hold true: for most Brazilian and South African workers, rapid economic growth was not accompanied by increased wages through the mid 1970s, and saturated domestic markets could be supplemented by export sales, rather than by raising wage levels or extending credit to even relatively skilled workers. Until factory-based organizations disrupted production processes—and, in South Africa's case, increased the threat of international sanctions—neither states nor large employers appeared eager to extend either political rights or economic benefits to the majority of their country's populations.

In both Brazil and South Africa, business opposition to state policies revolved around problems for private capital rather than around authoritarian rule. While business leaders complained about exclusion from policy-making even when growth rates soared, these complaints remained relatively muted while economies boomed. Economic growth supported a broad consensus between state policymakers and industrialists—until, for reasons related to a changing international economic climate and to dependence on international investment, both Brazil and South Africa confronted recession. The international climate following the 1973 oil crisis clearly altered developmental possibilities. In Brazil, industrialists who had counted on state support now viewed state investments as posing a potential threat to their access to funds and markets; in South Africa, similar concerns were reinforced by fears that apartheid would provoke international sanctions. As both states adopted policies to shore up national security instead of continuing to support dynamic industries, business leaders became increasingly concerned about how their interests were represented within policymaking circles.

Militant labor movements first emerged—or rather, first demonstrated some degree of success—during times of conflict between industrialists and the state. At points when the state-business consensus was most fragile, years of clandestine organizing could blossom into what were represented as spontaneous strikes. In both cases, broad-based labor movements emerged only as workers and union activists strategically took advantage of new political opportunities, building organizations on the shop floor and in their communities and gradually challenging the state and dominant classes to recognize and respond to new demands.

A crucial part of this story seems to lie in changes in the labor process and the laborers themselves during the period of industrial expansion. Where authoritarian states denied most workers any real voice in policies, "modernization" does not appear to have involved any "fundamental process of democratization," in the sense of rights gradually extended to workers; but in both cases, industrialization apparently resulted in democratization of a different kind. The expansion in heavy industrial production was accompanied by a rise in the importance of semi-skilled operatives in industry and growing reliance by employers on a more stable population of industrial workers. In South Africa, this process was especially obvious, since skilled white workers were increasingly replaced by semi-skilled and skilled black workers; but even in Brazil, patterns of industrialization gathered relatively educated semi-skilled workers together in the large factories that marked the crucial metal industry. Despite widespread unemployment and persistent layoffs, workers in dynamic industries were relatively privileged compared with those in agriculture or mining, or even in more traditional labor-intensive industries.

Changes in labor processes—linked to the adoption of new technologies under authoritarian industrialization strategies—seem to have meant that in both cases, when industrial employers confronted demands for increased wages and new labor relations frameworks, they seemed reluctant to respond with direct repression. Especially when business leaders were already declaring their independence from state policymakers, after the Soweto uprising in South Africa and during a period of growing elite opposition in Brazil, unionization seems to have appeared far less threatening than wildcat strikes. While union organizing remained an extremely dangerous activity for individuals, the gradual strengthening of a factory-based movement reflected both renewed efforts by activists and a growing acceptance by industrialists that without channels of negotiation and representation, workers would continue to disrupt production.

In both cases, however, workers viewed factory and community grievances as closely linked. Seeking higher wages and better working conditions, both Brazilian and South African workers rediscovered the possibilities offered by militant strike actions; demands escalated as organization spread. In both cases, rapid industrialization had been accompanied by rapid urbanization, under states that denied working-class communities access to basic social resources. Overt state and employer intervention in working-class communities, in workers' daily lives, meant that labor organizations could not restrict their concerns to the workplace: although they began with campaigns for union recognition and a new labor relations framework, labor movements began to take up community concerns. Within unions, women workers may have been especially likely to insist that unions engage in community-related campaigns; but most workers who lived in impoverished peripheral communities clearly viewed community and factory struggles as two sides of an effort to raise the general level of reproduction.

Instead of behaving as labor aristocracies, relatively skilled industrial workers demanded changes that would benefit a much broader population, redefining political and economic relationships between states, dominant classes, and those who considered themselves members of the working class. At the same time, instead of viewing labor demands as separate from concerns about collective consumption, the residents of poor communities reinterpreted demands for housing, education, and services as responses to state policies designed to assist private capital accumulation. Exploitive class relations, explicitly reinforced by state action, lowered living standards in residential areas, as well as limiting wages. In both cases, community-based movements were closely linked to rising labor activism, supporting union struggles and participating in the redefinition of citizenship in terms of socioeconomic rights—essentially, in terms of class identities.

"Social-movement unionism," then, seems to have emerged from the crucible of authoritarian industrialization, where rapid industrialization strategies reshaped the working class and working-class communities, while it altered the relationship between authoritarian states and industrialists. During periods of rapid growth, state policies designed to attract investment into heavy industry had been linked to policies designed to control labor, and to policies whose consequences included impoverishment of the urban poor; in both Brazil and South Africa, those policies were successful only as long as international capital and markets continued to flow. In both South Africa and Brazil, slowed growth ended elite consensus.

In both cases, however, semi-skilled workers, organized first in factories and increasingly in impoverished urban communities, took advantage of conflict in elite circles to formulate demands for more far-reaching changes. While business leaders demanded inclusion in policy-making, urban industrial workers used militant strikes to demand inclusion in the benefits of growth. Spreading beyond factories, popular organizations escalated their demands, not only for higher wages, but also for improved living standards for the majority of the population: authoritarian states faced disruption in communities, just as employers faced disruption at the workplace. Gradually overcoming regional differences and strategic disagreements, surviving attempts at repression and division, broad opposition movements emerged, demanding improved wages and living standards for working-class constituencies, and expanded possibilities for political participation and citizenship.

Again, it is worth emphasizing this point: although they were formed in opposition to "savage capitalism," both workers' movements were shaped by the processes of that capitalism, which changed the capacity of workers to disrupt production and affected the relationship between employers and the state. But these processes also changed the relationship between industrial workers and urban communities in ways that further strengthened both labor movements. Many studies of European and North American labor movements have emphasized the importance of appeals to a preindustrial past, where ethnic collectivities help reinforce bonds within labor movements. In both Brazil and South Africa, widespread support for new movements suggests that recent experiences in the industrial urban world shaped workers' behavior and loyalties far more than did their rural past. The collective identities developed within workers' organizations were situational, reflecting the creation of new kinds of communities, new social relationships.

Instead of drawing on real or imagined historical identities, labor and community activists appealed to new ones, based in the rapid industrialization and urbanization of the previous two decades. The collective identities developed within these movements seem to have been based on the lived experience of workers and their families in an urban context: in factories and in communities, the "lived experience" of class under "savage capitalism" gave rise to what can only be called class consciousness and class-conscious movements.

Changes in industrial structures, then, changed the possibilities available to workers' movements. Taking advantage of new potential capacities—arising from employers' increased dependence on semi-skilled workers and from the links between those workers and urban communities—workers' movements inserted class-based demands into the public arena at points of conflict between states and employers, expanding their constituencies in the process. From the strikes of the mid 1970s emerged movements formed in opposition to basic patterns of authoritarian industrialization. Maria Hermínia Tavares de Almeida's description of this process in Brazil could also apply to South Africa, as participants in these broad-based movements "identified a common experience of social and political exclusion under the authoritarian regime." Defining existing labor and political arrangements as inadequate, in both cases, workers' opposition to authoritarianism was based in "something else, a latent demand that made the workers' movement a collective actor unified in opposition to authoritarianism: the recognition of the dignity of labor, [and the right to] equality in the political arena."[8]

MILITANT WORKERS' MOVEMENTS
IN COMPARATIVE PERSPECTIVE

This study has offered a fairly detailed comparison between two workers' movements, chosen not because they were representative of workers' movements in newly industrialized countries but because they seemed unusual in their breadth and militance. Beginning from questions about why militant labor movements should have taken similar forms in such different contexts, the comparison was not designed to consider the extent to which explanations of underlying similarities might illuminate trends in other newly industrialized countries. Indeed, it is often suggested that historical configurations do not lend themselves to broader generalization; Charles Ragin, for example, suggests that two-case comparisons are more useful for understanding specific cases than for developing broader theoretical perspectives.[9] Authoritarian industrialization strategies in Brazil and South Africa have parallels in other parts of the world, however, and the explanations offered for these cases hold theoretical implications for a larger set.

Neither Brazil nor South Africa is unique in the extent to which its rapid industrialization policies relied on imported technologies and capital, or in the way state incentives helped change labor processes, fundamentally altering the nature of industrial work and the urban working class. From prerevolutionary Russia to post–World War I Germany, and to Italy in the 1960s, industrial workers discovered that the organization of work in heavy industry offered new potential for shop-floor militance.[10] Throughout the late twentieth century, examples abound: in Barcelona, Spain, and in Córdoba, Argentina, industrial workers have responded to the organizational possibilities offered by new technologies to challenge employers' control at the workplace.[11]

But the comparison between Brazil and South Africa emphasizes the way a specific pattern of industrialization shaped the possibilities for workers' movements, not only in terms of increased workplace capacity for organization, but also in terms of relationships between workers and communities and workers and the state. Furthermore, the similarities between these configurations underscore once again the importance of the international context for late twentieth-century industrialization. While state policies shape capitalist industrialization patterns—not only in terms of incentives and protection, but also in terms of labor controls—this comparison suggests some of the ways in which international pressures influence domestic actors in ways that may create new opportunities for worker mobilization in dependent capitalism.

Almost certainly, the trends that seem to explain the unusual degree of militance and mobilization in both Brazil and South Africa do not appear in identical form anywhere in the world; indeed, they are not identical in these two cases. Nevertheless, other cases of authoritarian industrialization do display marked parallels, in state policies toward capital and labor, in the direction of economic and social change, and in the capacity of industrial workers to challenge employers and the state. In the 1980s, the country whose industrialization strategy perhaps most closely resembled that followed by South Africa and Brazil was South Korea, where an authoritarian state combined assistance to private capital and direct intervention to build up both lighter and heavy industries, and where corporatist labor legislation restricted worker organization as well as political participation. In the mid 1960s, the military state in South Korea embarked on a conscious industrialization strategy, providing strong support to large conglomerates known as *chaebols*. Compared with either Brazil or South Africa, the industrializing South Korean state was relatively protective of domestic capital, channeling loans to domestic capital rather than inviting direct foreign investment, and relying more on private conglomerates than on state enterprises.[12] Marked by extreme concentration of capital—with the 1983 net sales of the largest thirty *chaebols,* equaling about three-quarters of the national output[13]—South Korea's capitalist class was extremely cohesive and tightly allied to the state.

In the 1970s, the state embarked on a rapid industrialization program, concentrating on capital-intensive heavy industries and chemical production. With this turn, the military regime encouraged joint ventures between Korean and foreign firms in order to attract new capital and technology: by 1978, foreign firms owned about 19 percent of Korean manufacturing, concentrated in industrial chemicals, electronics, and machinery.[14] During the 1980s, South Korea's industries grew rapidly, geographically concentrated in large industrial zones. Between 1965 and 1987, industry's share of the gross domestic product rose from 25 to 43 percent, while agricultural production declined from 38 to 11 percent.[15] In the same period, the non-agricultural work force increased from about one-third to about three-quarters of the economically active population.[16]

Like Brazil and South Africa, the South Korean state maintained strict control over political channels throughout most of the period of rapid growth: the Korean War left a legacy of military control over government that lasted into the 1990s, and from the early 1960s on, successive military regimes, in alliance with leading conglomerates, "chose growth over redistribution as the basis of political legitimacy."[17] To a greater extent than the governments of other East Asian NICs, the South Korean state was willing to resort to direct repression. Corporatist legislation provided strict controls on trade unions, which were tightened repeatedly in the 1960s and 1970s to prevent work stoppages and limit union organization. From 1969 on, South Korea's labor legislation looked quite similar to Brazil's: it required unions to provide assistance to members and prohibited most strikes.[18] Unlike in Brazil, real wages rose in the late 1970s, partly because expanded heavy industries were competing for skilled workers; but a 1980 military coup resulted in further restrictions on labor organization. In 1981, the military government limited wage increases; new labor laws decentralized union organization and "increased the government's power in the mediation of disputes, subjected collective action to prior government approval, and prohibited the involvement of outside groups, including grass-roots church organizations and students, in labor disputes." Labor organizers "and other political dissidents" risked placement in "re-education camps."[19]

Even in the early 1980s, when South Korea's development strategy was perhaps closest to that followed earlier by Brazil and South Africa, significant differences persisted. First, the South Korean state appears to have been far more successful in maintaining at least the appearance of political support from the business elite than either the Brazilian or South African states. Although South Korean business leaders have occasionally complained about state policies, the state has maintained both high growth rates and business support; to expand export-oriented automobile production in the 1980s, for example, the state could count on the availability of a "homogeneous and very nationalistic big business class," vertically integrated and dependent on state assistance with financing and international marketing, "to carry out the government's objectives in terms of domestic and overseas investments and external trade."[20] At least through the mid 1980s, the South Korean state retained far greater control over domestic capital by centralizing financial resources (including foreign loans) and occasionally by disciplining leading businesses by unilaterally declaring firms "insolvent."[21]

Since growth was the key to legitimacy, and since private capital involvement was critical for growth, Korean leaders relied on "a target group of leading entrepreneurial talents with their singular advantage of organization, personnel, facilities and capital resources," using institutional mechanisms to link the private sector to the state.[22] Perhaps as a result of this kind of control—what Stephan Haggard calls the South Korean state's "dirigist style" of economic policy implementation[23]—the state-business alliance appears to have weathered crises more successfully than either the Brazilian or South African authoritarian regimes. Moreover, rather than creating conflict, as in Brazil and South Africa, national security concerns were considered new opportunities for private investment in heavy industries—and for the growth of large, "octopus-like" conglomerates[24]—perhaps because the state generally relied on private investors instead of creating state-owned companies.

In the 1980s, a militant opposition movement demanded political liberalization and an end to human rights violations, but it apparently received little support from business leaders: in 1987, the election of a president closely linked to the military suggested that stability remained a key goal, although the presence of opposition parties in the National Assembly opened up new possibilities for public dissension. Electoral support for a regime allied to the military has been attributed to several factors, including disunity among the political opposition;[25] but it may also reflect a relative absence of divisions within the state-business alliance over critical questions of economic and political policy. The South Korean state, Bruce Cumings writes, has simultaneously substituted for a capitalist class and performed a class-making role;[26] in contrast to business leaders in Brazil and South Africa, that class has shown relatively little overt interest in mounting an overt challenge to an authoritarian state.

The relative weakness of the political opposition in South Korea, including the labor movement, may stem from a close alliance between the state and business leaders, which offered few opportunities for the opposition to expand beyond campuses and factories during the 1980s. But there is a second important distinction between South Korean, Brazilian, and South African industrialization strategies. Although income inequality is greater in South Korea than in other East Asian NICs, it remains less obvious there than in either Brazil or South Africa, while the potential for individual mobility is far greater.[27] Following American advice after the Korean War, a land reform program simultaneously created would-be industrialists, in the shape of (compensated) former landlords looking for investment opportunities, and a class of independent farmers; during industrialization, especially with expansion of educational programs, South Korea developed a visible middle class, which has tended to support growth-oriented strategies. Even for workers, state-funded education has been relatively easily available: primary school enrollment was nearly universal for school-age children by 1960, overall literacy had reached 80 percent by 1963, and by 1984, 94 percent of 11- to 17-year-olds were in secondary school.[28] Perhaps most important, despite repression of labor organization, incomes were more equitably distributed in South Korea than in either Brazil or South Africa: land reform, educational opportunities, and state policies designed to avoid encouraging further stratification meant that rapid industrialization occurred in a somewhat different context. While income inequality increased somewhat during the 1980s, it was still far less severe in South Korea than in the other two cases. Haggard suggests that South Korea's export-led growth policies created incentives for increased use of unskilled and semi-skilled labor, which, in the context of relatively slow population growth rates, reduced labor market dualism.[29] Real wages in manufacturing more than doubled between 1969 and 1979, especially in heavy industries;[30] they rose by about 25 percent more by 1985. At least until the late 1980s, on average, South Korean workers appear to have been able to count on improved incomes as long as growth continued.

Not all workers could have been so optimistic, however. In a strictly sex-segregated labor market, women workers in light industries, and later in export-oriented electronics industries, probably had less hope that conditions would improve; their best option was probably marriage, which usually meant leaving factory work. Militant strikes among South Korea's young, relatively unskilled single women may well reflect the fact that, as Soon Kyoung Cho argues, they are "more willing to risk losing their jobs than male workers who hold supervisory or technical positions."[31] On the other hand, the demands of these workers, who generally come from rural areas and live in single-sex hostels rather than in residential communities, have rarely been reflected in the agendas of corporatist unions, dominated by male workers.[32]

In Brazil and South Africa, labor militance emerged during times of conflict between business leaders and the state; workers in both cases had experienced intensified income stratification along with industrialization and turned to peripheralized working-class communities for support. In comparison with these cases, South Korea's industrialization strategy has been remarkably successful: relatively persistent growth rates, relatively strong elite cohesion, and relatively good opportunities for improved living conditions almost certainly reduced the broad appeal of militant unionism.

On the other hand, by the late 1980s, South Korea displayed more parallels to South Africa or Brazil than may immediately have been obvious. Economic growth alone may no longer legitimate an authoritarian state, Hagen Koo suggests, because heavy industrialization has meant that the South Korean state now seeks to manage

> an increasingly complex and politically sophisticated society. The continuing ability of the state to lead the process of development is now widely questioned, and big business seriously challenges it. As capitalist and working classes have become increasingly potent political forces, so the state has lost a considerable degree of the relative autonomy and institutional insulation that were essential to the major shift in development strategy of the early 1960s. The capitalist class has grown too strong to be easily dominated by the state, and workers are not as docile and quiescent as they once were. At the same time the presence . . . of a relatively large, well-educated middle class exerts pressure on the state for political democratization.[33]

Several observers have noted a general relationship between political conflict and an upsurge in South Korean labor militance: the 1987 election campaign, for example, coincided with a dramatic increase in labor disputes and new worker organization. If political conflict were to deepen—for example, if the state proved unable to sustain economic growth, or if business leaders backed some alternative to state-directed development strategies—would labor militance increase? Would new, militant unions among workers in heavy industry develop the kinds of alliances with working-class communities that marked social-movement unionism in Brazil and South Africa?

This possibility seemed especially realistic by the early 1990s. In the late 1980s, rapid growth appeared to have slowed; economists frequently attributed this trend to rising labor costs and "labor difficulties" that made Korean goods "less competitive on the world market."[34] Although real wages rose in the late 1980s, the "popular perception [is] that the distribution of wealth is badly skewed, and unjust. It is as if the frustration and resentment generated during 25 years of political repression were now being expressed, not just in the form of opposition to authority, but also in the form of extreme sensitivity to what is regarded as the unfair allocation of rewards."[35] Statistical data reflected and reinforced these perceptions: one estimate suggested that as much as 30 percent of the population lived below the poverty line,[36] while another study concluded that in 1989, despite a 54-hour work week, average wages in manufacturing covered only 40 percent of the minimum cost of living for a family of five. Steady increases in the length of workdays and in industrial accidents reflected growing pressure at the workplace. Nearly two-thirds of white- and blue-collar Korean workers interviewed said that considering their efforts at work, their living standards were at a low or very low level.[37]

By the mid 1980s, chances for individual mobility appeared slim. Although rural South Koreans still viewed a move into the urban working class as offering new opportunities, the likelihood of individual mobility within industry was apparently lower in South Korea than in other East Asian NICs.[38] In the 1990s, analysts predicted a steady increase in the labor force participation of "married women, especially from urban low-income households," for whom factory work could no longer be considered a temporary phase.[39] Collective organization may increasingly appear attractive to workers hoping to improve wages and living conditions.

By the mid 1980s, workers in South Korea's heavy industries lived in stable working-class communities, where labor militance was strengthened by church, student, and community activists who emphasized the inadequacy of existing channels for workers' political participation. In major industrial centers, to the extent that residents viewed exclusion from the state and from the benefits of economic growth as intimately linked, working-class communities may begin to develop popular demands reminiscent of those of the peripheralized communities of Brazil and South Africa.

South Korea's industrial workers have hardly been quiescent. Especially with the deepening of export-oriented industrialization in the 1980s, South Korean labor disputes took on a pattern that looked increasingly similar to the strikes that began in Brazil and South Africa during the 1970s. Dramatic work stoppages challenged employers' control over labor, forcing employers and the state to negotiate over basic labor relations frameworks. Women and migrant workers in the labor-intensive textiles and electronics industries engaged in militant strikes, but the relatively well-paid workers in heavy industries were rather more successful in creating workplace-based organizations. Supported by a student movement and by working-class communities, these "new unions" have generally emphasized workplace issues and union recognition outside the corporatist framework. As in Brazil and South Africa, workers in heavy industry, particularly in the automobile sector, have proved able to exploit their location in relation to the state's industrial strategy—a strategy dependent on increasing exports. Frederic Deyo writes: "The occasional militance and power of South Korean workers in the automobile, mining, shipbuilding and other heavy industries bears greater resemblance to the experience of auto workers in São Paulo than to that of industrial workers in the other Asian NICs."[40]

In 1987, following political and labor dissension, labor laws were revised, removing some restrictions on unions and on collective bargaining; by 1990, more than three thousand new "democratic" unions had been formed, with a combined membership of over a quarter of a million and a militant vision of worker activism. A quasi-clandestine federation linked these new unions, providing an alternative to corporatist unions,[41] suggesting that further labor militance lay in the future. By the early 1990s, tensions were emerging between business leaders and the state over economic policy. As Haggard concludes, "the insulation of economic policymaking from domestic social forces had clearly declined, generating new distributional pressures on the state."[42]

Macro-level comparative studies of this kind rarely allow predictions: there are too many mediating factors, too many points of variation, to expect similar trends to lead to identical outcomes in completely different contexts. The comparison between Brazil and South Africa is designed neither to show that they are identical despite different contexts nor to explain differences. Rather, it is an attempt to tease out tendencies that might explain relatively similar patterns of mobilization in very different contexts, to understand why, in both cases, militant labor movements emerged to challenge existing definitions of citizenship. South Korea's recent history is hardly parallel to that of either Brazil or South Africa; and yet authoritarian industrialization strategies seem to have produced roughly comparable capacities in the industrial working class, and at least a possibility of comparable workers' movements. While South Korea's industrialization strategy has differed in important ways from the other two cases—especially in terms of the relative cohesion of elites and equality of income—similarities in terms of rapid industrial growth, barriers to individual mobility, and constraints on labor organization and political expression suggest that Korea's labor movement may yet spread far beyond its factories.

LABOR MOVEMENTS IN LATE INDUSTRIALIZERS

Reinhard Bendix was hardly the first social theorist to predict that industrialization would be linked to increased worker militance: the bourgeoisie, Marx wrote, creates its own grave-diggers. But labor in newly industrialized countries may confront a situation with contours different from those Marx would have recognized. In late-nineteenth-century Europe, state policies designed to promote industrialization were sometimes linked to wage restraints, and state policies often sought to prohibit or control workers' organizations. In the late twentieth century, are workers in newly industrialized countries simply repeating the experiences of workers in nineteenth-century Europe, a century later?

Clearly, generalizations about late-industrializing countries are problematic: most have attempted to design specific development strategies, which almost certainly offer different possibilities for labor. Each country has a unique alliances between the state and capital, as well as a specific relationship between the state, employers, and labor. Moreover, development strategies tend to emphasize growth in specific sectors, with very different implications for labor processes. Among countries committed to capitalist growth, developing countries differ dramatically in the extent to which they emphasize export of primary commodities, or succeed in attracting and directing private investment into industries. Alternative economic models, different natural endowments, different cultural attributes, and, of course, different timing and international contexts—all these have been suggested as factors that help explain variation in industrialization strategies, and variation in growth.

The comparison between labor movements in Brazil and South Africa has suggested some factors one might consider in looking to explain worker mobilization under authoritarian industrialization. What does this comparison suggest for how we understand labor movements in countries experiencing different kinds of growth? Rather than focusing primarily on the internal dynamics of unions, or even on alliances between unionists and politicians, it suggests that we should begin by looking outside labor organizations, at the structural changes that shape the potential for worker mobilization and militance. Authoritarian industrialization reshaped workers' lives, and changed workers' ability to insert their demands in the public arena; other patterns of economic change must alter relationships between classes, and between states and classes, in ways that affect workers' organizational capacities, unions' appeal to broader constituencies, and labor movements' ability to redefine political issues in class terms.

In Brazil and South Africa, the salience of a discourse based on class in the late 1980s seems to reflect the history of labor organization from the mid 1970s onward—a history that in turn reflected the impact of broad structural change in the previous decade. In other cases, with

different patterns of economic growth, labor activists are likely to confront different possibilities and to employ different strategies; to what
extent are labor's possibilities, and those strategies, shaped by a specific
national development policy? Specific industrialization strategies clearly
affect workers in different ways; rather than assuming that all workers
in Third World countries face the same *capitalismo selvagem,* perhaps
we should recognize that different capitalist growth patterns will produce different experiences, different possibilities for labor, different
working-class movements.

The Brazil–South Africa comparison underlines an important aspect
of late industrialization: the competitive international context of the
late twentieth century may greatly reduce states' willingness to resolve
labor conflicts by expanding domestic markets or offering concessions
to a privileged section of the working class. In the late twentieth century, states seeking new avenues to economic expansion are likely to
see international markets as the key to growth and to view cheap labor
as a kind of comparative advantage with which to attract investment
and build sales. At a very general level, dependent development may
limit the willingness of states and dominant classes to respond to demands from the popular sector for distributive policies: in the effort to
attract foreign capital and technology, and to sell industrial products
internationally, states and employers may be especially unwilling to
share the benefits of economic growth, or to raise real wages. But, as
the South African and Brazilian cases suggest, when industrializing
states fail to ensure that the benefits of growth trickle down to their
populations, industrial workers may discover that they can use their
expanded capacity on the shop floor to build highly militant and politicized labor movements.

Over time, as states and employers recognize unions and engage in
collective bargaining, such labor movements may become institutionalized, part of the regular pattern of labor relations in their countries;
social-movement unionism may well be a transitory phase, as relatively
privileged workers create channels through which to articulate interests. On the other hand, if the constituencies of new labor movements
extend beyond the industrial work force, and if these unions retain a
broader vision, we may discover that in its efforts to promote industrialization, the bourgeoisie has, after all, inadvertently created a force
that will challenge the savage inequalities of peripheral capitalism.

Notes

INTRODUCTION

1. See, e.g., Munck, *New International Labor Studies,* 117–22; Webster, "Rise of Social-Movement Unionism."

2. Portelli, "Death of Luigi Trastulli," 25.

3. The worker, Marx writes, must be able to work today and repeat the process tomorrow; moreover, if labor power is to be supplied in the future, the worker's subsistence must include the means to provide for children. The means of subsistence "must therefore be sufficient to maintain him in his normal state as a laboring individual. His natural wants, such as food, clothing, fuel and housing, vary according to the climatic and other physical conditions of his country. On the other hand, the number and extent of his so-called necessary wants, as also the modes of satisfying them, are themselves the product of historical development, and depend therefore to a great extent on the degree of civilization of a country, more particularly on the conditions under which, and consequently on the habits and degree of comfort in which, the class of free laborers has been formed. In contradistinction therefore to the case of other commodities, there enters into the determination of the value of labor-power a historical and moral element. Nevertheless, in a given country, at a given period, the average quantity of the means of subsistence necessary for the laborer is practically known." Marx, *Capital,* in *Marx-Engels Reader,* 350. This definition of social-movement unionism was prompted by a discussion in Sader, "Quando novos personagens entrarem," introduction.

4. See, e.g., Berg and Butler, "Trade Unions"; Kerr et al., *Industrialism and Industrial Man;* Huntington, *Political Order.*

5. Di Tella, "Working-Class Organization"; Valenzuela, "Labor Movements in Transitions."

6. Early dependency theorists generally focused on mobilization among peasants who faced impoverishment with spreading capitalism and constituted the majority of the poor in underdeveloped societies; urban industrial workers were considered relatively privileged, and likely to pursue narrowly defined interests. Amin, *Unequal Development;* Frank, *Capitalism and Underdevelopment.* This perspective is criticized by Peace, "Lagos Proletariat" and Waterman, "Labour Aristocracy in Africa."

7. Luckhardt and Wall, *Organize . . . Or Starve!;* Erickson, *Brazilian Corporative State;* Spalding, *Organized Labor in Latin America* .

8. Van der Merwe, "Trade Unions and the Democratic Order," 112.

9. Cohen, "Benevolent Leviathan".

10. Cardoso and Faletto, *Dependent Development in Latin America.*

11. Some of these variations are discussed in Haggard, *Pathways from the Periphery;* and Gereffi and Wyman, *Manufacturing Miracles.*

12. Coincidentally, scholars of European and North American labor organizations are revising their own labor histories, rediscovering forgotten patterns of militance in early periods of industrialization. See, e.g., Katznelson and Zolberg, eds., *Working-Class Formation;* Montgomery, *Workers' Control in America;* Scott, *Gender and the Politics of History;* Wilentz, *Chants Democratic.*

13. Lipietz, *Mirages and Miracles.*

14. Bonnell, *Roots of Rebellion;* Cronin and Sirianni, *Work, Community and Power;* MacDaniel, *Autocracy.*

15. Arrighi and Silver, "Labor Movements and Capital Migration."

16. Balfour, *Dictatorship, Workers and the City.*

17. Dahrendorf, *Class and Class Conflict;* Huntington, *Political Order;* Offe and Wiesenthal, "Two Logics of Collective Action"; Lenin, "What Is to Be Done?" in *Selected Works,* 29.

18. Aminzade, *Class, Politics and Early Industrial Capitalism;* Biernacki, "Cultural Construction of Labor"; Haydu, *Between Craft and Class;* Smelser, *Social Change in the Industrial Revolution.*

19. Beinin and Lockman, *Workers on the Nile;* Crisp, *Story of an African Working Class;* Freund, *African Worker*; Holmstrom, *Industry and Inequality;* Higginson, *Working Class in the Making;* Roxborough, *Unions and Politics in Mexico.*

20. Evans, "Transnational Linkages."

21. Lipietz, "How Monetarism Has Choked Third World Industrialization," 75.

22. Amsden, "Third World Industrialization"; Brenner and Glick, "Regulation Approach"; Gordon, "Global Economy"; Ruccio, "Fordism."

23. Bergquist, *Labor in Latin America;* Deyo, *Beneath the Miracle* .
Most comparative studies of race relations emphasize unlike outcomes in settings that might have been expected to have similar dynamics. See Cell, *Highest Stage of White Supremacy;* Degler, *Neither Black nor White;* Frederickson, *White Supremacy;* Greenberg, *Race and State in Capitalist Development.* However, in 1981, Michael Burawoy suggested that a comparison of surprisingly similar outcomes might be used to examine the relationship between the state

and race and class in Brazil and South Africa ("State and Social Revolution in South Africa").

24. Moore, *Social Bases of Dictatorship and Democracy;* Skocpol, *States and Social Revolutions.*

25. Collier and Collier, *Shaping the Political Arena,* esp. 15–18.

26. Tilly, *Class Conflict and Collective Action,* 15.

27. Burawoy, *Manufacturing Consent.*

1. MILITANT LABOR MOVEMENTS IN BRAZIL
    AND SOUTH AFRICA

1. See, e.g., O'Donnell and Schmitter, *Transitions from Authoritarian Rule.*

2. Despite the literature's general focus on elite negotiations, Adam Prze-worski points out that in a majority of cases of transition away from authoritarianism, grass-roots pressures existed to one extent or another, often interacting with divisions within elites to provoke liberalization. See id., *Democracy and the Market,* 56–57.

3. Valenzuela, "Labor Movements in Transitions." However, for a different approach, see Alvarez, *Engendering Democracy in Brazil;* Keck, *Workers' Party and Democratization;* and Paine, "Working-Class Strategies."

4. Pastore and Skidmore, "Brazilian Labor Relations," 45.

5. Hindson, "Union Unity," 105.

6. Giddens, *Class Structure of Advanced Societies,* 201.

7. Schorske, *German Social Democracy.*

8. Huntington, "Reform and Stability."

9. Bendix, *Nation-building and Citizenship,* 361–434.

10. For South Africa, see Smollan, *Black Advancement.* For Brazil, see Rodrigues, *Sindicato e desenvolvimento,* 21, 180.

11. Bendix, *Nation-building and Citizenship,* 361–434.

12. Moore, *Injustice.*

13. Quoted by Michael Parks, "SA Black Unions Lead Fight against Apartheid," *Los Angeles Times,* Sept. 9, 1987.

14. Lange and Ross, *Change and Crisis,* 207–91.

15. Collier and Collier, *Shaping the Political Arena,* esp. 169–95, 360–402, 507–70, and 745–74.

16. Bergquist, *Labor in Latin America.*

17. Deyo, *Beneath the Miracle.*

18. Cohen, "Benevolent Leviathan"; Erickson, *Brazilian Corporative State;* Rodrigues, "Trabalhadores e sindicatos."

19. This argument is presented in works as diverse as Kerr et al., *Industrialism and Industrial Man* and Ehrensaft, "Phases in the Development of South African Capitalism." See also du Toit, *Capital and Labour;* McShane et al., *Power!*

20. Unlike South Africa's, Brazil's data use self-placement to put individuals in racial categories. Obviously, the use of these categories reflects changing attitudes toward and ideologies of race: Charles H. Wood has pointed out that in Brazil the line between "white" and other categories has been far more constant

than the shifting line between the main "nonwhite" groups (essentially, "brown" and "black"). Wood and Carvalho, *Demography of Inequality*, 140–43, and Wood, in Andrews, *Blacks and Whites in São Paulo*, 249–58. See also Araújo, "Classificação de 'cor.' " For demographic, educational, and income differences between blacks and whites in Brazil, see Berquo, "Demografia da desigualdade"; Wood and Carvalho, *Demography of Inequality*.

21. Andrews, *Blacks and Whites in São Paulo*, 198–99.

22. P. K. Leballo, in police records, 1960; cited by Gerhart, *Black Power*, 219. Similar sentiments run through the history of popular organizing in South Africa, perhaps especially, but not by no means only, in rural areas and among recent urban migrants. Bradford, *Taste of Freedom*; Lodge, *Black Politics*.

23. Skidmore, *Experiment in Democracy*, 62–64; Erickson, *Brazilian Corporative State*, 22; Santos, *Cidadania e justica*, 95.

24. Kowarick, *Trabalho e vadiagem*, 103.

25. Dean, *Industrialization of São Paulo*.

26. Simons and Simons, *Class and Color*, 95; Hirson, *Yours for the Union*, 10–13.

27. 1914 Commission, in Davies, "South Africa's Industrial Relations Legislation," 73.

28. O'Meara gives a detailed description of the process through which conservative unionists moved into the leadership of some white unions in *Volkscapitalisme*, 89–95 and 248–51.

29. Hirson, *Yours in the Union*, esp. chs. 7–14.

30. Ncube, *Black Trade Unions*, ch. 3.

31. S.A. Minister of Labour Ben Schoeman, in Bunting, *South African Reich*, 35.

32. Note, however, that the 1954 labor law reforms, which closed registered union membership to all but white workers, were opposed by several employers' associations. These associations argued that industrial peace would be better maintained if "nonwhite" industrial workers had some channel through which to articulate grievances—an argument that would reappear in the 1970s. See Ncube, *Black Trade Unions*, ch. 3.

33. Ensor, "TUCSA's Relationship with African Trade Unions."

34. Kenneth Luckhardt and Brenda Wall describe many of these unions in *Organize . . . or Starve!*

35. Formed in 1952 after the National Party began to implement its apartheid policies, the Congress Alliance was a multiracial body joining different political groupings, each representing a different racial group. In addition to the ANC and SACTU, the alliance included the white Congress of Democrats, the South African Indian Congress, and the South African Coloured People's Organization.

36. Simons and Simons, *Class and Colour*, 621–22.

37. French, *Brazilian Workers' ABC*, pt. 2.

38. On this period in Brazilian labor history, see, among others, Andrade, "Movimento trabalhista e sindicatos"; Harding, "Political History of Organized Labor in Brazil"; Vianna, *Liberalismo e sindicato*; Neves, *O Comando*

Geral; Weffort, *O populismo na política* and "Os sindicatos na política". For more specific case studies, see Araújo, *Operários em luta;* Sarti, *Porto vermelho;* Loyola, *Os sindicatos e o PTB.*

39. In a survey of delegates—all union officials—at the 1960 Third Congress of Metalworkers, Sarah Chucid and Michael Lowy found overwhelming objections to state control over union affairs. Chucid and Lowy, "Pesquisa das opinões e atitudes de líderes sindicais metalúrgicos."

40. Santos, *Cidadania e justiça,* 71–79.

41. Foster, "Workers' Struggle"; Moisés, "Qual é a estratégia," 32.

42. This line of reasoning dates to Selig Perlman's 1928 classic, *Theory of the Labor Movement,* but it is often repeated in works such as Ralph Dahrendorf's *Class and Class Conflict.* Lenin makes a rather similar argument in "What Is to Be Done?" in *Selected Works,* 29. Jonathan Zeitlin discusses this aproach in "Shop Floor Bargaining," 5–8.

43. Marx, "Manifesto," in *Marx-Engels Reader,* 480–81.

44. Thompson, "Peculiarities of the English," 357.

45. Katznelson, "Working-Class Formation," 20.

46. See, e.g., Amin, *Unequal Development;* Huntington, *Political Order,* 283–88.

47. Katznelson, "Working-Class Formation," 20.

48. See interviews in História Imediata, ed., *A greve.*

49. Former MAWU organizer, interview, Botswana, June 1987.

50. Levy and Associates, in *Weekly Mail,* Feb. 5–11, 1988.

51. This is particularly true of go-slows, industrial sabotage, and other less visible forms of worker protest. These unofficial worker actions were common in South Africa, and they seem to have been used extensively in Brazil during the most repressive years of the dictatorship. Frederico, *A vanguarda operária,* 57–85.

52. S.A. Department of Labour, in *Survey of Race Relations, 1968,* 117.

53. Compiled by the NEPP-UNICAMP. See Almeida, "Difícil caminho," 330–36, and Noronha, *Greve e conjuntura.*

54. Labour Monitoring Group, quoted by Swilling, "Stayaways," 23.

55. Levy and Associates, in *Weekly Mail,* Feb. 5–11, 1988.

56. This section draws heavily on methodological discussions in Shorter and Tilly, *Strikes in France.*

57. Alves, *State and Opposition,* table A-9, note.

58. Moisés, *Lições de liberdade,* 187.

59. This definition, which follows both South African labor laws and the experience of union organizers, excludes agricultural and domestic labor, as well as administrative and managerial personal. It also excludes workers in homelands, where unions were generally illegal at the time of the estimate, although it includes migrants to "white-designated" South Africa. Lewis and Randall, "State of the Unions," 75; and Bonner, "Independent Trade Unions," 30–31.

60. The earlier figure comes from Erickson, *Brazilian Corporative State,* 31. The later figure is from CEDI, *Trabalhadores urbanos no Brasil 82/84,* 54.

Margaret Keck has kindly reminded me that some of the increased membership reflects the creation of new unions for rural workers and urban professionals in the 1980s.

61. Moisés, "Qual é a estratégia," 15–16.

62. Almedia, "Difícil caminho," 331

63. Friedman, *Building Tomorrow Today,* 122–28.

64. Levy and Associates, *Industrial Action Monitor,* 11.

65. Ferreira, in CEDI, *Aconteceu Especial* 16, 26.

66. Keck, "From Movement to Politics," and her more recent *Workers' Party and Democratization;* and Meneguello, *PT: A formação,* pt. 1.

67. Alves, "Grassroots Organization"; Friedman, *Building Tomorrow Today,* 231–32, 236–37, 252–56.

68. Almeida, "Desarrollo capitalista y accion sindical"; Sutcliffe and Wellings, *Strike Action.*

69. Seekings, "Black Townships of the Transvaal," 201.

70. An early Brazilian example is from 1973, when bus transport was a major demand in the Massey-Ferguson strike. In South Africa, transport issues come up regularly in the Works and Liaison Committee minutes included in the FOSATU archives. See, e.g., "Minutes of Alusaf Zulu Liaison Committee," March 4, 1974: even after the chairman explained that workers living in townships could not be given a traveling allowance, "the problem of inadequate transport to and from work was raised again."

71. Faria, "A experiência operária," 239.

72. Sader, "Quando novos personagens entraram," ch. 1.

73. Castells, *City and the Grass Roots,* 326–31.

74. Luís Inácio da Silva, electoral campaign speech, BBC transmission, December 14, 1989.

75. The parallel with T. H. Marshall's discussion of different definitions of citizenship is not accidental; intellectuals sympathetic to both the Brazilian and South African labor movements often cited Marshall's *Citizenship and Social Development.* See, e.g., Weffort, "Why Democracy?"; Evans, "Hegemony in Repressive Regimes."

76. Thomson, *Making of the English Working Class.*

77. For South Africa: interviews, former labor organizers, Johannesburg, April 1987; Harriet Bolton, Harare, 1989. For Brazil, Ibrahim, "História do movimento."

78. Nunes, "Carências urbanas," 73.

79. Piven and Cloward, *Poor People's Movements,* ch. 1.

2.   CONDITIONS FOR INDUSTRIAL GROWTH, 1960–1973

1. Tilly, *Conflict and Collective Action,* 15.

2. Tilly and Tilly, eds., *Big Structure, Large Processes,* 63–64.

3. Although they did not coin the term NICs, Fernando Henrique Cardoso and Enzo Faletto were among the first to point out that some late industrializing countries had created industrial bases, although those economies remained vul-

nerable to pressures from the world economy in ways that differed significantly from the vulnerabilities of earlier industrializers.

4. Berman and Lonsdale, "Crises of Accumulation"; Block, "Ruling Class Does Not Rule"; Canak, "Peripheral State Debate"; Hamilton, *Limits of State Autonomy;* Krasner, "Approaches to the State."

5. Evans, "After Dependency."

6. Munck, *New International Labor Studies,* 206–14.

7. Lipietz, *Mirages and Miracles.*

8. Arrighi and Silver, "Labor Movements and Capital Migration"; Marks, *Unions in Politics.*

9. See, e.g., Wallerstein, "Collapse of Democracy."

10. Hirschman, "Turn to Authoritarianism in Latin America," and Remmer and Merkx, "Bureaucratic-Authoritarianism Revisited."

11. Brant et al., *São Paulo: Growth and Poverty;* Hewlett, *Cruel Dilemmas of Development.*

12. Frank, *Capitalism and Underdevelopment,* 174.

13. António Carlos, in Weffort, *O populismo na política,* 49.

14. Vianna, *Liberalismo e sindicato,* 153–242; Costa, *Estado e controle sindical,* 19–79.

15. Dean, *Industrialization of São Paulo;* Dulles, *Brazilian Communism;* Levine, *Vargas Regime;* Vianna, *Liberalismo e sindicato.*

16. Baer, *Industrialization and Economic Development,* 264.

17. Ministério da Fazenda figures, in Baer, *Industrialization and Economic Development,* 266.

18. Baer, *Industrialization and Economic Development,* 263.

19. Cardoso, *Ideologia do desenvolvimento.*

20. In fact, the distinction between "national capital" and other dominant fractions was overdrawn: while it is certainly possible to discern the distinct concerns of domestic capital, foreign capital, and large landowners in the debates of the 1950s, their economic interests often overlapped.

21. Weffort, "Sindicatos na política" and "Democracia e movimento operária."

22. Mericle, "Brazilian Motor Vehicle Industry."

23. Baer, *Industrialization and Economic Development,* 107.

24. It is sometimes argued that the full potential of Brazil's new industrial capacity would only be realized when income concentration, exacerbated in the 1960s, created a domestic market. Bacha, "Issues and Evidence"; Malan and Bonelli, "Brazilian Economy in the Seventies."

25. Skidmore, *Politics of Military Rule,* 12.

26. Erickson, *Brazilian Corporative State,* 31.

27. Neves, *O Comando Geral,* ch. 2.

28. A survey of Metalworkers' Union officers in about 1962 found nearly half considered themselves radicals, three-quarters believed the government favored employers, and about half believed strikes were "the workers' best arm against the bosses." Almost 80 percent believed unions should unite and mobilize workers at the point of production rather than provide the assistential ser-

vices offered by conservative unions. Chucid and Lowy, "Pesquisa das opinões e atitudes de líderes sindicais metalúrgicos," 12.

29. Andrade, "Movimento trabalhista e sindicatos"; Moisés, "Classes populares e protesto urbano"; Weffort, "Sindicatos e política," ch. 4:34.

30. Diario de Noticias, Mar. 23, 1964, in Stepan, Military in Politics, 199.

31. Azevedo, As Ligas camponeses; Neves, O Comando Geral, 100–137.

32. Alves, State and Opposition, 38–43. The military regime reserved the right to enforce cassação, or withdrawal of all legal and political rights, against potential members of the opposition.

33. Alves, State and Opposition, ch. 1.

34. Arquidiocese de São Paulo, ed., Brasil: Nunca mais, 124.

35. Figueirido, "Intervenções sindicais," and "A politíca governamental e funções sindicais," ch. 2.

36. O'Donnell, Modernization and Bureaucratic Authoritarianism.

37. The first edition of the magazine Brasil Industrial (1972) was titled "A conjuntura favoravel."

38. Fishlow, "Economic Policy," 80.

39. Alves, State and Opposition, 75–76.

40. Baer, Brazilian Economy, 94.

41. Ibid., 97.

42. Martins, Estado capitalista e burocracia, 51–53.

43. Baer, Brazilian Economy, 148.

44. Based on figures from Foxley, Latin American Experiments, 28.

45. Martins, Estado capitalista e burocracia, 67.

46. Baer, Brazilian Economy, 150–52.

47. Ibid., 155.

48. Ibid., 126.

49. Foxley, Latin American Experiments, 24–27.

50. Fajnzylber, A sistema industrial e exportação.

51. Baer, Brazilian Economy, 130, 149.

52. Skidmore, Politics of Military Rule, 36–37

53. Evans, Dependent Development, 78.

54. Cardoso and Faletto, Dependency and Development in Latin America, introduction.

55. Evans, Dependent Development, 119.

56. Ibid., 142.

57. Ibid., 120.

58. World Bank, Brazil: Industrial Policies, 119.

59. Andrade, "Brasil: A economia de capitalismo selvagem," 141.

60. Morley and Smith, "Effect of Changes," 129.

61. Pereira, Development and Crisis, 165.

62. The exact decline in real wages is disputed; government and union figures differ markedly. These differences are discussed in Almeida, Política salarial, 18–20.

63. Based on figures presented by the Ministério do Planejamento, IPEA, Diário do Congreso Nacional, Sept. 29, 1974, 3964.

64. DIEESE, Divulgação, No. 1/76 (April, 19, 1976), 10.

65. Singer, "Mais pobres e mais ricos."

66. Lei 4330, June 14, 1964; Decreto 3, Jan 27, 1966; Article 482 of the CLT.

67. Figueirido, "Intervenções sindicais."

68. Oliveira and Teixeira, *(Im)prévidencia social,* 196–97.

69. Alves, *State and Opposition,* 86.

70. Erickson, *Brazilian Corporative State,* 169.

71. Weffort, "Participação e conflito industrial," 21–50.

72. Ibrahim, "História do movimento de Osasco."

73. Weffort, "Participação e conflito industrial"; Ibrahim, "História do movimento de Osasco," 13–15.

74. In 1981, Lula told a meeting of the newly formed Partido dos Trabalhadores, "We must stop being afraid. What are we afraid of? Are we afraid of being arrested?" Maria Helena Moreira Alves writes, "From the back of the room a worker shouted back at him, 'We are afraid of being tortured! I was tortured!' There was a moment of distinct and uncomfortable silence, and then Lula responded, 'Yes, my friend. We are afraid of being tortured. But we must stop being afraid of torture. There is no worse torture than to see your child crying for a plate of food or a glass of milk and to know that your salary is not sufficient for you to buy it.'" Alves, *State and Opposition,* 126. See also Arquidiocese de São Paulo, ed., *Brasil: Nunca mais,* 124–31.

75. Arquidiocese de São Paulo, ed., *Brasil: Nunca mais,* 73; Alves, *State and Opposition,* 131.

76. Rodrigues, "Trabalhadores e sindicatos," 149.

77. See, e.g., strategic discusssions within the metalworkers of Baixada Santista during the early 1970s, described by Araújo, *Operários em luta.*

78. Erickson, *Brazilian Corporative State,* 160.

79. Quoted in Frederico, *Consciência operária,* 63.

80. Cohen, "Benevolent Leviathan."

81. Although the two systems initially ran simultaneously, workers almost inevitably opted for the FGTS, apparently believing they would not keep their jobs if they chose the older system. Ferrante, *FGTS.*

82. Ferrante, *FGTS,* 130 and 197.

83. Humphrey, *Capitalist Control and Workers' Struggle,* 87–99.

84. Faria, "Desenvolvimento, urbanização e mudanças," 146–47.

85. Singer, *Dominação e desigualdade,* table 37.

86. World Bank, *Brazil: Industrial Policies,* 10, 13–15.

87. Ibid., 19.

88. Pereira, "Um perfil da classe operária," *Movimento,* Apr. 24, 1980.

89. Based on figures in Sousa, "Concentração industrial," 21.

90. Brasil, Instituto Brasileiro de Geografia e Estatístico (IBGE), *Anuários estatísticos,* 1975 and 1983.

91. Unpublished DIEESE data, in Humphrey, *Capitalist Control and Workers' Struggle,* table 2–6.

92. Araújo, "Mudanças na estrutura social," 39.

93. Ibid., 50.

94. Humphrey, *Capitalist Control and Workers' Struggle,* 99, 144.

95. Sousa, "Concentração industrial," 14.
96. Rodrigues, *Industrialização e atitudes operárias*, 45.
97. Andrade, "Brasil: A economia do capitalismo selvagem."
98. Instituto Brasileiro de Geografia e Estatístico, *Censo demográfico, 1970*. Bernard Sorj discusses the changing class structure of the countryside in *Estado e classes sociais*.
99. Oliveira et al., *Nordestinos em São Paulo*, 73–79.
100. Santos, *Cidadania e justiça*, 76.
101. Dean, *Industrialization of São Paulo*.
102. Gonçalves, *Carteira de trabalho*, 7
103. John Humphrey, personal communication, São Paulo, 1986.
104. Lago and Lima, *Estrutura ocupacional*, 130.
105. Keck, "New Unionism," 260.
106. Moisés, *Lições de liberdade*, 60–61.
107. *Volkshandel* commented in June 1948: "It must be acknowledged that the non-white worker already constitutes an integral part of our economic structure, that he is now so enmeshed in the spheres of our economic life that for the first fifty/hundred years (if not longer) [of National Party rule], total segregation is pure wishful thinking." In O'Meara, *Volkscapitalisme*, 175.
108. Verwoerd, *Verwoerd Speaks*, 83.
109. Wolpe, "Capitalism and Cheap Labour-Power."
110. Lever, "Capital and Labour in South Africa."
111. Lodge, *Black Politics*, 201–317.
112. Luckhardt and Wall, *Organize...or Starve*, 402–37.
113. Lacey, *Working for Boroko*, 224–29.
114. SAR reports, in Lewis, *Industrialisation and Trade Union Organisation*, 75–76.
115. Solomon, "Transport," 98–99, 108.
116. Lewis, *Industrialisation and Trade Union Organization*, 75–76.
117. O'Meara, *Volkscapitalisme*, 36.
118. Holloway Commission report, para. 122; in Lumby, "Industrial Development," 215.
119. S.A. Department of Census and Statistics, *Statistics for Fifty Years*, L-26.
120. Lumby, "Development of Secondary Industry," 231–32.
121. Falkena, *South African State and Its Entrepreneurs*, 38.
122. Lumby, "Secondary Industrial Development," 234.
123. Seidman and Seidman, *U.S. Multinational Corporations*, 66.
124. Wassenaar, *Assault on Private Enterprise*, 123.
125. O'Meara, *Volkscapitalisme*, 250.
126. Clark, "South African State Corporations," 99.
127. Nattrass, *South African Economy*, 83.
128. O'Meara, *Volkscapitalisme*, esp. 96–118 and 167–76.
129. Verwoerd in Lipton, *Capitalism and Apartheid*, 286; see also Verwoerd, *Verwoerd Speaks*, 181–82.
130. Sampson, *Black and Gold*, 86.
131. Chase Manhattan's David Rockefeller helped arrange the loan to

South Africa. Curiously, Nelson Rockefeller played a parallel role in arranging U.S. government assistance to Brazil's military government immediately after the 1964 coup. Skidmore, *Politics of Military Rule*, 104, 158.

132. Chase Manhattan Bank, in Sampson, *Black and Gold*, 87.

133. Suckling, "Foreign Investment," 18, 23, table 11.

134. John Blashill, "Proper Role of US Corporations in South Africa," *Fortune*, July 1972, 49.

135. *South Africa: A Guide to Foreign Investors*, 61

136. U.S. Department of the Army, *South Africa: A Country Study*, table 13.

137. Economist Intelligence Unit Ltd., *Quarterly Economic Review Annual Supplement*, 1974.

138. Lumby, "Development of Secondary Industry," 232.

139. Solomon, "Transport."

140. Bloch, "Room at the Top?" 51.

141. AECI, "Document for the Private Placing of 12m Ordinary Shares," in Innes, *Anglo American*, 201.

142. Innes, *Anglo American*, 194–202.

143. Bloch, "Room at the Top?" 55

144. Whitaker, "The Economy," 188.

145. Meyer, *Role of Exports*, 32.

146. Jones, "History of Black Involvement," table 18.

147. O'Meara, "Analysing Afrikaner Nationalism," 71.

148. Figures from Lipton, *Capitalism and Apartheid*, tables 9 and 10.

149. Jones, "History of Black Involvement," 18

150. S.A. Central Statistical Services, *South African Statistics*, 1982.

151. Nattrass, *South African Economy*, 25 and 164; Torchia, "Business of Business," 423.

152. Based on S.A. Department of Statistics figures, *South African Statistics*, 1964, M7–M25; and 1976, 12.8–12.

153. Figures cited by Greenberg, *Race and State*, 402.

154. Lipton, *Capitalism and Apartheid*, 145–46.

155. Sadie, "Labour Supply in South Africa," 20.

156. Maree, "Dimensions and Causes of Unemployment," 34.

157. S.A. Department of Manpower, *Manpower Survey*, nos. 8 and 14.

158. Bendix, in *Survey of Race Relations, 1977*, 243.

159. Lewis, *Industrialisation and Trade Union Organization*, 111–56.

160. This practice did not end with the erosion of racial job reservation: employers clearly continued to pay workers for less-skilled positions through the early 1980s. See, e.g., correspondence between the Industrial Council for the Iron, Steel, Engineering and Metallurgical Industry and the Engineering and Allied Workers' Union regarding the case of Stephen Tladi, an EAWU member who was paid as a laborer although he worked as a forklift driver; despite the inclusion of three affidavits swearing that he had operated the forklift, the council found Tladi had never worked as a driver and ruled that there was therefore no question of paying him at the scheduled rate. FOSATU archives, Engineering and Allied Workers' Union, Nov. 27, 1979–May 29, 1980.

161. Kraak, "Uneven Capitalist Development"; Meth, "Are There Skill Shortages?" 25.
162. Simkins and Hindson, *Division of Labour*, 4 and 15.
163. Sitas, "African Worker Responses," 224.
164. Wright, "Changing Labor Process."
165. Maree, "Dimensions and Causes of Unemployment," 23.
166. Bell, "Industrial Decentralization," 209.
167. Jones, "History of Black Involvement in the Economy," 15.
168. Saul and Gelb, *Crisis in South Africa*, 149.
169. Institute for Industrial Education, *Durban Strikes, 1973*, 48.
170. Roux, "Division of Labour at Ford," 31.

3. BUSINESS OPPOSITION AND ITS LIMITS

1. Gereffi, "Paths of Industrialization," 21.
2. Tarrow, *Struggle, Politics and Reform*, 32–38. See also McAdam, *Political Process*, ch. 1.
3. Jessop, *Capitalist State*, 228–59.
4. O'Donnell, *Modernization and Bureaucratic Authoritarianism*; Remmer and Merkx, "Bureaucratic-Authoritarianism Revisited"; Schamis, "Reconceptualizing Latin American Authoritarianism."
5. Alves, *State and Opposition*, 9.
6. Greenberg, *Race, State and Capitalist Development*, 402–3.
7. See, however, Bonnell, *Roots of Rebellion*; Marks, *Unions in Politics*, 50–76. Clearly, the fact that some workers could vote in Britain, Germany, and the United States makes these cases quite different from that of prerevolutionary Russia.
8. See, e.g., Kerr et al., *Industrialism and Industrial Man*.
9. Claudio Bardella, Severo Gomes, José Mindlin, António Ermírio de Moraes, Paulo Villares, Paulo Vellinho, Laerte Setubal, and Jorge Gerdou, "Só democracia absorve tensões sociais: Manifesto de oito empresários paulistas," *Folha de São Paulo*, June 26, 1978, 20.
10. Laerte Setubal Filho, "Os conflitos que a carta da Conclap não eliminou," *Exame* 140 (Nov. 1977): 12–14.
11. See, e.g., Warren Dean's discussion of how capital from coffee plantations was reinvested in industrial projects, in *Industrialization of São Paulo*; and Boris Fausto's description of the close ties between agricultural and industrial elites during the initial period of import-substitution industrialization, in *Revolução de 1930*. See also Diniz, "O empresariado e o momento."
12. Martins, *Estado capitalista e burocracia*.
13. Oposição Sindical Metalúrgica de São Paulo, "História do movimento."
14. Pereira, *O colapso de uma aliança*.
15. Evans, "Re-inventing the Bourgeoisie."
16. Alves, *State and Opposition*, 155–66.
17. In 1969, Amnesty International's report on Brazilian torture was the first of a series of international reports on human rights violations in Brazil.

Although the Nixon administration continued to maintain cordial relations with the military regime, international public opinion certainly assisted the domestic human rights movement.

18. Einar Kok, "O medo da liberdade," *IstoÉ*, Feb. 21, 1980, 65.

19. Diniz, "A transição política"; Skidmore, *Politics of Military Rule*, 201.

20. Malan and Bonelli, "Brazilian Economy."

21. Official figures initially put the inflation rate for 1973 at 20.5 percent, up about 3 percent from the three previous years' average. However, as the following chapter discusses in greater detail, a successful suit by the Metalworkers' Union in 1977 proved that the government had purposely distorted the inflation rate and the index on which workers' salaries were based.

22. Banco Central figures, in Kucinski, *Abertura*, 27, 29.

23. World Bank, *Brazil: Industrial Policies*.

24. Kucinski, *Abertura*, 26. Tilman Evers argues in "Sobre o comportamento das classes médias" that the reduction in consumer credit and economic opportunities played a part in creating a middle-class opposition. Largely in response to industry's demands for a more technically skilled labor force, the government had greatly expanded opportunities for university education; by reducing the credit available to middle-class consumers, the economic crisis would intensify political alienation among the educated technicians created by the government's own previous policies.

25. Geisel, in Skidmore, *Politics of Military Rule*, 176.

26. Ibid., 115.

27. Lamounier, "O voto em São Paulo, 1970–1978," 35.

28. Skidmore, *Politics of Military Rule*, 188–98.

29. Evans, "Re-inventing the Bourgeoisie," S225.

30. Diniz and Lima, *Modernização autoritária*, 32.

31. Trebat, *Brazil's State-Owned Enterprises*, 59.

32. Martins, *Estado capitalista e burocracia*, 43.

33. Skidmore, *Politics of Military Rule*, 208.

34. Diniz and Lima, *Modernização autoritária*, 45.

35. Lessa, *A estratégia de desenvolvimento, 1974–1976*.

36. McDonough, "Mapping an Authoritarian Power Structure."

37. Cardoso, "O papel dos empresários," 12.

38. Abranches, "Divided Leviathan," 168.

39. Boschi, *Elites industriais e democracia*, 152.

40. Rolf Juntz, "Empresário perde sempre no jogo oficial sem regras," *Indústria e Desenvolvimento* 9, no. 7 (July 1976): 22–23.

41. Boschi, *Elites indústriais e democracia*, 154.

42. "Estatização, segundo a Fiesp," *Gazeta Mercantil*, Sept. 4, 1975, 1–5. However, Malan dates business concern over state enterprises from 1974, in "O debate sobre 'estatização,' " 30–32.

43. Affonso Almiro, "Para que desestatizar," *Carta Mensal* 22 (Oct. 1976): 1–7.

44. Diniz and Lima, *Modernização autoritária*, 62.

45. Pereira, *O colapso de uma aliança*, 120.

46. Thomaz António Pompeu, in Pereira, *O colapso de uma aliança*, 97.

47. A. T. Milanesi, "Hora de ouvir a voz dos empresários," *Indústria e Desenvolvimento* 10, no. 11 (Nov. 1977): 21–23.

48. "Os conflitos que a carta da Conclap não eliminou," *Exame* 140 (Nov. 1977): 12–14.

49. *Gazeta Mercantil*, Sept. 13, 1977.

50. Cardoso, "O papel dos empresários," 15n.

51. Interview with Severo Gomes, "O que a economia separa, a política une," *Movimento*, Jan. 23, 1978, 4.

52. Study of business's economic and political demands reported in *Jornal do Brasil*, Jan. 1, 1977, in Boschi, *Elites indústriais e democracia*, 215.

53. Vianna, *A classe operária e a abertura*, 93–105.

54. Abramo, "Empresários e trabalhadores," 5–10.

55. Einar Kok, "Um sindicalismo inspirado no modelo americano," *Exame* 151 (May 10, 1978): 17–18.

56. Kok, "Um sindicalismo inspirado no modelo americano," 17–18.

57. Keck, "New Unionism in the Brazilian Transition," 263.

58. Luís Inácio da Silva, "O avanço sindical," *IstoÉ*, Feb. 21, 1980.

59. Humphrey, *Capitalist Control and Workers' Struggle*, 150–53, 165; Moisés, "Qual é a estratégia," 15–16.

60. Pereira, *O colapso de uma aliança*, 147.

61. "Quais são os limites para as reivindicações?" *Exame* 150 (Apr. 26, 1978); Einar Kok, interview, *Exame* 151 (May 10, 1978); Roldão Oliveira, "O fim do medo e do silencio?" *Movimento*, Jan. 5, 1978.

62. Pereira, *O colapso de uma aliança*.

63. Abramo, "Empresários e trabalhadores," 6, esp. fn. 7.

64. Future FIESP president Luís Eulálio Bueno Vidigal, in *Folha de São Paulo*, June 16, 1978.

65. See, e.g., "Quais são os limites para as reivindicações," *Exame* 150 (Apr. 26, 1978): 12–13; Kurt Lenhard, "As mudanças que a abertura impõe as empresas," *Exame* 178 (June 20, 1979): 72–73; Laerte Setubal Filho, "O papel dos entitades de classe," *Escritorio Moderno* 8, no. 1 (May–June 1980): 40–44.

66. Jones Santos Neves, "Empresa como instrumento de ação social," *Indústria e Productividade* 14, no. 149 (May 1981): 34–35.

67. Luís Eulálio de Bueno Vidigal Filho, "Abertura chega à indústria paulista," *Indústria e Desenvolvimento* 14, no. 6 (1980): 6–10.

68. João Donato, new president of the Federation of Industries of Rio de Janeiro, argued that his election, like Vidigal's, reflected a new level of business activism. "A preocupação social dos novos líderes," *Tendência* 8, no. 82 (Oct. 1980): 11.

69. Cardoso, "O papel dos empresários," 21.

70. Fishlow, "Tale of Two Presidents," 108.

71. Diniz, "Empresário e transição política," 23.

72. Cardoso, "O papel dos empresários," 23.

73. Diniz, "Empresário e transição política," 28.

74. Souza, "As duas vertentes da democracia."

75. Diniz, in "A transição política no Brasil," 335n., suggests that his per-

spective differs from Alves's in the weight she gives to the regime's capacity to control opposition, especially business elites.

76. Lipton, *Capitalism and Apartheid,* 372.

77. Marks and Atmore, *Economy and Society;* and Marks and Trapido, *Politics of Race, Class and Nationalism.*

78. See, e.g., Burawoy, "Capitalist State in South Africa"; and Bonacich, "Capitalism and Race Relations in South Africa."

79. Wolpe, "Capitalism and Cheap Labour-Power."

80. Ncube, *Black Trade Unions.*

81. Lipton, *Capitalism and Apartheid,* 160–65; Greenberg, *Race and State in Capitalist Development,* 207.

82. Ncube, *Black Trade Unions.*

83. "Proposal to Ease Racial Tension," *Commercial Opinion,* July 1960; in Greenberg, *Race and State in Capitalist Development,* 203.

84. Wolpe, *Race, Class and the Apartheid State,* 73, 85–87.

85. Calculated from figures in Giliomee, "Afrikaner Economic Advance," 170–71.

86. O'Meara, *Volkscapitalisme,* 250.

87. *Volkshandel,* June 1948; in Posel, " 'Providing for the Legitimate Labour Requirements," 201.

88. *Volkshandel* Oct. 1960; in Greenberg, *Race and State in Capitalist Development,* 204.

89. *The Manufacturer,* Sept. 1960, 5, and May 1961, 11. Emphasis in original.

90. Torchia, "Business of Business," 438; Sampson, *Black and Gold,* 84–103.

91. *Industry and Trade,* Dec. 1963, 36.

92. Unilever Special Committee, in Sampson, *Black and Gold,* 89.

93. Hutt, *Economics of the Colour Bar,* 1964, 137; quoted in Torchia, "Business of Business," 440.

94. O'Dowd, "Stages of Economic Growth," 37.

95. *Industry and Trade,* Dec. 1968, 5.

96. Verwoerd, 1959, in *Verwoerd Speaks,* 271.

97. Glaser, "Periodisation," 37–38.

98. Marsh gives detailed examples of such objections in *Failures of Apartheid Industrial Decentralization,* 69–77.

99. Bell, "Is Industrial Decentralization a Thing of the Past?" 208–11.

100. Tomlinson and Addleson, "Is the State's Regional Policy in the Interest of Capital?" 67–68.

101. Greenberg, *Legitimating the Illegitimate,* 62.

102. Ibid., 56–84. Posel's careful discussion of the conflict between state and business over labor supplies, and of the process through which accommodation was reached, was published after this volume was already in press, but her analysis underlines the point. See Posel, *The Making of Apartheid,* esp. 116–80, 248–55.

103. For example, in 1961, the Educational Panel of the University of the Witwatersrand warned that since nearly all economically active whites were

engaged in skilled work, any "new recruits to the skilled ranks . . . must be non-whites." In 1964, the Bureau of Economic Research at Stellenbosch warned that "if, in certain sectors of the skilled labour market, the required white manpower supply has been exhausted, and sufficient numbers cannot be recruited by means of immigration, present needs dictate that recruits be sought in other sectors of the population." Second Report of the 1961 Education Panel, 1966, 25, and Bureau of Economic Research, University of Stellenbosch, 1963, 31; both in Webster, *Cast in a Racial Mould*, 157–58.

104. IMS Bienniel Conference Minutes, in Webster, *Cast in a Racial Mold*, 60.

105. Webster, *Cast in a Racial Mould*, 158; Lewis, *Industrialization and Trade Union Organisation*, 159–75.

106. Industrial Aid Society, "Skilled Workers" (mimeo, IAS archives, Johannesburg, n.d.).

107. Webster, *Cast in a Racial Mould*, 116–17.

108. Ibid., 106.

109. Friedman, *Building Tomorrow Today*, 52.

110. Adam, "South African Power Elite."

111. Adam, *Modernizing Racial Domination*, 147–48, 179.

112. O'Meara, *Volkescapitalisme*, 251.

113. Adam, *Modernizing Racial Domination*, 174–75; Asheron, "Race and Politics in South Africa," 67.

114. Charney, "National Party, 1982–1985," 6.

115. Federated Chamber of Industries, *Annual Report 1971*, 13, 16–17.

116. Lipton, *Capitalism and Apartheid*, 152.

117. U.S. Senate Foreign Relations Committee, Subcomittee on African Affairs, hearings on South Africa, Sept. 6, 1976, quoted in Sampson, *Black and Gold*, 90–91, 120–21.

118. Friedman, *Building Tomorrow Today*, 40.

119. Institute for Industrial Education, *Durban Strikes*, 38–52.

120. Ibid., 144–45.

121. Ibid., 39–40.

122. Nattrass and Duncan, "Study of Employer Attitudes," found that larger employers in Durban moved faster than smaller ones to form works committees, although there was no significant difference in the attitudes expressed by employers in factories of different sizes.

123. *Financial Mail*, Feb. 16, 1973.

124. Ibid., Dec. 21, 1973.

125. Verster, "Liaison Committees," 92.

126. Douwes-Dekker, "Are Works Committees Trade Unions?" 22.

127. Friedman, *Building Tomorrow Today*, 134.

128. Harry Openheimer, speech to Institute for Personnel Management, Sept. 1973; in Lipton, *Capitalism and Apartheid*, 167.

129. The FCI was supporting an earlier call by the Chamber of Commerce, *Star*, May 22, 1975.

130. Anglo American to Transport and Garment Workers' Union, Aug. 18, 1976; Chris Albertyn to TUACC, July 26, 1976, report on visit to Anglo's industrial relations department; in FOSATU archives.

131. Friedman, *Building Tomorrow Today*, 94, 125.

132. United Kingdom, House of Commons Select Committee in Respect of British Companies Operating in South Africa, *British Companies in South Africa*, 49.

133. Friedman, *Building Tomorrow Today*, 103n.

134. Until 1979, South Africa could still purchase oil from Iran; after the fall of the Shah, it was forced to buy on the more expensive spot market in Europe rather than directly from producing countries.

135. P. W. Botha, 1973 Defence White Paper; in Cawthra, *Brutal Force*, 22.

136. Kaplan, "South Africa's Changing Place," 159–60.

137. Rupert, *Priorities for Coexistence*, 36–45.

138. Calculated from figures in Seidman and Seidman-Makgetla, *Outposts*, 81.

139. The United Nations had first imposed an arms embargo in 1963, but strengthened it during the 1970s.

140. Cawthra, *Brutal Force*, 81–82, 88, 100.

141. Botha, in ibid., 26–31.

142. Harry Oppenheimer, in *South Africa Foundation News*, July 1973; in Torchia, "Business of Business," 426.

143. Institute for Industrial Education, *Durban Strikes*, 70–71, 105.

144. *Rand Daily Mail*, May 8, 1973. Lipton, *Capitalism and Apartheid*, 163, argues that capital-intensive industries could afford higher black wages more easily than labor-intensive ones, because wages made up a smaller component of the total cost of production.

145. Reynders Commission, 1972; in Lipton, *Capitalism and Apartheid*, 241; see also Simkins, *South African Development*.

146. Johnson, *How Long Will South Africa Survive?* 88–90.

147. Thomas, "Economic Crisis or Transformation?"; Black and Stanwix, "Manufacturing Development and the Economic Crisis."

148. *Rand Daily Mail*, May 8, 1973; Lipton, *Capitalism and Apartheid*, tables 10 and 11. Even with rising unemployment during the mid 1970s, a government decision to reduce recruitment from outside South Africa's borders and to rely more on migrants from bantustans threatened mine owners with a reduced pool of potential workers. In order to compete with manufacturing employers for black South African workers, even mining employers were forced to raise wage levels, while a gold price set so high it reached historic levels eased mining company concerns about labor costs. In 1971, black miners received only 33 percent of black workers' average wages in manufacturing; by 1978, black miners' wages had reached 70 percent of blacks' average wages in manufacturing. Martin, "Cycles, Trends or Transformations?" 173; James, *Our Precious Metal*, 20–21.

149. S.A. Central Statistical Services, *South African Statistics, 1982*, 7.6, 7.8, 7.10. Although average black manufacturing wages continued to rise slowly, average real black incomes would further decline between 1975 and 1980. Keenan, "Trickle Up," 186.

150. Hirson, *Year of Fire, Year of Ash*, 97–99. Crowding was worsened by a change in the school system that combined Standard 5 and Standard 6 students in Form I classes in 1976.

151. Vorster's speech to the Motor Industries Federation on Oct. 3, 1973; in Lipton, *Capitalism and Apartheid,* 60.

152. Levy, "Racism and the Distribution of Skills," 27–31.

153. Lipton, *Capitalism and Apartheid,* 59.

154. The major exception was mining, where a strong white union managed to retain job reservation until the mid 1980s. Rafel, "Job Reservation on the Mines."

155. Percentages compiled from figures in Simkins and Hindson, "Division of Labour," 34.

156. FCI, *Annual Report, 1977,* 8–11.

157. Seidman and Seidman-Makgetla, *Outposts,* 59.

158. Kaplan, "South Africa's Changing Place," 169.

159. Sampson, *Black and Gold,* 129–30.

160. *Financial Mail,* Nov. 18, 1977.

161. Harry Oppenheimer, in Karon, "Urban Foundation," 140.

162. The only exception was the South African German Chamber of Commerce. *Survey of Race Relations, 1977,* 44–46.

163. Mann, "Business in the Age of Reform," 69.

164. *Rand Daily Mail,* Dec. 1, 1977.

165. *Survey of Race Relations, 1978,* 46.

166. Harry Oppenheimer and J. H. Steyn, in Karon, "Urban Foundation," 124.

167. Barlow-Rand executive in Karon, "Urban Foundation," 128.

168. Oppenheimer and another businessman, in Mann, "Business in the Age of Reform," 64.

169. Wassenaar, *Assault on Private Enterprise,* 86, 153.

170. Cooper, *Strikes in South Africa, 1979,* 46–54.

171. Mann, "Business in the Age of Reform," 60–62.

172. *Survey of Race Relations, 1977,* 6.

173. FCI, ACI, and ASSOCOM submissions to the Wiehahn Commission, in the FOSATU archives.

174. Initially, the government tried to block migrant workers from joining registered unions; when the independent unions refused, registration was opened to unions whose membership include migrants from "independent" bantustans and neighboring states.

175. Seidman, *Face-lift Apartheid.*

176. Friedman, *Building Tomorrow Today,* 172n.

177. Mann, "Business in the Age of Reform," 63, 78.

178. Ibid., 63, 78.

179. Godsell, "Reform Process in South Africa," 304.

180. Saul and Gelb, *Organic Crisis in South Africa,* 137.

181. Associated Press, Nov. 11, 1985.

182. Huntington, "Reform and Stability."

183. Skidmore, *Politics of Military Rule,* 165, 167, 170.

184. South Africa, State President's Council, *First Report of the Constitutional Committee of the President's Council,* 35–40.

185. Godsell, "Reform Process in South Africa," 305.

4. THE EMERGENCE OF "NEW UNIONISM"

1. Berger, *Organizing Interests,* introduction; Katznelson, "Working-Class Formation," 20.
2. Wright, "Exploitation, Identity," 206–7; see also Brenner, "Work Relations," 184–90.
3. Calhoun, "What's New about New Social Movements?"
4. Cohen, "Benevolent Leviathan."
5. South African Congress of Trade Unions, submission to the International Labor Organization, 1976, FOSATU archives.
6. Marks, *Unions in Politics,* 54. This pattern was apparently true even of the relatively conservative American Federation of Labor in the nineteenth century. Tomlins, *State and the Unions,* 60–70.
7. Lange and Ross, "French and Italian Union Development," 218.
8. Moore, *Injustice.*
9. Biernacki, *Cultural Construction of Labor.*
10. Aminzade, *Class, Politics and Early Industrial Capitalism;* Sewell, "Artisans, Factory Workers"; Wilentz, *Chants Democratic;* Lubeck, "Class Formation at the Periphery."
11. Inkeles and Smith, *Becoming Modern,* esp. 154–74.
12. Rodrigues, *Sindicatos e desenvolvimento,* 180.
13. Van Onselen, *Chibaro.*
14. Bergquist, *Labor in Latin America,* 8.
15. Crisp, *Story of an African Working Class;* Higginson, *Working Class in the Making.*
16. Collier and Collier, *Shaping the Political Arena.*
17. Katznelson, "Working-Class Formation," 17–20.
18. Cronin, "Labor Insurgency and Class Formation."
19. Oestreicher, *Solidarity and Fragmentation,* 61.
20. Marks, *Unions in Politics,* 16–17.
21. Menezes, "A supresa"; see also *Movimento,* May 22, 1978, 3; Maroni, *A estratégia da recusa,* 72–73.
22. Rainho and Bargas, *As lutas operárias,* 55–68.
23. Alves, *State and Opposition,* 194.
24. Moisés, "Qual é a estratégia."
25. Weffort, "Sindicatos e política," ch. 4 and appendix.
26. Gilson Luiz Correa de Menezes, in Rainho and Bargas, *As lutas operárias,* 67.
27. Luís Inácio da Silva, May 14, 1978, in Antunes, *As formas da greve,* 148.
28. Rodrigues, "Trabalhadores e sindicatos."
29. Almeida, "Desarrollo capitalista y accion sindical."
30. Humphrey, *Capitalist Control and Workers' Struggle,* 98–102.
31. Ibid., 76–77.
32. From essays on "How I Spent My Day," written during adult courses given by the Metalworkers' Union of São Bernardo, 1976–78; in Abramo, "O resgate da dignidade," 60.

33. In Abramo, "O resgate da dignidade," 25.

34. Lula was questioned by the commander of the Second Army, and most news of the strikes was censored. However, the state did not intervene in the Metalworkers' Union, and some articles did appear; the television program Vox Populi was permitted to air an interview with Lula, along with government statements about the rights of those who wished to continue working. Rainho and Bargas, *As lutas operárias,* 83–84.

35. In 1977, Saab-Scania had fired, rehired, and fired again several workers from its São Bernardo factory for "spreading union propaganda"; when the 1978 strike began, Saab's workers in Sweden threatened to strike in support of the Brazilian workers' demands. Rainho and Bargas, *As lutas operárias,* 67; História Imediata, ed., *A greve,* 33–35.

36. História Imediata, ed., *A greve;* Rainho and Bargas, *As lutas operárias,* 80–84.

37. Vidigal Neto and Aldo Lorenzetti, "Quais são os limites aos reivindicações," *Exame* 10 (Apr. 26, 1978): 12–13; Einar Kok, interview, *Exame* 151 (May 10, 1978): 17–18.

38. Rainho and Bargas, *As lutas operárias,* 120.

39. Luís Inácio da Silva, interview, in, História Imediata, ed., *A greve,* 57.

40. *Bilhetes do João Ferrador,* 53. A comment from one auto worker, years later, suggests how popular these letters were: "I didn't read João Ferrador's letters, I ate them." Abramo, "O resgate da dignidade," 129.

41. "Metalúrgicos querem mudar as regras," *Movimento,* Mar. 20, 1978.

42. Alves, *State and Opposition,* 197.

43. Strike details in Centro Ecumenico de Documentação e Informações (CEDI), *Trabalhadores 78.*

44. Rainho and Bargas, *As lutas operárias,* 90.

45. Abramo, "Empresários e trabalhadores," 3.

46. See, e.g., discussion of this strategy by officers of the Metalworkers of Baixada Santista, in Araújo, *Operários em luta,* 149–78.

47. Communist Party activists tended to work within established unions, while activists from Catholic Action tended to stress factory commissions and shop-floor organization. The different approaches, which emerged most clearly after 1979, are summarized in Keck, "New Unionism in the Brazilian Transition," 273.

48. At the time of the Osasco and Contagem strikes of 1968, the rather unusual bishop of Santo André came under harsh government criticism for comparing Jesus' sacrifice, celebrated by the mass, with that of workers on strike.

49. Martins, "Igreja e movimento operário," 223.

50. Ação Católica Operária, "A realidade operária."

51. Gabeira, *O qué é isso, companheiro?* 186–89.

52. Mainwaring, *Catholic Church and Politics in Brazil.*

53. Oposição Sindical Metalúrgica de São Paulo, "História do movimento," 10.

54. Faria, "A experiência operária," 169.

55. Interview with metalworker in Rodrigues, *Comissão de fábrica,* 61.

56. Faria, "A experiência operária," 180–86.

57. Maroni, *A estratégia da recusa*, 53.

58. OMS member, in Faria, "A experiência operária," 98.

59. Congresso dos Trabalhadores nas Industrias Metalúrgicas, Mecânicas e de Material Elêtrico do Estado de São Paulo, *Organização e estrutura sindical* (8th congress, Praia Grande, Nov. 26–29, 1974).

60. Quoted in Frederico, *A vanguarda operária*, 62; see also Antunes, "As formas da greve."

61. Frederico, *Consciência operária*, 90–92; Frederico, *A vanguarda operária*, 105–13; Maroni, *A estratégia da recusa*, 74.

62. "Movimento operário," *Cadernos do CEAS* 50 (July-Aug. 1977): 34–35; "A luta por um sindicato de base," *Cadernos do CEAS* 63 (Sept. 1979): 8–11.

63. Leite, "Reivindicações sociais," 9–10.

64. Barrelli, "Inflação e reivindicações trabalhistas." For a sympathetic description of how activists in registered unions tried to challenge wage policy and other forms of state control over union activities, see Araújo, *Operários em luta*, 140–78.

65. DIEESE was created in 1955 by unionists who wanted independent data sources for inflation indexing. The *reposição* campaign reflects the extent to which data and norms of a "just" wage make a difference only when there is popular mobilization. DIEESE published data throughout the 1960s, but its data were not used in determining wage levels until unions began to emphasize worker mobilization in the mid 1970s. Chaía, "DIEESE: Saber intelectual."

66. CEDI, *Trabalhadores 78*, 3.

67. Rainho and Bargas, *As lutas operárias*, 52–53.

68. Morel, *Lula, o metalúrgico*.

69. Lula, cited in Rainho and Bargas, *As lutas operárias*, 55.

70. "Metalúrgicos querem mudar as regras," *Movimento*, Mar. 20, 1978.

71. "A festa virou protesto," *Movimento*, July 31, 1978, 9.

72. Theses approved by the First Congress of the Oposição Sindical Metalúrgica de São Paulo, 1979; in Giannotti and Neto, *CUT: Por dentro*, 24.

73. "A luta dos operários," *Cadernos de CEAS* 56 (July 1978): 21.

74. Santos and Chaves, *Metalúrgicos de Niteroi*.

75. Rodrigues, "Trabalhadores de uma indústria automobilística," 2.

76. In 1985, a study of union officers found that 40 percent were under forty years of age; at the time of the 1964 coup, they would have been under twenty. Grondim, *Perfil dos dirigentes sindicais*, 89.

77. Luís Inácio da Silva, interview with Antunes et al., 53.

78. Interviews with Lula, Miguel Galhardo, and Joaquim dos Santos Andrade, in História Imediata, ed., *A greve*, 56–61.

79. Venceslau, "Metalúrgicos: Eleições sindicais," 48. Andrade was also sometimes referred to as the "arch-pelego." José Carlos Ruy, "Pelegos levam ferro," *Movimento*, Jan. 19, 1981.

80. Joaquim dos Santos Andrade, in Silva, *Os sindicatos e a transição democrática*, 24, 209.

81. José Carlos Ruy, "Pelegos levam ferro," *Movimento*, Jan. 19, 1981.
82. Silva, "Brasil: Sindicatos y transicion democratica," 118.
83. Neves, "Trabalho, o capitalismo adiantado e a classe operária"; Leite, "Reivindicações sociais."
84. Araújo, *Operários em luta*.
85. Alves, *State and Opposition*, 201.
86. "Contra as horas-extra," *Movimento*, Feb. 12, 1979, 4; SIMESP memorandum cited in Rainho and Bargas, *As lutas operárias*, 118.
87. Rainho and Bargas, *As lutas operárias*, 116–61; Lula, speeches of May 1979, included as appendix in Rainho and Bargas, *As lutas operárias*, 236–46.
88. Paula et al., *Ação e razão dos trabalhadores*, 47; CEDI, *História dos metalúrgicos de São Caetano*, 59.
89. Associação Beneficente e Cultural dos Metalúrgicos de São Bernardo do Campo e Diadema, *Fundo de Greve*, 9–10.
90. *Balanço Anual das Greves, 1979*, 18, 25. These figures are only rough estimates, based on newspaper accounts; the overall figures may have been even higher (18fn).
91. "A alegria dos peões," *Movimento*, Aug. 27, 1979.
92. In Belo Horizonte, for example, striking construction workers physically ejected a conservative union president from a meeting where Lula and other metalworkers' leaders had come to speak.
93. "O povo explode, agora no Maranhao," *Movimento*, Sept. 24, 1979; *Balanço Anual das Greves, 1979*.
94. Olívio Dutra, in "Ainda não foi desta vez," *Movimento*, Sept. 24, 1979, 7.
95. Almeida, "Sindicalismo brasileiro e pacto social," 23–25.
96. Silva, "Sindicato e sociedade," 227.
97. CEDI, *Trabalhadores urbanos no Brasil/1980*, 16; Brito, *A tomada da Ford*; Silva et al., *Organização dos trabalhadores nos locais de trabalho*; Oposição Sindical Metalurgica (SP), *Comissão da fábrica*.
98. Abramo, "Empresários e trabalhadores," 22.
99. Lula, interview in História Imediata, *A greve*, 56.
100. Lula claimed the government refused to let Termomecânica negotiate when it asked permission to do so. Luís Inácio da Silva, interview by Ricardo Antunes et al., 27.
101. Details from CEDI, *Aconteceu especial: 1980, ABC da greve*. A photograph of this scene is reprinted in CEDI, *Imagens da luta, 1905–1985*, 202.
102. CEDI, *Aconteceu especial: Trabalhadores urbanos, 1981* and *1982–1984*; *Boletim do DIEESE* no. 1-1 (1982): 3.
103. Brazilian Department of Labor figures cited in Skidmore, *Politics of Military Rule*, 224.
104. Menezes, "Do CGT a CUT," 13.
105. Erickson, *Brazilian Corporative State*, 32; CEDI, *Trabalhadores urbanos no Brazil 82/84*, 54.
106. Rodrigues, *Comissão de fábrica*, 54–57.
107. Compiled from data in CEDI, *Trabalhadores urbanos no Brasil 82/84*.

108. *Boletim do DIEESE* no. 1-1 (1982): 13.

109. Jaco Bitar, 31 Dec. 1980; in CEDI, *Trabalhadores urbanos no Brasil/ 1980,* 16–17.

110. "Carta da comissão Pro-CUT ao presidente da república," *Cadernos do CEAS* 76 (Nov.–Dec. 1981): 15–17.

111. This debate is described in Bastos, "A CONCLAT," 11–13.

112. For example, between 1983 and 1986, between a third and a half of CUT's executive had been workers in heavy industry. Rodridgues, *CUT: Os militantes,* table 16.

113. Giannotti and Neto, *CUT: Por dentro e por fora,* 42–52; Rodrigues, *CUT: Os militantes,* 71–82.

114. Bonelli, *A class média do "milagre" à recessão,* 42–67.

115. Although some Communist Party activists left the party and joined the CUT, the more official Communist Party line supported the CGT. CONCLAT, "A carta de Praia Grande," *Cadernos do CEAS* 89 (Jan.–Feb. 1984): 21–23; Gonçalves, "Duas vertentes."

116. Silva, "Sindicato e sociedade," 229.

117. Giannotti and Neto, *CUT: Por dentro e por fora,* 54.

118. Keck, "New Unionism in the Brazilian Transition," 278.

119. The third federation was called the Força Sindical.

120. CUT unionist, in Gonçalves, "As duas vertentes," 8.

121. XI Congress of Metal, Mechanical, and Electrical Workers of the State of São Paulo, Jan. 1979.

122. Luís Inácio da Silva, May 1978; in Rachel Meneguello, *PT: A Formação,* 52.

123. Keck, *From Movement to Politics,* 180–216; see also Meneguello, *PT: A Formação,* esp. 52–64.

124. Partido dos Trabalhadores, "Declaração política," Oct. 13, 1979.

125. Luís Inácio da Silva, during the November 1982 election campaign; in Rachel Meneguello, *PT: A formação,* 114.

126. Most contemporaneous observers interpreted the flag as a traffic control device rather than an indication of political sympathies. Although the image was certainly suggestive, no striker or sympathetic observer at the time publicly acknowledged any political significance to the flag for fear of repression. By 1985, on the other hand, red flags at South African demonstrations were invariably considered an indication of clandestine Communist Party presence. It seems reasonable to speculate that even in 1973, some workers would have been perfectly aware of the flag's political overtones.

127. Institute for Industrial Education, *Durban Strikes,* 9–16.

128. Luckhardt and Wall, *Working for Freedom,* 23.

129. IIE, *Durban Strikes,* 47–52.

130. Harriet Bolton, in Friedman, *Building Tomorrow Today,* 59.

131. Interview, Johannesburg, Apr. 1987; IIE, *Durban Strikes,* 53–55.

132. Jeannette Curtis, testimony before the Schlebusch Commission, 1974.

133. Sideris, *Sifuna Imali Yethu;* Paula Ensor to Jenny Curtis, letter quoted in Schlebusch Commission Report, 1974, ch. 17.

134. University of Cape Town SRC, Industry and Economy Commission, "Report on the Wage Board Sitting on the 20th July, Inquiring into the Wages and Working Conditions in the Stevedoring Industry" (Feb. 27, 1972), FOSATU archives, "University Wages Commissions."

135. Labour History Group, *Organizing at the Cape Town Docks.*

136. Evidence submitted by the UCT Wages Commission, 1972, FOSATU archives, "University Wages Commissions."

137. FOSATU, "A History of the Chemical Workers' Industrial Union, 1974–1984."

138. TUACC, "Background Document Presented by the TUACC to the Ad Hoc Feasibility Committee of Proposed Federation of Trade Unions, April 1979," FOSATU archives, box 1.

139. Minutes of Industrial Aid Society meetings, Jan.–June 1975, and "Memorandum on the Industrial Aid Society," n.d.; in MAWU and Industrial Aid Society archives.

140. Interview, Harriet Bolton (not a SACTU member in 1973), Harare, October 1989. For a more acerbic description of SACTU's 1972 organizing efforts, see the Institute for Industrial Education, "Notes for a Seminar on African Trade Unions" (n.d.): the IIE notes remark disdainfully that SACTU officials collected subscriptions at the office rather than on the shop floor—a fact borne out by interviews with the officials themselves. The IIE study notes claim this indicates that SACTU was more a channel for political expression than a federation of factory-based unions. FOSATU archives, "IIE."

141. Interview, former SACTU/Trade Union Advisory and Coordinating Council organizer, Johannesburg, May 1987.

142. Friedman, *Building Tomorrow Today*, 43.

143. Two of these students, both white, may have attended a SACTU conference in 1974 (interview, former IAS member, Johannesburg, Mar. 1987). One of these students, Jeannette Curtis, became a SACTU officer when she went into exile after her banning. She and her young daughter, Katryn Schoon, were killed in Angola in 1984.

144. Webster, "A Profile of Unregistered Union Members," 51, 63. More than half of respondents listed other ANC figures as the most important leaders, but the frequent mention of Mabhida (spelled Mabheda in the survey) is particularly important because it reflects the strength of the SACTU tradition in the region. Moses Mabhida went into exile in 1960 when a warrant for his arrest was issued during the Hammarsdale clothing factory strike. In exile, he served on the ANC executive committee from 1962 and in the ANC's armed wing from 1963, becoming secretary-general of the South African Communist Party in 1981. He died in exile in 1987, and his body was buried in Pietermaritzburg. Hundreds of workers attended the funeral despite police harassment. I am grateful to Eddie Webster for pointing out the significance of these findings.

145. MAWU (PMB) report, June 1974, FOSATU archives, "TUACC Union Reports 1974."

146. See, e.g., MAWU Report to the Fourth TUACC Meetings, Aug. 1975, FOSATU archives, "TUACC." See also Webster, *Cast in a Racial Mould*, 208.

147. Minutes of TUACC meetings, 1973–75, FOSATU archives, "TUACC," esp. minutes of Feb. 7 and June 16, 1974, and 24 May, 1976.

148. Forbo-Krommeni (Pty) Ltd. to Forbo-Betriebs AG, 12 Sept. 1978; in MAWU and Industrial Aid Society Archives.

149. Notes from meetings with employers in the East London area, quoted by Theo Heffer, *Trade Unions*, 41.

150. TUACC council meetings minutes, Aug. 24, 1975, and Oct. 26, 1975, FOSATU archives, "TUACC."

151. Interview, former MAWU (Tvl) organizer, Botswana, June 1987.

152. MAWU, "TUACC Report" (June 1974), FOSATU archives.

153. TUACC to ICFTU Education Department, Dec. 13, 1977; Joint Legal Defense Fund, "Overall Assessment of the Operation and Function of the JLDF since its Inception in 1977 to July 1979"; FOSATU Policy Proposals, based on Interim Committee Meeting, Oct. 1979, principle five; FOSATU Interim Secretary's Report, Oct. 1978–Mar. 1979; all in FOSATU archives.

154. Averages based on figures from *Surveys of Race Relations*, 1966–80.

155. "Report of the National Union of Textile Workers to the TUACC Council Meeting" (Feb. 1976), FOSATU archives, "TUACC." For examples of liaison and works committee discussions with union participation, see minutes of Alusaf (Pty) Ltd. Zulu Liaison Committee meetings, nos. 2/75 and 4/75 (n.d. and Mar. 4, 1975), FOSATU archives, "MAWU." At Raleigh Cycles (Nutfield) Management/Works Committee Meetings 60 and 61 (n.d. and Sept. 13, 1979), topics discussed included management refusals to allow trade union meetings on premises; protective clothing and toilet facilities; overfull buses to townships; transport for late shifts; and the possibility of employer intervention to assist in the distribution of poll-tax refunds.

156. MAWU (Pmb), "TUACC Report" (June 1974). FOSATU archives, "TUACC."

157. SEIFSA, Memo on Bantu Labour Relations Regulation Act, Aug. 1973; in Webster, *Cast in a Racial Mould*, 135. Webster discusses SEIFSA's labor policies at some length, 127–55.

158. "Strikes in the Metal Industry," *WIP* 22(April 1982): 26–28, and Webster, "Stoppages in the East Rand Metal Industry."

159. Council of Industrial Workers of the Witwatersrand, "Report for the Period Jan. 77–June 77," FOSATU archives, box 4.

160. Kirkwood, "The Defy Dispute."

161. For historical reasons, there were two separate unions called the Metal and Allied Workers' Union in the mid 1970s: MAWU (Transvaal) and MAWU (Natal), but they cooperated closely and finally merged in 1979. Even before the merger, the distinction between the two was an organizational one rather than a clear matter of strategy or ideology.

162. Apparently, the company was advised not to negotiate by SEIFSA, which at that point rejected the principle of black worker organization. MAWU, "Further Report on the Dispute at Heinemann Electric Co. in March 1976 and Subsequent Events," FOSATU archives. "Workers under the Baton: An Examination of the Labour Dispute at Heinemann Electric Company," *SALB* 37(June 1977): 49–60; interviews, former Heinemann worker,

Johannesburg, Apr. 1987, and former MAWU (Tvl) organizer, Botswana, 1987.

163. Minister of Justice Jimmy Kruger, in the *Johannesburg Star,* May 8 and 14, 1976.

164. *Johannesburg Star,* Mar. 30, 1976.

165. "Cops Club Workers in Baton Charge," *Rand Daily Mail,* Mar. 27, 1976; "Unions Slam Police Violence," id., Mar. 31, 1976.

166. "New Wave of Unrest Could Cripple Economy," *Sunday Tribune,* Apr. 4, 1976.

167. Hirson, *Year of Fire, Year of Ash,* 253–55.

168. *Rand Daily Mail,* Apr. 3, 1976.

169. Sitas, "African Worker Responses," 274, 323.

170. Interview, former MAWU activist, Johannesburg, Mar. 1987.

171. The Black Consciousness movement generally argued that blacks needed to free themselves of the psychological effects of racism, including a sense of inferiority; activists often argued that only in separate, independent groups would blacks develop the self-reliance and pride needed for liberation.

172. Private notes of FOSATU coordinating committee member, from meeting of coordinating committee, Durban, Aug. 26, 1980.

173. The unionist was Calvin Nkabinde, general secretary of the Engineering and Allied Workers' Union.

174. David Webster, "A Review of Some 'Popular' Anthropological Approaches."

175. Interviews, union members, Mphophomeni, Natal, Apr. 1987.

176. Baskin, *Striking Back: A History of COSATU,* 129–33, 316–42.

177. See, however, Eddie Webster, "Taking Labour Seriously," 60–61.

178. The National Union of Motor Assembly and Rubber Workers of South Africa (NUMARWOSA) was FOSATU's largest single union, with 4,500 members. Primarily composed of "Coloured" workers in the automobile industry of the Eastern Cape, NUMARWOSA had been registered since 1967 as a parallel union. Under its general secretary Fred Sauls, it had attempted to organize at the shop floor since 1969 and had left TUCSA in 1975 over the white federation's refusal to admit independent African unions. Perhaps because of the union's previous experience, Sauls and other NUMARWOSA officers urged the independent unions to form a new federation, recognizing the advantages a broader organization of workers could offer. "Report on Meeting in Johannesburg on 23 March 1977 to Discuss the Possible Formation of a New Union Federation"; "Minutes of Feasibility Committee Meeting on 13 June 1977, Johannesburg," FOSATU archives.

179. These five represented workers in the chemical, food and beverages, jewellery, and other smaller industries. Only the textile workers union, with 2,360 paid-up members, came close to the average size of the four metal unions. "FOSATU Report, April 1979–April 1980," FOSATU archives.

180. Steve Friedman, *Building Tomorrow Today,* 197n.

181. "Minutes of Interim Tvl Committee of FOSATU, 13 Dec. 1978"; and "Minutes of the Interim Central Committee of FOSATU, 10th and 11th March 1979, Wilgespruit," FOSATU archives.

182. Webster, *Cast in a Racial Mould*, 278.

183. Kraak, "Uneven Capitalist Development"; Sitas, "African Worker Responses," 179–225.

184. Webster, *Cast in a Racial Mould*, 231–44.

185. Meth, "Trade Unions, Skill Shortages," 76.

186. Roux, "Daily Events"; Maree, "1979 Port Elizabeth Strike," and Favis, "The Ford Workers' Committee."

187. Ferreira, "Collective Bargaining," 81. See also Roux, "Managerial Strategies at Ford."

188. "The Support Alliance," *WIP* 19 (1981): 6–12.

189. Roux, "The Division of Labour at Ford."

190. See, e.g., Council of Industrial Workers of the Witwatersrand, "Background Document Submitted to the Ad Hoc Feasibility Committee Considering the Formation of a Federation of South African Trade Unions and Worker Organization" (n.d.), MAWU and Industrial Aid Society archives.

191. "Report on Meeting in Johannesburg on 23 March 1977 to Discuss the Possible Formation of a New Union Federation"; "Minutes of the the Meeting of the Feasibility Committee Established in Terms of the Resolution Adopted at the Preliminary Federation Meeting on the 23rd March 1977"; "Resolution of the Consultative Committee"; "Minutes of Feasibility Committee Meeting on 13 June 1977, Johannesburg"; "Minutes of the Interim Central Committee of FOSATU, 10 and 11 March 1979, Wilgespruit"; Alec Erwin, "FOSATU Interim Secretary's Report, Oct. 1978 to March 1979" (Mar. 8, 1979); FOSATU "Draft Policy Resolutions" (agreed on at interim committee meeting, Mar. 1979), FOSATU archives.

192. TUACC and FOSATU executive committee meetings, 1974–80, FOSATU archives; and Meer, "Community and Unions" and "Conflict in the Communities."

193. Favis, "The Ford Workers' Committee," 44.

194. This debate is summarized in Plaut, "Political Significance of COSATU," esp. 66–69; and von Holdt, "Response to Plaut."

195. In 1975, 25 percent of black union members surveyed said they had first heard about the union in the township; 43 percent said they were approached by work mates, and 32 percent had been approached by a union organizer. Webster, "Profile of Unregistered Union Members," 52. However, interviews and minutes of meetings suggest unionists often sought to publicize their presence in the relatively safe area of the community before trying to approach workers within the factory, to avoid victimization. See "Minutes of Extraordinary TUACC Council Meeting, 26 Oct. 1975," FOSATU archives, and Maree, "SAAWU in the East London Area, 1979–1981."

196. Community Action Support Community, "We Do Not Buy Fattis and Monis" (mimeo, n.d.), South African Institute of Race Relations (SAIRR) archives.

197. Community Action Support Committee, "The Fattis and Monis Strike Boycott" (mimeo, n.d.), SAIRR archives.

198. Christiane M. Elias, "Report of the Labour Dispute at Fattis and Monis" (mimeo, n.d.), 15, SAIRR archives.

199. Fattis and Monis Ltd. and Its Subsidiaries, *Annual Report to Year End, 31 Jan 1979*, SAIRR archives. Profits dropped from R 363,000 in the first half of 1978 to R 186,000 in the first half of 1979. "Trading Better—Fattis," *Cape Times*, Oct. 9, 1979.

200. McGregor, "The Fatti's and Moni's Dispute," 127.

201. Leatt, "Role of Pressure Groups in Labour Relations"; "This Is What Consumer Power Can Do," *Cape Herald*, Oct. 26, 1979. Friedman suggests that another reason for Fatti's and Moni's sudden decision to negotiate was that an overseas partner became embarrassed by the negative publicity. *Building Tomorrow Today*, 200n.

202. During the negotiations to settle the issue, union organizers warned that a community activist, leader of the nonracial sports group that had led the Simba Quix boycott, might not call off the boycott when the union asked him to. The activist, however, insisted he had always planned to accept the union's decision. Hassan Howa, in "Fattis Strike: Talks with Howa Soon," *Cape Herald*, Oct. 3, 1979. However, unionist Jan Theron had apparently warned company representatives that Howa and SACOS were unlikely to support a compromise that did not include unconditional reinstatement of striking workers. Leatt, "Role of Pressure Groups in Labour Relations," 6. See also "The Support Alliance," *WIP* 19(1981): 6–12; Food and Canning Workers' Union, "Search for a Workable Relationship."

203. "A Warning to South Africa's Big Companies," *Cape Herald*, Aug. 25, 1979.

204. Chemical Workers' Industrial Union, "Why Are Workers Calling for a Boycott?" (n.d.), FOSATU archives. WPGU, "The Cape Town Meat Strike"; interview, labor organizer, Johannesburg, 1982.

205. See, e.g., "Report 5: Glacier Bearings and the MAWU" (Feb. 8, 1979), FOSATU archives.

206. See *Focus on Wiehahn*, a special issue of the *South African Labour Bulletin*, 5, no. 2 (1979): passim.

207. Union distrust of the state ran so deep that no arguments in favor of registration appeared in labor journals until one was offered by academics living in England, where the argument that "compromises can never be avoided" had become more acceptable among left-wing activists. Bob Fine and fellow authors argued that unions should not "fetishize illegality," but should try to distinguish "between those compromises which promote and those which retard the workers' movement"; they suggested that perhaps unions should register to gain access to industrial courts and industrial councils. Fine et al., "Trade Unions and the State."

208. "Critiques of the Wiehahn Commission and the 1979 Amendments to the Industrial Conciliation Act," and "Some Initial Reactions to Wiehahn," *SALB* 5, no. 2(1979): 75–79; Cheadle, "A Guide to the Industrial Conciliation Act of 1979"; FOSATU, "Statement on Wiehahn and Its Implications"; FOSATU, WPGU, FCWU, and AFCWU, "Press Statement on Industrial Conciliation Act"; Nicol, "Legislation, Registration and Emasculation"; General Workers' Union, "Reply to Fine, de Clercq and Innes"; Cornell and Kooy, "Wiehahn Part 5 and the White Paper."

209. Resolutions, Conference of Trade Unions, Langa, Cape Town, Aug. 8, 1981, FOSATU archives.

210. FOSATU, "Parallel Union Thrust," Nov. 8, 1989. See also Hendler, "Organization of Parallel Unions."

211. Heffer, *Trade Unions*, 42–48.

212. Sitas and Webster, "Stoppages," 5.

213. Morris, "Capital's Responses"; Sideris, "MAWU Enters the Industrial Council"; "MAWU Moves Forward," *FOSATU Worker News,* no. 19 (Mar. 1983).

214. Federated Chamber of Industries, "Guidelines for Industrial Relations in the 1980s" (Dec. 12, 1980); ASSOCOM, "Restatement of Policy: Recognition of Trade Unions" (Nov. 29, 1980), FOSATU archives.

215. Interview, labor organizer, Johannesburg, July 1982.

216. Natal Labor Research Committee, "Control over a Workforce—The Frame Case," 21, 30; Keenan, "Migrants Awake," 16–17.

217. Keenan, "Effect of the 1978–1982 Industrial Cycle," 36.

218. "Second FOSATU Union Joins Industrial Council," *FOSATU Worker News,* no. 26 (Nov.–Dec. 1983); and "PWAWU Steps Up Its Fight," *FOSATU Worker News,* no. 30 (June–July 1984).

219. Alec Erwin, in Didi Moyle, "Mass Resistance," 7; see also FOSATU, "Pensions Panic" (FOSATU occasional publication, 1981), FOSATU archives.

220. FOSATU, "Executive Committee Report for the Year April 1979–April 1980, to Be Tabled at the First AGM of the FOSATU CC Meeting, 26 and 27 April 1980," FOSATU archives

221. Foster, "The Workers' Struggle: Where Does FOSATU Stand?"

222. "Strive to Build a Strong Working Class Movement," *FOSATU Worker News,* no. 25 (Oct. 1983).

223. "The Workers' Struggle in South Africa," 9; and Toussaint, "A Trade Union Is Not a Political Party."

224. Chris Dlamini in "May Day Call for Unity," and "Profile: Chris Dlamini," *FOSATU Worker News,* no 21 (May 1983).

225. "We Say No," describing the FOSATU campaign against the 1984 constitution, and "FOSATU Decides Not to Join UDF," both in *FOSATU Worker News,* no. 26 (Nov.–Dec. 1983).

226. Sydney Mufamadi, interview.

227. Oberty and Swilling, "MAWU and UMMAWUSA."

228. Webster, *Cast in a Racial Mould,* 278.

5. COMMUNITY STRUGGLES AND THE REDEFINITION OF CITIZENSHIP

1. For South Africa, see Hirson, *Yours for the Union,* esp. 200, and Fine with Davis, *Beyond Apartheid,* esp. chs. 5–9. For Brazil, see Moisés, "Classes populares," and Weffort, "Sindicatos e política."

2. Kowarick, "Pathways to Encounter," 79.

3. Cardoso, "Movimentos sociais," 27–28.

4. Moisés, "Qual é a estratégia," 32.

5. See, e.g., Haydu, *Between Craft and Class,* conclusion; Berger, "Gender and Working-class History"; Cronin, "Labor Insurgency and Class Formation."

6. Cooper, "Urban Space, Industrial Time," 37, 43.

7. Castells, *City and the Grass Roots,* 291–336.

8. Holmstrom, *Industry and Inequality,* 260.

9. Di Tella, "Working-Class Organization," 33, 40.

10. Deyo, *Beneath the Miracle,* 203–4.

11. Calhoun, "What's New about New Social Movements?" 9.

12. Marks, *Unions in Politics,* 14.

13. Bonnell, *Roots of Rebellion.*

14. Mosely, "Contested Terrains," 12.

15. Cooper, "Urban Space, Industrial Time," 25.

16. The double meaning lies in the title of an important collection of studies of popular movements in São Paulo. See Singer and Brant, *O povo em movimento.*

17. Between 1974 and 1984, there were at least seventy-one violent riots on the trains of Rio de Janeiro and São Paulo; in São Paulo, where these incidents only began to occur after 1979, the link to rising labor activism is unmistakable. Nunes and Jacobi, "A cara nova do movimento popular"; Nunes, "Inventário dos quebra-quebras"; Moisés and Martinez-Aliér, "A revolta dos suburbanos".

18. Camargo et al., "Communidades eclesiais de base"; Petrini, *CEBs;* Mainwaring, "A igreja católica e o movimento popular".

19. Sader, "Quando novos personagens entrarem."

20. Afonso and Azevedo, "Cidade, poder público," 127–31.

21. Nunes and Jacobi, "A cara nova do movimento popular," 79; Neves, "Invasões e acesso a terra urbana," 31–32.

22. Boschi, *A arte da associação,* 46; For discussions of specific movements, see e.g., Jacobi, "Carências de saneamento básico"; Mucoucah, "A coletiva seletiva de lixo"; Kowarick, *As lutas sociais e a cidade.*

23. Singer, "Movimentos de bairro," 93–98, 103.

24. *IstoÉ,* Feb. 3, 1982; in Renato Raul Boschi, *A arte da associação,* 41.

25. Caldeira, "A luta pela voto."

26. In 1979, for example, a priest helping residents resist removal from Catumbi, in Rio, was imprisoned. After his return, he "never said much about prison. He appeared battered and missing teeth." Santos, *Movimentos urbanos no Rio de Janeiro,* 196n.

27. Brant, "Da resistência aos movimentos sociais," 13–14.

28. Jacobi, "Movimentos populares e resposta do estado," 163.

29. Gohn, *A força da periferia,* 159.

30. In 1979, the organization, composed primarily of working- and middle-class women, merged with other groups to become the Movement against Neediness (Movimento contra Carestia). See Evers, "O caso do Movimento do Custo de Vida"; Sader, "Quando novos personagens entrarem," 210–19.

31. Telles, "Anos 70: Experiências, práticas."

32. Santos, *Movimentos urbanos no Rio de Janeiro,* 171.

33. Caldeira, *A política dos outros,* 150–52.

34. Pereira, *O coração da fábrica*, 179.

35. Sader, "Quando novos personagens entrarem," 211, 222.

36. Martins, *Igreja e movimento operário*, 223; Faria, *A experiência operária*, 241–42; Sader, "Quando novos personagens entrarem," 195–275.

37. This took both overt and clandestine forms. In a 1968 television interview, Dom Jorge Marcos, a priest in Santo André, compared the sacrifice of God in the mass to the sacrifice of workers on strike. On Catholic Worker Youth (Juventude Operária Católica) activists within the metalworkers of São Bernardo do Campo from the 1960s, see Martins, *Igreja e movimento operário*, 157 and 177.

38. Almeida, *Novos demandas, novos direitos*, 14–21; Almeida, *Projeto transformações*, 12; Leite, *Reivindicações sociais*.

39. Causa Operária, "Como e porqué foi suspensa a greve do dia 25?" (mimeo, Oct. 26, 1983).

40. By 1986, virtually none of the members of the original factory commission at the Ford plant in São Bernardo still held their old jobs (John Humphrey, personal communication, 1986).

41. Sader, "Quando novos personagens entrarem," 15–16, 30–32.

42. Abramo, "Greve metalúrgica em São Bernardo," 216.

43. Bava, "A luta nos bairros e a luta sindical."

44. Lamounier, *1985: O voto em São Paulo*, table 9.

45. Oliveira, *Luiza Erundina*, 109–27.

46. Valladares, "Estudos recentes sobre a habitação," 47.

47. Sorj, *Estado e classes sociais na agricultura*.

48. Censos Demográficos, in Bolivar Lamounier, "Representação política," 237.

49. FIBGE, Censos Demográficos, in Sousa, "Concentração industrial," 14.

50. Kowarick, "O preço do progresso," 33.

51. Brant et al., *São Paulo: Growth and Poverty*, 21.

52. Grondim, "Sindicalismo na Grande São Paulo," 34.

53. Bonduki, "Habitação popular," 141–43; Blay, *Eu não tenho onde morar*.

54. Maricato, *A política habitacional*, 66. The percentage of renters living on the periphery was even higher, reaching over 60 percent in 1980. Brant et al., *São Paulo: Trabalhar e viver*, 88.

55. For a discussion of rural racial identities and how they change with urbanization, see Bandeira, *Territorio negro em espaço branco*, esp. 22, 325–29; and for a discussion of the effect of race on life chances nationally, see Wood and Carvalho, *Demography of Inequality in Brazil*.

56. Brant et al., *São Paulo: Growth and Poverty*, 89. See also Moura, "Organisações negras."

57. Moisés, *Classes populares e protesto urbano*.

58. Valladares, "Estudos recentes sobre a habitação."

59. Figures from Coordenação Geral do Planejamento, in Maricato, *A política habitacional*, 71.

60. I am grateful to Teresa Pires do Rio Caldeira for describing this process in detail.

61. Study by PROPERIFERIA, in Brant et al., *São Paulo: Trabalhar e viver,* 82n; Krischke, in "Loteamentos clandestinos," 47.

62. Figures from COGEP, EMBRAESP, and DIEESE, in Kowarick, "São Paulo: Metropole do subdesenvolvimento industrializado," 38.

63. Maricato, *A política habitacional,* 71.

64. Moisés and Martinez-Aliér, "A revolta dos suburbanos," 26–29.

65. Centro de Pastoral Vergueiro, *Movimento popular: Transporte coletivo;* Doimo, *Movimento social urbano.*

66. The BNH was the executive agent of a housing financial fund (*Sistema Financeira Habitação*).

67. Lei 4380, August 1964, in Portes, "Housing Policy, Urban Poverty," 6.

68. Perlman, *Myth of Marginality.*

69. Maricato, *A política habitacional,* 38.

70. Portes, "Housing Policy, Urban Poverty," 10 and 14.

71. Carlos Nelson Ferreira dos Santos describes the successful struggle against the removal of Bras de Piña, a *favela* of nearly nine hundred families, in *Movimentos urbanos no Rio de Janeiro.*

72. See, e.g., the testimony of residents and workers recorded in Rainho, *Os peões do Grande ABC,* 131; and in Bohadana, "Guararapes: A luta pela cidadania," 55, 63.

73. BNH, 1975; in Portes, "Housing Policy, Urban Poverty," 19–20.

74. BNH figures, in Maricato, *A política habitacional,* 45.

75. Rainho, *Os peões do Grande ABC,* 130–31; Maricato, *A política habitacional,* 38.

76. BNH figures, in Portes, "Housing Policy, Urban Poverty," 7.

77. *A Construção São Paulo,* May 6, 1974, 22.

78. Maricato, *A política habitacional,* 39–40.

79. Nunes, "Carências urbanas."

80. Jacobi, "Atores sociais e estado," 13.

81. Kowarick, "O preço do progresso," 37n.

82. Ibid., 38.

83. Maricato, *A política habitacional,* 65.

84. Valladores, "Estudos recentes sobre a habitação no Brasil: Resenha da literatura," 47.

85. Brant et al., *São Paulo: Growth and Poverty,* ch. 2.

86. Ibid., 31–32.

87. Kowarick, "O preço do progresso," 38.

88. Brant et al., *São Paulo: Growth and Poverty,* 40n.

89. Rossi, "Somos humanos, não peças do capitalismo," 13.

90. EMPLASMA data, in Caldeira, *A política dos outros,* 57.

91. Caldeira, *A política dos outros,* 57.

92. Somarriba et al., *Lutas urbanas em Belo Horizonte,* 21.

93. Maricato, *A política habitacional,* 26–27. Similar ideas are also developed in Harvey, *Consciousness and the Built Environment.*

94. Fortes et al., *Análise das greves de maio de 1978,* 32.

95. *Favela* activist, 1981, in Bava, "A luta nos bairros e a luta sindical," 307.

96. Centro de Estudos do Trabalho, "O trabalhador e o transporte coletivo."

97. Kowarick, "O preço do progresso," 38.

98. Antunes, *As formas da greve*, 107–25.

99. This interaction is discussed at length in, among others, Petrini, *CEBs;* and Mainwaring, "A igreja católica e o movimento popular."

100. Gitahy et al., "Operárias: Sindicalização," 91, 110; Schminck, "Women and Urban Industrial Development," 139; Alvarez, "Politicizing Gender and Engendering Democracy," 211.

101. FIBGE, in Brant et al., *São Paulo: Trabalhar e viver*, 42–43.

102. Gitahy et al., "Operárias: Sindicalização," 106.

103. Schminck, "Women and Urban Industrial Development," 144–46.

104. Gitahy et al., "Operárias: Sindicalização," 93.

105. Frederico, *Consciencia operária*, 56–59.

106. Humphrey, *Gender and Work*, 128–34.

107. Gitahy et al., "Operárias: Sindicalização," 101.

108. Ibid., 112–16.

109. Jelin, "Citizenship and Identity," 195.

110. Caldeira, "Women, Daily Life and Politics," 64.

111. Alvarez, "Politicizing Gender," 210. See also Schminck, "Women in Brazilian *Abertura* Politics."

112. Gitahy et al., "Operárias: Sindicalização," 113–16. See also Leite, *A operária metalúrgica.*

113. Alvarez, *Engendering Democracy in Brazil*, esp. 126–33.

114. Movimenta da Luta pela Creches, "Manifesto" (May 1979), in Alvarez, "Politicizing Gender," 226.

115. Luís Inácio da Silva, interview, in História Imediata, ed., *A greve*, 58.

116. Chinchilla, "Marxism, Feminism," 296–97.

117. Sader, "Quando novos personagens entrarem," 27–32.

118. Marshall, *Citizenship and Social Development.*

119. Moisés, *Lições de liberdade*, 174–184. This issue is also discussed at length in DaMatta, *A casa e a rua*, 55–80; Santos, *Cidadania e justiça*, 71–82; Viana, *A classe operária*, 149–51; Weffort, "A cidadania dos trabalhadores."

120. Weffort, "Why Democracy," 330.

121. Caldeira, "A luta pelo voto."

122. Sader and Silverstein, *Without Fear of Being Happy*, 79.

123. Meneguello, *PT: Formação*, 130–60.

124. Moacir Gadottia and Otaviano Pereira, in Sader and Silverstein, *Without Fear of Being Happy*, 79.

125. Dirceu, "Os desafios do PT," 41.

126. Sader, "O qué é qué está escrito na estrela?" 166–67.

127. Luiza Erundina de Souza, in Oliveira, *Luiza Erundina*, 158.

128. Partido dos Trabalhadores, "Circular from the National Directory" (1987), in Sader and Silverstein, *Without Fear of Being Happy*, 91.

129. Keck, *Workers' Party and Democratization.*

130. Singer, "Collor na periferia," 148.

131. Gavin Evans, "Holomisa at Giant CDF Conference," *Weekly Mail,*

Dec. 7, 1989. The meeting had 500 trade union delegates; other categories were religious (200), political (25), youth (65), civic (64), business (36), students (32), rural (28), women (23), teachers and education (27), cultural (18), and unemployed (4). One hundred international observers were also admitted.

132. Saul, "South Africa: Between Barbarism and Structural Adjustment."

133. Wolpe, *Race, Class and the Apartheid State,* ch. 2, esp. 58.

134. Seekings, "Political Mobilization," 201.

135. Barrell, "United Democratic Front and National Forum," 12, 17–18.

136. Seekings, "Political Mobilization," 201.

137. Ibid., 215–16.

138. Friedman, "Struggle within the Struggle."

139. Swilling, "Beyond Ungovernability."

140. In June 1986, the Federated Chamber of Industries called on the government to release union leaders detained under South Africa's state of emergency.

141. UDF First National Conference, Aug. 20, 1988, "Resolution on Workers," UDF archives.

142. "Thousands Support Stayaway Call as Anger Rises in Transvaal Townships," *FOSATU Worker News,* nos. 33/34 (Oct.–Nov. 1984).

143. S. Mufamadi, "None but Ourselves," in COSATU, *The Crisis,* 18.

144. "Chris Dlamini Renews Call for Unity," *FOSATU Worker News,* no. 32 (Sept. 1984).

145. See, however, Fadal, "Assessing Our Strengths and Weaknesses" (speech at NUTW Congress, June 27, 1987), in COSATU, *The Way Forward,* 27.

146. Webster, "Stayaways and the Black Working Class" (the author has reassessed the strategy since writing this article—Eddie Webster, personal communication, 1990); Moss, "Stay Aways: Mass Strike or Demonstration?"; Fadal, "Assessing Our Strengths and Weaknesses," 27.

147. Mufamadi, interview, *WIP,* 19–22; Njikelana, "Unions and the UDF."

148. Baskin, *Striking Back!* ch. 3.

149. Matiwana and Walters, *The Struggle for Democracy,* 34–36.

150. Foster, "The Workers' Struggle."

151. Cooper and Ensor, *PEBCO: A Black Mass Movement,* 28–32.

152. Heffer, *Trade Unions: Threat or Challenge?*

153. Lodge, *Black Politics.*

154. Marais, "SAAWU in the East London Area."

155. Obery and Swilling, "MAWU and UMMAWSA Fight."

156. Moses Mayekiso, in Labor and Community Resources Project Johannesburg, *Comrade Moss,* 94–96.

157. Meer, "Community and Unions in Natal," and "Conflict—in the Community."

158. Mzala, *Gatsha Buthelezi,* 165–81. See also Shula Marks, *Ambiguities of Dependence,* 116–25.

159. Meer, "Community and Unions in Natal" and "Conflict—in the Community."

160. Barayi, "COSATU: An Assessment," 4.

161. Mfeka, "Working-Class Leadership."

162. Head Office General Circular No. 25, 1967, "Settling of Non-Productive Bantu Resident in European Areas, in the Homelands," in Platzky and Walker, *Surplus People,* 28.

163. Platsky and Walker, *Surplus People,* 105.

164. Gelb and Saul, *Crisis in South Africa,* 149.

165. *The Star* (Johannesburg), Apr. 27, 1984. Another two million laborers worked on farms in white-designated areas.

166. Calculated from figures in *Survey of Race Relations, 1977,* 386.

167. Hindson and Lacey, "Influx Control and Labour Allocation."

168. International Commission of Jurists and Bindman, *South Africa: Human Rights and the Rule of Law,* 29–33. For discussion of changing state policies toward migrant labor, see Posel, *Making of Apartheid,* and Greenberg, *Legitimating the Illegitimate.*

169. Ramphele, "Dynamics of Gender Politics in the Hostels."

170. Keenan, "Migrants Awake"; McGregor, "Fatti's and Moni's Dispute."

171. Labour Research Committee, "State Strategy and the Johannesburg Municipal Strike," 85.

172. Sitas, "African Worker Responses," 250–51; Institute for Industrial Education, *Durban Strikes.*

173. The importance of black consciousness ideology throughout South Africa's postwar history is eloquently described in Gerhart, *Black Power in South Africa.*

174. *The Star* (Johannesburg), Jan. 14, 1961, in Rogerson, "From Coffee-Cart to Industrial Canteen," 189.

175. NUMAROWSA objections to PEBCO, discussed in "The Support Alliance: Trade Unions and Community," 11; and Food and Canning Workers' Union, "Search for a Workable Relationship."

176. Baskin, "Growth of a New Worker Organ," 47.

177. COSAS Transvaal Region, "Workers, Workers, Build Support for the Students' Struggle in the Schools" (1984), COSAS archives.

178. ANC, "The Workers' Way Forward Is the Strongest Way Forward" (pamphlet circulated anonymously in Cape Town, 1987).

179. Lelyveld, *Move Your Shadow,* 127–31.

180. President's Council report on urbanization, in *Survey of Race Relations, 1985,* 223

181. Mann and Segal, "Transport Industry," 20.

182. Republic of South Africa, "Second Interim Report of the Commission of Inquiry into Bus Transportation in the Republic of South Africa" (1983), paras. 3.44–3.45, in McCarthy and Swilling, "Transport and Political Resistance," 32.

183. Interviews, labor organizers, Johannesburg, May 1987, and Harriet Bolton, Harare, Oct. 1989. Transport boycotts seem to have often preceded other forms of collective action. The 1973 Durban strikes were preceded by an attempted train boycott, while in March 1976, three months before the Soweto

uprising, residents of KwaThema boycotted buses to protest a fare increase, walking ten kilometers into Durban and back for a month. *Survey of Race Relations, 1976,* 179.

184. McCarthy and Swilling, "Transport and Political Resistance," 28 and 30.

185. *Putco News,* Apr. 1982; in Perlman, "Bus Boycotts," 30.

186. Alexandra bus boycotter, 1984, in Perlman, "Bus Boycotts," 24.

187. Obery, "East Rand Bus Drivers," 24–25. Community activists also organized consumer boycotts during strikes by bus and train workers. Sello Ntai, interview, *WIP* 50(1987): 56–58.

188. For descriptions of this process in Durban and the Eastern Cape, see McCarthy and Swilling, "Transport and Political Resistance"; for a description of the Alexandra boycott, see Perlman, "Bus Boycotts," esp. 23–27.

189. McCarthy and Swilling, "Transport and Political Resistance," 38. The authors stress class differences in responses, with higher income respondents slightly more likely than poorer ones to list "crime" as a serious problem, but across income levels, the degree of agreement on the seriousness of transport issues is remarkably high. During the 1983 bus boycott against raised fares, Mdantsane residents risked severe repression to travel the twenty-five kilometers to East London on foot or by train rather than by bus; mass arrests, killings, and torture in a stadium provoked an international outcry. Haysom, *Ruling with the Whip.*

190. Although most members of the South African Railway and Harbour Workers Union (SARHWU) were migrants housed in single-sex hostels, they managed to gain support from most Soweto residents by reaching them during the commute and by tying their demands to ongoing community campaigns for political goals. Interview, SARHWU organizer, Johannesburg, June 1987.

191. Musa Zondi, "At 50k/ph on the 6:15, You Can Hardly Hear the Hymns for the Toyi-Toyi Next Door," *Weekly Mail,* Mar. 31–Apr. 7, 1988.

192. *Survey of Race Relations, 1977,* 398–99. People classified as Indian or Coloured, who made up about 12.5 percent of the population, fared only slightly better. Although they could buy homes in areas assigned to their racial category, in 1976 the government estimated that nearly 79,000 houses were needed for these groups.

193. *Survey of Race Relations, 1976,* 50, 431.

194. Cole, *Crossroads,* 9, 11–15.

195. Hindson, "Orderly Urbanization," 78.

196. Hindson and Lacey, "Influx Control," 109–10.

197. More than 1,400 of these were in Soweto, primarily for homes of very wealthy residents. Wilkinson, "Housing," 272.

198. Cole, *Crossroads,* 40 (see also p. 73, however).

199. Obery and Swilling, "MAWU and UMMAWSA Fight," 12.

200. Cobbett, "A Test Case for Planned Urbanization."

201. Chaskalson et al., "Rent Boycotts," 56.

202. UNISA Bureau of Market Research study, in Chaskalson et al., "Rent Boycotts," 55–56.

203. Mabin, "Struggle for the City," esp. 10–14.

204. Alexandra Residents' Association, 1985, in Jochelson, "Reform, Repression and Resistance," 4.

205. State vs. Moses Mayekiso and Four Others, testimony of Moses Mayekiso; and an anonymous discussion paper, "Organising for People's Power," circulated in 1986; both cited in Jochelson, "Reform, Repression and Resistance," 6, 13.

206. *Voice of the Alexandra Youth Congress* (1983, 1984), in Carter, " 'We Are the Progressives,' " 206.

207. Chaskalson et al., "Rent Boycotts," 68.

208. J. Molatsi, "1987: The Year the Mineworkers Take Control," 12–13.

209. However, see Berger, "Gender and Working-Class History."

210. I am grateful here for the insights of Lydia Kompe—former metalworker, former metalworkers' organizer, and community organizer; of Leila Patel, former education officer for the Federation of Transvaal Women; and of Jenny Schreiner, former secretary of the United Women's Organization.

211. Pillay, "Women and Employment," 25.

212. Based on figures from the S.A. Department of Manpower, *Manpower Survey*, 8 (1969) and 14 (1981).

213. For a detailed discussion of textile employers' evaluations of this new labor source, see Mager, "Moving the Fence."

214. Barrett et al., *Vukani Mawethu*, 22.

215. For discussions of the impact of the migrant labor system on women classified as African, see Ramphele, "Dynamics of Gender Politics in the Hostels"; Walker, "Gender and the Development of the Migrant Labour System."

216. "Workshop on Women," *SALB 93 (1983):* 14.

217. COSATU, *Women's Conference, 22–24 April 1988, 1.*

218. "Women's Resolution," COSATU inaugural congress, Dec. 1985.

219. Klugman, "Women Workers in the Unions."

220. See, e.g., Baard, *My Spirit Is Not Banned*, 22–31; and Walker, *Women and Resistance in South Africa.*

221. Jaffee, "Women in Trade Unions and the Community," 76.

222. Jeremy Seekings suggests that women's participation decreased as the mid-1980s uprising became more violent. However, his examination of how existing gender ideologies shaped women's political participation tends to emphasize more radical forms of organization; he virtually rejects the possibility that nonconfrontational civic associations or unions might provide alternative avenues to mobilization and politicization. The fact that women activists were rarely prominent in "youth" organizations hardly means women were completely demobilized. Seekings, "Gender Ideology," 77–88. See, however, Friedman et al., "African Women in the Durban Struggle"; and Hassim, "Gender, Social Location and Feminist Politics."

223. VOW member, 1984, in Barrett et al., *Vukani Mawethu*, 252.

224. Berger, "Gender and Working-Class History"; Scott, *Gender and the Politics of History*, 104–8.

225. In 1979, a spokesperson for the ANC's women's secretariat said, in a relatively typical statement, "In our society women have never made a call for the recognition of their rights as women, but always put the apsirations of the

whole African and other oppressed people of our country first." Mavis Nhlapo, in Kimble and Unterhalter, " 'We Opened the Road for You,' " 13.

226. Sidney Mafumadi, "None but Ourselves" (speech delivered at the launching of South Natal Region of COSATU, Mar. 2, 1986), in COSATU, *The Crisis*, 18.

227. Various draft Workers' Charters were circulated in late 1989 by CO-SATU, SACTU, and the SACP.

228. Evans, "Hegemony in Repressive Regimes."

229. Pietie du Plessis, in Baskin, *Striking Back!* 262.

230. Baskin, *Striking Back!* 463.

231. Ibid., 353.

232. Drew Forrest, "COSATU's Angry Call Stirs up a Storm in a Teacup," *Weekly Mail*, Mar. 13–19, 1992.

CONCLUSION

1. Interview, CUT delegate to COSATU Fourth Congress, Johannesburg, July 1991.

2. As late as 1985, ASSOCOM's executive director, Raymond Parsons, was describing needed political reform in terms of "principles to facilitate negotiations for African participation in the political system" and "meaningful dialogue" between African leaders and the government, rather than explicitly proposing a system of universal franchise. *Survey of Race Relations, 1985*, 62.

3. Glaser, "Ruling Groups and Reform in the mid-1980s."

4. Bendix, *Nation-Building and Citizenship*, 361, 402.

5. Ibid., 66–126.

6. See, e.g., Lipset, *Political Man*, 45–76.

7. Lipietz, *Mirages and Miracles*.

8. Almeida, "Sindicalismo brasileiro," 207.

9. Ragin, *Comparative Method*.

10. Cronin and Sirianni, *Work, Community and Power;* Marks, *Unions in Politics*, esp. ch. 3; MacDaniel, *Autocracy, Capitalism and Revolution in Russia;* Sabel, *Work and Politics*.

11. Arrighi and Silver, "Labor Movements and Capital Migration"; Balfour, *Dictatorship, Workers and the City;* Deyo, *Beneath the Miracle*, esp. 135–40, 187–208; Rock, "The Survival and Restoration of Peronism."

12. Between 1961 and 1986, Brazil relied on direct foreign investment for 23.0 percent of net foreign investment; only 11.8 percent of foreign capital in South Korea came as direct investment, while 67.6 percent came in the form of private bank loans. Of the ten largest companies in Brazil in 1987, six were state-owned, and three were foreign-owned (the tenth was owned by private local capital); in South Korea, nine were private local conglomerates, and only one, Pohang Iron and Steel, was controlled directly by the state. Stallings, "Role of Foreign Capital," 62; and Gereffi, "Big Business and the State," 93–94.

13. Koo, "Interplay of State, Social Class, and World System in East Asia," 176.

14. Deyo, *Beneath the Miracle*, 30, 36, 40.

15. Gereffi, "Paths of Industrialization," 9.

16. Brandt, "South Korean Society," 83.

17. Cheng, "Political Regimes and Development Strategies," 159.

18. Deyo, *Beneath the Miracle*, 93 and 135.

19. Haggard, *Pathways from the Periphery*, 134.

20. Gereffi, "Big Business and the State," 98, 105.

21. Cheng, "Political Regimes and Strategies," 166. See also Johnson, "Political Institutions and Economic Performance," 149.

22. Kim, 1976, in Haggard, *Pathways from the Periphery*, 72.

23. Haggard, *Pathways from the Periphery*, 74.

24. Cheng, "Political Regimes and Strategies," 164–68; and Stallings, "Role of Foreign Investment," 79.

25. Han, "South Korea: Politics in Transition," 285–92.

26. Cumings,"Abortive Abertura," 14.

27. In 1989, the ratio between average incomes for the top and bottom quintiles in Brazil was about 33:1. In South Korea, the ratio was closer to 8:1. Gereffi, "Paths of Industrialization," 14. See also Evans, "Class, State and Dependence in East Asia," 203–6.

28. Haggard, *Pathways from the Periphery*, 239–40.

29. Ibid., 232, 247.

30. Deyo, *Beneath the Miracle*, 93

31. Cho, "Labor Process and Capital Mobility," 212.

32. Deyo, *Beneath the Miracle*, 189–96.

33. Koo, "Interplay of State, Social Class, and World System," 178.

34. Koo, "Korean Economy," 55.

35. Brandt, "South Korean Society," 85–86.

36. Korea Development Institute estimate, in Brandt, "South Korean Society," 85.

37. Korea Labor Institute figures, in Kim, "Analysis of Labor Disputes in Korea and Japan," 18, 20.

38. Cheng, "Political Regimes and Strategies," 161.

39. Park, "Labor Issues in Korea's Future," 102.

40. Deyo, *Beneath the Miracle*, 211.

41. Brandt, "South Korean Society," 89–90.

42. Haggard, *Pathways from the Periphery*, 138.

Bibliography

ARCHIVES CONSULTED

Centro de Pastoral Vergueiro, São Paulo. 1971–85.

Congress of South African Students archives. 1984. Church of the Province of South Africa Records, University of the Witwatersrand, Johannesburg.

Federation of South African Trade Unions [FOSATU] archives, including records of the Institute for Industrial Education, Trade Unions Coordinating Council, University Wages Commissions, and member unions of FOSATU. 1973–85. Church of the Province of South Africa Library, University of the Witwatersrand, Johannesburg.

Metal and Allied Workers' Union and Industrial Aid Society archives. 1974–77. Church of the Province of South Africa Library, University of the Witwatersrand, Johannesburg.

Private archives, organizer, Metal and Allied Workers' Union. 1980–86.

South African Institute of Race Relations [SAIRR] archives. "Fattis and Monis Strike." 1979. Church of the Province of South Africa Library, University of the Witwatersrand, Johannesburg.

United Democratic Front [UDF] archives. 1983–84. Church of the Province of South Africa Library, University of the Witwatersrand, Johannesburg.

FREQUENTLY CITED PERIODICALS

abcd jornal (São Bernardo do Campo). 1979.

Aconteceu (Centro Ecumenico de Documentação e Informações [CEDI]). 1978–85.

Balanço Anual das Greves (DIEESE). 1978–79.

Boletim do DIEESE (São Paulo). 1982–85.

Cadernos de CUT (São Paulo). 1985–87.

Cadernos do CEAS (São Paulo). 1976–84.
Divulgação (Departimento Inter-sindical de Estatística e Estudos Socio-Económicos [DIEESE]). 1976.
FOSATU Worker News (Johannesburg). Feb. 1983–Nov. 1985.
Indústria e Desenvolvimento (São Paulo). 1974–79.
Industria e Produtividade (São Paulo). 1975–76.
Movimento (São Paulo). 1976–82.
New Nation (Johannesburg). 1987–98.
South African Labour Bulletin (SALB) (Durban). 1974–89.
South African Review (Johannesburg). 1983–88.
Survey of Race Relations (South African Institute of Race Relations [SAIRR], Johannesburg). 1966–85.
Weekly Mail (Johannesburg). 1985–90.
Work in Progress (WIP) (Johannesburg). 1978–89.

GOVERNMENT PUBLICATIONS CITED

Brasil. Congreso Nacional. *Diario.* 1960–80.
Brasil. Instituto Brasileiro de Geografia e Estatístico. *Anuários estatísticos.* 1960–80.
———. *Censos demográficos.* 1960–80.
South Africa. Bureau of Census and Statistics. *Union Statistics for Fifty Years, 1910–1960.*
South Africa. Central Statistical Services. *South African Statistics.* 1982–85.
South Africa. Department of Manpower. *Manpower Survey.* 1980–83.
South Africa. Department of Statistics. *South African Statistics.* 1954–82.
South Africa. State President's Council. *First Report of the Constitutional Committee of the President's Council.* Cape Town: Government Printer, 1982.
United Kingdom. Parliament. House of Commons Select Committee in Respect of British Companies Operating in South Africa. *British Companies in South Africa.* London: Christian Concern for Southern Africa, 1974.
United States. Department of the Army. *South Africa: A Country Study.* Edited by Harold Nelson. Washington, D.C.: U.S. Department of the Army, 1981.

WORKS CITED

"A luta dos operários." *Cadernos do CEAS* 56 (July 1978): 20–23.
Abramo, Lais Wendel. "Empresários e trabalhadores: Novas ideías e velhos fantasmas." *Coleção Cadernos do CEDEC* 7 (1985).
———. "Greve metalúrgica em São Bernardo: Sobre a dignidade do trabalho." In *As lutas sociais e a cidade: São Paulo, passado e presente,* ed. Lucio Kowarick, 207–245. São Paulo: CEDEC/Paz e Terra/UNESCO, 1988.
———. "O resgate da dignidade: A greve de 1978 em São Bernardo." Master's thesis, FFLCH/University of São Paulo, 1986.
Abranches, Sérgio. "The Divided Leviathan: State and Economic Policy Formulation in Authoritarian Brazil." Ph.D. diss., Cornell University, 1978.

Ação Católica Operária. "A realidade operária vista e sentida pelos trabalhadores." Mimeo. Recife: 1971.

Adam, Heribert. *Modernizing Racial Domination: The Dynamics of South African Politics.* Berkeley and Los Angeles: University of California Press, 1971.

———. "The South African Power Elite: A Survey of Ideological Commitment." In *South Africa: Sociological Perspectives,* ed. Heribert Adam, 73–102. London: Oxford University Press, 1971.

Adam, Heribert, and Herman Giliomee. *Ethnic Power Mobilized: Can South Africa Change?* New Haven: Yale University Press, 1979.

Afonso, Mariza Rezende, and Sérgio de Azevedo. "Cidade, poder público e Movimento de Favelados." In *Movimentos Sociais em Minas Gerais,* ed. Malori Pompermayer, 111–39. Belo Horizonte: Eda. UFMG, 1987.

Alavi, Hamza. "The State in Post-Colonial Societies: Pakistan and Bangladesh." *New Left Review* 74 (Aug. 1972): 59–81.

Alexander, Robert J. *Organized Labor in Latin America.* New York: Free Press, 1965.

Almeida, Fernando Lopes de. *Política salarial, emprego e sindicalismo, 1964–1981.* Petrópolis: Eda. Vozes, 1982.

Almeida, Maria Hermínia Tavares de. "Desarrollo capitalista y accion sindical." *Revista Mexicana de Sociologia* 40, no. 2 (Apr. 1978): 467–92.

———. "Difícil caminho: Sindicatos e política na construção da democracia." In *A democracia no Brasil: Dilemas e perspectivas,* ed. Fábio Wanderley Reis and Guillermo O'Donnell, 327–67. São Paulo: Edições Vertice, 1988.

———. "Novas demandas, novos direitos: Experiências do sindicalismo Paulista na última decada." Mimeo. São Paulo: CEBRAP, n.d.

———. "O sindicalismo brasileiro entre a conservação e a mudança." In *Sociedade e política no Brasil Pós-64,* ed. Bernardo Sorj and Maria Hermínia Tavares de Almeida, 191–212. São Paulo: Eda. Brasiliense, 1983.

———. "Sindicalismo brasileiro e pacto social." *Novos Estudos CEBRAP* 13 (Oct. 1985): 14–28.

———, ed. *Projeto "Transformações do sistema de relações trabalhistas no Brasil."* Mimeo. São Paulo: CEBRAP, 1986.

Alvarez, Sonia. *Engendering Democracy in Brazil: Women's Movements in Transition Politics.* Princeton: Princeton University Press, 1990.

———. "Politicizing Gender and Engendering Democracy." In *Democratizing Brazil,* ed. Alfred Stepan, 205–51. New York: Oxford University Press, 1989.

Alves, Maria Helena Moreira. "Grassroots Organization, Trade Unions and the Church: A Challenge to the Controlled Abertura in Brazil." *Latin American Perspectives* 11, no. 1, issue 40 (1984): 73–102.

———. *State and Opposition in Military Brazil.* Austin: University of Texas Press, 1985.

Amin, Samir. *Unequal Development: An Essay on the Social Formations of Peripheral Capitalism.* New York: Monthly Review Press, 1976.

Aminzade, Ronald. *Class, Politics and Early Industrial Capitalism.* Albany: State University of New York Press, 1981.

Amsden, Alice. "Third World Industrialization: 'Global Fordism' or a New Model?" *New Left Review* 82 (July-Aug. 1990): 5–31.

Andrade, Regis de Castro. "Brasil: A economia do capitalismo selvagem." In *Brasil: Do "milagre" à "abertura,"* ed. Paulo J. Krischke, 121–50. São Paulo: Cortez Editora, 1982.

———. "Movimento trabalhista e sindicatos sob o nacional-populismo no Brasil." Mimeo. São Paulo: CEBRAP, 1974.

Andrews, George Reid. *Blacks and Whites in São Paulo, Brazil, 1888–1988.* Madison: University of Wisconsin Press, 1991.

Antunes, Ricardo. "As formas da greve: O confronto operário no ABC Paulista, 1978/9." Ph.D. diss., University of São Paulo, 1986.

Araújo, Bras José de. "Mudanças na estutura social." In *Brasil: Do "milagre" á "abertura,"* ed. Paulo J. Krischke, 23–52. São Paulo: Cortez Editora, 1982.

———. *Operários em luta: Metalúrgicos da Baixada Santista, 1938–1983.* Rio: Paz e Terra, 1985.

Araújo, Tereza Cristina N. "A classificação de 'cor' nas pesquisas do IBGE: Notas para uma discussão." *Cadernos de Pesquisa* 63 (1987): 14–16.

Arquidiocese de São Paulo, ed. *Brasil: Nunca mais.* Introduction by Dom Paulo Evaristo, Cardinal Arns. Petrópolis: Eda. Vozes, 1985).

Arrighi, Giovanni, and Beverly Silver. "Labor Movements and Capital Migration: The U.S. and Western Europe in World-Historical Perspective." In *Labor in the Capitalist World Economy,* cd. C. Bergquist, 183–216. Beverly Hills, Calif.: Sage Publishers, 1984.

Asheron, Andrew. "Race and Politics in South Africa." *New Left Review* 53 (Jan. 1969): 55–67.

Associação Beneficente e Cultural dos Metalúrgicos de São Bernardo do Campo e Diadema. *Fundo de Greve: Da resistência a autonomia sindical.* São Paulo: Associação Beneficente e Cultural dos Metalúrgicos de São Bernardo do Campo e Diadema, n.d.

Associação Nacional dos Fabricantes de Veículos Automotores [ANFAVEA]. *Indústria automobilística Brasileira: Anúario estatístico, 1957/1987.* São Paulo: ANFAVEA, 1986.

Associated Chambers of Commerce [ASSOCOM]. "Assocom Restatement of Policy." *Information Digest* 47 (Nov. 29, 1980): 1.

Azevedo, Fernando António. *As Ligas camponeses.* Rio: Paz e Terra, 1982.

Baard, Frances, as told to Barbie Schreiner. *My Spirit Is Not Banned.* Harare: Zimbabwe Publishing House, 1986.

Bacha, Edmar. "Issues and Evidence on Recent Brazilian Economic Growth." *World Development 5,* nos. 1–2 (1977): 47–68.

Baer, Werner. *The Brazilian Economy: Its Growth and Development.* Columbus: Grid Publishing Company, 1979.

———. *Industrialization and Economic Development in Brazil.* Homewood, Ill.: Economic Growth Center, Yale University, and Richard Irwin, Inc., 1965.

Balfour, Sebastian. *Dictatorship, Workers and the City: Labour in Greater Barcelona since 1939.* Oxford: Clarendon Press, 1989.

Bandeira, Maria de Lourdes. *Territorio negro em espaço branco.* São Paulo: Eda. Brasiliense, 1988.

Banfield, Edward. *The Moral Basis of a Backward Society.* New York: Free Press, 1958.

Barelli, Walter. "Inflaçao e reivindicações trabalhistas." *Revista Civilização Brasileira* 16 (Nov. 1967): 159–70.

Barrell, Howard. "The United Democratic Front and National Forum: Their Emergence, Composition and Trends." *South African Review Two* (1984): 6–20.

Barrett, Jane, Aneene Dawber, Barbara Klugman, Ingrid Obery, Jennifer Shindler, and Joanne Yawitch. *Vukani Makhosikazi: South African Women Speak.* London: CIIR, 1985.

Baskin, Jeremy. "Growth of a New Worker Organ: The Germiston Shop Stewards' Council." *SALB* 7, no. 8 (July 1982): 42–53.

———. *Striking Back! The History of COSATU.* Johannesburg: Ravan Press, 1991.

Bastos, Ana Cecilia de Sousa. "A CONCLAT e a organisação nacional dos trabalhadores." *Cadernos do CEAS* 76 (Nov.–Dec. 1981): 1–15.

Bava, Sílvio Caccia. "A luta nos bairros e a luta sindical." In *As lutas sociais e a cidade,* ed. Lucio Kowarick, 288–313. São Paulo: CEDEC/Paz e Terra/ UNESCO, 1988.

Beall, Jo, Michelle Friedman, Shireen Hassim, Ros Posel, Lindy Stiebel and Alison Todes. "African Women in the Durban Struggle, 1985–1986: Towards a Transformation of Roles?" *South African Review Four* (1987): 93–103.

Beinin, Joel, and Zachary Lockman. *Workers on the Nile: Nationalism, Communism, Islam and the Egyptian Working CLass, 1882–1954.* Princeton: Princeton University Press, 1987.

Bell, Trevor. "Industrial Decentralization: A Thing of the Past?" In *Regional Restructuring under Apartheid,* ed. Richard Tomlinson and Mark Addleson, 207–221. Johannesburg: Ravan Press, 1987.

Bendix, Reinhard. *Force, Fate and Freedom.* Berkeley and Los Angeles: University of California Press, 1984.

———. *Nation-building and Citizenship: Studies of Our Changing Social Order.* 2d ed. Berkeley and Los Angeles: University of California Press, 1977.

Berg, Elliot, and Jeffrey Butler. "Trade Unions." In *Political Parties and National Integration in Africa,* ed. James Coleman and Carl Rosberg, 340–81. Berkeley and Los Angeles: University of California Press, 1964.

Berger, Iris. "Gender and Working-Class History: South Africa in Comparative Perspective." *Journal of Women's History* 1, no. 2 (1989): 117–33.

Berger, Suzanne, ed. *Organizing Interests in Western Europe.* Cambridge: Cambridge University Press, 1981.

Bergquist, Charles. *Labor in Latin America: Comparative Essays on Chile, Argentina, Venezuela, and Colombia.* Stanford: Stanford University Press, 1986.

———. "What Is Being Done? Some Recent Studies on the Urban Working Class and Organized Labor in Latin America." *Latin American Research Review* 16, no. 2 (1981): 203–23.

———, ed. *Labor in the Capitalist World Economy.* Beverly Hills, Calif.: Sage Publications, 1984.

Berman, Bruce, and John Lonsdale. "Crises of Accumulation, Coercion and the

Colonial State: The Development of the Labor Control System in Kenya, 1919–1929." *Canadian Journal of African Studies* 14, no. 1 (1980): 54–81.

Berquo, Elza. "Demografia da desigualdade." *Novos Estudos CEBRAP* 21 (1988): 74–84.

Biernacki, Richard "The Cultural Construction of Labor: A Comparative Study of Late Nineteenth-Century German and British Textile Mills." Ph.D. diss., University of California, Berkeley, 1988.

Bilhetes do João Ferrador. Preface by Lula [Luís Inácio da Silva]. São Paulo: Eda. Grafite, 1980.

Black, Anthony, and John Stanwix. "Manufacturing Development and the Economic Crisis: Restructuring in the 1980s." *Social Dynamics* 13, no. 1 (1987): 47–60.

Blay, Eva Alterman. *Eu não tenho onde morar: Vilas Operárias na cidade de São Paulo*. São Paulo: Nobel, 1985.

Bloch, Graeme. "Room at the Top? The Development of South Africa's Manufacturing Industry, 1939–1969." *Social Dynamics* 7, no. 2 (1981): 47–57.

Block, Fred. "The Ruling Class Does Not Rule: Notes on the Marxist Theory of the State." *Socialist Revolution* 7, no. 3, issue 33 (May 1977): 6–28.

Bohadana, Estrella, ed. *A cidade é nossa*. 2 vols. Rio de Janeiro: Eda. Codecri, 1983.

———. "Guararapes: A luta pela cidadania." In *A cidade é nossa*, ed. Estrella Bohadana, 1: 43–78. Rio de Janeiro: Eda. Codecri, 1983.

Bonacich, Edna. "Capitalism and Race Relations in South Africa: A Split Labor Market Analysis." *Political Power and Social Theory*, no. 2 (1981): 239–77.

Bonduki, Nabil Georges. "Habitação popular: Contribuição para o estudo da evolução urbana de São Paulo." In *Repensando a habitação no Brasil*, ed. Licia do Prado Valladores, 135–168. Rio de Janeiro: IUPERJ/Zahar, 1982.

Bonelli, Maria da Gloria. *A class média do "milagre" á recessão: Mobilidade social, expectativas e identidade colectiva*. São Paulo: IDESP, 1989.

Bonnell, Victoria. *Roots of Rebellion: Workers' Politics and Organization in St. Petersburg and Moscow, 1900–1914*. Berkeley and Los Angeles: University of California Press, 1983.

Bonner, Philip. "Independent Trade Unions since Wiehahn." *SALB* 8, no. 4 (Feb. 1983): 16–35.

Boschi, Renato Raul. *A arte da associação: Política de base e democracia no Brasil*. Rio de Janeiro: Edições Vertice e IUPERJ, 1987.

———. *Elites industriais e democracia: Hegemonia burguesa e mudança política no Brasil*. Trans. P. Burglin. Rio: Edições Graal, 1979.

———, ed. *Movimentos coletivos no Brasil urbano*. Rio de Janeiro: Zahar Edas., 1983.

Bozzoli, Belinda, ed. *Labour, Townships and Protest*. Johannesburg: Ravan Press, 1979.

Bradford, Helen. *A Taste of Freedom: The History of the ICU in South Africa*. New Haven: Yale University Press, 1987.

Brandt, Vincent S. R. "South Korean Society." In *Korea Briefing 1990*, ed. Chong-Sik Lee, 75–95. Boulder, Colo.: Westview Press, 1991.

Brant, Viniculus Caldeira. "Da resistência aos movimentos sociais: A emergência das classes populares em São Paulo." In *O povo em movimento*, ed. Paul Singer and Viniculus Caldeira Brant, 9–27. Petrópolis: Eda. Vozes/CEBRAP, 1980.

———, coordinator. *São Paulo: Trabalhar e viver*. São Paulo: Eda. Brasiliense/Comissao Justica e Paz de São Paulo, 1989.

Brant, Viniculus Caldeira, Maria Herminia Tavares de Almeida, Lucio Kowarick et al. *São Paulo: Growth and Poverty*. London: Bowerdean Press/CIIR, 1978.

Brenner, Johanna. "Work Relations and the Formation of Class Consciousness." In *The Debate on Classes*, ed. Erik Olin Wright et al., 184–90. London: Verso Press, 1989.

Brenner, Robert, and Mark Glick. "The Regulation Approach: Theory and History." *New Left Review* 188 (July 1991): 45–121.

Brito, José Carlos Aguiar. *A tomada da Ford: O nascimento da um sindicato livre*. Petrópolis: Eda. Vozes, 1983.

Bunting, Brian. *The Rise of the South African Reich*. Harmondsworth: Penguin Books, 1964.

Burawoy, Michael. "The Capitalist State in South Africa: Marxist and Sociological Perspectives on Race and Class." *Political Power and Social Theory* 2 (1981): 279–335.

———. "The Contours of Production Politics." In *Labor in the Capitalist World Economy*, ed. C. Bergquist, 23–47. Beverley Hills, Calif.: Sage Publications, 1984.

———. *Manufacturing Consent: Changes in the Labor Process under Monopoly Capital*. Chicago: University of Chicago Press, 1979.

———. *The Politics of Production*. London: Verso, 1985.

———. "State and Social Revolution in South Africa: Reflections on the Comparative Perspective of Greenberg and Skocpol." *Kapitalistate* 9 (1981): 93–122.

Burawoy, Michael, and Theda Skocpol, eds. *Marxist Inquiries: Studies of Labor, Class and States*. Supplement to the *American Journal of Sociology* 88 (1982).

Caldeira, Teresa Pires do Rio. "A luta pela voto em um bairro da periferia." *Cadernos CEBRAP*, no. 1 (1984).

———. *A política dos outros: O cotidiano dos moradores da periferia e o que pensam do poder e dos poderosos*. São Paulo: Eda. Brasiliense, 1984.

———. "Women, Daily Life and Politics." In *Women and Social Change in Latin America*, ed. E. Jelin, 47–78. London: Zed Press, 1990.

Calhoun, Craig. "What's New about New Social Movements? The Early Nineteenth Century Reconsidered." Paper presented at the Social Science History Association, New Orleans, Nov. 3, 1991.

Camargo, Cándido Procópio Ferreira de, Beatriz Muniz de Souza, and Antónia Flávio de Oliveira Pierucci. "Communidades eclesiais de base." In *O povo em movimento*, ed. Paul Singer and Vinícius Caldeira Brant, 59–82. Petrópolis: Eda. Vozes/CEBRAP, 1980.

Canak, William. "The Peripheral State Debate: State Capitalist and Bureaucratic-Authoritarian Regimes in Latin America." *Latin American Research Review* 19, no. 1 (1984): 3–36.

Cardoso, Fernando Henrique. "O papel dos empresários no processo de transição: O caso brasileiro." *Dados* 26, no. 1 (1983): 9–27.

Cardoso, Fernando Henrique, and Enzo Faletto. *Dependency and Development in Latin America.* Trans. M. Urquidi. Berkeley and Los Angeles. University of California Press, 1979.

Cardoso, Miriam Limoeiro. *Ideologia do desenvolvimento no Brasil: JK-JQ.* Rio de Janeiro: Paz e Terra, 1978.

Cardoso, Ruth Corrêa Leite. "Movimentos sociais na America Latina." *Revista Brasileira de Ciencias Sociais* 1, no. 3 (Feb. 1987): 27–37.

Carter, Charles. " 'We Are the Progressives': Alexandra Youth Congress Activists and the Freedom Charter, 1983–1985." *Journal of Southern African Studies* 17, no. 2 (1991): 197–220.

Castells, Manuel. *The City and the Grass Roots.* Berkeley and Los Angeles: University of California Press, 1983.

Cawthra, Gavin. *Brutal Force: The Apartheid War Machine.* London: International Defense and Aid, 1986.

Cell, John. *The Highest Stage of White Supremacy: The Origins of Segregation in South Africa and the American South.* Cambridge: Cambridge University Press, 1982.

Centro de Estudos do Trabalho. "O trabalhador e o transporte coletivo." In *Cadernos do CUT.* Serie trabalhador 2. Rio de Janeiro: Centro de Estudos do Trabalho, 1979.

Centro de Pastoral Vergueiro. *Movimento popular: Transporte coletivo.* São Paulo: Centro de Pastoral Vergueiro, 1985.

Centro Ecumenico de Documentação e Informações [CEDI]. *História dos metalúrgicos de São Caetano.* Contribuição ao Debate 2. São Paulo: CEDI, 1987.

———. *Imagens da luta, 1905–1985.* São Bernardo: Sindicato dos Trabalhadores nas Indústrias Metalúrgicas, Mecânicas e de Material Elétrico de São Bernardo do Campo e Diadema, 1987.

Chaía, Miguel Wady. "DIEESE: Saber intelectual e prática sindical." *Lua Nova* 19 (Nov. 1989): 141–77.

Charney, Craig. "The National Party, 1982–1985: A Class Alliance in Crisis." In *The State of Apartheid,* ed. Wilmot James, 5–33. Boulder, Colo.: Lynne Reinners, 1987.

Chaskalson, Matthew, Karen Jochelson, and Jeremy Seekings. "Rent Boycotts and the Urban Political Economy." *South African Review Four* (1987): 53–74.

Chauí, Marielena. "PT 'leve e suave'?" In *E agora PT? Caráter e identidade,* ed. Emir Sader, 43–99. São Paulo: Eda. Brasiliense, n.d.

Cheadle, Halton. "A Guide to the Industrial Conciliation Act of 1979." *SALB* 5, no. 2 (Aug. 1979): 102–12.

Cheng, Tun-Jen. "Political Regimes and Development Strategies: South Korea and Taiwan." In *Manufacturing Miracles: Paths of Industrialization in*

Latin America and East Asia, ed. Gary Gereffi and Donald Wyman, 139–78. Princeton: Princeton University Press, 1990.

Chilcote, Ronald. *The Brazilian Communist Party.* Oxford University Press: New York, 1974.

Chinchilla, Norma Stoltz. "Marxism, Feminism and the Struggle for Democracy in Latin America." *Gender and Society* 5, no. 3 (Sept. 1991): 291–310.

Cho, Soon Kyoung. "The Labor Process and Capital Mobility: The Limits of the New International Division of Labor." *Politics and Society* 14, no. 2 (1985): 185–222.

Chucid, Sarah, and Michael Lowy. "Pesquisa das opinões e atitudes de líderes sindicais metalúrgicos." Mimeo. São Paulo: DIEESE, n.d.

Clark, Nancy. "South African State Corporations: 'The Death Knell of Economic Colonialism'?" *Journal of Southern African Studies* 14, no. 1 (Oct. 1987): 99–122.

Cobbett, William. "A Test Case for Planned Urbanization: Bloemfontein, Botshabela, Thaba N'chu." *Work in Progress,* no. 42 (May 1986): 25–30.

Cohen, Yousseff. "The Benevolent Leviathan." *American Political Science Review* 76, no. 1 (Mar. 1982): 46–59.

Cole, Josette. *Crossroads: The Politics of Reform and Repression, 1976–1986.* Johannesburg: Ravan Press, 1987.

Coleman, Francis L., ed. *Economic History of South Africa.* Pretoria: Haum Publishers, 1983.

Collier, David, ed. *New Authoritarianism in Latin America.* Princeton: Princeton University Press, 1980.

Collier, David, and Ruth Berins Collier. *Shaping the Political Arena.* Princeton: Princeton University Press, 1991.

Collier, Ruth Berins. "Labor and Politics in Brazil." In *Brazil and Mexico: Patterns in Late Development,* ed. S. Hewlett and Richard Weinert, 57–109. Philadelphia: Institute for the Study of Human Issues, 1982.

Congresso dos Trabalhadores nas Indústrias Metalúrgicas, Mecânicas e de Material Elétrico do Estado de São Paulo. *Organisação e estrutura sindical.* Report to the 8th congress, Praia Grande, Nov. 26–29, 1974.

Congress of South African Trade Unions [COSATU]. *The Crisis: Speeches by COSATU Office Bearers.* Johannesburg: COSATU, 1986.

———. *The Way Forward.* Johannesburg: COSATU, 1987.

———. *Women's Conference, 22–24 April 1988.* Johannesburg: COSATU, 1988.

Conniff, Michael. "Populism in Brazil, 1925–1945." In *Latin American Populism in Comparative Perspective,* ed. M. Conniff, 67–91. Albuquerque: University of New Mexico Press, 1982.

Cooper, Carole. *Strikes in South Africa, 1979.* Johannesburg: South African Institute of Race Relations, 1980.

Cooper, Carole, and Linda Ensor. *PEBCO: A Black Mass Movement.* Johannesburg: South African Institute of Race Relations, n.d..

Cooper, David. "Ownership and Control of Commercial Agriculture." *South African Review Four* (1987): 568–80.

Cooper, Frederick. "Urban Space, Industrial Time, and Wage Labor in Africa." In *Struggle for the City: Migrant Labor, Capital and the State in Urban Africa*, ed. Frederick Cooper, 7–50. Beverly Hills, Calif.: Sage Publications, 1983.

Cooper, Linda, and Dave Kaplan, eds. *Selected Research Papers on Aspects of Organization in the Western Cape*. Cape Town: Department of Economic History, University of Cape Town, 1982.

Cornell, Jud, and Alide Kooy. "Wiehahn Part 5 and the White Paper." *SALB* 7, no. 3 (Nov. 1981): 51–74.

Costa, Sérgio Amad. *Estado e controle sindical no Brasil*. São Paulo: T. A. Quieroz, 1986.

Crisp, Jeff. *The Story of an African Working Class: Ghanaian Miners' Struggles, 1870–1980*. London: Zed Press, 1985.

"Critiques of the Wiehahn Commission and the 1979 Amendments to the Industrial Conciliation Act." *SALB* 5, no. 2 (Aug. 1979): 75–79.

Cronin, James. "Labor Insurgency and Class Formation: Comparative Perspectives on the Crisis of 1917–1920 in Europe." In *Work, Community and Power: The Experience of Labor in Europe and America, 1900–1925*, ed. James Cronin and Carmen Sirianni: 20–48. Philadelphia: Temple University Press, 1983.

Cronin, James, and Carmen Sirianni, eds. *Work, Community and Power: The Experience of Labor in Europe and America, 1900–1925*, ed. James Cronin and Carmen Sirianni: 20–48. Philadelphia: Temple University Press, 1983.

Cumings, Bruce. "The Abortive Experience in South Korea in the Light of the Latin American Experience." *New Left Review* 173 (Jan.–Feb. 1989): 5–32.

Dahrendorf, Ralph. *Class and Class Conflict in Industrial Society*. Stanford: Stanford University Press, 1959.

DaMatta, Roberto. *A casa e a rua: Espaço, cidadania, mulher e morte no Brasil*. São Paulo: Eda. Brasiliense, 1985.

Daniel, John. "Peasant Revolts in South Africa." Ph.D. diss., University of Michigan, 1975.

Davies, Robert. "The Class Character of South Africa's Industrial Relations Legislation." In *Essays in Southern African Labour History*, ed. Eddie Webster, 69–81. Johannesburg: Ravan Press, 1978.

———. "The 1922 Strike and the Political Economy of South Africa." In *Labour, Townships and Protest*, ed. Belinda Bozzoli, 298–324. Johannesburg: Ravan Press, 1979.

Dean, Warren. *The Industrialization of São Paulo, 1880–1945*. Austin: University of Texas Press, 1969.

Degler, Carl. *Neither Black nor White: Slavery and Race Relations in Brazil and the United States*. New York: Macmillan, 1971.

Deyo, Frederic. *Beneath the Miracle: Labor Subordination in the New Asian Industrialism*. Berkeley and Los Angeles: University of California Press, 1989.

———. "State and Labor: Modes of Exclusion in East Asian Development." In

The Political Economy of the New Asian Industrialism, ed. Frederic Deyo, 182–202. Ithaca, N.Y.: Cornell University Press, 1987.

———, ed. *The Political Economy of the New Asian Industrialism.* Ithaca, N.Y.: Cornell University Press, 1987.

Diniz, Eli. "O empresariado e o momento político: Entre a nostalgia do passado e o temor do futuro." *Cadernos de Conjuntura* 1 (Oct. 1985).

———. "O empresariado e a Nova República: Algumas considerações." *Cadernos de Conjuntura* 5 (1986).

———. "Empresário e transição política no Brasil: Problemas e perspectivas." *Cadernos de Conjuntura* 22 (Feb. 1984).

———. "A transição política no Brasil: Uma reavaliação da dinâmica da abertura." *Dados* 23, no. 8 (1985): 329–46.

Diniz, Eli, and Olavio Brasil de Lima Junior. *Modernização autoritária: O empresariado e a intervenção do estado na economia.* Serie Estudos no. 47. Rio de Janeiro: Instituto Universitario de Pesquisas do Rio de Janeiro (IUPERJ), 1986.

Dirceu, José. "Os desafios do PT." In *E agora PT?: Carater e identidade,* ed. Emir Sader. São Paulo: Eda. Brasiliense, 1986.

Di Tella, Torcuato. "Working-Class Organization and Politics in Argentina." *Latin American Research Review* 26, no. 2 (1981): 33–56.

Doimo, Ana Maria. *Movimento social urbano, igreja e participação popular: Movimento de Transporte Coletivo de Vila Velha, Espirito Santo.* Petrópolis: Eda. Vozes, 1984.

Douwes-Dekker, L. C. G. "Are Works Committees Trade Unions?" Mimeo. Johannesburg: South African Institute of Race Relations, 1973.

Dulles, John Foster. *Brazilian Communism, 1935–1945.* Austin: University of Texas Press, 1983.

Du Toit, Darcy. *Capital and Labour in South Africa: Class Struggles in the 1970s.* Boston: Kegan and Paul International, 1981.

Ehrensaft, Philip. "Phases in the Development of South African Capitalism: From Settlement to Crises." In *The Political Economy of Contemporary Africa,* ed. P. Gutkind and I. Wallerstein, 64–93. 2d ed. Beverly Hills, Calif.: Sage Publications, 1985.

Elias, Christiane M. "Report of the Labour Dispute at Fattis and Monis." Mimeo. Johannesburg: South African Institute of Race Relations, n.d.

Ensor, Linda. "TUCSA's Relationship with African Trade Unions: An Attempt at Control 1954–1962." In *Essays in Southern African Labour History,* ed. Eddie Webster, 216–31. Johannesburg: Ravan Press, 1978.

Erickson, Kenneth. *The Brazilian Corporative State and Working-Class Politics.* Berkeley and Los Angeles: University of California Press, 1977.

Erickson, Kenneth, and Patrick Peppe, "Dependent Capitalist Development, U.S. Foreign Policy and Repression of the Working Class in Chile and Brazil." *Latin American Perspectives* 3, no. 1, issue 8 (Winter 1976): 19–44.

Evans, Ivan. "Hegemony in Repressive Regimes: South Africa in the 1980s." Paper presented at the American Sociological Association, Washington, D.C., 1990.

Evans, Peter. "After Dependency: Recent Studies of Class, State and Industrialization." *Latin American Research Review* 20, no. 2 (1985): 149–60.

———. "Class, State and Dependence in East Asia: Lessons for Latin Americanists." In *The Political Economy of the New Asian Industrialism,* ed. Frederic Deyo, 203–226. Ithaca: Cornell University Press, 1987.

———. *Dependent Development: The Alliance of Multinationals, State and Local Capital in Brazil.* Princeton: Princeton University Press, 1979.

———. "Re-inventing the Bourgeoisie: State Entrepreneurship and Class Formation in Dependent Capitalist Development." In *Marxist Inquiries: Studies of Labor, Class and States,* ed. Michael Burawoy and Theda Skocpol, Supplement to the *American Journal of Sociology* 88 (1982): S210–S247.

———. "Transnational Linkages and the Economic Role of the State: An Analysis of Developing and Industrialized Nations in the Post-World War II Period." In *Bringing the State Back In,* ed. Peter Evans, Dieter Reuschemeyer and Theda Skocpol, 192–226. Cambridge: Cambridge University Press, 1985.

Evans, Peter, and John Stephens. "Development and the World Economy." Institute for Comparative Development Studies, Brown University, Working Paper no. 8/9 (1987).

Evans, Peter, Dieter Reuschemeyer, and Theda Skocpol, eds. *Bringing the State Back In.* Cambridge: Cambridge University Press, 1985.

Evers, Tilman. "Sobre o comportamento das classes médias no Brasil, 1963–1977." In *Brasil: Do "milagre" à "abertura,"* ed. Paulo J. Krischke, 83–102. São Paulo: Cortez Editora, 1982.

———. "Os movimentos sociais urbanos: O caso do Movimento do Custo de Vida." In *Alternativas populares da democracia: Brasil, anos 80,* ed. J. A. Moisés et al., 73–98. Petrópolis: Eda. Vozes, 1982.

Fadal, M. H. "Assessing Our Strengths and Weaknesses." Speech at NUTW Congress, June 27, 1987. In *The Way Forward,* ed. COSATU, 25–29. Johannesburg: COSATU, 1987.

Fajnzylber, Fernando. *Sistema industrial e exportação de manufaturados: Análise da experiência brasileira.* Rio de Janeiro: IPEA/IMPES, 1970. Relatorio de pesquisa (Instituto de Planejamento Economico e Social, Instituto de Pesquisas), no. 7.

Falkena, H. B. *The South African State and Its Entrepreneurs.* Johannesburg: A. D. Donner, 1979.

Faria, Hamilton José Barreto. "A experiência operária nos anos de resistência: A Oposição Sindical Metalúrgica de São Paulo e a dinâmica do movimento operário (1964–1978)." Master's thesis, PUC-São Paulo, 1986.

Faria, Vilma. "Desenvolvimento, urbanização e mudanças na estrutura de emprego: A experiência Brasileira nos ultimo trinta anos." In *Sociedade e política no Brasil pós-64,* ed. Bernard Sorj and Maria Hermínia Tavaras de Almeida, 118–63. São Paulo: Eda. Brasiliense, 1984.

Fausto, Boris. *A Revolução de 1930: Histografia e história.* São Paulo: Eda. Brasiliense, 1970.

Favis, Merle. "The Ford Workers' Committee: A Shop-Flawed Victory?" *SALB* 6, no. 2–3 (Sept. 1980): 38–45.

Federation of South African Trade Unions [FOSATU]. *A History of the Chemical Workers Industrial Union, 1974–1984.* Johannesburg: FOSATU, 1984.
———. "The Parallel Union Thrust." Nov. 8, 1979. Reprinted in *SALB* 5, nos. 6–7 (1980): 76–98.
———. "Statement on Wiehahn and Its Implications." *SALB* 5, nos. 6–7 (March 1980): 12–16.
Ferrante, Vera Lucia B. *FGTS: Ideologia e repressão.* São Paulo: Eda. Atica, 1978.
Ferreira, Fred H. "Collective Bargaining: Dealing With a Black Union." *SALB* 6, nos. 2–3 (Sept. 1980): 78–83.
Figueirido, Angela Cheibub. "Intervenções sindicais e o 'Novo Sindicalismo.' " *Dados,* no. 17 (1978): 135–55.
———. "A política governamental e funções sindicais." Master's thesis, Department of Social Sciences, University of São Paulo, 1975.
Fine, Bob, Francine de Clercq, and Duncan Innes. "Trade Unions and the State: the Question of Legality." *SALB* 7, nos. 1–2 (Sept. 1981): 39–68.
Fine, Bob, with Denis Davis. *Beyond Apartheid: Labour and Liberation in South Africa.* Johannesburg: Ravan, 1991.
Finnemore, M., and R. van der Merwe. *Introduction to Industrial Relations in South Africa.* Johannesburg: McGraw-Hill, 1986.
Fishlow, Albert. "Some Reflections on Economic Policy." In *Authoritarian Brazil,* ed. Alfred Stepan, 69–118. New Haven: Yale University Press, 1973.
———. "A Tale of Two Presidents: The Political Economy of Crisis Management." In *Democratizing Brazil,* ed. in Alfred Stepan, 83–119. New York: Oxford University Press, 1989.
Food and Canning Workers' Union. "Search for a Workable Relationship." *SALB* 7, no. 8 (July 1982): 54–58.
Fortes, Narcekubi S., Ferdinando B. Silveira, Aurea M. Machado, and Josue K. Bermudes. *Contribuição para análise das greves de maio de 1978.* São Paulo: 13 de Maio Núcleo de Educação Popular, 1979.
Foster, Joe. "The Workers' Struggle: Where Does FOSATU Stand?" Keynote address to the 2d FOSATU Congress, 1982; reprinted in *Review of African Political Economy,* no. 24 (1982): 99–114.
Foxley, Alejandro. *Latin American Experiments in Neoconservative Economics.* Berkeley and Los Angeles: University of California Press, 1983.
Frank, André Gunder. *Capitalism and Underdevelopment in Latin America.* New York: Monthly Review Press, 1967.
Frankel, P., N. Pines, and M. Swilling, eds. *State, Resistance and Change in South Africa.* London: Croom Helm, 1988.
Frederickson, George. *White Supremacy: A Comparative Study in American and South African History.* New York: Oxford University Press, 1981.
Frederico, Celso. *Consciência operária no Brasil.* São Paulo: Eda. Atica, 1979.
———. *A vanguarda operária.* São Paulo: Edições Simbolo, 1979.
French, John D. *The Brazilian Workers' ABC: Class Conflict and Alliances in Modern São Paulo.* Chapel Hill: University of North Carolina Press, 1992.
Freund, Bill. *The African Worker.* Cambridge: Cambridge University Press, 1988.

Friedman, Steve. *Building Tomorrow Today: African Workers in Trade Unions, 1970–1984.* Johannesburg: Ravan Press, 1987.

———. "Idealised Picture of Township Organization." *Die Suid-Afrikaan* 22 (Aug.–Sept. 1989): 28–29.

——— "The Struggle within the Struggle: South African Resistance Strategies." *Transformation* 3 (1987): 58–70.

Gabeira, Fernando *O qué é isso, companheiro?* Rio: Eda. Nova Fronteira, 1982.

General Workers' Union. "Reply to Fine, de Clercq and Innes." *SALB* 7, no. 3 (Nov. 1981): 16–25.

Gereffi, Gary. "Big Business and the State." In *Manufacturing Miracles: Paths of Industrialization in Latin America and East Asia,* ed. Gary Gereffi and Donald L. Wyman, 90–109. Princeton: Princeton University Press, 1990.

———. "Paths of Industrialization: An Overview." In *Manufacturing Miracles: Paths of Industrialization in Latin America and East Asia,* ed. Gary Gereffi and Donald Wyman, 3–31. Princeton: Princeton University Press, 1990.

Gereffi, Gary, and Donald L. Wyman, eds. *Manufacturing Miracles: Paths of Industrialization in Latin America and East Asia.* Princeton: Princeton University Press, 1990.

Gerhart, Gail. *Black Power in South Africa: The Evolution of an Ideology.* Berkeley and Los Angeles: University of California Press, 1978.

Giannotti, Vito, and Sebastião Neto. *CUT: Por dentro e por fora.* Petrópolis: Eda. Vozes, 1990.

Giddens, Anthony. *The Structure of the Advanced Capitalist Societies.* New York: Harper & Row, 1975.

Giliomee, Herman. "The Afrikaner Economic Advance." In *Ethnic Power Mobilized: Can South Africa Change?* ed. Heribert Adam and Herman Giliomee, 145–76. New Haven: Yale University Press, 1979.

Giliomee, Herman, and Lawrence Schlemmer, eds. *Up Against the Fences: Poverty, Passes and Privilege in South Africa.* New York: St Martin's Press, 1985.

Gitahy, Leda, Helena Hirata, Elizabeth Lobo, and Rosa Lucia Moyses. "Operárias: Sindicalização e reivindicações, 1970–1980." *Revista de Cultura e Política* 8 (June 1982): 90–116.

Glaser, Daryl. "A Periodisation of South Africa's Industrial Dispersal Policies." In *Regional Restructuring under Apartheid: Urban and Regional Policies in Contemporary South Africa,* ed. Richard Tomlinson and Mark Addleson, 28–54. Johannesburg: Ravan Press, 1987.

Godsell, Robert. "The Reform Process in South Africa: Some Thoughts about the Relationship between Government and the Private Sector." In *Up Against the Fences: Poverty, Passes and Privilege in South Africa,* ed. Herman Giliomee and Lawrence Schlemmer, 304–8. New York: St Martin's Press, 1985.

Gohn, Maria da Gloria Marcondes. *A forca da periferia: A luta das mulheres por creches em São Paulo.* Petrópolis: Eda. Vozes, 1985.

Gonçalves, Emilio. *Carteira de trabalho e prévidencia social.* São Paulo: Eda. Saraiva, 1977.

Gonçalves, Francisco Luiz Salles. "Duas vertentes e dois projectos no sindicalismo brasileiro." *Coleção Cadernos do CEDEC*, no. 6 (1985).

Gondim, Linda M. de Pontes. "Planners in the Face of Power: The Case of the Metropolitan Region of Rio de Janeiro, Brazil." Ph.D. diss., Cornell University, 1986.

Gordon, David. "Global Economy: New Edifice or Crumbling Foundation?" *New Left Review* 168 (March 1988): 24–65.

Greenberg, Stanley B. *Legitimating the Illegitimate: State, Markets and Resistance in South Africa.* Berkeley and Los Angeles: University of California, 1987.

———. *Race and State in Capitalist Development.* New Haven: Yale University Press, 1980.

Grondim, Marcelo. *Perfil dos dirigentes sindicais na Grande São Paulo.* São Paulo: CECODE, 1985.

———. "Sindicalismo na Grande São Paulo." *Socialismo & Democracia* 1 (Jan.–Mar. 1984): 26–40.

Gutkind, Peter, and I. Wallerstein, eds. *The Political Economy of Contemporary Africa.* 2d ed. Beverly Hills, Calif.: Sage Publications, 1985.

Haggard, Stephan. *Pathways from the Periphery: The Politics of Growth in the Newly Industrialized Countries.* Ithaca, N.Y.: Cornell University Press, 1990.

Hamilton, Nora. *The Limits of State Autonomy: Post-Revolutionary Mexico.* Princeton: Princeton University Press, 1982.

Han, Sung-Joo. "South Korea: Politics in Transition." In *Democracy in Developing Countries,* ed. S. Diamond, J. Linz, and S. M. Lipset, vol. 3: 267–303. Boulder, Colo.: Lynne Reinners, 1989.

Harding, Timothy Fox. "The Political History of Organized Labor in Brazil." Ph.D. diss., Stanford University, 1973.

Harvey, David. *Consciousness and the Built Environment.* Baltimore: Johns Hopkins Press, 1985.

Hassim, Shireen. "Gender, Social Location and Feminist Politics in South Africa." *Transformation,* no. 15 (1991): 65–82.

Haydu, Jeffrey. *Between Craft and Class: Skilled Workers and Factory Politics in the United States and Britain, 1890–1922.* Berkeley and Los Angeles: University of California Press, 1988.

Haysom, Nicholas. *Ruling with the Whip: A Report on the Violations of Human Rights in the Ciskei.* University of the Witwatersrand Centre for Applied Legal Studies Occasional Paper No. 5. Johannesburg: Centre for Applied Legal Studies, 1983.

Heffer, Theo. *Trade Unions: Threat or Challenge?* Occasional Paper No. 7 (Jan. 1984). Stellenbosch: University of Stellenbosch Business School.

Hendler, Paul. "The Organization of Parallel Unions." *SALB* 5, nos. 6–7 (1980): 99–115.

Hewlett, Sylvia Ann. *The Cruel Dilemmas of Development: Twentieth-Century Brazil.* New York: Basic Books: 1980.

Hewlett, Sylvia Ann, and Richard Weinert, eds. *Brazil and Mexico: Patterns in Late Development.* Philadelphia: Institute for the Study of Human Issues, 1982.

Higginson, John. *A Working Class in the Making: Belgian Colonial Labor Policy, Private Enterprise and the African Mineworker, 1907–1951.* Madison: University of Wisconsin Press, 1989.

Hindson, Doug. "Orderly Urbanization and Influx Control: From Territorial Apartheid to Regional Spatial Ordering in South Africa." In *Regional Restructuring under Apartheid*, ed. Richard Tomlinson and Mark Addleson, 74–105. Johannesburg: Ravan Press, 1987.

———. "Union Unity." *South African Review Two* (1984): 90–107.

Hindson, Doug, and Marion Lacey. "Influx Control and Labour Allocation: Policy and Practice since the Riekert Commission." *South African Review One* (1983): 97–113.

Hirsch, Allan, and A. Kooy. "Industry and Employment in East London." *SALB* 7, nos. 4–5 (Feb. 1982): 50–64.

Hirschman, Albert. "The Turn to Authoritarianism in Latin America and the Search for Its Economic Determinants." In *Transitions from Authoritarian Rule: Tentative Conclusions about Uncertain Democracies*, ed. G. O'Donnell and P. Schmitter, 98–135. Baltimore: Johns Hopkins University Press, 1986.

Hirson, Baruch. *Year of Fire, Year of Ash: The Soweto Revolt.* London: Zed Press, 1979.

———. *Yours for the Union: Class and Community Struggles in South Africa, 1930–1947.* London: Zed Press, 1989.

História Imediata, ed. *A greve na voz dos trabalhadores: Da Scania à Itu.* São Paulo: Alpha Omega, 1979.

Hobsbawm, Eric. *Workers: Worlds of Labor.* New York: Pantheon Books, 1982.

Holmstrom, Mark. *Industry and Inequality: The Social Anthropology of Indian Labour.* Cambridge: Cambridge University Press, 1984.

Horowitz, I. L., ed. *Revolution in Brazil.* New York: E. P. Dutton, 1964.

Humphrey, John. *Capitalist Control and Workers' Struggle in the Brazilian Auto Industry.* Princeton: Princeton University Press, 1982.

———. *Gender and Work in the Third World: Sexual Divisions in Brazilian Industry.* London: Tavistock Publications, 1987.

Huntington, Samuel. *Political Order in Changing Societies.* New Haven: Yale University Press, 1968.

———. "Reform and Stability in a Modernizing, Multi-Ethnic Society." *Politikon: South African Journal of Political Science* 8, no. 2 (Dec. 1981): 8–26.

Ibrahim, José. "A história do movimento de Osasco." In *Cadernos do Presente 2: Greves operárias (1968–1978)*, 7–15. Belo Horizonte: Eda. Aparte S/A, 1978.

Inkeles, Alex, and David H. Smith. *Becoming Modern: Individual Change in Six Developing Countries.* Cambridge, Mass.: Harvard University Press, 1974.

Innes, Duncan. *Anglo American and the Rise of Modern South Africa.* New York: Monthly Review Press, 1984.

Institute for Industrial Education. *The Durban Strikes, 1973.* Durban: Ravan Press/IIE, 1974.

International Commission of Jurists and Geoffrey Bindman, eds. *South Africa: Human Rights and the Rule of Law.* London: Pinter Publishers, 1988.

Jacobi, Pedro. "Atores sociais e estado: Movimentos reivindicatórios urbanos e estado—dimensões da ação coletiva e efeitos político-institucionais no Brasil." *Espaço & Debates* 26 (1989): 10–21.

———. "Carências de saneamento basico e demandas sociais: Os movimentos por agua na cidade de São Paulo na decada de 70." *Espaço & Debates* 22 (1987): 54–65.

———. "Movimentos populares e resposta do estado: Autonomia e controle vs. cooptação e clientilismo." In *Movimentos coletivos no Brasil urbano,* ed. Renato Raul Boschi, 145–79. Rio de Janeiro: Zahar Edas., 1983.

Jaffee, Georgina. "Women in Trade Unions and the Community." *South African Review Four* (1987): 75–92.

James, Wilmot. *Our Precious Metal: African Labour in South Africa's Gold Industry, 1970–1990.* Cape Town: David Philip, 1992.

———, ed. *The State of Apartheid.* Boulder, Colo.: Lynne Reinners, 1987.

Jelin, Elizabeth. "Citizenship and Identity: Final Reflections." In *Women and Social Change in Latin America,* ed. Elizabeth Jelin, 184–207. London: Zed Books, 1990.

———, ed. *Women and Social Change in Latin America.* London: Zed Books, 1990.

Jessop, Bob. *The Capitalist State.* New York: New York University Press, 1982.

Jochelson, Karen. "Reform, Repression and Resistance in South Africa: A Case Study of Alexandra Township, 1979–1989." *Journal of Southern African Studies* 16, no. 1 (1990): 1–32.

Johnson, Chalmers. "Political Institutions and Economic Performance: The Government-Business Relationship in Japan, South Korea and Taiwan." In *The Political Economy of the New Asian Industrialism,* ed. Frederic Deyo, 136–64. Ithaca, N.Y.: Cornell University Press, 1987.

Johnson, Richard. *How Long Will South Africa Survive?* London: Macmillan, 1977.

Johnstone, Frederick. *Class, Race and Gold: A Study of Class Relations and Racial Discrimination in South Africa.* London: Routledge & Kegan Paul, 1976.

Jones, Stuart. "The History of Black Involvement in the South African Economy." In *Black Advancement in the South African Economy,* ed. Roy Smollan, 1–30. New York: St. Martin's Press, 1986.

Kane-Berman, John. *South Africa's Silent Revolution.* Johannesburg: South African Institute of Race Relations, 1990.

Kaplan, David. "South Africa's Changing Place in the World Economy." *South African Review One* (1983): 158–70.

Karon, Tony. "The Urban Foundation: Government Supporters and Critics." In *Selected Research Papers on Aspects of Organization in the Western Cape,* ed. Linda Cooper and Dave Kaplan, 114–49. Cape Town: Department of Economic History, University of Cape Town, 1982.

Katznelson, Ira. "Working-Class Formation: Constructing Cases and Comparisons." In *Working-Class Formation: Nineteenth-Century Patterns in West-*

ern Europe and the United States, ed. Ira Katznelson and Aristides Zolberg, 3–41. Princeton: Princeton University Press, 1986.

Katznelson, Ira, and Aristides Zolberg, eds. *Working-Class Formation: Nineteenth-Century Patterns in Western Europe and the United States.* Princeton: Princeton University Press, 1986.

Keck, Margaret. "From Movement to Politics: The Formation of the Workers' Party in Brazil." Ph.D. diss., Columbia University, 1986.

———. "The New Unionism in the Brazilian Transition." In *Democratizing Brazil,* ed. Alfred Stepan, 252–96. Oxford: Oxford University Press, 1989.

———. *The Workers' Party and Democratization in Brazil.* New Haven: Yale University Press, 1992.

Keenan, Jeremy. "The Effect of the 1978–1982 Industrial Cycle on Sowetan Household Incomes and Poverty Levels." In *Studies in Urbanisation in South Africa,* ed. E. A. Kraayenbrink, 33–36. Johannesburg: South African Institute of Race Relations, 1984.

———. "Migrants Awake: The 1980 Johannesburg Municipality Strike." *SALB* 6, no. 7 (May 1981): 4–60.

———. "Trickle Up: African Income and Unemployment." *South African Review One* (1983): 184–92.

Kerr, Clark, John Dunlop, Frederick Harbison, and Charles Meyers. *Industrialism and Industrial Man: The Problems of Labor and Management in Economic Growth.* Cambridge, Mass.: Harvard University Press, 1960.

Kim, Dong-One "Analysis of Labor Disputes in Korea and Japan: The Search for an Alternative Model." *European Sociological Review,* forthcoming.

Kimble, Judy, and Elaine Unterhalter. " 'We Opened the Road for You, You Must Go Forward': ANC Women's Struggles, 1912–1982." *Feminist Review,* no. 12 (1982): 11–35.

Kirkwood, Mike. "The Defy Dispute." *SALB* 2, no. 1 (May–June 1975): 55–63.

Klugman, Barbara, et al. "Women Workers in the Unions." *SALB* 14, no. 4 (Oct. 1989): 14–36.

Koo, Bon-Ho. "The Korean Economy: Structural Adjustment for Future Growth." In *Korea Briefing, 1990,* ed. Chong-Sik Lee, 55–73. Boulder, Colo.: Westview Press, 1991.

Koo, Hagen. "The Interplay of State, Social Class, and World System in East Asian Development: The Cases of South Korea and Taiwan." In *The Political Economy of the New Asian Industrialism,* ed. Frederic Deyo, 165–81. Ithaca, N.Y.: Cornell University Press, 1987.

Kowarick, Lucio. "The Pathways to Encounter: Reflections on the Social Struggle in São Paulo." In *New Social Movements and the State in Latin America,* ed. David Slater, 73–125. Amsterdam: CEDLA, 1985.

———. "O preço do progresso: Crescimento econômico, pauperização e espoliação urbana." In *Cidade, povo e poder,* ed. José Alvaro Moisés et al., 30–50. Rio de Janeiro: CEDEC e Paz e Terra, 1981.

———. "São Paulo: Metropole do subdesenvolvimento industrializado." In *As lutas sociais e a cidade: São Paulo, passado e presente,* ed. Lucio Kowarick, 29–46. São Paulo: CEDEC, Paz e Terra e UNESCO, 1988.

———. *Trabalho e vadiagem: A origem do trabalho livre no Brasil.* São Paulo: Eda. Brasiliense, 1987.

———, ed. *As lutas sociais e a cidade: São Paulo, passado e presente.* São Paulo: CEDEC, Paz e Terra e UNESCO, 1988.

Kraak, André. "Uneven Capitalist Development: A Case Study of Deskilling and Reskilling in South Africa's Metal Industry." *Social Dynamics* 13, no. 2 (1987): 14–31.

Kraayenbrink, E. A., ed. *Studies in Urbanisation in South Africa.* Johannesburg: South African Institute of Race Relations, 1984.

Krasner, Stephen D. "Approaches to the State: Alternative Conceptions and Historical Dynamics." *Comparative Politics* 16, no. 2 (Jan. 1984): 223–46.

Krischke, Paulo J., ed. *Brasil: Do "milagre" a "abertura."* São Paulo: Cortez Editora, 1982.

———. "Loteamentos clandestinos: Autonomia ou dependencia." In *A cidade é nossa,* ed. Estrella Bohadana, 2: 47–63. Rio de Janeiro: Eda. Codecri, 1983.

———, and Scott Mainwaring, eds. *A igreja nas bases em tempo de transição (1974–1985).* Porto Alegre: L&PM Edas. e CEDEC, 1986.

Kronish, Rich, and Kenneth Mericle, eds. *The Political Economy of the Latin American Motor Vehicle Industry.* Cambridge, Mass.: MIT Press, 1984.

Kucinski, Bernard. *Abertura: A história de uma crise.* São Paulo: Eda. Brasil Debates, 1982.

Labor and Community Resources Project Johannesburg. *Comrade Moss.* Johannesburg: Learn and Teach Publications, 1989.

Labour History Group. *Organizing at the Cape Town Docks.* Cape Town: LHG, March 1984.

Labour Research Committee. "State Strategy and the Johannesburg Municipal Strike." *SALB* 7, nos. 1–2 (Sept. 1981): 61–86.

Lacey, Marion. *Working for Boroko: The Origins of a Coercive Labour System in South Africa.* Johannesburg: Ravan Press, 1981.

Lago, Luiz A. Correa do, and Beatriz M. F. de Lima. *Estrutura ocupacional, educação e formação de mao-de-obra.* Rio de Janeiro: Fundação Getúlio Vargas, 1983.

Lamounier, Bolivar. "Representação política: A importância de certos formalismos." In *Direito, cidadania e participação,* ed. Bolivar Lamounier, Francisco Weffort, and Maria Victoria Benevides, 233–60. São Paulo: T. A. Queiroz, 1981.

———. *Voto de desconfiança: Eleições e mudança política no Brasil, 1970–1979.* São Paulo: Eda. Vozes and CEBRAP, 1980.

———. "O voto em São Paulo, 1970–1978." In *Voto de desconfiança: Eleições e mudança política no Brasil, 1970–1979,* ed. Bolivar Lamounier, 15–80. São Paulo: Eda. Vozes and CEBRAP, 1980.

———, ed. *De Geisel à Collor: O balanço da transição.* São Paulo: IDESP/Eda. Sumare, 1990.

———. *1985: O voto em São Paulo.* São Paulo: Instituto de Estudos Econômicos, Sociais e Políticos, 1986.

Lamounier, Bolivar, Francisco Weffort, and Maria Victoria Benevides, eds. *Direito, cidadania e participação.* São Paulo: T. A. Queiroz, 1981.

Lange, Peter, and George Ross. *Unions, Change and Crisis: French and Italian Strategy and the Political Economy, 1945–1980.* London: George Allen & Unwin, 1982.

Leatt, James. "A Case Study of the Role of Pressure Groups in Labour Relations." Mimeo. Unit for Futures Research, University of Stellenbosch, Sept. 1980.

Lee, Chong-Sik, ed. *Korea Briefing, 1990.* Boulder, Colo.: Westview Press, 1991.

Leite, Marcia de Paula. "Reivindicações sociais dos metalúrgicos." *Coleção Cadernos do CEDEC,* no. 3 (1984).

Leite, Rosalina de Santa Cruz. *A operária metalúrgica: Estudo sobre as condições de vida e trabalho de operárias metalúrgicas na cidade de São Paulo.* São Paulo: Eda. Semente, 1982.

Lelyveld, Joseph. *Move Your Shadow: South Africa, Black and White.* New York: Times Books, 1985.

Lenin, V. I. "What Is to Be Done?" In *V. I. Lenin: Selected Works,* 1: 92–241. Moscow: Progress Publishers, 1977.

Lessa, Carlos. *A estratégia de desenvolvimento, 1974–1976: Sonho e fracasso.* Rio de Janeiro: Reproarte, 1979.

Lever, Jeff. "Capital and Labour in South Africa: The Passage of the Industrial Conciliation Act, 1924." In *Essays in Southern African Labour History* ed. Eddie Webster, 82–110. Johannesburg, Ravan Press, 1978.

Levine, Robert. *The Vargas Regime: The Critical Years, 1934–1938.* New York: Columbia University Press, 1970.

Levy, Andrew, and Associates. *Industrial Action Monitor: An Analysis of Strike Action in South Africa, 1979–1986.* Johannesburg: Andrew Levy and Associates, 1986.

Levy, Norman. "Racism and the Distribution of Skills: Employment, Education and Manpower Training." Paper presented to the Annual Meeting of the African Studies Association, Nov. 19–23, 1987.

Lewis, Jon. *Industrialization and Trade Union Organisation in South Africa, 1924–1955.* Cambridge: Cambridge University Press, 1984.

Lewis, Jon, and Estelle Randall. "The State of the Unions." *SALB* 11, no. 2 (Oct.–Dec. 1985): 60–88.

Lipietz, Alain. "How Monetarism Has Choked Third World Industrialization." *New Left Review* 145 (May 1984): 71–87.

———. *Mirages and Miracles: The Crises of Global Fordism.* Trans. D. Marcey. London: Verso Press, 1987.

Lipset, Seymour Martin. *Political Man.* Garden City, N.Y.: Doubleday, 1959.

Lipton, Merle. *Capitalism and Apartheid: South Africa, 1910–1986.* Cape Town: David Philip, 1986.

Lodge, Thomas. *Black Politics in South Africa since 1945.* Johannesburg: Ravan Press, 1983.

Loyola, Maria Andrea. *Os sindicatos e o PTB: Estudo de um caso em Minas Gerais.* Petrópolis: Vozes/CEBRAP, 1980.

Lubeck, Paul. "Class Formation at the Periphery: Class Consciousness and Islamic Nationalism among Nigerian Workers." *Research in the Sociology of Work* 1 (1981).

Luckhardt, Kenneth, and Brenda Wall. *Organize . . . or Starve! The History of the South African Congress of Trade Unions.* London: International Publishers, 1980.

————. *Working for Freedom: Black Trade Union Development in South Africa throughout the 1970s.* Geneva: World Council of Churches, 1981.

Lumby, A. B. "Industrial Development Prior to the Second World War." In *Economic History of South Africa,* ed. F. L. Coleman, 195–205. Pretoria: Haum Publishers, 1983.

Mabin, Alan. "Struggle for the City: Urbanization and Political Strategies of the South African State." *Social Dynamics* 15, no. 1 (1989): 1–28.

————, ed. *Organisation and Economic Change.* South African Studies Vol. 5. Johannesburg: Ravan Press, 1989.

McAdam, Doug. *The Political Process and the Development of Black Insurgency.* Chicago: University of Chicago Press, 1983.

McCarthy, Jeff, and Mark Swilling. "Transport and Political Resistance: Bus Boycotts of 1983." *South African Review Two* (1984): 26–44.

MacDaniel, Timothy. *Autocracy, Capitalism and Revolution in Russia.* Berkeley and Los Angeles: University of California Press, 1987.

McDonough, Peter. "Mapping an Authoritarian Power Structure: Brazilian Elites during the Medici Regime." *Latin American Research Review* 16, no. 1 (1981): 57–106.

McGregor, Liz. "The Fatti's and Moni's Dispute." *SALB* 5, nos. 6–7 (March 1980): 122–30.

McShane, Denis, Martin Plaut, and David Ward. *Power! Black Workers, Their Unions and the Struggle for Freedom in South Africa.* Boston: South End Press, 1984.

Mager, Ann. "Moving the Fence: Gender in the Ciskei and Border Textile Industry, 1945–1986." *Social Dynamics* 15, no. 2 (1989): 46–62.

Magubane, Bernard. *The Political Economy of Race and Class in South Africa.* New York: Monthly Review Press, 1979.

Mainwaring, Scott. *The Catholic Church and Politics in Brazil, 1916–1985.* Stanford: Stanford University Press, 1986.

————. "A igreja católica e o movimento popular: Nova Iguaçu, 1974–1985." In *A igreja nas bases em tempo de transição (1974–1985),* ed. Paulo Krischke and Scott Mainwaring, 73–100. Porto Alegre: L&PM Edas. e CEDEC, 1986.

Makgetla, Neva, and Ann Seidman. *Outposts of Monopoly Capitalism: Southern Africa in the Changing Global Economy.* London: Zed Press, 1980.

Malan, Pedro Sampaio. "O debate sobre 'estatização' no Brasil." *Dados* 24, no. 1 (1981): 25–36.

Malan, Pedro Sampaio, and Regis Bonelli. "The Brazilian Economy in the Seventies." *World Development* 5, nos. 1–2 (1977): 19–46.

Mann, Michael. "The Giant Stirs: South African Business in the Age of Reform." In *State, Resistance and Change in South Africa*, ed. P. Frankel, N. Pines and M. Swilling, 52–86. London: Croom Helm, 1988.

Mann, Michael, and Simon Segal. "The Transport Industry: Carrying Apartheid's Burden." *Work in Progress* 38 (Aug. 1985): 19–23.

Maree, Johann. "Democracy and Oligarchy in Trade Unions: The Independent Trade Unions in the Transvaal and the Western Province General Workers Union in the 1970s." *Social Dynamics* 8, no. 1 (1982): 41–52.

———. "The Dimensions and Causes of Unemployment in South Africa." *SALB* 4, no. 3 (May 1978): 15–50.

———. "The 1979 Port Elizabeth Strike and an Evaluation of the UAW." *SALB* 6, nos. 2–3 (Sept. 1980): 13–30.

———. "SAAWU in the East London Area 1979–1981." *SALB* 7, nos. 4–5 (Feb 1982): 34–49.

Maricato, Ermínia. *A política habitacional do regime militar: Do milagre brasileiro à crise econômica*. Petrópolis: Eda. Vozes, 1987.

Marks, Gary. *Unions in Politics: Britain, Germany, and the United States in the Nineteenth and Early Twentieth Century*. Princeton: Princeton University Press, 1989.

Marks, Shula. *The Ambiguities of Dependence: Class, Nationalism and the State in Twentieth-Century Natal*. Baltimore: Johns Hopkins University Press, 1986.

Marks, Shula, and Anthony Atmore, eds. *Economy and Society in Pre-Industrial South Africa*. Hong Kong: Longman's, 1980.

Marks, Shula, and Stanley Trapido, eds. *The Politics of Race, Class and Nationalism in Twentieth-Century South Africa*. New York: Longman's, 1984.

Maroni, Amneris. *A estratégia da recusa: Análise das greves de maio/78*. São Paulo: Eda. Brasiliense, 1982.

Marsh, Pearl-Alice. "The Failures of Apartheid Industrial Decentralization Policies and the Rise of the Independent Trade Union Movement in South Africa, 1968–1982." Ph.D. diss., University of California, Berkeley, 1984.

Marshall, T. H. *Citizenship and Social Development and Other Essays*. Cambridge: Cambridge University Press, 1950.

Martin, William G. "Cycles, Trends or Transformations? Black Labor Migration to the South African Gold Mines." In *Labor in the Capitalist World-Economy*, ed. Charles Bergquist, 157–79. Beverly Hills, Calif.: Sage Publications., 1984.

Martins, Heloisa Helena Teixeira de Souza. "Igreja e movimento operário no ABC, 1954–1975." Ph.D diss., FFLCH/USP, 1986.

Martins, Luciano. *Estado capitalista e burocracia no Brasil pós-64*. Rio de Janeiro: Paz e Terra, 1985.

Marx, Karl. *Capital*. Vol. 1. Excerpted in *The Marx-Engels Reader*, ed. Robert C. Tucker. 2d ed. New York: Norton, 1978.

Mashinini, Emma. *Strikes Have Followed Me All My Life*. New York: Routledge, 1991.

Matiwana, Mazina, and Shirley Walters. *The Struggle for Democracy: A Study of Community Organisations in Greater Cape Town from the 1960's to 1985.* Cape Town: University of the Western Cape, 1986.

Mbeki, Govan. *The Peasants' Revolt.* 1964. London: IDAF, 1984.

Meer, Shamim. "Community and Unions in Natal." *SALB* 13, no. 3 (Mar.–Apr. 1983): 75–84.

———. "Conflict—in the Community and in the Factories." *SALB* 13, nos. 4–5 (June–July 1983): 66–86.

Meli, Francis. *South Africa Belongs to Us: A History of the ANC.* Harare: Zimbabwe Publishing House, 1988.

Meneguello, Rachel. *PT: A formação de um partido, 1979–1982.* São Paulo: Eda. Paz e Terra, 1989.

Menezes, Clarice Melamed. "Do CGT a CUT." Mimeo. São Paulo: ANPOCS, 1984.

Menezes, Gilson, "A supresa." In *A greve na voz dos trabalhadores: Da Scania à Itu,* ed. História Imediata, 6–10. São Paulo: Alpha Omega, 1979.

Mericle, Kenneth S. "The Brazilian Motor Vehicle Industry." In *The Political Economy of the Latin American Motor Vehicle Industry,* ed. Rich Kronish and Kenneth Mericle, 1–40. Cambridge, Mass.: MIT Press, 1984.

Meth, Charles. "Are There Skill Shortages in the Furniture Industry?" *SALB* 4, no. 7 (Nov. 1978): 7–40.

———. "Trade Unions, Skill Shortages and Private Enterprise." *SALB* 5, no. 3 (Oct. 1979): 59–89.

Meyer, W. N. *The Role of Exports in South Africa's Economic Development, 1961–1976.* Research Paper C-16. Port Elizabeth: University of Port Elizabeth, 1979.

Mfeka, Monde. "Working-Class Leadership and the Liberation Struggle." *Work in Progress* 49 (1987): 38–39.

Moisés, José Alvaro. "Classes populares e protesto urbano." Ph.D. diss., University of São Paulo, 1978.

———. *Lições de liberdade e de opressão: O novo sindicalismo e a política.* Rio de Janeiro: Paz e Terra, 1982.

———. "Qual é a estratégia do novo sindicalismo?" In José Alvaro Moisés et al., *Alternatives populares da democracia: Brasil, anos 80,* 13–39. São Paulo: Eda. Vozes, 1982.

Moisés, José Alvaro, and Verena Martinez-Aliér. "A revolta dos suburbanos ou 'Patrão, o trem atrasou.'" In José Alvaro Moisés et al., *Contradições urbanas e movimentos sociais,* 13–63. Rio de Janeiro: CEDEC e Paz e Terra, 1985.

Moisés, José Alvaro, et al. *Alternatives populares da democracia: Brasil, anos 80.* São Paulo: Eda. Vozes, 1982.

Moisés, José Alvaro, et al. *Cidade, povo e poder.* Rio de Janeiro: CEDEC e Paz e Terra, 1981.

Moisés, José Alvaro, et al. *Contradições urbanas e movimentos sociais.* Rio: CEDEC e Paz e Terra, 1985.

Molatsi, J. "1987: The Year the Mineworkers Take Control." In COSATU, *The Way Forward,* 12–13. Johannesburg: COSATU, 1987.

Montgomery, David. *The Fall of the House of Labor: The Workplace, the State, and American Labor Activism, 1865–1925.* Cambridge: Cambridge University Press, 1987.

———. *Workers' Control in America.* Cambridge: Cambridge University Press, 1979.

Moore, Barrington, Jr. *The Social Origins of Dictatorship and Democracy.* Boston: Beacon Press, 1966.

———. *Injustice: The Social Bases of Obedience and Revolt.* White Plains, N.Y.: M. E. Sharpe, 1978.

Morel, Mário. *Lula, o metalúrgico: Anatomia de uma liderança.* Rio de Janeiro: Eda. Nova Fronteira, 1981.

Morley, Samuel, and Gordon Smith. "The Effect of Changes in the Distribution of Labor, Foreign Investment and Growth in Brazil." In *Authoritarian Brazil: Origins, Policies and Future,* ed. Alfred Stepan, 119–41. New Haven: Yale University Press, 1973.

Morris, Mike. "Capital's Responses to African Trade Unions Post-Wiehahn." *SALB* 7, nos. 1–2 (Sept. 1981): 69–85.

Mosely, K. P. "Contested Terrains: Social Relations of Production." *African Journal of Political Economy* 2 (Aug. 1987): 1–38.

Moss, Glenn. "Stay Aways: Mass Strike or Demonstration?" *Work in Progress,* no. 25 (Feb. 1983): 29–34.

Moura, Clovis. "Organizações negras." In *O povo em movimento,* ed. Paul Singer and Vinícius Caldeira Brant, 143–75. Petrópolis: Eda. Vozes e CEBRAP, 1980.

"Movimento operário em ritmo da resistência." *Cadernos do CEAS* 50 (July–Aug. 1977): 32–42.

Moyle, Didi. "Mass Resistance to Pensions Bill." *SALB* 7, no. 3 (Nov. 1981): 4–7.

Mucoucah, Paulo Sérgio. "A coletiva seletiva do lixo." São Paulo: Núcleo de gestao municipal do Polis, 1990.

Mufamadi, Sydney. Interview. *Work in Progress,* no. 31 (May 1984): 19–22.

———. "None but Ourselves." In COSATU, *The Crisis: Speeches by COSATU Office Bearers,* 14–18. Johannesburg: COSATU, 1986.

Munck, Ronaldo. *The New International Labour Studies: An Introduction.* London: Zed Press, 1988.

———. "State and Capital in Dependent Social Formations: The Brazilian Case." *Capital and Class* 8 (Summer 1979): 34–53.

Myers, Desaix. *Labor Practices of U.S. Corporations in South Africa.* London: Praeger/IRRC, 1977.

Mzala. *Gatsha Buthelezi: Chief with a Double Agenda.* London: Zed Press, 1988.

Nash, June, and Helen Safa (eds.) *Women and Change in Latin America.* Massachusetts: Bergin & Garvey, 1986.

Natal Labor Research Committee. "Control over a Workforce—The Frame Case." *SALB* 6, no. 5 (Dec. 1980): 17–47.

Nattrass, Jill. *The South African Economy: Its Growth and Change.* Cape Town: Oxford University Press, 1981.

Nattrass, Jill, and I. G. Duncan. "A Study of Employer Attitudes toward African Worker Representation." Durban: Department of Economics, University of Natal, 1975.

Ncube, Don. *The Influence of Apartheid and Capitalism on the Development of Black Trade Unions in South Africa.* Johannesburg: Skotaville Pubs., 1985.

Neves, Estela. "Invasões e acesso a terra urbana." In *A cidade é nossa*, ed. Estrella Bohadana, 2: 25–44. Rio de Janeiro: Eda. Codecri, 1983.

Neves, Joana. "Trabalho, o capitalismo adiantado e a classe operária: Um novo sindicalismo." Mimeo. Universidade Federal de Paraiba, Feb. 1985.

Neves, Lucília de Almeida. *O Comando Geral dos Trabalhadores no Brasil, 1961–1964.* Belo Horizonte: Eda. Vega, 1981.

Nicol, Martin. "Legislation, Registration and Emasculation." *SALB* 5, nos. 6–7 (March 1980): 44–56.

Njikelana, Sisa. "Unions and the UDF." *Work in Progress* 28 (*Aug.* 1983): 38–40.

Nolan, Mary. 1986. "Economic Crisis, State Policy and Working-Class Formation in Germany, 1870–1900." In *Working-Class Formation,* ed. I. Katznelson and A. Zolberg, 352–96. Princeton: Princeton University Press.

Noronha, Eduardo *Greve e conjuntura, 1978–1986.* Campinas: NEPP-NICAMP, 1987.

Ntai, Sello. Interview. *Work in Progress* 50 (*Oct.* 1987): 56–58.

Nunes, Edson. "Carências urbanas, reivindicações sociais e valores democráticos." *Lua Nova* 17 (1989): 67–69.

———. "Inventário dos quebra-quebras nos trens e onibus em São Paulo e Rio de Janeiro, 1977–1981." In Jose Alvaro Moisés et al., *Cidade, povo e poder,* 92–108. Rio de Janeiro: CEDEC e Paz e Terra, 1981.

Nunes, Edson, and Pedro Jacobi. "A cara nova do movimento popular." *Lua Nova* 1, no. 3 (Oct.–Dec. 1984): 75–79.

Obery, Ingrid. "East Rand Bus Drivers: Between Commuters and Community." *Work in Progress*, no. 38 (Aug. 1985): 24–25.

Obery, Ingrid, and Mark Swilling. "MAWU and UMMAWUSA Fight for the Factories." *Work in Progress*, no. 33 (Aug. 1984): 4–12.

O'Donnell, Guillermo. *Modernization and Bureaucratic Authoritarianism.* New Haven: Yale University Press, 1973.

———. "Tensions in the Bureaucratic-Authoritarian State and the Question of Democracy." In *New Authoritarianism in Latin America,* ed. David Collier, 285–318. Princeton: Princeton University Press, 1980.

O'Donnell, Guillermo, and P. Schmitter, eds. *Transitions from Authoritarian Rule: Tentative Conclusions about Uncertain Democracies.* Baltimore: Johns Hopkins University Press, 1986.

O'Dowd, M. C. "The Stages of Economic Growth and the Future of South Africa." In *Change, Reform and Economic Growth in South Africa,* ed. Lawrence Schlemmer and Eddie Webster, 28–50. Johannesburg: Ravan Press, 1978.

Oestreicher, Richard. *Solidarity and Fragmentation: Working People and Class Consciousness in Detroit, 1875–1900.* Urbana: University of Illinois Press, 1986.

Offe, Claus, and Helmut Wiesenthal. "Two Logics of Collective Action: Theoretical Notes on Social Class and Organizational Form." In *Political Power and Social Theory,* ed. Maurice Zeitlin, *vol.* 1: 67–115. Greenwich, Conn.: JAI Press, 1980.

Oliveira, Antónia Alves de, Iúlio Gomes Almeida, and Miguel Mahfoud e Silvana Cavichioli. *Os nordestinos em São Paulo.* São Paulo: Edições Paulinas, 1982.

Oliveira, Elvira de. *Luiza Erundina: Uma grauna no Ibirapuera.* São Paulo: Eda. Busca Vida, 1988.

Oliveira, Jaime de Araujo, and Sonia M. Fleury Texeira. *(Im)prévidencia social: 60 anos de historia da Prévidencia no Brasil.* Petrópolis: Eda. Vozes and ABRASCO, 1986.

O'Meara, Dan. "Analysing Afrikaner Nationalism: The 'Christian National' Assault on White Trade Unionism in South Africa, 1934–1948." *African Affairs* 77, no. 306 (Jan. 1978): 45–72.

———. *Volkscapitalisme: Class, Capital and Ideology in the Development of Afrikaner Nationalism, 1934–1948.* Johannesburg: Ravan Press, 1983.

Oposição Sindical Metalúrgica de São Paulo. *Comissão da fábrica: Uma forma de organização operária.* Petrópolis: Eda. Vozes, 1981.

———. "História do movimento operário-sindical no Brasil de 1900 ate 1970." Mimeo. São Paulo: Aug. 1970.

———. *Nas raizes da democracia operária: A história da Oposição Sindical Metalúrgica de São Paulo.* São Paulo: Instituto de Planejamento Regional e Urbano da PUC, 1982.

Paine, Leigh. "Working-Class Strategies in the Transition to Democracy in Brazil." *Comparative Politics* 23, no. 2 (1991): 221–38.

Park, Se-il. "Labor Issues in Korea's Future." *World Development* 16, no. 1 (1988): 99–119.

Pastore, José, and Thomas Skidmore. "Brazilian Labor Relations: A New Era?" MS., 1985.

Paula, Edemir de, Ivo Soares Ferreira, José Carlos da S. Barbosa, Mauro Rodrigues do Prado, and Mauricio R. Monteiro. *Ação e razão dos trabalhadores da General Motors de São José dos Campos.* São José dos Campos: Fundo de Greve dos Metalurgicos de São José dos Campos, 1985.

Peace, Adrian. "The Lagos Proletariat: Labour Aristocrats or Populist Militants?" In *The Development of an African Working Class,* ed. R. Sandbrook and R. Cohen, 281–301. London: Harlow, 1975.

Pereira, Luiz Carlos Bresser. *O colapso de uma aliança de classes.* São Paulo: Eda. Brasiliense, 1978.

———. *Development and Crisis in Brazil, 1930–1983.* Trans. Marcia van Dyke. Boulder, Colo.: Westview Press, 1984.

Pereira, Vera Maria Cándido. *O coração da fábrica.* Rio de Janeiro: Eda. Campus Ltda, 1979.

Perlman, Janice. *The Myth of Marginality: Urban Poverty and Politics in Rio de Janeiro.* Berkeley and Los Angeles: University of California Press, 1976.

Perlman, John. "Bus Boycotts, Monopolies and the State." *Work in Progress* 31 (May 1984): 23–37.

Perlman, Selig. *A Theory of the Labor Movement.* New York: Macmillan, 1928.

Petrini, João Carlos. *CEBs: Um novo sujeito popular.* São Paulo: Paz e Terra, 1984.

Pillay, Pundy. "Women and Employment: Some Important Trends and Issues." *Social Dynamics* 11, no. 2 (1985): 20–37.

Piven, Frances Fox, and Richard Cloward. *Poor People's Movements.* New York: Pantheon Books, 1977.

Platzky, Laureen, and Cherryl Walker. *The Surplus People.* Johannesburg: Ravan Press, 1985.

Plaut, Martin. "The Political Significance of COSATU." *Transformation, no.* 2 (1986): 62–72.

Pompermayer, Malori, ed. *Movimentos sociais em Minas Gerais.* Belo Horizonte: Eda. UFMG, 1987.

Portelli, Alessandro. "The Death of Luigi Trastulli: Memory and the Event." In id., *The Death of Luigi Trastulli and Other Stories: Form and Meaning in Oral History,* 1–26. Albany: State University of New York Press, 1991.

Portes, Alejandro. "Housing Policy, Urban Poverty and the State: The *Favelas* of Rio de Janeiro, 1972–1976." *Latin American Research Review* 14, no. 2 (1979): 3–24.

——."Political Primitivism, Differential Socialization, and Lower-Class Radicalism." *American Sociological Review* 36, no. 5 (1971): 820–35.

Portes, Alejandro, and John Walton. *Labor, Class and the International System.* New York: Academic Press, 1981.

Posel, Deborah. " 'Providing for the Legitimate Labour Requirements of Employers': Secondary Industry, Commerce and the State in South Africa During the 1950s and Early 1960s." In *Organisation and Economic Change,* ed. Alan Mabin, 199–220. South African Studies Vol. 5. Johannesburg: Ravan Press, 1989.

——. *The Making of Apartheid, 1948–1961: Conflict and Compromise.* Oxford: Clarendon Press, 1991.

Przeworski, Adam. *Democracy and the Market: Political and Economic Reforms in Eastern Europe and Latin America.* Cambridge: Cambridge University Press, 1991.

——. "Material Interests, Class Compromise and the Transition to Socialism." *Politics and Society* 10, no. 2 (1980): 125–53.

——. "Social Democracy as an Historical Phenomenon." *New Left Review* 122 (July–Aug. 1980): 27–58.

Rafel, Robyn. "Job Reservation on the Mines." *South African Review Four* (1987): 265–82.

Ragin, Charles. *The Comparative Method: Moving beyond Qualitative and Quantitative Strategies.* Berkeley and Los Angeles: University of California Press, 1987.

Rainho, Luiz Flávio. *Os peões do Grande ABC.* Petrópolis: Eda. Vozes, 1980.

Rainho, Luiz Flávio, and Oswaldo Bargas. *As lutas operárias e sindicais dos metalúrgicos em São Bernardo, 1977/79.* São Bernardo do Campo: Associação Beneficiente e Cultural dos Metalúrgicos de São Bernardo do Campo e Diadema, 1983.

Ramphele, Mamphela. "The Dynamics of Gender Politics in the Hostels of Cape Town: Another Legacy of the South African Migrant Labour System." *Journal of Southern African Studies* 15, no. 3 (April 1989): 393–414.

Randall, Peter, ed. *Power, Privilege and Poverty: Report of the Economics Commission of the Study Project on Christianity in Apartheid Society.* Johannesburg: SPRO-CAS, 1972.

Reis, Fábio Wanderley, and Guillermo O'Donnell, eds. *A democracia no Brasil: Dilemas e perspectivas.* Rio de Janeiro: Vertice, 1988.

Rock, David. "The Survival and Restoration of Peronism." In *Argentina in the Twentieth Century,* ed. David Rock, 179–221. Pittsburgh: University of Pittsburgh Press, 1975.

Rodrigues, Iram Jacome. *Comissão de fábrica e trabalhadores na indústria.* São Paulo: Cortez Editora, 1990.

Rodrigues, José Albertino. *Sindicato e desenvolvimento no Brasil.* 2d ed. São Paulo: Edições Simbolo, 1979.

Rodrigues, Leôncio Martins. *CUT: Os militantes e a ideologia.* Rio: Paz e Terra, 1990.

———. *Industrialisação e atitudes operárias.* São Paulo: Eda. Brasiliense, 1970.

———. "Trabalhadores de uma indústria automobilística: Perfil social e participação sindical." Paper presented at the llth annual ANPOCS meeting, Aguas de São Pedro, Oct. 1987.

———. "Trabalhadores e sindicatos no processo de industrialisação." Tese de livre-dociência, University of São Paulo, 1972.

Rogerson, Chris. "From Coffee-Cart to Industrial Canteen: Feeding Johannesburg's Black Workers, 1945–1965." In *Organisation and Economic Change,* ed. Alan Mabin, 168–98. Southern African Studies Vol. 5. Johannesburg: Ravan Press, 1989.

Rolnik, Raquel. "De como São Paulo virou à capital do capital." In *Repensando a habitação no Brasil,* ed. Lícia do Prado Valladares, 109–34. *Debates Urbanos* 3. Rio de Janeiro: Zahar Edas., 1982.

Rossi, Waldemar. "Somos humanos, nao peças do capitalismo." In *O Papa e os operários em São Paulo,* ed. Comissão Justica e Paz de São Paulo, Pastoral do Mundo do Trabalho. São Paulo: Grafica da Associação dos Advogados de São Paulo, n.d.

Roux, A., P. Stewart, and M. Roux. "East London and the Politics of Decentralization." In *Studies in Urbanization in South Africa,* ed. E. A. Kraayenbrink, 61–74. Johannesburg: South African Institute of Race Relations, 1984.

Roux, Marianne. "Daily Events of the Wildcat Strike." *SALB* 6, nos. 2–3 (Sept. 1980): 3–12.

———. "The Division of Labour at Ford." *SALB* 6, nos. 2–3 (Sept. 1980): 31–37.

———. "Managerial Strategies at Ford." *SALB* 6, nos. 2–3 (Sept. 1980): 84–91.

Roxborough, Ian. *Unions and Politics in Mexico: The Case of the Auto Industry.* Cambridge: Cambridge University Press, 1984.

Ruccio, David F. "Fordism on a World Scale: International Dimensions of Regulation." *Review of Radical Political Economics* 21, no. 4 (1989): 33–53.

Rupert, Anton. *Priorities for Coexistence.* Cape Town: Tafelberg, 1981.

Sabel, Charles. *Work and Politics: The Division of Labor in Industry.* Cambridge: Cambridge University Press, 1982.

Sader, Eder. "Quando novos personagens entraram em cena: Experiências, falas e lutas dos trabalhadores da Grande São Paulo (1970–1980)." Doctoral thesis, FFLCH/University of São Paulo, 1987.

Sader, Eder, and Paulo Sandroni. "Lutas operárias e táticas da burguesia—1978/80." Special issue. *Cadernos PUC,* no. 7 (1981).

Sader, Emir. "O qué é qué está escrito na estrela?" In *E agora PT? Caráter e identidade,* ed. Emir Sader. São Paulo: Eda. Brasiliense, n.d.

———, ed. *E agora PT? Caráter e identidade.* São Paulo: Eda. Brasiliense, n.d.

Sader, Emir, and Ken Silverstein. *Without Fear of Being Happy: Lula, the Workers Party and Brazil.* London: Verso Press, 1991.

Sadie, J. L. "Labour Supply in South Africa." Paper presented at the National Labour Conference, April 29–30, 1971.

Sampson, Anthony. *Black and Gold: Tycoons, Revolutionaries and Apartheid.* London: Hodder & Stoughton, 1987.

Sandbrook, R., and R. Cohen, eds. *The Development of an African Working Class.* London: Harlow, 1975.

Santos, Abdias José dos, and Ercy Rocha Chaves. *Consciência operária e luta sindical: Metalúrgicos de Niteroi no movimento sindical Brasileiro.* Rio de Janeiro: Eda. Vozes, 1980.

Santos, Carlos Nelson Ferreira dos. *Movimentos urbanos no Rio de Janeiro.* Rio de Janeiro: Zahar Edas., 1981.

Santos, Wanderley Guilherme dos. *Cidadania e justiça: A política social na ordem brasileira.* Rio de Janeiro: Eda. Campus, 1979.

Sarti, Ingrid. *Porto vermelho: Os estivadores Santistas no sindicato e na política.* Rio de Janeiro: Paz e Terra, 1981.

Saul, John. "The State in Post-Colonial Societies: Tanzania." *Socialist Register,* 1974. Reprinted in John Saul, *The State and Revolution in East Africa,* 167–99. New York: Monthly Review Press, 1979.

———. "South Africa: Between Barbarism and Structural Adjustment." *New Left Review,* no. 188 (July/Aug. 1991): 1–43.

Saul, John, and Stephen Gelb. *Crisis in South Africa.* 2d ed. New York: Monthly Review Press, 1986.

Schamis, Hector E. "Reconceptualizing Latin American Authoritarianism in the 1970s: From Bureaucratic-Authoritarianism to Neoconservatism." *Comparative Politics* 23, no. 4 (1991): 201–20.

Schlemmer, Lawrence, and Eddie Webster, eds. *Change, Reform and Economic Growth in South Africa.* Johannesburg: Ravan Press, 1978.

Schminck, Marianne. "Women and Urban Industrial Development in Brazil." In *Women and Change in Latin America,* ed. J. Nash and Helen Safa, 136–64. Massachusetts: Bergin & Garvey, 1986.

———. "Women in Brazilian *Abertura* Politics." *Signs* 7, no. 1 (1981): 115–35.

Schorske, Carl. *German Social Democracy.* Cambridge, Mass.: Harvard University Press, 1955.

Scott, Joan Wallach. *Gender and the Politics of History.* New York: Columbia University Press, 1988.

Seekings, Jeremy. "Gender Ideology and Township Politics in the 1980's." *Agenda,* no. 10 (1991): 77–88.

———. "Political Mobilization in the Black Townships of the Transvaal." In *State, Resistance and Change in South Africa,* ed. P. Frankel, N. Pines, and M. Swilling, 197–228. London: Croom Helm, 1988.

Seidman, Ann, and Neva Seidman. *South Africa and U.S. Multinational Corporations.* Westport, Conn.: Lawrence Hill, 1977.

Seidman, Judy. *Face-lift Apartheid.* London: International Defense and Aid, 1980.

Setubal Filho, Laerte. "O papel dos entitades de classe no momento brasileiro." *Escritorio Moderno* 8, no. 1 (May–June 1980): 40–44.

Sewell, William H., Jr. "Artisans, Factory Workers and the Formation of the French Working Class, 1789–1848." In *Working-Class Formation,* ed. I. Katznelson and A. Zolberg, 45–70. Princeton: Princeton University Press, 1986.

Shane, S., and J. Farnham. *Strikes in South Africa, 1960–1984.* National Institute for Personnel Research Report No. 338. Pretoria: NIPR, 1985.

Shefter, Martin. "Trade Unions and Political Machines: The Organization and Disorganization of the American Working Class in the Late Nineteenth Century." In *Working-Class Formation,* ed. I. Katznelson and A. Zolberg 197–278. Princeton: Princeton University Press, 1986.

Shorter, Edward, and Charles Tilly. *Strikes in France.* Cambridge: Cambridge University Press, 1974.

Sideris, Tina. "MAWU Enters the Industrial Council." *Work in Progress* 27 (June 1983): 10–13.

———. *Sifuna Imali Yethu: The Life and Struggles of Durban Dockworkers, 1940–1981.* Oral History Series No. 3. Johannesburg: South African Institute of Race Relations, 1983.

Silva, Luís Inácio da. Interview with Ricardo Antunes, António Rago Filho, Maria Dolores Prades, and Paulo Douglas Barsotti, July 1981. *Ensaio 9* (Jan. 1982): 13–54.

Silva, Roque Aparecido da. "Brasil: Sindicatos y transición democrática." *Nueva Sociedad* (Venezuela) 83 (May–June 1986): 115–24.

———. "Sindicato e sociedade na palavra dos metalúrgicos." In *Comision de Movimientos Laborales de CLASCO,* 227–34. Santiago de Chile: Comision de Movimientos Laborales de CLASCO, 1985.

———, ed. *Os sindicatos e a transição democrática: O que pensam os interessados.* São Paulo: IBRART/OIT, 1986.

Silva, Roque Aparecido da, Ana Amelia da Silva, Daisy Camargo, and Patricio Gastelo. "A organização dos trabalhadores nos locais de trabalho: Os casos da Asama, Volkswagen, MWM, Coldex-Frigor e Bardella, Borriello, Eletro-Mecânica SA." Mimeo. São Paulo: CEDEC, 1984.

Simkins, C. E. W. *South African Development in International Perspective, 1950–1975.* Working Paper. Pietermaritzburg: University of Natal Development Studies Research Group, 1979.

Simkins, C. E. W., and Doug Hindson. *The Division of Labour in South Africa, 1969–1977.* Working Paper. Pietermaritzburg: University of Natal Development Studies Research Group, 1979.

Simons, Jack, and Ray Simons, *Class and Colour in South Africa.* 2d ed. London: IDAF, 1983.

Singer, André. "Collor na periferia: A volta por cima do populismo." In *De Geisel à Collor: O balanço da transição,* ed. Bolivar Lamounier, 135–52. São Paulo: IDESP/Eda. Sumaré, 1990.

Singer, Paul. *Dominação e desigualdade: Estrutura de classes e repartição da renda no Brasil.* Rio de Janeiro: Paz e Terra, 1981.

———. "Mais pobres e mais ricos." *Opinião* 116 (Jan. 24, 1975).

———. "Movimentos de bairro." In *O povo em movimento,* ed. Paul Singer and Vinícius Caldeira Brant, 83–107. Petrópolis: Eda. Vozes e CEBRAP, 1980.

Singer, Paul, and Vinícius Caldeira Brant, eds. *O povo em movimento.* Petrópolis: Eda. Vozes e CEBRAP, 1980.

Sitas, Ari. "African Worker Responses on the East Rand to Changes in the Metal Industry, 1960–1980." Ph.D. diss., University of the Witwatersrand, 1983.

Sitas, Ari, and Eddie Webster. "Stoppages in the East Rand Metal Industry." Mimeo. Johannesburg: n.d.

Skidmore, Thomas. *Politics in Brazil, 1930–1964: An Experiment in Democracy.* London: Oxford University Press, 1967.

———. *The Politics of Military Rule in Brazil, 1964–1985.* Oxford: Oxford University Press, 1988.

Skocpol, Theda. "Emergent Agendas and Recurrent Strategies." In *Vision and Method in Historical Sociology,* ed. Theda Skocpol, 356–91. Cambridge: Cambridge University Press, 1984.

———. *States and Social Revolutions.* Cambridge: Cambridge University Press, 1979.

———, ed. *Vision and Method in Historical Sociology.* Cambridge: Cambridge University Press, 1984.

Slater, David, ed. *New Social Movements and the State in Latin America.* Amsterdam: CEDLA, 1985.

Smelser, Neil. *Social Change in the Industrial Revolution.* Chicago: University of Chicago Press, 1959.

Smollan, Roy, ed. *Black Advancement in the South African Economy.* New York: St. Martin's Press, 1986.

Sofer, Eugene. "Recent Trends in Latin American Historiograpy" and "Dependency versus Working Class History." *Latin American Research Review* 15, no. 1 (1980): 167–82.

Solomon, V. E. "Transport." In *Economic History of South Africa,* ed. F. L. Coleman, 89–124. Pretoria: Haum Publishers, 1983.

Somarriba, Maria da Merces G., Maria Gezica Valadares, and Mariza Rezende Afonso. *Lutas urbanas em Belo Horizonte.* Petrópolis: Eda. Vozes, 1984.

Sorj, Bernard *Estado e classes sociais na agricultura brasileira.* Rio de Janeiro: Zahar, 1980.

Sorj, Bernard, and Maria Hermínia Tavaras de Almeida, eds. *Sociedade e política no Brasil pós-64.* São Paulo: Eda. Brasiliense, 1983.

Sousa, Maria Tereza Sadek R. de. "Concentração industrial e estrutura partidaria: O processo eleitoral no ABC, 1966–1982." Doctoral thesis, University of São Paulo, 1984.

South Africa: A Guide to Foreign Investors. Johannesburg: Erudita Publisherss, 1976.

Souza, Amaury de, and Bolivar Lamounier. "Governo e sindicatos no Brasil: A perspectiva dos anos 80." *Dados* 24, no. 2 (1981): 139–59.

Souza, Herbert de. "As duas vertentes da democracia." In *Brasil: Do "milagre" à "abertura,"* ed. Paulo J. Krischke, 151–65. São Paulo: Cortez Editora, 1982.

Spalding, Hobart, Jr. *Organized Labor in Latin America: Historical Case Studies of Workers in Dependent Societies.* New York: New York University Press, 1977.

Stallings, Barbara. "The Role of Foreign Capital in Economic Development." In *Manufacturing Miracles: Paths of Industrialization in Latin America and East Asia,* ed. Gary Gereffi and Donald L. Wyman, 55–89. Princeton: Princeton University Press, 1990.

Stepan, Alfred. *The Military in Politics: Changing Patterns in Brazil.* Princeton: Princeton University Press, 1971.

———, ed. *Authoritarian Brazil: Origins, Policies and Future.* New Haven: Yale University Press, 1973.

———, ed. *Democratizing Brazil.* Oxford: Oxford University Press, 1989.

"Strikes in the Metal Industry." *Work in Progress,* no. 22 (Apr. 1982): 26–28.

Suckling, John. "The Nature and Role of Foreign Investment in South Africa." In J. Suckling, Ruth Weiss, and Duncan Innes, *The Economic Factor: Foreign Investment in South Africa,* 11–48. London: Africa Publications Trust, 1975.

"The Support Alliance: Trade Unions and Community." *Work in Progress,* no. 19 (Aug. 1981): 6–12.

Sutcliffe, Michael, and Paul Wellings. *Strike Action in the South African Manufacturing Sector: A Socio-Spatial Analysis.* Durban: University of Natal Development Studies Unit, 1985.

Swilling, Mark. "Stayaways, Urban Protest and the State." *South African Review Three* (1986): 20–50.

———. "Beyond Ungovernability: Township Politics and Local-Level Negotiations." Mimeo. Johannesburg: Centre for Policy Studies, 1989.

Tarrow, Sidney. *Struggle, Politics and Reform: Collective Action, Social Movements and Cycles of Protest.* Occasional Paper No. 21. Ithaca, N.Y.: Cornell

University Center for International Studies, Western Societies Program, 1991.

Telles, Vera da Silva. "Anos 70: Experiências, práticas e espaços políticos." In *As lutas sociais e a cidade: São Paulo, passado e presente*, ed. Lucio Kowarick, 247–83. São Paulo: CEDEC, Paz e Terra e UNESCO, 1988.

Thomas, Wolfgang. "Economic Crisis or Transformation? South Africa's Economy in the Late 1980s." *Social Dynamics* 13, no. 1 (1987): 1–12.

Thompson, E. P. *The Making of the English Working Class*. New York: Vintage Press, 1963.

————. "The Peculiarities of the English." In *Socialist Register, 1965*, ed. Ralph Miliband and John Saville. London: Merlin Press, 1966.

Tilly, Charles. *Class Conflict and Collective Action*. Beverly Hills, Calif.: Sage Publishers, 1981.

Tilly, Charles, and Louise Tilly, eds. *Big Structures, Large Processes, Huge Comparisons*. New York: Russell Sage, 1984.

Tolliday, Steven, and Jonathan Zeitlin, eds. *Shop Floor Bargaining and the State: Historical and Comparative Perspectives*. Cambridge: Cambridge University Press, 1985.

Tomlins, Christopher. *The State and the Unions: Labor Relations, Law and the Organized Labor Movement*. Cambridge: Cambridge University Press, 1985.

Tomlinson, Richard, and Mark Addleson. "Export Processing and Free Enterprise Zones: Regional Economic Policy in South Africa." In *Regional Restructuring under Apartheid: Urban and Regional Policies in Contemporary South Africa*, ed. Richard Tomlinson and Mark Addleson, 278–93. Johannesburg: Ravan Press, 1987.

————. "Is the State's Regional Policy in the Interests of Capital?" In *Regional Restructuring under Apartheid: Urban and Regional Policies in Contemporary South Africa*, ed. Richard Tomlinson and Mark Addleson, 55–73. Johannesburg: Ravan Press, 1987.

————, eds. *Regional Restructuring under Apartheid: Urban and Regional Policies in Contemporary South Africa*. Johannesburg: Ravan Press, 1987.

Torchia, Andrew. "The Business of Business: An Analysis of the Political Behavior of the South African Manufacturing Sector under the Nationalists." *Journal of Southern African Studies* 14, no. 3 (Apr. 1988): 421–45.

Toussaint [pseud.]. "A Trade Union Is Not a Political Party: A Critique of the Speech 'Where FOSATU Stands.'" *African Communist* 93 (2d quarter 1983): 35–46.

Trebat, Thomas J. *Brazil's State-Owned Enterprises: A Case Study of the State as Entrepreneur*. Cambridge: Cambridge University Press, 1983.

Turrell, Robert. *Capital and Labour on the Kimberley Diamond Field, 1871–1890*. Cambridge: Cambridge University Press, 1987.

United Kingdom. Parliament. House of Commons Select Committee in Respect of British Companies Operating in South Africa. *British Companies in South Africa*. London: Christian Concern for Southern Africa, 1974.

Valenzuela, Samuel. "Labor Movements in Transitions to Democracy." *Comparative Politics* 21, no. 4 (1989): 445–72.

Valladores, Licia do Prado. "Estudos recentes sobre a habitação no Brasil: Resenha da literatura." In *Repensando a habitação no Brasil,* ed. Licia do Prado Valladores, 21–78. Rio de Janeiro: IUPERJ–/–Zahar, 1983.

———, ed. *Repensando a habitação no Brasil.* Rio de Janeiro: IUPERJ–/–Zahar, 1983.

Van der Merwe, Roux. "Trade Unions and the Democratic Order." In *Introduction to Industrial Relations in South Africa,* ed. M. Finnemore and R. van der Merwe, 106–14. Johannesburg: McGraw-Hill, 1986.

Van Onselen, Charles, *Chibaro: African Mine Labour in Southern Rhodesia.* Nottingham: Pluto Press, 1976.

Van Zyl, I. J. "South Africa's Strike Statistics: A Quantitative Analysis." *Productivity South Africa* 13, no. 1 (Feb. 1987): 6–11.

Venceslau, Paulo de Tarso. "Metalúrgicos: Eleições sindicais." *Socialismo & Democracia* 4 (Dec. 1984): 47–53.

Verster, R. "Liaison Committees in the South African Industry: Their Present Functioning and Constitution." Mimeo. University of the Orange Free State, Personnel Research Division, Bloemfontein, 1974.

Verwoerd, Hendrick. *Verwoerd Speaks: Speeches, 1948–1966.* Edited by A. N. Pelzer. Johannesburg: APB Pubs., 1966.

Vianna, Luiz Werneck. *A classe operária e a abertura.* São Paulo: CERIFA, 1983.

———. *Liberalismo e sindicato no Brasil.* Rio de Janeiro: Paz e Terra, 1978.

Von Holdt, Karl. "The Political Significance of COSATU: Response to Plaut." Mimeo. Johannesburg, 1987.

Walker, Cherryl. "Gender and the Development of the Migrant Labour System c. 1850–1930." In *Women and Gender in Southern Africa to 1945,* ed. Cherryl Walker, 168–96. Cape Town: David Philip, 1990.

———. *Women and Resistance in South Africa.* London: Onyx Press, 1982.

———, ed. *Women and Gender in Southern Africa to 1945.* Cape Town: David Philip, 1990.

Walker, Neuna Aguiar. "The Organization and Ideology of Brazilian Labor." In *Revolution in Brazil,* ed. I. L. Horowitz, 242–56. New York: E. P. Dutton, 1964.

Wallerstein, Immanuel. *The Capitalist World Economy.* Vol. 1. Cambridge: ambridge University Press, 1979.

Wallerstein, Michael. "The Collapse of Democracy in Brazil: Its Economic Determinants." *Latin American Research Review* 15, no. 3 (1980): 3–44.

Wassenaar, A. D. *Assault on Private Enterprise.* Cape Town: Tafelberg, 1977.

Waterman, Peter. "The 'Labour Aristocracy' in Africa: Introduction to a Debate." *Development and Change* 6, no. 3 (1975): 57–74.

Webster, David. "A Review of Some 'Popular' Anthropological Approaches to the Understanding of Black Workers." *South African Labour Bulletin* 3, no. 1 (1976): 52–62.

Webster, Eddie. *Cast in a Racial Mould: Labor Process and Trade Unionism in the Foundries.* Johannesburg: Ravan Press, 1985.

———. "A Profile of Unregistered Union Members in Durban." *SALB* 4, no. 8 (Jan. 1979): 43–74.

————. "The Rise of Social-Movement Unionism: The Two Faces of the Black Trade Union Movement in South Africa." In *State, Resistance and Change in South Africa*, ed. P. Frankel, N. Pines and M. Swilling, 174–96. London: Croom Helm, 1988.

————. "Stayaways and the Black Working Class: Evaluating a Strategy." *Labour, Capital and Society* 14, no. 1 (Apr. 1981): 10–38.

————. "Taking Labour Seriously: Sociology and Labour in South Africa." *South African Sociological Review* 4, no. 1 (1991): 50–72.

————, ed. *Essays in Southern African Labour History*. Johannesburg: Ravan Press, 1978.

Weffort, Francisco. "A cidadania dos trabalhadores." In *Direito, cidadania e participação*, ed. Bolivar Lamounier, Francisco Weffort, and Maria Victoria Benevides, 140–50. São Paulo: T. A. Queiroz, 1981.

————. "Democracia e movimento operária." *Revista de Cultura Contemporânea* 1, nos. 1 and 2 (Jan. and Aug. 1979): 3–11 and 11–34.

————. *Participação e conflito industrial: Contagem e Oscasco, 1969.* Mimeo. São Paulo: CEBRAP, 1972.

————. *O populismo na política brasileira.* Rio de Janeiro: Paz e Terra, 1980.

————. Tese de livre-dociência, University of São Paulo, 1978.

————. "Os sindicatos na política (Brasil: 1955–1964)." *Ensaios de Opinão* 7 (1978): 18–27.

————. "Why Democracy." In *Democratizing Brazil*, ed. Alfred Stepan, 327–50. New York: Oxford University Press, 1989.

Western Province General Workers Union. "The Cape Town Meat Strike." *SALB* 6, no. 5 (Dec. 1980): 49–78.

Whitaker, Donald P. "The Economy." In *South Africa: A Country Study*, ed. Harold Nelson, 161–218. Washington, D.C.: U.S. Department of the Army, 1981.

Wilkinson, Peter. "Housing." *South African Review One* (1983): 271–77.

Wilentz, Sean. *Chants Democratic: New York City and the Rise of the American Working Class, 1788–1850.* New York: Oxford University Press, 1984.

Wolpe, Harold. "Capitalism and Cheap Labour-Power in South Africa: From Segregation to Apartheid." *Economy and Society* 111, no. 4 (1972): 425–56.

————. *Race, Class and the Apartheid State.* London: James Currey, OAU and UNESCO, 1988.

Wood, Charles H., and Jose Alberto Magno de Carvalho. *The Demography of Inequality in Brazil.* Cambridge: Cambridge University Press, 1988.

"Workers' Struggle in South Africa—A Comment." Mimeo. Johannesburg: n.d.

"Workers under the Baton: An Examination of the Labour Dispute at Heinemann Electric Company." *SALB* 3, no. 7 (June 1977): 49–60.

World Bank. *Brazil: Industrial Policies and Manufactured Exports.* Washington, D.C.: World Bank, 1983.

Wright, Erik Olin. "Exploitation, Identity, and Class Structure: A Reply to My Critics." In Erik Olin Wright et al., *The Debate on Classes*, 184–90. London: Verso Press, 1989.

Wright, Erik Olin, with Ume Becker, Johanna Brenner, Michael Burawoy, Val

Burris, Guglielmo Carchedi, Gordon Marshall, Peter Meiksins, David Rose, Arthur Stinchcombe, and Philippe Van Parijs. *The Debate on Classes.* London: Verso Press, 1989.

Wright, I. D. "The Changing Labor Process and Its Consequences: A Case Study of a General Engineering Firm in Natal." *SALB* 4, no. / (Nov. 1978): 55–62.

Zeitlin, Jonathan. "Shop Floor Bargaining and the State: A Contradictory Relationship." In *Shop Floor Bargaining and the State: Historical and Comparative Perspectives,* ed. Steven Tolliday and Jonathan Zeitlin, 1–45. Cambridge: Cambridge University Press, 1985.

Index

ABC/ABCD region (São Paulo), 66, 67, 68, 157, 158, 162, 163, 171, 176, 203, 216
ABC Metalworkers' Union, 152, 162, 165
Abertura (liberalization), 112, 140. *See also* "Controlled liberalization" (Brazil)
Abramo, Lais Wendel, 152
Abranches, Sérgio, 106
Absenteeism, 144, 147
Activists, 42, 43, 92-93, 141, 142, 143-44, 195, 197, 198-99; in Brazil, 61, 92-93, 95, 111, 116, 145, 154, 155, 157, 158-59, 160, 163, 168, 171, 193, 203-9, 217, 218-19, 223, 224, 226, 295 n. 64; in South Africa, 1, 14, 23, 116, 176, 181, 227, 229, 237-38, 241, 251-52, 302 n. 202
Adam, Heribert, 123
"African" labor (South Africa), 133, 137, 138, 179, 182, 186, 188, 193, 234, 243
African National Congress. *See* ANC
Afrikaans (language), 74, 75, 80, 85; Afrikaans-speaking businessmen, 97, 118-19, 123, 125, 135-36
Afrikaanse Handelsinstituut, 118, 119, 124, 188
Aggett, Neil, 182
Agrarian elites. *See* Landowners/agrarian elites
Agriculture, 200; in Brazil, 67; in South Africa, 73, 117, 118, 123, 247

AI-5 (Institutional Act Number 5, Brazil), 53, 61, 101, 103
Alexandra township, 245
Almeida, Maria Hermínia Tavares de, 151, 264
Alvarez, Sonia, 221
Alves, Maria Helena Moreira, 53, 94, 100, 283 n. 74, 288 n. 75
ANC (African National Congress), 14, 16, 26, 39, 72, 174, 183, 187, 227, 228, 232, 233-34, 239, 245, 250-52, 278 n. 35, 298 n. 114, 311 n. 225
Andrade, Joaquim dos Santos, 160, 161
Andrade, Regis de Castro, 67
Andrews, George Reid, 22
Anglo American Corporation (South Africa), 75, 77, 80-81, 120, 127, 138
Anti-apartheid groups, 131, 172, 181, 190-91, 228, 230, 251-52, 257-58. *See also* ANC (African National Congress); UDF (United Democratic Front)
Apartheid, 1, 25, 26, 70-72, 84, 117, 119, 124, 125, 234-37, 238, 239, 255-56, 257-58; dismantling of, 116; legislation, 14; race, class and, 227-28; and racial differentiation, 23; racial stratification and, 21, 22, 255
Apprenticeship programs: in Brazil, 160; in South Africa, 122, 132
ARENA party (Brazil), 103, 104, 108
Arms industry (South Africa), 130
Arns, Cardinal, 101
Artisans, 6, 47, 185

"Asians" (South Africa). *See* Indians
Assistentialism, 21, 60, 62, 145, 154, 220, 281 n. 28
Associated-dependent development, 44, 57, 88, 89
Associationalism, 198
ASSOCOM (Associated Chambers of Commerce, South Africa), 190, 312 n. 2
Authoritarian industrialization, 12, 40, 45, 69
Authoritarian states, 11, 12, 13, 15, 17, 21, 42, 90, 91-92, 94, 95, 115-16, 139, 141, 142, 150, 170, 194, 196, 199, 201, 203, 215, 253, 256, 258-59, 262, 263, 264, 265-66, 267-68, 272, 273
Authoritarianism, 17, 18, 47, 95, 199; bureaucratic, 53, 94
Automobile industry workers, 36, 37, 194, 271; in Brazil, 36, 37, 48, 51, 57, 63, 66-67, 69, 108-10, 112, 152-54, 185; in South Africa, 36, 37, 78, 80, 81, 158, 178, 184, 185, 231, 300 n. 178

Back, S. R., 124
Baer, Werner, 50
Bank Workers' Union (Brazil), 163
Banks, 77, 128, 134; Barclays, 77; Chase Manhattan, 77, 125, 284 n. 131
Bantustans, 18, 70, 71, 88, 120-21, 126-27, 234-37, 240, 245, 247, 291 n. 148
Barcelona, 5, 265
Bardella, Claudio, 108
Barlow Rand, 181
Baskin, Jeremy, 239, 251
Bell, Trevor, 87
Belo Horizonte, 38, 61, 204, 210, 296 n. 92
Bendix, Reinhard, 18, 19, 258, 259, 272
Bergquist, Charles, 9, 21, 147
Biernacki, Richard, 146
Biko, Steve, 133, 181. *See also* Black Consciousness movement (South Africa)
"Black" (South African terminology), 14
Black Consciousness movement (South Africa), 133, 181, 182, 300 n. 171, 309 n. 173
BNH (Banco National de Habitação—National Housing Bank), 213-14
Bonnell, Victoria, 201
Botha, P. W., 129, 130, 136, 137
Botha, Thozamile, 231
Boycotts (South Africa): bus, 231, 241, 309 n. 183; consumer, 38, 187-88,

229, 231, 250, 302 n. 202, 310 n. 187; rent, 228, 229, 244, 248
Brant, Vinícius Caldeira, 205
Brazil: business opposition to state, 99-114; citizenship, 222-27; class identity, 215-22, 234; community struggles, 203-27; controls over labor, 20-23; and "economic miracle" (*see* Growth); end of "miracle," 106, 260; industrial strategies, 48-69, 281 n. 24; and mobilization of labor, 29-41 (*see also* Mobilization); pattern of industrialization, 210-15; and strikes (*see* Strikes); and trade unions (*see* Trade unions)
Britain: business with South Africa, 128, 131; in EEC, 131; labor movements in, 149
Burawoy, Michael, 12, 276 n. 23
Business (Brazil): calls for democratization, 111-13, 137, 138-39, 141, 142; challenge from below, 108-11; collapse of alliance with state, 99-102; controls on labor, 60-63; *empresariado*, 104, 107-8, 109, 113, 117, 137; and military, 52-60; policymaking, 111-14; reshaping the labor force, 63-68; Second Development Plan, 104-8
Business (South Africa): accommodation with state, 118-25, 140-42; industrial strategies, 72-75; liberal attitudes, 120, 127, 133, 137, 139, 140; opposition to state, 114-18, 125-33, 256-57; reshaping the labor force, 83-89; and separate development, 70-72; and "unrest," 133-42
"Business consultative conference" (South Africa), 256-57
Buthelezi, Chief Mangosuthu, 183, 186, 233

Caldeira, Teresa Pires do Rio, 206-7, 216, 224
Calhoun, Craig, 143, 201
Cape Town, 87, 241, 244
Capital accumulation (Brazil): foreign, 50, 56, 103; private, 54, 55, 56, 63, 94, 223, 253, 254, 259, 263; state, 53, 54, 55
Capital accumulation (South Africa): foreign, 75-76, 77-80, 259; private, 75; state (*see* Parastatal corporations)
Capital flight (South Africa), 74, 117, 136
Capital-intensive industry, 6, 140, 141,

145, 260; in Brazil, 64-65, 69, 84, 171, 219; in South Africa, 84, 86, 87, 121, 125, 131, 185

Capitalism, 5, 7, 8, 12, 46-47; as eroding apartheid, 120, 124; and state, 126, 135, 138, 191, 257-58, 265-66, 274

Capitalist industrializers, 44-45, 47, 93-94, 191, 206, 216

Cardoso, Fernando Henrique, 4, 57, 108, 113, 280 n. 3

Cardoso, Ruth, 198

Carteira (work records), 24, 67-68

Cassação (removal of political rights), 53, 282 n. 32

Castells, Manuel, 39, 199

Catholic church (Brazil), 11, 41, 101, 154, 157, 187, 202, 204, 207, 304 n. 26; and Workers' Pastoral, 154-55, 207

Catholic unionists (Brazil), 52, 187, 305 n. 37

Catholic Worker Action (Ação Católica Operária), 154, 294 n. 47

Central Única dos Trabalhadores. *See* CUT

CGT (Confedereação Geral dos Trabalhadores—General Workers' Federation), 168, 169, 225, 297 n. 115. *See also* CONCLAT

Chaebol (Korean conglomerates), 266

Chamber of Mines (South Africa), 118

Citizenship demands, 3, 5, 10-11, 12, 15, 16-17, 33, 40, 142, 150, 197-209, 222-27, 251-52, 258, 263, 272; in Brazil, 110, 114; in South Africa, 172, 233-34, 251-52, 256

Civic associations (South Africa), 228

Civil society, and state, 168, 217

"Civilized labor policy" (South Africa), 24, 71

Clandestine activism, 10, 41, 43, 193, 261; in Brazil, 154-55, 156; in South Africa, 173, 174, 176, 232. *See also* Activists

Clark, Nancy, 75

Class: and citizenship, 222-27; and class consciousness, 11, 145-47, 148, 177, 237-42, 252-54, 264; and class-based action, 29-30, 31; and class-based discourse, 2, 199, 234, 245, 249-50, 252, 273; and identity (Brazil), 215-22, 226; and race, 227-28, 234, 239; and unions, 193-96, 198-99, 249-54

CLT. *See* Labor code

Cloward, Richard, 42

Coffee, 23-24, 48, 49

Collective bargaining, 19, 96, 98, 259,

274; in Brazil, 109, 165; in South Africa, 23, 25, 117, 135, 139

Collier, Richard and Ruth, 9, 20, 147-48

Colonialism: in Brazil, 23-24; in South Africa, 24, 74

Color bar (South Africa), 122, 133

"Coloured" (South Africa), 14, 25, 85, 132, 133, 138, 172, 179, 182, 186, 241, 310 n. 192

Communist Party: in Brazil, 49, 50, 51, 100, 155, 168, 294 n. 47, 297 n. 126; in South Africa, 14, 26, 71, 174, 175, 250-52, 297 n. 126, 298 n. 144

Community support, and labor movements, 3, 37-38, 39, 40, 42, 141, 142, 197-203, 252-54; in Brazil, 61, 108-9, 146, 161, 162, 163, 171, 203-27; in South Africa, 133-39, 187-93, 227-54, 262

Commuting. *See* Transport, public

Comparative labor studies, 2, 4-5, 9, 11, 12, 13, 41-42, 46-47, 193-96, 264-74

CONCLAT (Coordenação Nacional da Classe Trabalhadora—National Working-Class Coordination), 168

Conference of the Working Class (Brazil), 167

Congress Alliance (South Africa), 26, 278 n. 35

Congress of Industrial Workers (Brazil), 159

Congress of the Productive Classes (Brazil), 108

Conservative unions, 4; in Brazil (*pelegos*), 27, 52, 160, 161, 296 n. 92; in South Africa, 25, 82, 114, 144, 182, 278 n. 28, 281 n. 28

Consolidação das Leis Trabalhadores (CLT), 50, 51. *See also* Labor code

Consumer boycotts. *See* Boycotts (South Africa)

Consumer demands, 38, 39, 202

Consumer durables, 98, 260

Consumers: in Brazil, 53, 54, 56, 57, 206; in South Africa, 78, 80, 89, 178

Contagem strike. *See* Strikes (Brazil)

Contract labor (South Africa), 236, 237

"Controlled liberalization" (Brazil), 112, 114, 139, 140, 142, 144

Cooper, Frederick, 202-3

Córdoba (Argentina), 265

Corporatist labor legislation, 2, 4, 49, 50, 266

Corporatist unions (Brazil), 21, 110, 144, 161, 168, 178, 225

COSAS (Congress of South African Students), 239

COSATU (Congress of South African Trade Unions), 171, 183, 92, 230, 233-34, 248, 250-52, 255
Cost of Living Movement (Movimento do Custo da Vida), 206, 208, 221, 222, 304 n. 30
Craft unions, 6, 24, 27, 198, 209
Culture, and tradition, 21, 47, 146
Cumings, Bruce, 268
CUT (Central Única dos Trabalhadores—Unified Workers' Central), 167-68, 169, 170-71, 185, 208, 225, 297 n. 115

Dahrendorf, Ralph, 6, 279 n. 42
De Klerk, President F. W., 256
Decentralization, industrial (South Africa), 120-21, 123, 124, 236, 247
Democratization, 10, 15, 40, 199, 252-54, 258, 259, 261; in Brazil, 99-100, 112, 139, 159, 170, 216; in South Africa, 123, 136, 139, 140, 142, 196
Demonstrations: in Brazil, 38, 151, 155; in South Africa, 250
Dependency, 3-4, 44, 95-96, 276 n. 6
Dependent capitalism, 265; development, 274; industrialization, 47
De-skilling, 6
Developing nations. See Newly industrialized countries (NICs)
"Developmentalism," 7; in Brazil, 50-52, 69, 94
Deyo, Frederic, 9, 21, 200, 271-72
Di Tella, Torcuato, 200
DIEESE (Brazil), 157-58, 166, 295 n. 65
Diniz, Eli, 107, 115, 288 n. 75
Diretas já!, 37. See also Elections/direct elections
Discrimination, racial, 227, 234, 238
Dockworkers' strikes (South Africa). See Strikes
Dominant classes, 8, 223, 227, 261, 262, 263, 269
Durban, 87, 241. See also Strikes (South Africa)
Dynamic industries: in Brazil, 58, 90, 97, 114, 262; in South Africa, 80, 90, 137

East London, 231, 241, 310 n. 189
East Rand, 181, 187, 237, 244. See also Strikes (South Africa)
Eastern Cape, 88, 183, 185, 186, 187, 231, 241, 300 n. 178
Education: in South Africa, 132, 135, 238; in South Korea, 268
Elections/direct elections, 17, 18, 23, 25,

135, 139, 252, 257, 259; in Brazil, 203, 224
Elites, economic, 45, 89, 92, 96-97, 98, 141, 259; in Brazil, 49, 99, 100, 101, 114, 286 n. 11
Elitist politics (Brazil), 223, 225, 256, 262, 277
Employers: as collaborating with state, 240-41, 243, 246, 252-53, 259; and influx control (South Africa), 235-37; and state, 193-94, 235-37, 265-66; subsidized by labor (Brazil), 217, 218; and unions (South Africa), 176-77, 179; and women (Brazil), 219-20
Empresariado. See Business (Brazil)
"Endorse out" (South Africa), 89, 237. See also Victimization
English-speaking businessmen (South Africa), 118-19
ESCOM (Electricity Supply Commission, South Africa), 74, 135
Evans, Peter, 7, 57, 100

Factory-based organizations, 3, 10, 11, 12, 33, 39, 155, 161, 177, 184-93, 196, 203, 217, 226, 231, 246, 252-54, 260-62, 272
Faletto, Enzo, 4, 57, 280 n. 3
Family labor: in Brazil, 218-22; in South Africa, 246-49
Favelas. See Squatter settlements
FCI (Federated Chamber of Industry, South Africa), 119, 121, 124, 127, 131, 134, 190, 308 n. 140
Ferrador, João, 153, 294 n. 40
Ferrante, Vera Lucia B., 63
FGTS (Fundo por Tempo de Serviço—Unemployment Fund), 62-63, 155, 213, 214, 283 n. 81
FIESP (Federation of Industry of São Paulo), 107, 109, 111, 112
Figueirido, Angela, 60
Figueirido, President João Batista de Oliveira, 111, 112
Filho, Laerte Setubal, 108
Filho, Luis Eulálio de Bueno Vidigal, 111-12
Filho, Manoel Fiel, 155
Fishlow, Albert, 54, 112-13
Forced removals (South Africa), 139, 232
Ford Motor Company: in Brazil, 111, 164, 305 n. 40; in South Africa, 78, 88, 186, 231
Fordism, 5, 7-8, 260
Foreign debt: in Brazil, 48, 51, 56, 103, 104, 112; in South Africa, 77, 129, 138

FOSATU (South Africa), 167, 183-85, 186-87, 190-92, 231, 280 n. 70, 300 n. 178
FOSKOR (South Africa), 74
Foster, Joe, 191, 231
France, labor movement in, 146
Free enterprise, 141; in South Africa, 134-35, 136, 138

Galhardo, Miguel, 160
Geisel, President Ernesto, 43, 100, 103, 104, 105-6, 107, 111
Gender: ideologies in Brazil, 219, 220, 221, 222, 246; ideologies in South Africa, 249, 311 nn. 215, 222; and workforce, 11, 38, 46, 246-49
Gereffi, Gary, 91
Germany, labor movement in, 5, 145, 146, 149, 265
Ghana, labor movement in, 147
Godsell, Bobby, 138, 141-42
Gomes, Severo, 107, 108, 130
Good Hope summit, 138
Go-slows (Brazil), 33, 144, 156-57, 279 n. 51
Goulart, President João, 28, 52
"Gradual liberalization" (South Africa), 126
Greenberg, Stanley B., 95, 120-22
Grileiro (dishonest subdivider), 211
Grobbelaar, Andries, 180
Group Areas. See Influx control (South Africa)
Growth, of world economy, 45, 91-92, 102
Growth rates, 19, 36-37, 43-44, 45, 46, 48, 58, 140, 255, 259, 261, 263, 267, 273; Brazil's decline, 103, 104-5, 106, 111; Brazil's "economic miracle," 45, 46, 48-49, 54, 63, 69, 90; South Africa's "economic boom," 45, 46, 48, 69-89, 90, 116, 123, 136, 138-39
Grupo 14 (employers), 152-53

Haggard, Stephan, 267, 269, 272
Heavy industry, 46, 78, 86, 87, 89, 194, 196, 253, 258-59, 260, 261, 263, 264, 271; in Brazil, 164, 219, 297 n. 112; in South Africa, 178, 184. See also Consumer durables
Heinemann strike. See Strikes (South Africa)
Herzog, Vladimir, 101
Hirschman, Albert, 47
"Hoggenheimer," 75, 123. See also Oppenheimer, Ernest

Holmstrom, Mark, 200
Homelands. See Bantustans
Hostels, migrant: in South Africa, 201, 236, 237, 243, 244, 246; in South Korea, 269
Housing: in Brazil, 210-11, 213-14, 216, 218, 253; family (South Africa), 240, 243, 246; "informal" (South Africa), 244-46; patterns, 202-3, 204-5, 210-11, 310 n. 192; in South Africa (black), 134, 135, 233, 238, 242-46, 247, 253
Human rights (Brazil), 100-101, 286 n. 17
Humphrey, John, 63, 66, 67, 151-52
Huntington, Samuel, 6, 17, 140

Import substitution: in Brazil, 49, 51-52, 89, 103; in South Africa, 72, 73, 76, 81, 89, 90, 116-17, 118
Indebted industrialization (Brazil), 104
India, 7, 200
Indians (in South Africa), 14, 25, 85, 132, 133, 138, 172, 179, 182, 241, 310 n. 192
Industrial "deepening," 46, 47, 51, 89, 90; in Brazil, 103, 139, 140; in South Africa, 73, 89, 140
Industrial Development Corporation (South Africa), 74
Industrial relations, 23, 31, 77, 141, 145, 209-10, 271
Industrial unrest (South Africa), 31, 133-39, 250
Industrialization, 3, 4, 5, 7, 18-20, 43, 44, 64, 95, 195; dependent, 47-48; early, 5, 7, 17, 20, 29, 30, 47, 96, 120, 145, 146, 147, 193, 199, 201, 259, 260, 276 n. 12; late, 4, 5, 6, 7, 9, 10, 12, 30, 44, 46, 47, 96, 147, 148, 199-200, 260, 265, 272-74; rapid, 45, 64, 89-90, 149, 200, 203, 227-28, 247, 252, 258-62, 263, 264, 269
Inequality, 8, 12, 17, 19, 57-58, 203; in Brazil, 216, 223, 227, 255, 257
Inflation: in Brazil, 51, 56, 58-59, 102, 105, 111, 112, 157-58, 219, 287 n. 21, 295 n. 65 (see also DIEESE); in South Africa, 69, 129, 247
Influx control (South Africa), 119, 121-22, 138, 246, 250, 254-57; Group Areas and, 70, 71, 234-37
Infrastructure, urban (Brazil), 203-27
Inkatha Yenkululeko Yesize, 183, 233; and UWUSA (Union of Workers of South Africa), 183, 223

Inkeles, Alex, 147
Innes, Duncan, 80
Institute for Industrial Education (IIE), 298 n. 140
International contexts, 4, 7, 8, 19, 265, 271. See also "Triple alliance"
International Monetary Fund (IMF), 134
ISCOR (Iron and Steel Corporation of South Africa), 74, 78
Italy, 265

Job reservation system (South Africa), 84-85, 86, 115, 122-23, 124, 132, 179, 285 n. 160, 292 n. 154
Joint ventures, 89-90, 140, 260, 266; in Brazil, 56, 57, 105, 109; in South Africa, 76, 77, 80

Katznelson, Ira, 29, 148
Keck, Margaret, 68, 169-70, 279 n. 60
Kok, Einar, 109-10
Koo, Hagen, 270
Kowarick, Lucio, 198

Labor aristocracy, 3, 30, 67, 69, 88-89, 151, 262
Labor bureaus (South Africa), 88, 121
Labor code (Brazil), 27, 50, 51, 52, 60, 150, 167, 173
Labor contracts (South Africa), 235-36
Labor Department (South Africa), 121
Labor federations: in Brazil, 40, 52, 145-46, 166-71, 193; in South Africa, 175, 183-93
Labor institutions (South Africa), 176, 178, 179
Labor movements. See Workers' movements
Labor Party (Brazil), 52. See also PT (Partido dos Trabalhadores)
Land: in Brazil, 211, 212; in South Africa, 116, 139; in South Korea, 268
Land Acts (South Africa), 71, 234
Landowners/agrarian elites (Brazil), 50, 97, 99
Layoffs (Brazil), 162, 208, 262
Leballo, P. K., 23
Lenin, V. I., 6, 279 n. 42
Lessa, Carlos, 106
Liaison committees (South Africa), 127, 133, 137, 299 n. 155
Liberation movement (South Africa), 37, 39, 41, 144, 187
Liberation theology (Brazil), 41, 202, 294, 219, 221
Lipietz, Alain, 5, 7-8, 260
Lipton, Merle, 115

Literacy (Brazil), 23, 24, 50, 68, 223
"Living wage" campaign (South Africa), 39, 233, 250
Lockouts (Brazil), 162
Low-income housing (Brazil), 201 5
Low-wage industries, 210, 131
Lula. See Silva, Luís Inácio da ("Lula")

Mabhida, Moses, 175, 298 n. 144
Mandela, Nelson, 227, 257
Mann, Michael, 138
Marginalization, 254; in Brazil, 58
Marks, Gary, 145, 149, 201
Marshall, T. H., 223, 259, 280 n. 75
Martins, Heloisa Helena Texeira de Souza, 154
Marx, Karl, 2, 29, 272, 273, 275 n. 3
Mashinini, Emma, 13
"Mass democratic movement" (South Africa), 234, 250
MAWU (Metal and Allied Workers' Union, Transvaal), 175, 177, 179-80, 185, 190, 299 n. 161
Mayekiso, Moses, 143, 191-92, 232, 238
Mdabtsane township, 242
MDB (Movimento Democrático Brasileiro), 103-4
Medici, President Emilio Garrastazzú, 61, 103
Mello, Fernando Collor de, 226
Metal industry workers, 36, 37, 194; in Brazil, 36, 37, 155, 156, 157, 158, 161-62, 164, 217, 261; in South Africa, 36, 37, 86, 178, 184, 189
Metalworkers' Union Opposition (Brazil), 155, 156, 159, 281 n. 28, 287 n. 21
Metalworkers' unions: in Brazil, 160, 161, 162, 167, 169, 207, 208-9, 220; in South Africa, 232
Migrant labor, 36, 67, 146-47; in Brazil, 210-15; in South Africa, 71-72, 89, 121-22, 124, 125, 131, 137, 183, 189, 234-37, 241
Militance, 3, 4, 5, 7, 12, 16, 18, 40, 42, 47, 52, 96, 141, 144-45, 148, 149, 255, 262, 264, 269, 273-74; in Brazil, 109-11, 159-64, 220-21; in South Africa, 127, 176-79, 239
Militant labor movements, 2, 15, 143, 145, 253, 259, 261-72, 276 n. 12
Militants, shop-floor (Brazil), 159, 163, 164-66
Military (Brazil), 11, 16, 17, 49, 94, 128, 258; and civilian rule, 37; distancing from other elites, 106; and industrial strategy, 171; leaves office, 256; and

opposition from business, 99-114; and repression, 60-63, 92, 94; take-over, 28, 52-60
Military (South Korea), 266-72
Mindlín, José, 110
Mining: in Brazil, 55; in South Africa, 71-74, 117, 118, 192
Ministry of Labor (Brazil), 49, 50, 53, 59, 60, 150, 151, 152, 158, 159, 162, 163, 165, 166, 167
Mobilization, 11, 15, 29, 30, 31, 32, 38, 40, 41-42, 43, 48, 92, 93, 141, 272; in Brazil, 112-13, 201-2, 203, 222, 223, 224, 226, 257, 295 n. 65; in South Africa, 71-89, 123, 133-39, 228-37, 241-42, 245-46, 249, 251-52, 253-54, 257, 258-59
Modernization, 3, 4, 19, 44, 94, 95, 115, 147, 258, 261
Moisés, José Alvaro, 33, 68-69
"Monopoly capital" (South Africa), 80
Moore, Barrington, Jr., 9, 19, 146
Morely, Samuel, 58
Mosely, K. P., 202
Mothers' Clubs (Brazil), 203-4, 207, 221
Movement against Neediness (Movimento contra Carestia), 304 n. 30
Movement for Health (Brazil), 206
Mufamadi, Sidney, 249-50
Multinational capital, 36-37, 45, 47, 53; in Brazil, 56, 57; in South Africa, 124-25
Munck, Ronaldo, 46-47
Municipal authorities (South Africa), 242-46

Natal, 233
National Confederation of Industry (Brazil), 107-8
National Party (South Africa), 25, 25, 70, 71, 72, 74, 84, 116, 117, 118, 123, 124, 129, 135, 136, 256
Nationalization (Brazil), 54
Native reserves (South Africa), 70, 71
Negotiations, direct, 109-10, 169, 194, 196
Neves, President Tancredo, 113
New unionism, 10, 16, 31, 61, 143-96, 197, 199, 271-72; in Brazil, 150-71, 207, 208, 209, 221; in South Africa, 171-93
Newly industrializing countries (NICs), 2-8, 12, 41, 44, 94, 260, 264-65, 266, 272-74, 280 n. 3; and labor movement, 41, 94, 146-47, 266-67, 268, 271, 272-74
Nigeria, labor movement in, 146

Nonracial capitalism, 139, 194. See also Capitalism
Nonracial unions (South Africa), 31, 145, 171, 177, 182, 183-93, 230-34, 244, 246, 278 n. 32
NUSAS (National Union of South African Students), 173

OBAN (Operação Bandeirantes), 61-62
O'Donnell, Guillermo, 53, 94
O'Dowd, M. C., 120
Oestreicher, Ricard, 149
Ofte, Claus, 6
Oil: and boycott against South Africa, 128, 291 n. 134; and world recession, 90, 92, 98, 102, 105, 125, 128, 130, 261
Oppenheimer, Ernest, 75
Oppenheimer, Harry, 127, 130-31, 132, 134, 135, 139
Osasco strike. See Strikes (Brazil)

PAC (Pan Africanist Congress), 23, 72
Parastatal corporations: in Brazil, 75, 105; in South Africa, 72, 74, 75, 80, 84, 98, 122
Pass laws (South Africa), 2, 71-72, 88, 118, 119, 121, 139, 187, 235, 236, 243
"Pass-bearing natives" (South Africa), 25, 68, 71, 72, 88
Peasants, 46, 148, 200, 210
Pelegos (conservative unionists, Brazil), 27, 60, 158
Pereira, Luiz Carlos Bresser, 58, 100, 107
Pereira, Vera Maria Cándido, 207
Peres, Aurelio and Conceição, 207
Periferia (Brazil), 11, 22, 38, 204, 206, 209-15, 253, 305 n. 54
Peripheral countries, 4, 7-8
Peripheralization: in Brazil, 209-15, 216, 217, 218, 226, 237, 239-40, 242, 252, 254; in South Africa, 237-42, 252, 254; in South Korea, 269, 271
Perlman, Selig, 279 n. 42
Petite bourgeoisie (South Africa), 238
Pickets, 38; in Brazil, 209
Pingentes (illegal train passengers, Brazil), 212. See also "Staff-riders" (South Africa)
Piven, Frances Fox, 42
PMDB (Partido Movimento Democrático Brasileiro), 223, 225
Police: in Brazil, 162-63, 165; in South Africa, 127, 133, 172, 173, 176-77, 180-81

"Political opportunity structure," 6, 93, 96
Political strikes, 32; in Brazil, 36, 164; in South Africa, 32, 33, 229-33
Political unionism, 2, 3, 32, 33, 36, 41, 253, 274
Poor whites (South Africa), 73
Popular Action (Ação Popular), 154
Populism, 3, 39; in Brazil, 27, 101, 155, 158, 159, 160, 170, 223-24
Port Elizabeth, 87, 88, 185, 231
Poverty, 12, 263, 270; in Brazil, 203-15, 216; political creation of, 212, 225; in South Africa, 236
Primary goods, 23-24, 44, 48, 81-82, 286 n. 11
Privatization (Brazil), 135-36
Progressive Federal Party (South Africa), 135
Proletarianization, 6, 64, 147
PT (Partido dos Trabalhadores—Workers' Party), 37, 39, 166, 169-70, 171, 191, 197, 209, 223-25, 226, 227, 283 n. 74
PWV (Pretoria/Witwatersrand/Vereeniging), 87, 183, 231, 232, 233, 236, 244, 246

Quebra-quebras ("break-breaks"), 204, 207, 212, 218. See also Transport, public

Race: in Brazil, 22, 211, 255; in South Africa, 22, 227-28, 255-56
Racial capitalism (South Africa), 116, 139, 305, n. 55
Racial classification: in Brazil, 277 n. 20; in South Africa, 22-23, 86, 122, 228, 234-37
Racial democracy (Brazil), 22, 23, 211
Racial unions (South Africa), 23, 188-89
Ragin, Charles, 265
Rallies (Brazil), 158, 208, 209, 224
Ramaphosa, Cyril, 16, 251
Redistribution, 8, 16, 251-52; in Brazil, 89, 111, 216; in South Africa, 197, 233, 234
Reinvention of business class, 139-42
Rent, increases (South Africa), 244-46. See also Boycotts
Reposição (salary reposition campaign), 157-59, 163, 171, 173, 295 n. 65
Repression, 8, 10, 19, 21, 30, 42, 45, 47, 92, 94-95, 96, 142, 145, 148, 193, 201, 202, 266-67, 270; in Brazil, 94-95, 153, 154, 171, 205, 223; in South

Africa, 72, 95, 172, 180-81, 229, 251-52, 255, 263
Reproduction, sphere of, 203, 215-22, 253, 262
Residential patterns, 200-201
Residents' associations: in Brazil, 205; in South Africa, 238, 241, 245
Re-skilling, 6, 86
Riekert Commission (South Africa), 137
Rio de Janeiro, 38, 204-5, 206, 210, 213, 215
Rodrigues, José Albertino, 147
Rodrigues, Leôncio Martins, 151
Rupert, Anton, 129
Rural: migrants, 19, 20, 67; race identities (Brazil), 305 n. 55; unions (Brazil), 51
Russia, 6, 201, 265, 286 n. 7

Saab-Scania strike (Brazil). See Strikes
SAAWU (South African Allied Workers' Union), 231-32
SACP (South African Communist Party). See Communist Party
SACTU (South African Congress of Trade Unions), 26, 72, 82, 142, 145, 173, 174-75, 182, 187, 251, 278 n. 35, 298 nn. 140, 144
Sampson, Anthony, 76
Sanctions (South Africa), 98, 118, 119, 128, 129, 131, 139, 256, 260, 261; after 1976, 180-81; arms embargo, 130; oil embargo, 128
Santos, Carlos Nelson Ferreira dos, 206
Santos, Wanderley Guilherme dos, 67
São Bernardo do Campo, 208-9, 215, 305 n. 40
São Paulo, 24, 38, 97, 154, 155, 159, 163, 203, 205-6, 209, 210, 211, 214-15, 216, 219; autoworkers, 36, 272; concentration of industry, 64, 65, 67, 155; manifesto (1978), 91, 99, 100, 106-7, 111; unions/activism in, 60, 61, 62, 108-9, 150-51, 155, 159, 160, 304 n. 17
SASOL (South African Coal, Oil and Gas Corporation), 74, 130
"Savage capitalism," 198, 217, 259, 263, 264, 274
Scabs, 171, 208
Security, national, 94-95, 98, 141, 261, 268; in Brazil, 100, 101, 105, 128, 130; in South Africa, 128-29, 130-31, 134-35
Seekings, Jeremy, 229, 311 n. 222
Segregation: racial (South Africa), 38,

71, 199, 211, 228, 238-41, 253, 284 n. 107; spatial (Brazil), 210, 211, 212, 215, 253

SEIFSA (Steel and Engineering Industries Federation of South Africa), 127, 178-79, 185, 190, 299 n. 157

Semi-peripheral areas, 6

Semi-skilled workers. *See* Workers, semi-skilled

"Separate development" (South Africa), 69, 70-72, 115, 124, 125. *See also* Apartheid

Sharecroppers (Brazil), 210. *See also* Peasants

Sharpeville township, 72, 76, 117, 119

Shop stewards, 186, 191; councils, 40, 239; training courses, 178

Shop-floor activism, 26, 28, 33, 39-40, 42, 69, 141, 142, 194; in Brazil, 109, 114, 156, 157, 159, 163; in South Africa, 117, 131, 164-66, 183-93, 225, 229-34, 237, 250, 253-54, 265, 274

Silva, Luís Inácio da ("Lula"), 16, 37, 39, 110, 150-51, 153, 158, 160, 162, 164-65, 167, 169, 170, 209, 222, 225-26, 283 n. 74, 294 n. 34, 296 n. 92

Silva, Roque Aparecido da, 168, 185

Simons, Ray Alexander, 26

Singer, Paul, 63

Skilled workers. *See* Workers, skilled

Skills: increasing levels, 96; semi-skilled to skilled, 66-67; shortages in Brazil, 152; shortages in South Africa, 36, 84-86, 90, 98, 122, 125, 130, 131, 261, 289 n. 103

Skocpol, Theda, 9

Slavery (Brazil), 22, 24

Slowdowns (Brazil), 156-57

Slum tenements (*cortiços*), 294, 205, 211

Smith, Gordon, 58

Social movements, 15, 16, 28, 143-44, 263-64

Social-movement unionism, 2-3, 4, 5, 9-10, 11, 12, 17, 28, 40, 41, 93, 143, 199-200, 208-9, 214-15, 253, 254, 263, 270, 274, 275 n. 3

Solidarity (Poland), 191

South Africa: business accommodation to state, 114-25; business opposition to state, 114-18, 125-33; citizenship, 242-52; class identity, 227-37; community struggles, 172-96, 249-52; controls over labor, 81-83; and "economic boom" (*see* Growth rates); foreign investment, 75-81; and mobiliza-

tion of labor (*see* Mobilization); reshaping labor force, 83-89; shop-floor organization, 183-93; and strikes (*see* Strikes [South Africa]); and trade unions (*see* Trade unions [South Africa])

South Korea, 9, 166-72, 312 n. 12, 313 n. 27

Soweto, 242, 262; 1976 uprising, 179-83, 242. *See also* Students

Squatter settlements: in Brazil (*favelas*), 201, 204, 205, 211, 213-14, 215, 216, 217, 306 n. 71; in South Africa, 228, 243-44, 246

"Staff-riders" (illegal train passengers, South Africa), 212. *See also Pingentes* (Brazil)

State of emergency (South Africa), 72, 229, 250

State-sponsored industry, 98, 129; in Brazil, 51, 53, 54, 55-56, 106-7; in South Africa, 72, 75, 116, 129. *See also* Parastatal corporations

"Statization" (*estatização*), 107

Stay-aways (South Africa), 38, 39, 133-39, 230, 250, 251

Stratification, 203, 257; in Brazil, 81, 90, 226, 257; in South Africa, 72, 81-83, 90

Street committees (South Africa), 229

Strike funds, 201; in Brazil, 171, 208; in South Africa, 187

Strikebreakers (Brazil), 161

Strikes (Brazil), 28, 30, 31-32, 38, 40, 60-61, 109-10, 142, 144, 145, 223, 264; Contagem (1968), 60-61, 155, 294 n. 48; metalworkers (1979), 163; metalworkers (1980), 165; and "new unionism," 159-64; Osasco (1968), 61, 155, 294 n. 48; Saab-Scania autoworkers (1978), 150-51, 152, 163, 217, 220, 272, 294 n. 35; in 1983, 169; in 1989, 169

Strikes (South Africa), 30, 31, 32, 38, 40, 125, 126, 128, 137, 140, 143-45; dockworkers (1972), 173-74, 175; Durban (1973), 88, 126-27, 128, 141-42, 172-76, 309 n. 183; East Rand (1981), 143; Heinemann Electric (1976), 179-80; "illegal" (1988), 250-51; municipal and flour mill workers (1980), 237; in 1973-79, 176-83, 229, 237; in 1979-80, 185-88; in 1981-82, 189-90; in the 1980s, 230

Students, 172, 173-74, 175, 176, 193; in

Students (continued)
  Brazil, 101, 111; and Soweto uprising, 121, 132, 133-39, 179-83, 228,
  239, 241
Sympathy strikes, 40; in South Africa,
  176, 250
Syndicalism, 161, 199

Tariffs/protection, 45, 46, 51, 53, 56, 57,
  90
Tarrow, Sidney, 93
Taxi-drivers' associations (South Africa),
  241
Technocratic alliance (South Africa), 138
Textiles, 57-58, 219
Third World, 4, 8, 44, 46
Thompson, E. P., 29, 41
Tilly, Charles, 10, 43, 47
"Total strategy" (South Africa), 181
Townships (South Africa), 38, 228-34,
  240, 242, 243, 256
Trade unions (Brazil), 26-28, 30; regis-
  tered, 27, 53
Trade unions (South Africa), 25-26, 30;
  nonracial (see Nonracial unions); rec-
  ognition of, 114; registered, 24-25,
  26, 33, 136-37, 292 n. 174; unregistered, 25, 26, 72, 127-28, 301 n. 195
Traditional industry: in Brazil, 64, 67,
  262; in South Africa, 87
Training/manpower (South Africa), 122,
  132, 133, 135, 138
"Transnational linkages," 7
Transport, public, 38-39, 280 n. 70; community struggles for, in Brazil, 203,
  204, 207, 212, 215, 216, 218, 239,
  240, 304 n. 17, 309 n. 183, 310 nn.
  187, 189; community struggles for, in
  South Africa, 231, 238, 239, 240-42,
  252-54; commuting (South Africa),
  239-41, 309 n. 183, 310 n. 189
Tricameral Parliament (South Africa),
  138, 244
"Triple alliance" (state, international capital, local business), 89, 140; in Brazil, 53, 57, 281 n. 20; in South Africa, 76, 116
TUACC (Trade Union Advisory and Coordinating Council), 174, 175, 177

UDF (United Democratic Front, South Africa), 39, 192, 228, 230, 232, 251
Unemployment, 200; in Brazil, 67, 166,
  205, 208, 216; in South Africa, 87,
  88, 89, 237, 291 n. 148
Unemployment fund (Brazil). See FGTS
  (Fundo por Tempo de Serviço)

"Union tax" (impôsto sindical), 27-28,
  51
United States, labor movement in, 5,
  146, 149
Unskilled workers. See Workers, un-
  skilled
Urban blacks (South Africa), 238, 240,
  243-44
Urban Foundation (South Africa), 134-
  35, 243
"Urban spoliation," 198, 203
Urbanization, 43, 253-54, 262, 264; in
  Brazil, 210-15, 216; in South Africa,
  87-88, 134, 235, 236, 242-46
"Useful vote" (voto útil), 213-14
UWUSA (Union of Workers of South Af-
  rica), 183, 233

Valladares, Licia do Pardo, 215
Vargas, President Getúlio, 27, 49, 50
Verkramptes (old-style Afrikaans nation-
  alists), 123
Verligtes (liberal Afrikaners), 124, 135
Verwoerd, H. F., 43, 75, 121
Victimization, 201; in South Africa, 89,
  176, 178, 190, 237, 301 n. 195

Wages, 30, 42, 46; in Brazil, 58-60, 63,
  103, 111, 112, 157, 206, 212, 219,
  226, 282 n. 62; in South Africa, 69,
  243, 247
Wages Commission (South Africa), 174,
  175
Wassenaar, Andreas, 135-36
Webster, Eddie, 185, 194
Weffort, Francisco, 223
"White" (South Africa), 14, 24, 83-87,
  234-37
Wiehahn Commission (South Africa),
  136-37, 141, 188
Wildcat strikes, 193, 196; in South Africa, 176
Wolpe, Harold, 71, 227
Women: and feminist movement, 220-
  21, 249; and strikes in South Africa,
  180; and strikes in South Korea, 269,
  271; in trade unions (Brazil), 220,
  222, 248; women's rights, in Brazil,
  203-4. See also Gender
Women, in labor force, 38, 262; in Brazil, 219-22, 248; in South Africa,
  246-49, 252
Work stoppages, 151, 193; in South Africa, 177-78
"Workerist" philosophy (South Africa),
  184, 195
Workers, semi-skilled, 5, 6, 28, 30, 36,

47, 64, 66, 67, 149, 176, 194, 261, 263; in Brazil, 167, 209, 216; in Europe, 149; in South Africa, 70, 84-85, 86, 89, 117, 122, 126, 133, 179, 184, 185, 186, 247
Workers, skilled, 194, 261; in Brazil, 66, 67, 69, 209; in South Africa, 84-85, 86, 122, 133, 185, 186, 237, 241, 289 n. 103
Workers, unskilled, 147; in Brazil, 66, 72; in South Africa, 24, 70, 86
Workers' movements, 17-22, 29-30, 143-46, 148-49, 171-72, 193-96, 252-54, 255-67

Working class, 5-6, 7, 8, 16, 17, 20, 29, 40, 46, 142, 144-49, 196, 199, 252-54, 262, 263, 269; in Brazil, 114, 166-71, 225-27, 237; in South Africa, 24, 185, 192, 234, 237-42, 248, 245-46
Works committees (South Africa), 127, 290 n. 122, 299 n. 155
World Bank, 56, 157

Zaire, labor movement in, 147
Zulu ethnicity/culture, 233

Compositor:	Maple-Vail Manufacturing Group
Text:	10/13 Sabon
Display:	Sabon
Printer and Binder:	Maple-Vail Manufacturing Group